A. J. Willard

An Examination of the Law of personal Rights

To discover the Principles of the Law

A. J. Willard

An Examination of the Law of personal Rights
To discover the Principles of the Law

ISBN/EAN: 9783337157760

Printed in Europe, USA, Canada, Australia, Japan

Cover: Foto ©Suzi / pixelio.de

More available books at **www.hansebooks.com**

AN EXAMINATION

OF THE

LAW OF PERSONAL RIGHTS,

TO DISCOVER

THE PRINCIPLES OF THE LAW,

AS ASCERTAINED FROM THE PRACTICAL RULES OF THE LAW, AND HARMONIZED WITH THE NATURE OF SOCIAL RELATIONS.

BY

A. J. WILLARD.

NEW YORK:
D. APPLETON AND COMPANY,
1, 3, AND 5 BOND STREET.
1882.

COPYRIGHT BY
D. APPLETON AND COMPANY,
1882.

CONTENTS.

CHAPTER	PAGE
I.—Origin in Nature of Law	7
II.—Nature and Origin of Rights, Obligations, and Powers	14
III.—Origin of Fundamental Social Law	22
IV.—The Nature of Institutional Law	37
V.—The Science of the Law	41
VI.—Common, Public, and Private Obligations	44
VII.—Private Obligations	49
VIII.—Capacity of Self-Obligation	55
IX.—Consideration	60
X.—Proper Subjects of Contracts	102
XI.—Terms and Conditions of Contracts	114
XII.—Obligation to Good Faith	122
XIII.—Effect of Executed Contracts	129
XIV.—Summary of the Origin and Nature of Obligations	133
XV.—General View of Rights and Powers	141
XVI.—Civil Powers	145
XVII.—Common Right to the Use of Natural Elements	148
XVIII.—Principles of Individual Sustenance	155
XIX.—Nurture	159
XX.—Individual Redress and Protection	171
XXI.—Nuisance	180
XXII.—Injuries to the Person by Force	189
XXIII.—Wrongs to Right of Person	194
XXIV.—Assault	199
XXV.—Self-Defense	204
XXVI.—Action of Assault and Battery	216

CHAPTER	PAGE
XXVII.—Injuries to the person by force, other than in personal encounter	249
XXVIII.—Volition considered as a right	277
XXIX.—Residence and change of place	286
XXX.—Residence	318
XXXI.—Wrongs to right of change of place	345
XXXII.—Liberty of speech	348
XXXIII.—Occupation, industry, and association	356
XXXIV.—Contracts	363
XXXV.—Companies	381
XXXVI.—Marriage	391
XXXVII.—The family	399
XXXVIII.—Association—communal and general	402
XXXIX.—Liberty of judgment	415
XL.—Liberty of self-gratification	427

THE PRINCIPLES OF THE LAW.

CHAPTER I.

ORIGIN IN NATURE OF LAW.

THAT man has a social nature is a proposition fundamental to a proper understanding of the place in nature that is occupied by the law. The demonstration of this proposition belongs to general philosophy rather than to legal science; but the question, from its close relation to the philosophy of the law, can not be altogether ignored. Society, more or less permanent, exists among the lower animals as well as among the human species, affording a wide range of proofs that social tendencies are an important and necessary part of the order of nature. That such a tendency should not exist in the most primitive state in which we can conceive mankind to have lived, but that it should have arisen simply as a product of mature experience, contradicts the principle that has firmly fastened itself upon the minds of reflecting men, that experience can have no greater force than that of formulating that which must be conceived as existing prior to any experience whatever. When we speak of a tendency, we mean more than a practice or habit, and no less than that from which all practices and habits must have their origin. Without doubt, tendencies of a particular character are produced in association with habits formed; but they are referable to some general tendency that lies back of all habits. A natural tendency is of that general character, as its name imports, and it can not be doubted that the social tendency existing among human beings is one of that class. The fact that animals of a lower nature than man partake of it is in itself a demonstration that such tendency existed in the nature of man anterior to any modification induced by advance in knowledge and experience.

Assuming, then, that man has a distinctly social nature which is essential to his existence and development, a step may be taken in the direction of developing the fundamental and essential character of the law. The primary notion of the social state is that of two or more persons coöperating together to accomplish some result for their mutual or common advantage. When the number thus coöperating is large, it is manifest that it is essential to the end of such coöperation that some means should exist of coercing such individuals as resist or antagonize that which is essential to complete the action of such society. There must, then, exist a rule of conduct, and a force competent to coerce such individuals as antagonize or neglect the common will and common good. Such a rule of conduct is the law.

The law of a society is its will in respect to the conduct of its members as among themselves and with strangers to it. As societies become integrated, and endowed with permanent organization tending to perpetuity, they are denominated communities, and as such must, as the condition of their continued existence, have a law binding on all that form a part of such communities, and where dominion over the place where such community exercises its powers is possessed, over all that intrude themselves into such place. If these communities are independent—that is, do not form parts of a still larger society or community—then the will of such community or its law is absolute. If, however, it is subject to a superior authority, it is limited or conditional.

The development of a distinctive will for any given society, whether of the simplest class or possessed of full governmental organization, is the product of natural necessity acted upon by motives of utility. This foundation of governmental authority is found in the instincts of the lower animal nature, as well as in the operations of the mind of man in the earliest of primitive associations. It is by no means essential to the idea of a common will that it should consist of the united volitions of the individual members of a community, or even of the major part of such community. The expression of that will may be by the consent or acquiescence of the community committed to a single individual, as in the case of absolute monarchies; it is none the less the common will in its relation to the conduct of the community and its individual members. Among gregarious animals a single powerful individual seems at times arbitrarily to determine the conduct of the community he governs.

In man there is a principle of individual equality which, though inactive in primitive states, yet in the progress of knowledge and experience asserts itself. It is through the operation of this principle of individual equality that man comes to discover that all the members of a community should participate in the expression of its will. In the earliest stages of human society, as in societies of animals of a lower type than man, the conception of equality is without force, and personal rather than collective rule is the practice, derived, beyond doubt, out of those instincts that form the parental relation, which appear to be identical in both man and many of the lower animals. The fact of the transition from parent to patriarch, or chieftain, and from that to monarch, would imply that the ideas characteristic of the parental relation would be carried over to the succeeding relation, until met by some modifying cause sufficient to give them a new force and interpretation. As, with man, the parental idea seeks to rehabilitate itself in the tribal condition, so, with the lower animals, the gregarious relation perpetuates the essential features of the precedent parental relation.

The question of the nature and origin of a common will in any society is a totally distinct one from that of the causes that have produced some particular mode of gathering and expressing such will prevalent in such society. What we have to consider at this time is the origin and nature of such common will apart from those causes that tend to modify the mode of its expression. It is material to find this foundation behind all formulated experiences and ideas in the instincts of mankind, and to accomplish this the most sure method is to trace it in the general animal instincts that accompany a social nature. We may assume on general principles that a common basis underlies the instincts of all animal natures, and that instinctive causes producing certain consequences in the case of the lower animals exist as tendencies in man when his conduct reflects similar consequences.

Starting from the idea that a common interest and a common will exist in some degree in all societies of lower animals, it becomes necessary to ascertain what are the elements that enter into the composition of that common will. It is manifest that the habit of the kind of animal in question is an important factor. That habit, as it exists at any moment of time, must be the general law of such society. It is, indeed, formulated from the instincts by the action of the animal and his ancestors linked together by heredity, but can not be considered as identical with the instinct in all respects. It is like the identity between rough metal and some object of utility or beauty made from such metal, identity of substance, as distinguished from that of form. What we recognize as instincts are tendencies to certain action inseparable from certain natures. It would not be inappropriate to call these instincts principles of the animal nature, using that term in the same sense in which we would those fundamental tendencies that exist in all moral or rational natures. This does not imply identity between animal instincts and moral tendencies, but that the two sustain like relations to the systems they support.

As animal instincts are the substance, and animal habit the form, of animal life, they must be regarded as factors in the formation of a common purpose and common will. The remaining factor is a conception of utility formed by the society, or by some individual in its behalf. An object or end is propounded as agreeable to the habit and instinct of the society that demands coöperation, and expression is given to this purpose as the common will by the voice or motions of a leader.

In the sketch just presented we have an outline of what takes place in human associations, as it regards the formation of a common will. In every community of men the habits of its individuals constitute a general law. These habits have been mainly derived by heredity, modified by various means. Certain tendencies have taken form more or less developed in these habits, and still continue to operate as modifying causes in the further development of habit. So far as these habits are essential to maintain the social state and attain its ends, they are imperative, and assume the form of law; that is, are embodied in the common will. Beyond this there must be an authority to select the means of maintaining the society and the ends it shall pursue, and to prescribe the conduct of individuals in reference to the community and to each other. This is the public law of society.

The usages, customs, and practices prevailing in any community are the aspect of the civilization of such community—indeed, they are its civilization in a formal sense. The social quality itself consists in conformity to common usages, customs, and practices. Considering all the various methods and formularies of action and speech that prevail in any community with the sanction of general consent, we may generalize these elements under the single term, the habit of the community. These habits, when imperatively exacted, as essential to the welfare of the community, and of the individuals composing it, are a part, and important part, of its laws. It is not necessary to assume that there ever has been any legislative expression of the common will rendering such habits imperative. Usages, customs, and practices prevailing generally throughout a community tend to formulate themselves as laws. All existing systems of law attest this fact, and, indeed, the bulk of what constitutes the body of the law is traceable to this source. As there must be in every community a legislative power, there is a possibility that habits of mutual conduct and dealing may be externally imposed upon the community at the suggestion of utility or imitative of other peoples; but this is a source from which modification, rather than original tendency, is to be expected, and in the main the primitive habit of a community will be found to account for all succeeding phenomena.

It is important to observe that fundamental to this habit lie certain tendencies that serve both to unify each community with all others, and to mark individual peculiarities. It is tendency that takes the form of habit, and therefore tendency is the reason of habit propounding limits within which particular habits are possible and others impossible. These tendencies are the exterior form of what we call principles. Conduct springing from a tendency indirectly springs from its principle, but its form may be very remote from what such principles properly understood would suggest. The rational quality in man enables him to become conscious of the principles that underlie the surface of his action, and through the knowledge of these principles he corrects his tendencies, and produces conduct conformable to such principles. The civilization of communities passes through a similar stage of enlightened self-consciousness. The tendencies of communities that are thus formulated into general and particular habits exist in consequence of certain deep-lying principles that admit of interpretation, and, as they are properly interpreted, produce modifications in the tendencies themselves, and in their superimposed habits.

Every organized community possesses a function through which it becomes self-conscious of its habits and tendencies. This function is allied with the possession of judicial power, which consists in the rectification of individual conduct when at variance with the common will. Through the exercise of this function, in the course of judicial action, those usages, customs, and practices that are generally accepted, and, according to the nature of society, vital to its maintenance and to the maintenance of social relations among the individuals of the community, are distinguished as imperative, and become standards of right and wrong by which to measure the conduct of individuals for the purpose of rectification. These cognitions constitute the main body of the law. The method by which the judicial function thus compares the conduct of the community with that of individuals involves the necessity of discovering and stating the principles that underlie the tendencies of the community as a means of interpreting conduct and intention. These principles, thus brought to light, constitute the principles of the law, and are the means by which judicial action unifies the habit of the community, the legislative expression of the common will, and the expression of individual will that imposes individual obligation.

All the obligations springing from these three sources constitute the law of the community as containing that of its individual members, and are reducible to a general obligation to conform to the habit of the community as it regards all usages, customs, and practices of an imperative nature; to conform to the common will specifically expressed, and to such obligations as spring from the individual power of self-obligation.

CHAPTER II.

NATURE AND ORIGIN OF RIGHTS, OBLIGATIONS, AND POWERS.

THAT which concerns the law of a community is the conduct of individuals. The idea of conduct embraces not only that of the actions of men, but of their omissions to act in given cases. As the object of government is to secure the coöperation of individuals to produce general and particular ends demanded by the common welfare, it is not only necessary that it should prevent obstructive action, but compel action that is material for such ends, or, what is subservient to the same purpose, should establish certain equivalences to compensate for improper actions performed and proper ones withheld. Its office is thus to coördinate action, and has therefore for its subject the conduct of individuals. Although a community has material interests, such as property to protect or manage, still this is accomplished by means of public duties imposed, for that purpose, upon particular individuals, so that the community attains all its ends by means of laws governing the conduct of individuals, and by the force it possesses for rendering these laws efficacious.

The proper function of the law is to establish and enforce obligations, rights, and powers. By obligations, in a legal sense, must be understood all limitations imposed by public authority upon the natural liberty of individuals to control their own actions, or those of others subjected to their authority. An obligation presupposes a certain degree of power or capacity over the subject of such obligation. Where no such power exists, no obligation exists, and hence it is that our law does not put the same estimation on conduct that results from overpowering necessity that it does upon the actions and omissions of those who have the capacity to conform to the law. It follows that the obligation of an individual is limited to the measure of his powers.

It is proper to observe that powers, in the sense here employed, are not restricted to that class known to the law by the technical term *powers*, such as a power to create a charge on the land of another or to bind another by a contract, which class of powers are here treated under the general denomination of *delegated powers*. Whatever capacity of action or abstention an individual possesses, capable of producing civil consequences, is a power in the sense here employed.

It is manifest that, among the many acts of which any individual is capable, in a natural sense, some are of such interest to the community that its welfare or orderly relations among its members demand that they should be performed; others are of such a nature that for the same reasons they should be omitted; others again are indifferent as it regards the welfare and duty of the community. Actions appertaining to the first two of these classes are the proper subject of obligations, imposed either expressly by the will of the community or implied from the nature of the social state, while the last class named embraces such actions as may be performed or omitted at the pleasure of the individual, including the great body of actions that an individual is capable of performing within the liberty allowed by the law. It would follow that every act within the natural capacity of any individual is the subject of an obligation of a civil character. If it is an act which must be performed or omitted, then, clearly, it is the subject of an obligation, binding the person capable of performing such act. If it may be performed or omitted at pleasure, then such performance or omission is a right protected by obligations imposed upon all others having a natural capacity to interfere with such right, binding them to respect it. It is obvious, therefore, that the civil obligations and rights of any individual, aggregated, are equal to his entire civil powers.

Each individual in a civil community possesses natural and

civil powers, to which may be added, according to the organic constitution of such community, political powers. Natural powers are such as result through the operation of the laws of nature; civil, such as result through the operation of the laws of the community; while political powers, where enjoyed, are delegated out of the civil right of the community considered as an individual.

Natural powers are such as may be conceived to exist in a state of nature apart from the existence of organized or civil society. The physical, moral, and intellectual forces of an individual, to the extent that they may exist apart from the influence of organized society, impose a limit to such natural powers. It may be assumed that the physical powers of man are in the largest development, at least in individual instances, in the natural state, as they must of necessity be then in constant and vigorous exercise to maintain his rights and enforce the obligations due him by others. Under the denomination of moral powers are included those influences which, apart from the exercise of physical strength, draw around man the family, the tribe, and the casual or permanent associations characteristic of a social state anterior to its attaining an organized condition. The basis of the sentiment on which the associative function of moral influence depends is the desire of the weak for protection from the strong, so that in a state of nature it may be affirmed that there is a distinct quantitative relation between the physical and the moral relations of individuals, thus reducing social power in that condition to physical superiority. Intellectual power, as the means of determining the action of others through the force of ideas, must of necessity receive immense enhancement from the means of culture afforded by organized society, and should be regarded as in an imperfect state until moral equilibrium is attained by the suppression of physical superiorities as acting on the motives that lead to conduct.

It is essential to the idea of society that some degree of liberty attached to the exercise of natural powers should be relinquished. Every association, for any purpose, presupposes an agreed line of conduct in some direction, and, to the extent and in the direction of such line, liberty of action is converted into necessity. This is the essential idea of law, the necessary condition of associated action. Thus it happens that when men are living together in communities, who are capable of separating themselves from such communities, there are implied in their conduct certain obligations, the nature and extent of which are determinable, in the absence of any statement of agreed conditions, by the nature of the object they have in view in thus becoming or remaining members of such community and the conditions essential to the accomplishment of such purpose. The law, in the course of its ordinary administration, assumes, from such sources, to state the conditions and agreements implied by the naked fact of association for a given purpose, and, applying the same principles to the condition of men living together in social communities, it has the means of stating the obligations that must be assumed as implied in such act of association.

Somewhere within that line that expresses the limits of the natural powers of the individual must be drawn another line, representing what liberty in the exercise of natural powers is consistent with the fact of association for the purposes of civil society. That which is bounded by this second line is the civil power, or right, or liberty of the individual, or what is called his *civil liberty*, as that term will be hereafter defined. That which is within natural liberty, but not within civil liberty, stands as the subject of an implied obligation that it shall not be exercised, being inconsistent with social conditions. That which is within the civil liberty of the individual, as it stands affected by the naked fact of the existence of civil society, is subject to still further encroachment. When that society, having attained an organic will, propounds certain specific objects to be pursued, there must be a further limitation of the liberty of the individual in order that aid may be obtained in moving along that line of purpose and that resistance along such line may be eliminated. For this a new line of individual liberty must be drawn within that marking the general civil liberty, which represents a still narrower definition of liberty, that we may define as legal liberty. This limitation is effected by public law; that is, by the legislative will of the community.

Again, this degree of liberty may be narrowed by the voluntary act of the individual himself. He may assume obligations of an imperative character, reducing his legal liberty below that which exists as consistent with social conditions, and as reduced by the exercise of the power of imposing obligations possessed by the community as a sovereign. It is from these sources that the various obligations arise that constitute the law, all being diminutions of natural liberty.

Civil powers may be defined as consisting of those natural powers of acting or omitting to act at pleasure that are not taken away as a consequence of being a member of a civil community and of the power of abstaining from the performance of such acts as are thus prohibited. That it is strictly accurate to enumerate among powers that of abstaining from action is readily made apparent. If an act is forbidden by law under penalties, and it is still performed, though under the coercion of overpowering necessity, the power of abstaining from such act being wanting, no culpability arises. This shows that what the law in such a case seeks to act upon is the power of abstaining, and, when that is wanting, takes no notice whether the act forbidden is or is not performed. This places the power of abstaining from action in the position of the subject to which the obligation relates.

Civil powers, as thus defined, represent the powers that would appertain to a citizen of a community if all expressions of its legislative will should be withdrawn and he should be affected by no obligation originating in the individual power of self-obligation. This definition makes a clear distinction between civil and legal powers, which appears to be demanded by the various senses applied to the term civil.

That which raises the quality of civil above that of natural powers is the circumstance that they are enforced by the authority and force of the whole community under which they are enjoyed. The immense energy that is imparted to the powers of an individual by bringing the irresistible force of the community to their enforcement is the motive to which we must ascribe the formation of civil society. The weaker members of a community derive the greatest benefit from the concentration of force; but still a motive remains for inducing even the strongest, who in a state of nature would have the greatest advantage, to enter into the civil state. In a state of nature the strongest may be compelled to yield to associated force, and hence the advantages of extraordinary individual force may prove so precarious as to be readily exchanged for diminished powers of a higher degree of certainty and stability.

The formation of civil society thus considered as a change brought about in the natural rights of the members of a community is a surrender of a certain freedom of action, in order to receive the aid of the community in the enforcement of such powers as are retained. It has, therefore, according to legal definition, the essential characteristics of a contract between the individuals of a community: modifying the powers belonging to the natural state, establishing certain fundamental obligations and correlative rights, and furnishing the means by which future modifications of such obligations and rights may be made.

That which distinguishes this obligatory transaction from all others is the fact that through it sovereign power comes into existence as delegated out of individual powers. It may be illustrated in this respect by the analogy of a contract, in virtue of which corporate rights come into existence through the operation of the law of the land. The new element, or legal being, is composed in part of the law of the land and in part of the aggregation of certain individual powers; and, once that it comes into existence, it can not be destroyed except by the concurrence of all the minds from which it emanated. It can not be disputed that there is an imperative law imposed on man's nature, independent of his volitions, rendering it necessary that he should be the subject of sovereign authority; and this law, by whatever name or character we may describe it, takes a part in the consequences that flow from the voluntary union of men in societies with a view to the formation of government. Some, looking to the phenomena of nature, where this law is found operative, prefer to call it natural law, from the association in which it is found; others, looking to causes rather than conditions, characterize it as the divine law, or the law of God. In both cases the object contemplated is the same. It follows, upon strictly legal principles, that the obligation imposed by the existence of society can not be dissolved without the concurrence of that supreme law that is one of its constituent elements; and such an act of concurrence is called an act of justice. It is the province of justice through its administration to dissolve that which has lost its legal sanction and vitality; and hence it is that war, the great agent for modifying and dissolving compacts of government, has uniformly, in ancient as well as modern times, been associated in idea with methods of administering justice. That as such it may be corrupt and corrupting is a view that may be taken of it in common with other modes of administering justice.

It is manifest that it is the interest of the individual that the aid afforded by government should extend to all his rights and powers. Having parted with the natural right of coercing the actions of others for the purpose of redress, powers, standing on the footing of merely natural powers, without any civil quality, and, therefore, without the possibility of enforcement through the aid of the community, would be worthless, as capable of giving rise to no enforceable obligation, and, for want of a corresponding civil obligation, could not become the subject of civil rights.

It is proper here to notice a common impression, that the right of self-defense has not acquired the status of a civil right, but is the unchanged remnant of former natural right. This is evidently a misconception, for the law not only recognizes the right of self-defense, but both places it under limitations and affords protection in its exercise. In this respect, which is decisive of the question, the right of self-defense is not distinguishable from all other rights arising under the civil law. No doubt the idea of self-defense is borrowed from the natural state, just as the law of the first occupancy of land and goods, waste and unclaimed, is borrowed from natural law; but both are recognized and regulated by the civil law, and can only be enjoyed by its permission.

It may be affirmed, in view of what has been said, that the law bases its action wholly on civil powers, though recurring constantly to natural powers as a means of interpreting those of a civil nature. It remains briefly to observe, in regard to political powers, that they are the creation of the action of the community, having no previous or independent existence, and as such are granted to individuals or withheld at the pleasure of the community. Under these powers are embraced the right of making laws and authorizing public agents, and constraining the actions of individuals through the administration of laws, whether enjoyed as a personal or sole prerogative, or in part with others, and whether exercised directly or indirectly through the choice of others authorized for such purpose.

CHAPTER III.

ORIGIN OF FUNDAMENTAL SOCIAL LAW.

WHILE, as has been seen, powers civil and political are the ultimate subjects of legal science, the method of that science is based upon the nature and incidents attached to obligations. In the practical treatment of the rights of persons and things, by the common law-writers the prominent place is given to rights, and obligations have been treated principally as the means of modifying rights. This would seem at variance with the statement that obligations instead of rights are the basis of the scientific method; but it must be remembered that the law has an art as well as a science, and that the composition of our law-books has been influenced more by the wants of the practical lawyer than by the demands of abstract investigation. The idea of a legal right has a positive value that gives it relative prominence where practical considerations are principally concerned, while it is equally accordant with the nature of scientific investigation that ideas of an abstract and analytical nature should become the basis of classification. In a work on practical engineering, the materials employed and the purposes for which they are designed dictate naturally the order in which the various subjects are treated, while, in a work devoted to a more general treatment of the same subjects in reference to the various laws to which they are or may be subjected, the order of treatment would be dictated by the nature of the principles and laws by which they are to be tested rather than by the particular nature or forms of the material substances themselves. It is in the sense just made clear that obligations constitute the basis of the methods of legal investigation.

The comments just made will be rendered clear when the exact relation between obligations and rights is considered. A right has for its subject either the control of material substances or the action of persons. The dominion and ownership of land or personal property is an instance of the first class, and a right to demand the performance or the withholding of an act of some kind is illustrative of the second class. This classification is not accurate or exhaustive, but presents with sufficient clearness the distinction that serves in the practical treatment of the subject, and is sufficient for the immediate purpose. We will, then, in the first place, inquire what we mean by a right of property in material substances. Apart from any question of the right of others to control a particular substance, the ability of a person to do so is one of natural capacity alone, into which no legal idea enters. It is only when such an act of control is obstructed by the act or claim of right of another, either actual or potential, that the capacity of such control becomes a legal question, for the obvious reason that the law deals directly only with the conduct of persons, and indirectly with the material substances upon which action may take place. It is only when an action of an individual affects some other individual that the idea of conduct is attached to it, and it becomes a ground of legal question. Property, in a legal sense and considered as a right, denotes the possibility that the person to whom it may be ascribed may perform rightfully certain acts, to the exclusion of all other persons from performing the same acts. It is this exclusion of others from doing what we ourselves may do that constitutes the principal element of the idea of property; and, as the ground upon which the means of such exclusion can be demanded of the community is the obligation imposed by the nature of society itself, it is apparent that the legal conception of property is fundamentally based upon the obligation that rests upon all individuals other than the one whom the law calls the owner to abstain from obstructing such acts as he, as owner, has an exclusive right to perform. In other words, the legal virility of a right is the means of its enforcement, and the legal basis of that right is the ground upon which the means of enforcement may be demanded.

As it regards the remaining class of rights involving a claim for the performance on the part of another of some act, it needs no elucidation to show that such rights consist in a claim to enforce some obligation, and thus fundamentally are based upon the obligation the existence of which is essential to the existence of the right itself.

It can not be doubted, then, that obligations are the fundamental entities on which the method of legal science rests, and must be taken as the basis and starting-point of legal classification for scientific purposes. While this is true, still, as has been already indicated, it does not necessarily follow that the distribution and sequence of the various topics that go to make up our books of practical law should be influenced by this consideration, but may depend upon certain external analogies between such topics conveniently connecting them in the mind for ready reference.

It is clear upon general principles, that hold good throughout all departments of investigation, that the primary obligation is that out of which all derivative obligations must spring, and therefore must contain in itself, in principle, all the elements that are found in all the various derived obligations in the various forms of modification, and hence must contain what we must properly understand as the universal principles of the law.

In order to form a clear conception of what is meant by the universal principles of the law, it is proper to notice that, from a scientific point of view, the law consists of formulated propositions that concern the conduct of mankind in society, establishing certain standards of legal right and wrong, and certain consequences as resulting from conformity or non-conformity with such standards. Certain of these propositions are only applicable under particular conditions that may or may not exist in any particular case, while others are in their nature applicable to all the members of a class of cases, large or small, and others again are of such a nature that they must be present as actual or potential elements in every case that can arise. The propositions that have the character last described are properly designated as the universal principles of the law, and are *universal constants* in all propositions embodying any conclusion of the law, either as an active or potential element.

It is, then, of prime importance that the precise nature of the fundamental obligation that must be regarded as existing between the members of a community should be understood, as the history of the development of legal rules and principles can not be complete without studying them at their source and in their origin. It is necessary here to distinguish clearly those obligations that spring from the nature of society from those positive dispositions that constitute the legal sanction of the government of such society. Constitutions of government, whether produced by enactment or derived by tradition and long-established usage, must be regarded as outgrowths of the act by which such society was formed and the foundation of its law laid, and not as identical with it, as will appear more clearly when the essential nature of the fundamental societary law comes to be considered more minutely.

Before proceeding to the subject just named, a word of explanation is necessary to prevent conclusions being drawn from the idea that civil government rests upon an implied obligation that belongs to other than the legal sphere of investigation.

The law takes but a single aspect of human affairs, and its principles and rules, while they should be true to what is observed in that aspect, do not necessarily embrace what can only be observed from some other distinct and independent point of view. It is not essential to the idea of the obligation inseparable from society that such an agreement should have been formally made. The methods of the law are such that it necessarily and constantly assimilates transactions of which the precise origin is unknown to transactions originated in a certain definable mode. This is the basis of its mode of implying contracts. To find, then, the origin of the principles and the rules of the law, it is not necessary that resort should be had to actual historical facts. Law is not history in the general sense, and, regarded as a science, its immediate subject is not the actual transactions that have taken place among mankind, but certain principles and rules of conduct; and, so far as it may be regarded as a history of such principles and rules, its office is to trace them back through successive derived forms to their original form. Nor does the law, as a science, deal with the external causes that have impressed those characteristics on the mind of man that, being studied, give rise to the idea of principles and rules of the law. Other branches of science deal with the nature of and connection between such causes, while the science of the law is confined to a narrower class of phenomena.

It is equally important to affirm that the principles and rules of the law are not cognate to any particular form, method, or principle of the organization or administration of government. They have their roots back of all forms of government, and the consequences flowing from them, though modified by the structure and principles of particular governments, are always such as the nature of their origin would suggest. The separation between law and politics is so complete that any attempt to blend them tends to produce that which is neither amenable to the principles of the law nor the precepts of political science.

Having premised thus much, we are ready to inquire what, according to the modes of investigation characteristic of the law, must be the nature of that obligation that attaches itself necessarily to every association for governmental purposes. As the primary object of such an association must, on the principles of legal construction, be taken to be the creation of a government of some kind for the society composed of those individuals entering into it, it must have for its leading feature the creation of sovereign power and its delegation to some agent for the purpose of exercise. Such sovereign power must, in the first instance, be considered as vested in the whole community, for the law must consider it possible that an entire community may be endowed with sovereign power prior to the creation of any agency or office through which it may be administered, whether by an absolute sovereign or by a more limited agency. To affirm the contrary would be to assert that the law can not conceive of sovereign power in its most generalized form, which would be denying it a capacity essential to full reasoning. The law is familiar with the idea of first creating a power or estate and afterward vesting it specifically for exercise, and in familiar instances supplies a want of such investment on the principles of trusts. It is a fundamental principle of construction, as applied especially to governmental compacts, that the grant of a power implies the grant of the necessary means of its exercise. Applying this principle to the case in hand, we must recognize, as part of the original intention of governmental society, such means as are necessary to effect the lodgment of such sovereignty for exercise in the hands of some agent capable of exercising it. It is clear that the whole community can not exercise sovereign authority, as an act of all its members, with the effect proper to such power, for, the moment such exercise should run counter to the will of any one of its members, that member refusing to coöperate, the actual exercise would be by a part of the society only, or not at all. It must, then, be concluded that the original delegation of sovereign authority involved the investiture of some part of the community with the power of its exercise. What part is that? In the absence of the specific indication of any particular part, resort must be had to the principles and rules of law to determine, constructively, what part was intended. And here we find a ready answer, for, wherever power of any kind is conferred upon a certain class or number of persons, the general rule is, that it may be exercised by the major part of the persons or class designated. There are exceptions to this rule, but when the nature of the power is such that it is practically valueless, unless exercised by less than the whole number prescribed, the general rule is necessarily applicable in the absence of any interfering limitation specifically imposed upon the power at its creation. This meets the whole case, and enables us to say that upon the principles of legal construction the original intention of society must be regarded as creating sovereign power and lodging it for exercise in the hands of the majority of the community.

If it is objected that the conclusion just stated is narrow, as resting on legal ideas alone, the answer is that it is only drawn for legal purposes, and must be drawn consistently with legal rules. There are only two modes in which the law can determine the character of an individual obligation; one is by actual proof of the facts and circumstances out of which it grew, and the other is by ascertaining its nature and object, and deducing its origin through the principles and rules of the law. Should it appear that any body of men capable of forming civil society had united in terms of agreement variant from that ascribed to such compacts in general, the law would construe such contract according to its nature as proved, without in the slightest degree interfering with the principles and rules from which the foregoing conclusions have been drawn. If it is objected that this deductive method is in itself objectionable when induction is possible, it is at once conceded that the law uniformly prefers induction to deduction as the basis of its inferences, and rests wholly on the latter only when an induction can not be made. The moment, then, that actual proof appears as to what any society intended, the law will act on such proof, but in its absence must employ such deductive means as are in harmony with its rules and principles.

The next question is whether the grant of sovereign power, by virtue of which the majority of the members of a community may impose laws on a non-consenting minority, should, on the principles of the law, be regarded as absolute or limited, as it stands prior to its delegation for exercise. In legal consideration, sovereign authority is not limited by anything contained in its own nature. If subjected to limitation, it must be by an authority competent to delegate or withhold it. Sovereign authority lodged in the hands of a monarch or legislative body is recognized as capable of restriction by the power from which it had its origin; but our law contains no means of limiting sovereign authority of a legislative character, except through the operation of express limitation to which its grant may have been subjected by the organic law out of which it has arisen. In this country, where the law is familiar with such limitations to the exercise of sovereign power in the hands of public agents, it is as destitute of the means of limiting the action and authority of the Constitution-making power as it is under the most absolute government. This is a distinct legal sanction for unlimited authority in the majority of the people of a community. It follows that, as sovereign authority is in its nature affected by no limitation, and as no principle or rule of law can be applied to the transaction of forming a society with such effect as to imply such a limitation, according to legal ideas and for legal purposes, the delegation of sovereign authority by the members of a society to be exercised by the major part of such society is absolute.

The conclusion just stated may seem harsh, and at variance with modern ideas of abstract justice; but that impression will disappear when it is considered that the law has a limited scope and force, and does not exclude, but, on the contrary, accommodates itself to the operation of the larger causes that have in their custody the development of civilization in harmony with the principles of abstract justice. This is merely expressing the proposition that the law does not contain within itself the means of independently advancing the political condition of mankind. An attempt will hereafter be made to demonstrate that the principles of the law contain, and always have contained, that of individual equality, which is the source from which the adaptation of government to the higher needs of man has proceeded; but it will also appear that these principles can not have an effective operation by calling into existence suitable institutional forms until they are discovered through their utility to conserve the interest and advance the condition of communities. While the inspiration from the principle of individual equality is the spirit of liberty, when once discovered, yet it must become embodied in the action of mankind before it can become efficacious in influencing forms of civilization. The law, though conscious of its principles, is powerless to put them in their proper forms. Society, acted upon by a plexus of motives, ordains forms, and it is the province of the reason of the law to interpret such forms by the principles that underlie them. The policy of states contains the germs of institutional forms; law as a rational system can only develop the relation of such forms to fundamental ideas, but can not mold them to its conceptions. It is like a silent hand-post that can point out the way, but can not compel the traveler to pursue it.

It is obvious that a delegation of unlimited sovereignty implies an obligation of unlimited obedience to that authority. It therefore becomes necessary to ascertain whether, upon the principles of legal construction, any distinctive features can be traced in the character of the obligation incident to the social state apart from that which delegates public authority. It has already been said that the compacting of society must be regarded, according to legal apprehension, as a transaction between individuals intended to secure both mutual and common advantages, and to that end creating governmental authority. To hold, then, that it can be construed as if of no more effect than a mere delegation of absolute sovereignty would be to separate the means called into existence from the purpose for which it was so created, which is contrary to the principles of legal construction. The reason of a contract, as well as its formal requirements, must have a part in its construction. Regarded as an implied contract between individuals, it must have the effect of calling into existence mutual obligations, as well as that common obligation to the community as a whole to which all the individuals concerned are equally subjected. It remains, then, to consider what interpretation the law places upon those features of the obligation that consist of mutual obligations between the individual members as distinguished from the common obligation incurred to the community as a whole.

We may here receive aid from historic data by ascertaining that human society has gone through several distinct stages in the course of development. We know, on reliable grounds, that human society existed prior to the development of organized government. The idea of organized government is that of the division and distribution of the powers of government as distinct functions, conferred upon individuals or collective bodies. Until such a division took place, civil law, as we understand it, could not exist. The law is, in one sense, the memory of the state of its past volitions; this is in its nature a reflex function demanding functional separation between the faculty that wills and that which formulates the consequences of the determinations of such will. Such an organized condition as that which is essential to confer upon law a civil character can not be regarded as existing in family or even patriarchal or tribal government, nor in some of the derived forms of an absolute character, such as we know historically to have preceded regular government. There are, then, three distinct historic periods in the development of society: that while in an inorganic condition as it regards government; that of an organized governmental condition; and that of a transition state from the one to the other, partaking of the peculiarities of both the precedent and the subsequent conditions. That such should be the case may be also deduced from the law of development, as that which is structureless must precede the perfecting of structure, and the two must be united by an interval characterized by imperfect or partially developed structural conditions.

It can not be assumed that the civil law is unconscious of the conditions of its own origin, or that it retains no impress of those conditions on its principles and rules. On the contrary, the adaptation of the law to embody in itself the elements of the social state out of which it sprung, and give them a place and office in its more mature system, is evinced in the most striking manner by two of its familiar principles. It recognizes the possibility that at this day, although the law has acquired the rigidity that belongs to maturity, usages and customs may spring up independently of public law, and become embodied as a fixed part of the law. Again, where a community having lived under one sovereign passes under another independent and even absolute sovereign, its laws and customs, so far as not abrogated or changed by the new sovereign, remain obligatory, having the presumed sanction of the new sovereign. These instances illustrate an important proposition applicable to the present inquiry: namely, that civil law at its origin, as such, was competent to, and must have embodied in itself, the usages, customs, and practices of the society out of which it was formed, retaining their substance and form, and conferring upon them the name and sanction of civil authority.

Accepting this historic fact and the principle of law just stated, our course is clear to ascertain in important respects the character that must be ascribed to the mutual obligations that are involved in the obligation inherent to society. It is not only a necessary presumption, but an historic fact, that many usages, customs, and practices existed among the primitive communities that had with them the force of law. The right of property was recognized, and could only exist as a right in virtue of such usages as had the force of law. Habits of dealing, entering into and forming part of their contracts and engagements, are known to exist on the same grounds, and could only exist in virtue of customs recognized as obligatory. So formularies and symbolical representations existed giving rise to practices generally recognized as elements of right. This group of usages, customs, and practices must be regarded as that which we describe under the name of natural law. In the strictest sense it is natural law, because it sprang up in the conduct of man without the influence of artificial systems of government. It is distinguished from civil law by the fact that the latter is the product, in part, of the influence of formal institutions and organic conditions.

It is proper here to correct an impression that has currency, that the natural law means some speculative or abstract system deduced by abstract reasoning alone. The law does not formulate rules of conduct from abstract rules or ideas. Its propositions are based on the usages, customs, and practices that have a fixed hold upon society. It derives from that general source its maxims, rules, and principles. Even where it gives force to the expressed legislative will of the community, it examines that expression by the usages, customs, and practices of the community as gathered up and expressed in its rules and principles, and its institutional and formal requirements founded on legislative enactment are the product of the correlation of such will with the antecedent habit of the community. Its principles and rules are thus strictly inductions from the facts of society. So far as ethical and moral principles are actually embodied in the conduct of mankind, so far the law recognizes these in its principles. It does not reach its general conclusions by reasoning from final causes, which is embraced within the function of politics, but, as it is in the largest form the memory of past actions, it reasons upon what it finds embodied in that memory. Those abstract speculations in which an attempt is made to formulate social conditions and institutions upon general views of the aims of mankind, and the means of attaining them, must be regarded as discussions within the province of politics rather than of the law. The science of the law can make no direct use of such ideas, however valuable in their proper sphere.

If the foregoing be assented to, it leads to the conclusion that civil law is, as it regards its origin, a transformation of natural law, consisting of the usages, customs, and practices held obligatory at the moment when that transformation took place. Such being the case, the constitution of society, upon which civil authority is based, must be regarded as having, at the moment it took effect, converted all existing natural rights, obligations, and powers into those of a civil nature of the same kind and measure, so far as it might be consistent with the nature of civil society, and subject to the sovereign power of the community delegated by such act.

It is not essential to the conclusion just stated, or to the conception upon which it rests, that there should have been any single moment of time when such a social transaction was consummated in form. Implied contracts arise out of facts and circumstances not necessarily concurring in point of time, but out of the consideration that a certain change has been wrought in the relative rights of certain parties, irrespective of the length of time occupied by such transition or the number of the transactions that have served to effect that change. It may be conceded, then, that the transition of society from an inorganic to an organic state may have occupied long periods of time, and proceeded by gradual steps, without in the least affecting the basis of the argument on which the legal estimation of such a transaction depends.

It follows from the foregoing that our law, apart from that which had its origin in the expressed will of the legislative mind, rests on the usages, customs, and practices of primitive society, consistent with the civil state and such as have sprung up in society since the commencement of civil authority. It is a consequence of this view that the principles and rules that were embodied in such usages, customs, and practices, and in the tendencies leading to them, whether recognized as such or latent, became, through the operation of the constitution of civil society, embodied in the civil law, and remain there so long as political society possesses vital conditions.

We have, then, the general elements necessary to construct the idea of the fundamental social obligation. It is an obligation binding upon all permanent members of the community, whether present at or absent from the place where the community exercises its powers, and upon all persons present at such place for either permanent or temporary purposes, and upon all persons having property or rights localized at such place to the extent of their control over such property or rights. It is a delegation of civil power of two kinds—of the fullest possible measure of public power embraced under the name of sovereign power, to the community as a whole—to be exercised according to the will of the major part of such community. It is also a delegation of civil power to each member of the community commensurate with the largest natural power capable of being enjoyed by man in civil society consistently with the nature of such society, subject absolutely to the sovereign power so granted, and diminished by withholding the natural power of using force against the person or property of another for the purpose of vindicating rights, enforcing obligations, or obtaining redress for wrongs, the last-named power being reserved for exercise by the community itself as a public power accompanied with the implied obligation that the community will fully protect the rights and enforce the obligations due to each individual.

It is an obligation binding each individual to conform his conduct to what is in its nature essential to the maintenance of civil society; to such usages, customs, and practices as by general recognition and acceptance are of imperative force; to the requirements of the public authority having due sanction; and to such obligations as may exist or arise under the exercise of the voluntary power of self-obligation.

It will be hereafter shown that these obligations contain an obligation of the individual to respect the rights of person and property of all others by abstaining from such acts as another has an exclusive right to perform; and from molesting or interfering with the person or subject of property of another; and an obligation to use that degree of prudence in the performance of acts within his own right that is sanctioned by the habit of the community to prevent the natural consequences of such uses of his own right from becoming a source of injury to the person or property of others; and also an obligation to use good faith in dealing with the community and all persons.

It will be observed that, according to this, the only obligation imposed absolutely upon the community is that of administering justice, which, though an imperfect obligation, as not being supplied with the means of enforcement, yet, according to the principles of the law, must be regarded as absolute, as it rests upon a particular consideration—namely, the surrender to the community of part of the natural right of the individual; and, as the sovereign power delegated is so delegated in part for the administration of justice, the very end propounded by the granting of such consideration, it is impossible that the end should be subordinated to the means, as it would be if the sovereign power granted could be used to destroy the force of the obligation to administer justice imposed upon the community.

It is not difficult to conceive of an obligation of an imperfect character being absolute, as this is necessarily the character of all absolute obligations binding a sovereign state.

If we suppose a community of persons to have made an express agreement of the character just stated, at the moment it became operative, and prior to any exercise of the sovereign power delegated, all questions as to the rights, obligations, and powers of individuals, and of the community considered as a community, would have to be tested by what was either expressed or implied in such agreement. In other words, such an agreement would to a people so circumstanced supply the full idea of the law, the elements of which would be the state of rights and obligations antecedently existing and those arising from the nature and objects of the agreement itself. As, then, we can affirm that the civil law is in its inception identical with the obligation resulting from the formation of civil society, we have ascertained both its origin and the key to its nature. If this view is correct, then it would be possible to trace all the conclusions of the law derived from its principles backward, until they meet in a single obligation such as would exist as the ordinary legal consequence of the mere fact of the union of men to form civil society, acting upon the habit of the community and the state of rights and obligations existing at the moment of its formation. The inquiry to be hereafter made to ascertain the principles of the law affords an opportunity to test the possibility of such a reduction.

CHAPTER IV.

THE NATURE OF INSTITUTIONAL LAW.

Our inquiry in the natural order must turn to the nature of the law. Its nature in the most general sense is that which we find contained in the broadest possible proposition that can be affirmed regarding it. We can state that proposition from what has gone before. It is an obligation of a perfect character, based on the consent of the individual, containing within itself unlimited means of self-modification in virtue of a delegation of power adequate for such purpose. But an inquiry into the nature of the law can not be satisfied by so generalized a statement, even though its implications argue a transcendent nature and sphere for the law.

The present inquiry concerns rather the science of the law than the substance of the law itself, but will be aided by an exact knowledge of the substantial nature of the phenomena and incidents with which it has to deal. The law in its primary form is *institutional*. It is the fundamental structural feature of government and society. It is not to be denied that other than legal elements enter into the structure of the institutions of society; but comparing those institutions together, as it regards the character of the elements entering into their structure, it will be found that the legal element is *constant* through the whole class, while all other elements are *variable* as affecting only particular institutions or particular groups. As that element which is constant throughout a class is fundamental to that class, it is apparent that the statement is sustained that the 'aw is fundamental to all the institutions of society and government.

From another point of view this same fact appears. The social aspect of man is the nature of the usages, customs, and practices prevailing in his communities. Those habits that are persistent in an individual or society are the basis of his or its character for the reason that their persistency determines within certain limits the character of its future development. It is this property of the habit of the individual which determines the line of future development that we term character or nature. Now, as the law consists of those social habits of man that are imperative and hence persistent, it is obvious that it is perfectly correct to say that the law is the expression of the character or nature of civil society. As such, it must be regarded as fundamental to all the institutions of society into which its habits are gathered up and both utilized and perpetuated.

The institutional character of the law depends upon the fact that it tends directly to connect men together in coöperating groups for mutual assistance and common effort by enforcing the compacts on which such associations depend. From a simple contract between two individuals by which they may interchange property or labor, or unite property and labor, to produce some result of mutual or common advantage, up to the most expanded and complicated institution that performs the largest social functions, the law prescribes the structural principles or skeleton, and sometimes a portion or the whole of the mechanism.

As associated effort is that which marks the highest animal and rational states, and is the means and power of civilization, that which gives effect to such associated effort stands in the place of the first essential of civilization. As this end is accomplished by the law as an institutional system, it becomes of the greatest interest to know by what adaptation of its principles it affords at once strength and stability with that elasticity that confers upon it the character of a mechanism capable of being at the same time employed by each individual, group of individuals, and the community at large, for the accomplishment of the purposes of each where such purposes are reconcilable with the common good.

This brings us to the recognition of the fact that the law, in its most comprehensive sense, embraces both public and private law. Public law is the will of a sovereign binding his subjects; private law is the will of the individual binding himself when carried into execution or expressed as part of an interchange with others of burdens and benefits. When two or more individuals unite in the expression of a common purpose for some end and by means that the law does not exclude, and upon conditions capable of creating an obligation between them, the expressed intention of such parties as it regards their mutual conduct respecting the subject of such agreement, together with all which is necessarily or reasonably to be implied therefrom, becomes the law of that particular transaction, and is technically designated as the law of the contract. This is private law as it regards its origin, but its obligation stands upon the same footing as it regards the general or particular exactions of the law as if it had obtained its origin in the public law purely. Public law, in its institutional character, assumes to give form and method in some degree to all transactions of an obligatory character, and in some cases to propound the ends to be pursued as well as the requisite form and method. It follows that the private law of every transaction of an obligatory character unites with the public law so far as the latter seeks to give form, method, or purpose to such transaction to form the law of the contract or the case; and, being thus incorporated together, the product is not distinguishable from that which we denominate the law in its largest sense. Thus the principle of the law is that of a mechanism receiving in itself the strain of all forces capable of producing permanent effect upon social interests, resolving and directing one part of such forces into lines of useful action, and of balancing and destroying the residue. But the singular peculiarity of this mechanism is the fact that within certain limits each individual, or group of individuals, may induce modifications fitting it to produce particular results in particular cases, not performed by it under other conditions. In this respect the mechanism that bears the closest analogy to it is the animal skeleton, which, while retaining a general form and method of action proper to a particular animal species, undergoes special individualization through the persistent habits of certain individuals, or classes of individuals. This circumstance shows that the law is an organic development, and not an artificial contrivance.

The law, thus considered as the very substance of civilization, gives rise to a science and an operative art, with the first-named of which we have at present specially to deal.

CHAPTER V.

THE SCIENCE OF THE LAW.

The science of the law is the cognition of its institutional actions, and of the principles and rules inherent in such actions, as well as of certain incomplete formulations consisting of axioms and unintegrated propositions. In order to place the idea that the science of the law is entitled strictly to that name upon the firmest foundation, it is proper to affirm that it is not composed of deductions from first principles arranged in a systematic manner, as an ideal up to which man and society should attempt to reach. The science of the law takes no notice of any principle, rule, or fact that is not found practically efficient within the body of the law, considered as an organic institutional system. The science of the law grows out of its previous action, precisely as the reason of man is the ripened product of his conduct. Thus the legal scientist, as the anatomist, deals with the body as it is, and thus is entitled to recognition among those who study the laws of Nature in Nature herself.

The general method of the science of the law will now be briefly stated as a means of disclosing its nature. It is not to be denied that abstract and speculative disquisition has a certain tentative value as possible to produce a good working theory, but the maker of speculative theory has the same place in science that the maker of tools useful to some art has in that art. The scientific method of the law is based upon what the law as a practical institution did in a certain case under known conditions, and the grounds and reasons upon which it acted. The primary facts of legal science are cases involving the actual conduct of men in their dealings with each other, and the deliberate judgment of the law based upon them. What practical law knows of the principles and rules that govern the conduct of men is derived from that conduct, and what the science of the law knows of such principles and rules is obtained from their practicalization in the action of the law as an institutional system.

The method itself is simple. It consists in resolving each case into its elements, or, what is the same, reducing complex relations between parties to simple, elemental relations. Cases are compared with cases. If a proposition containing an important truth, capable of being affirmed of a single case, is equally capable of being affirmed of all cases, that proposition contains a universal principle of the law. Where a proposition stated from a particular case is common to a great group of cases, leaving unclassified another great group, a general principle has been reached of the largest possible value. This statement, while it illustrates the ends that the science of the law seeks to reach, does not illustrate the steps necessary in order to reach them, for the actual progress of science is by gradual steps from particulars to generals. Propositions full and complete, and excluding all extraneous matter, must first be framed. Propositions recurring constantly throughout given classes of cases must be stated in their relation to the conditions under which they recur, and such statements constitute rules of law. The comparison and analysis of these rules leads to arranging them in classes in respect of fundamental propositions that are constant throughout large or small classes, and such propositions contain the principles of the law. Thus upward, step by step, the mind proceeds in its cognition of generals from particulars, and universals from generals.

A case is the record of a controversy between parties involving their conduct in relation to certain general or specific obligations, and as it regards a particular subject of dealing, containing a judicial solution, the result of a comparison between the conduct of such parties and the standards of right conduct recognized by the law, and the consequences of non-conformity with such standards. The usual elements of an adjudicated case are: 1. The habit of the community in a given case, as modified by public law and the individual obligations of the parties. 2. More or less of the process of comparing such case with the cases constituting some class, for the purpose of stating the relation of the case to a previously formulated rule. 3. The discussion of the various opinions that have been produced in the course of the consideration of the class of cases to which such case is referred; and 4. Some recognition of the principles assumed as contained in the rule applicable to it.

The value of such discussion is tentative merely, the fact of permanent value being the facts presented and the consequences derived from them in their bearing on the parties. Such a judicial act constitutes a primary fact as denoting the action of the law under given conditions. It is by the comparison and analysis of facts of this nature that the tendencies and underlying principles of the law are discovered, precisely as all phenomena of animal life are examined to determine the fundamental truths underlying such life. In rational action, which is the highest form of animal action, the same relations between phenomena and principles exist that exist in the lower phases of life; the subject of the relationship differs, but the relation itself is constant throughout all the departments of nature.

The method of the science of the law thus briefly stated links it in principle and practice with all other sciences, or, what is more accurate, with the general method by which the mind advances in exact knowledge, and places the science of the law abreast with all other sciences resting on inductive methods, even if it is not entitled on historical grounds to the leadership.

It is not within the direct purpose of the present treatment of the subject to give particular attention to the law as an operative art, but it is manifest, from what has already been said, that the reason of the law can not run beyond its practical action, and the practice of the law, thus occupying an empirical relation to its rational development, may bar or open the way to that development. No better office can be performed for the practice of the law, and none is more needed, than to exhibit to it the possibility of its influence, the material out of which higher motive is largely coined.

CHAPTER VI.

COMMON, PUBLIC, AND PRIVATE OBLIGATIONS.

We come next to consider more in detail the essentials and particular characteristics of obligations. If we are to consider the law as the expanded form of an obligation of a general nature, and that the process of development has transformed a simple form of obligation into a complex system of derived obligations, reducible in principle to the primary form, then it would follow that all obligations have certain common properties that define their common nature. The study of these common properties lays the foundation for an understanding of the specific differences between them.

Three distinct classes of obligations have already been recognized: first, those that arise, between men associating themselves for the purpose of forming civil society, out of the mere fact of such association, independently of any act performed by the community thus brought into being; second, those that are created by the expression of the sovereign will of the community, which have been already referred to as obligations arising by public law; and third, obligations created by individuals through the power of individual self-obligation.

Thus the members of any community are, as among themselves and in their relation to the community, under the operation of three classes of obligations. In the first place, they are under an obligation, fundamental to all others, that exists in consequence of their relation as members of such community, and which is interpreted from two sources: first, the habit of the community, and second, the nature of civil society. In the second place, they are bound by whatever declarations of the legislative will of such community have been made in the past that are of present force. In the last place, they are bound by all obligations that they have personally contracted, or have become subject to, by the acceptance of some benefit to which an obligation had been previously attached.

For the sake of definiteness, the obligations of the first class will be termed common obligations, from the fact that they are the source of that class of rights known as common rights. The second class will be termed public obligations, as embracing statutes and all other promulgations declarative of the public will. The third class will be termed private obligations, from the fact that they constitute private law, and their force is in establishing private right.

Our investigation embraces directly civil obligations—that is, obligations of such a nature that the law recognizes them, and assumes to give efficacy to them. Obligations that have not such binding force exist among men, and indeed their existence is essential to any complete conception of the social state; but such obligations form directly no part of the public or private law. It is true that, for some purposes, the law notices the existence of such obligations as it terms moral obligations, and attaches legal consequences to them, but only as an incident of the administration of legal rights having their origin in imperative obligations. The discussion of this subject will be reached in a later place.

The law being an organic system, capable of growth or development from its primitive forms and undergoing modification from the action of external causes and from its essential principles, it would follow that whatever principles and laws are of universal application to organic growth must determine fundamentally its development. One of these principles is, that all derivative forms must partake of the nature of that from which they are derived. As thus the law is the expanded form of the common obligations of society, all the obligations that come into existence must rest upon the nature of this common obligation.

As it appears that a distinct portion of the law rests upon

the common obligations, and consists of what is derivable out of these obligations, it is obvious that such part of the law must have some distinctive designation, and such a designation is afforded by the nature of its foundation. The term common law exactly defines that part of the body of the law that is not traceable to statutory sources, or, at least at this day, has no recognized relation to such sources. This is not using the term common law in an unusual sense. The common law of England expresses a modified idea of the common law in general, as localized in that country at some particular time. As the term common law is generally used, apart from any reference to its state in England, it must be regarded as embracing precisely that part of the law here described as resting upon the common obligations incident to society. Whether the demonstration that will be hereafter attempted, to show that that portion of the law does in fact arise from the sources that have been pointed out, is conclusive or otherwise, it is clear that such demonstration will not be complete unless it accounts for all that is understood as embraced under the term common law.

An obligation is a stable form of volition, the will being the substance, and the obligation its form, and its sanction being the ground of stability. When the volitions of an individual assume a coherent and logical relation as among themselves and adaptation to a definite end, that characteristic of the will is described as a purpose, and in the case of a community as a policy, from the fact that it gives promise of a definite result. The will of the individual and that of the community are the determining causes of all obligations. Public policy gives rise to public laws, and private purpose to private obligations, constituting private law.

The public law being, then, the embodied will of the community, a statute contains within itself the policy determining that will. But this proposition is subject to a very important restriction, as applied to interpretation based on the distinction between law and politics, and that is, that only so far as a policy is actually embodied in a law is it an element in the interpretation of that law. A producing cause can not be said to be embodied in a product unless there appears in that product some element of form due to the operation of such producing cause. This is an important deduction, as presenting the reason that lies at the basis of the rules of construction. In order to construct the policy of a law from an enactment, every inference must rest on some element of form contained within the act itself. The court making such construction, looking at the expressions of the law, must be able to say that the expression in some particular can not be accounted for unless a certain intention formed part of the policy that dictated it, in order to produce an inference having the force of a *necessary* implication; and in those cases where greater latitude is allowed in construction, and the *reasonableness* of an inference is allowed as its justification, although the court is not required to say that the form of the law can be accounted for in no other way than by assuming a certain policy to exist, yet it must be able to trace in the expression that which undoubtedly points to a particular inference, though possibly not excluding the possibility that it might have come from some other source.

It is obvious from the foregoing that the principles stated must be common to obligations of all classes.

As the common obligations that are inherent in civil associations are derived from the voluntary act of the individual, the principles that have just been stated are applicable to them. The fact that these obligations are only ascertainable by a process of implication does not affect this proposition. The essential nature of obligations is the same whether they are express or implied. In both cases there must be something to evidence a determination of the will; in the one case that evidence may consist in the direct declarations of the party, while in the other it is inferable only from conduct and declarations combined, or from conduct alone. So in applying the principles of construction that arise out of the essential nature of obligations, the conduct of the party replaces the declaration of intent in the other case as it regards the application of these principles. Private obligations may be implied; so that no difference, in this respect, exists between the two classes. It is therefore clear that common and private obligations are referable to the same type.

In order to assimilate all the sources from which obligations derive their nature so as to reduce them to a single typical original, it is necessary to inquire whether in nature a statute and an obligation are identical. No objection to its being in substance an obligation can arise from the fact that it is consummated through delegated powers, for that is one of the modes by which private obligations may be created. If the familiar definition be taken that a statute is a rule of conduct imposed by a superior upon an inferior, then it is clearly an obligation. The only case that it is necessary to examine in that connection is that of a statute granting some right coupled with no words of command or obligation. According to the view of rights that has been already presented, such a statute is in substance a command, to all others than the person or persons on whom such right is conferred, to desist from interference with the exercise of the right, and such a statute is a warrant to the law to fix upon all persons interfering with such right the charge of wrong-doing, which is in its nature the violation of some obligation. It must be concluded that the three obligations from which the law derives its power to act—namely, the common obligation of society itself, the public obligation imposed by statutes and other declarations of the public legislative will, and that created by the voluntary act of individuals—are identical in nature, and are resolvable into a single type of obligation.

CHAPTER VII.

PRIVATE OBLIGATIONS.

As private obligations are molded to the various purposes of life, and are thus developed in the greatest variety of form, their study will afford the best means of ascertaining the characteristics of obligations at large and of developing their principles. Private obligations, as has been said, are created by the exercise of the individual power of self-obligation. In order to create a private obligation there must be some specification of the grounds, conditions, and terms of such obligation from which it may be stated in form, either published as the common act of the parties, or disclosed in their acts and declarations in the course of their mutual dealings. To this statement of the intended form of the obligation the law applies the designation contract. The term agreement is also very commonly applied for the same purpose, but, as the term agreement is used in a general sense that includes other transactions than such as result in legal obligation, the term contract is to be preferred as conveying a definite sense.

The necessary elements of a contract according to established usage are:

1. That it must be the voluntary act of the contracting parties.
2. Such parties must have legal capacity to contract.
3. The contract must be made upon adequate consideration.
4. It must have a competent subject and terms of contract.
5. It must be free from fraud on the part of the person asserting its validity.

Before examining these necessary properties of contracts, it is proper to the present line of investigation to show that such properties are in substance, though not always in form, necessary elements of every legal obligation. This would involve the necessity of drawing an analogy between obligations created by public statutes of all kinds and private contracts. Obligations created by public authority being consummated by authority delegated for that purpose, must, according to the principles of the law, have the same effect as if such obligations were expressed in a contract identical with the common obligations out of which such delegative authority arose. The law justly imputes to every member of the community voluntary acquiescence in the fundamental sanctions on which public law rests. According to the principles and rules of law, men must be assumed to intend that which their conduct implies. This principle results from the common obligation to good faith. Conduct that misrepresents intention must be either accidental or intentionally deceptive. In either case the consequence of the misfortune, or the fault, as the case may be, must, on familiar principles, fall upon the unfortunate or the guilty party. Good faith excludes unintentional deception, or misfortune, as well as intentional. Hence the reasonableness of the rule that makes conduct the incontrovertible evidence of intention. Applying these principles to men living together in voluntary social relations, it obviously leads to the imputation of acquiescence in the existence of such state, or, what is equivalent, to acquiescence in the common obligations that are the sanction of such state. But there is still another and general ground in human nature for the same conclusion. Upon the same principle on which the law imputes to each individual a desire to preserve his natural life it must impute a desire to preserve the society that shelters him, for the civil life of the community is the civil life of each of its members, and its maintenance must be regarded as a necessity of the individual, forming his motives just as natural life is regarded as such necessity. In this respect each member of the community is bound by the obligations imposed by public authority on the ground of consent.

That legal capacity should be essential to the authority of

any enactment of the public law is manifest. As it must exist inferentially in all whose assent is essential to the sanction of government, so it must exist in the agents of expressing the public will. Where public powers are derived for exercise through written constitutions, their delegation and qualifications are directly evidenced, but whether so derived, or resting on usage or tradition, such powers must emanate from the sanction of society in order to give validity to their exercise. Usurped authority may be legitimatized, but when that takes place it is the result of acquiescence which is the foundation of the rule of *de facto* authority. That every legislative power may be so limited by the terms of its delegation as to give rise to legal question as to the legal capacity of a legislative body to impose particular obligations, is established by the doctrines of constitutional law as settled in this country. It may, then, be affirmed, equally of obligations created by public authority and those created by private authority, that such obligations can not exist apart from the presence of legal capacity competent for their creation.

That every public obligation has its force in the considerations upon which the common obligations rest has been sufficiently illustrated already. It is self-evident that, as it regards a subject-matter and terms, the reason of the requirement as to contracts applies equally to all obligations. As it regards the obligation to good faith, the law imputes good faith to all expressions of the legislative will, and thus supplies to all public obligations that necessary element.

We are, then, at liberty to say that what the law has administratively declared, in the case of private contracts as the necessary characteristics of such contracts in order to create obligations, is so declared as a consequence of the broader proposition that they are the essential attributes of the very idea of an obligation.

The power of self-obligation must be ranked as in the class of civil powers recognized by the law, and as it is the power that enables man to bring to his exertions the aid of associated power, it lies at the foundation of the distinction that places mankind above the brute creation, and therefore is the root and principle of all social, and consequently of all civil, powers. As this power embodies the efficacy of self-determined will, voluntariness must be its essential attribute. If, then, the will is determined independently of self-control, or the conduct independently of the will, the conditions upon which the power of self-obligation depend do not exist, and no effect properly ascribable to such power can exist.

The nature of what is implied by the word voluntary is readily derived from the principles and rules of law governing the effect of *duress* in vitiating contracts. *Duress* implies the absence of volition, and exists where external control is applied either to the body or to the mind. The character of volition in a physical sense is obvious. That external action which has the force to destroy the volitions of the mind may be applied either to the emotional or to the intellectual faculties. The ordinary form in which the mind is externally controlled on its emotional side is through fear. Where the source of that fear is the conduct of one seeking an advantage by coercing another to assume an obligation that, but for the influence of fear, would be declined, a want of volition may be found to exist. The conduct capable of producing fear of that class and degree may consist either in words or in actions. It must be in its nature a threat, either of some impending calamity, or the withholding of some necessary good, as implied in action apparently tending to that end, or in words apparently accompanied by the power and will to produce such result. This fear may have its roots in the love of self, or of offspring or friends, and its exciting cause may be the apprehension of destruction or great injury to life, member, health, reputation, or property. The elements of *duress* are: an intention to coerce the exercise of the power of self-obligation, conduct springing from such intention and apparently tending to that end, and the assuming of an obligation in consequence thereof through belief in its necessity and not through choice. It is not the fact that the mind is constrained by necessity that in a legal sense impairs the voluntariness of its action, but it arises from the fact that such necessity, either real or apparent, is produced by the conduct of a party seeking advantage or to do injury, and springing from an intention to compel an exercise of the power of self-obligation.

One may make a contract, as a choice of evils, with binding effect, which shows that there is a difference between voluntariness and the ability to do that which one would choose to do if free to act according to choice. The fact that it is the destruction of that power of choice by another as an act of wrong that impairs a contract based upon it, shows that it is the violation of the common obligation to good faith, and to respect the rights of others, that prevents an obligation from arising out of such circumstances.

It is manifest that this principle extends itself to a case where the mind is controlled through an intentional interference with the elements upon which its judgment is based. The doctrine of the law on the subject of deception as a cause of vitiating contracts clearly rests upon the same general principle. When, with intention to gain advantage by misdirecting the self-obliging power, one proceeds by usurping the channels through which the mind gains the material for its judgments, and when he misdirects the emotional tendencies of others as part of the same purpose, the wrong to the right of self-control is fundamentally of the same nature. In both cases the act producing the assumption of an obligation is a violation of the common obligation, and, therefore, can not be the means of deriving a valid obligation out of that fundamental source.

As we have already seen, it is the nature of every right to coexist with a commensurate obligation to respect it; also that wherever a civil power exists, unimpaired by any public obligation, its exercise is constituted as a right, and an obligation imposed on all to respect such right. We have already characterized the faculty of self-obligation as a civil power; and, as left free according to choice within its legal liberty, such right is attended by a corresponding common obligation binding all others to respect that power of choice. It follows that freedom of choice in assuming or rejecting obligations of this class is, according to the nature of the common obligations, the essential condition on which the power of self-obligation can be exercised, and that, when the producing cause of such an obligation is an act in violation of fundamental duty, its product must be rejected as vicious.

It is proper to remark in this connection that every instance of fraud or bad faith is in a sense the equivalent of *duress* and deception as it regards this principle, but fraud which is a particular case of general bad faith has a much wider influence than that of vitiating contracts, and is linked with a more general principle that will be presently discussed.

While the identity of the principles that underlie the doctrines of *duress* and deception have been traced, yet, as will hereafter be seen, the proper effect of deception, whether by misrepresentation or wrongful concealment, and other acts of bad faith, is to impair the consideration on which the contract affected by them rests. The discussion of the last-named subject will elicit a more full consideration of the particular application of the general principle as a test of the validity of obligations, and a statement of the reasons why the case of *duress* should be referred to the class of causes impairing the voluntary feature of obligations, while they affect the various recognized violations of good faith, should be treated under the head of consideration.

It will appear quite clear, from the foregoing principles, that the sufficiency of the causes alleged as destroying the voluntary character of an obligation by acting upon the mind must be determined by the rules that govern the action of the mind, the question being one of the sufficiency of a physical or intellectual cause to produce certain mental phenomena.

CHAPTER VIII.

CAPACITY OF SELF-OBLIGATION.

The rules of law that demand that capacity to contract must exist, in order to give efficacy to a contract, are clearly traceable to the first principles derivable from the view that has been taken of the common obligations. Capacity is endowment with power. We have already discussed certain general characteristics of the power of self-obligation that enter into the immediate question, but there are others that are yet to be considered, in which the question of the status of infancy is prominent. The power of self-obligation may exist in a perfect or in an imperfect condition. It is agreeable to the general laws of organic growth that that which comes into existence appears, in the first instance, in an imperfect form, the idea of imperfection being, in this instance, that of the want of certain developed attributes essential to a perfect state of development. The natural powers of man of every kind are subject to this law, and are imperfect until the progress of development has reached a certain stage. As this law embraces the intellectual and moral, as well as the physical powers, the natural power of self-obligation must be subject to it, and that power having taken a certain character and form under civil institutions, not denying its primitive nature, it would follow that the civil power of self-obligation must exist in the two stages of imperfect and perfect. The period during which such power necessarily exists in an imperfect condition, according to the universal law of development, is, in the case of mankind, termed infancy. From the reason of this imperfection it would be concluded that whenever, in point of fact, maturity of the will has arrived, the power of self-obligation would be considered perfect, and, until that condition arrives, should be regarded as imperfect. Although actual maturity arrives at different ages in different persons, yet, on grounds of utility, the law has instituted certain generalizations as to the period of life when maturity arrives in the place of the fact as it discloses itself in individual cases. The common law of England fixes, arbitrarily, the period of maturity as twenty-one years of age, while the Roman law divided the imperfect stage into two subordinate periods, with separate attributes, and postponed the period of perfect maturity beyond the time fixed by the common law of England. The simplification of the common law of England in this respect, as in other parallel cases, has produced a higher degree of convenience, though not adhering as strictly to the analogies of nature as did the Roman law. It can with propriety be said that the rule of the law, though arbitrary in its mode of measurement, rests strictly upon the principles of natural law, and its exposition must be sought in these principles.

Before developing the consequences of the view that has been taken of the imperfect power of self-obligation, it is proper to examine that idea in its relation to the proposition that the basis of civil obligation is the consent of the individual. It is apparent that, if the power of self-obligation is absent or imperfect, in the case of any individual, there is the absence of that full consent which is demanded by the proposition just stated. On the other hand, the infant, and persons deprived of rational power, are under perfect subjection to the law, although for such cases it may make special provision. It is not enough to say that such persons are excepted from the general rule on special grounds, for that which is properly excepted from a rule belongs under some other rule that should be in harmonious relations to the first. It is more accurate to say that the rule only embraces cases of matured powers.

It is evident that the rule is based on the idea of the equal civil right of individuals. An infant under the power of a parent can not be regarded as in that condition. That all men are born free and equal is only potentially, and not actually, true, and only true in that degree of such as have the capacity to attain to the maturity of their powers. The fact is, that children are born under the power of others. By the law of nature, children at their birth are under the perfect dominion of their parents. Civil institutions modify this relation by absorbing into themselves the dominion of the parent, transforming his natural dominion into civil power assimilated to that which it displaces. The parental idea transplanted into civil institutions develops into that of sovereignty. A proper adjustment among the powers of government results from equilibrium between the sovereign and equal individual powers. The parental idea, both in its natural state and as transformed under civil institutions, is the centralizing principle, that of equal civil right among individuals, the dispersing power. In the historical order the parental idea first attains dominance, and only yields to conceptions of individual equality when a certain stage of development is reached. The individual, in existing societies, attains to the full civil status by the same steps that were taken by societies of men in their collective advance toward balanced social conditions. It would follow that, as a civil fact, immaturity follows the consequences of parental power as that power is embodied in sovereignty, and thus the infant is a subject of law before possessing the capacity of exercising full choice in controlling his own actions or those of the community.

The basis of the parental idea is an obligation to protect those committed to its authority. When parental power passes into sovereignty its obligation passes with it. The obligation is imperfect, for the want of the means of enforcement, in both the natural and civil status, of the parental idea, but is absolute in the sense that it can not be rightfully denied.

This duality of government as to its principles leads to no confusion either in practice or theory, and is the result of its organic nature, assimilated to a duality existing in natural conditions. For the sake of clearness, the principles of government are usually discussed as if all the members of society possessed mature powers. This form of discussion is logically essential, and does not interfere with what is based upon the conception of immaturity, and will be pursued in this investigation.

The idea of imperfection is resolvable into two distinct conceptions. The imperfection that results from immaturity alone may be termed normal imperfection. In this sense an imperfect power is one that may do some things, but not all things, appropriate to its mature or perfect condition. This is the kind of imperfection ascribed to the power of self-obligation during infancy. The other idea of imperfection, as applied to organisms, is that of organic or functional derangement which may arise from arrested development, from abnormal development, and deterioration. Idiocy may be regarded as a case of arrested development. Insanity and various other diseases, as well as physical injury and vicious habits, are causes that may produce abnormal development and deterioration, while the latter may result from old age alone. Imperfections thus give rise to questions affecting the power of self-control, and of forming a deliberate judgment, that are both quantitative and qualitative.

The question of infancy considered by itself is one of the degree of normal development existing at a particular time. In the case of infancy the law, though founded on that of nature, does not strictly follow natural reason. Natural reason would suggest that some new degree of capacity would be discovered in the power of self-obligation at every step toward maturity, for all natural powers may be used with increasing advantage in every succeeding stage of their passage toward perfection. On grounds strictly of public utility the law generalizes the facts of infancy into an arbitrary rule by which the duration of infancy is fixed at a period the same for all persons, and a certain capacity ascribed as it regards self-obligation, which is substantially the same through the whole period of infancy.

Stated in the most general terms, the law denies validity to the contracts of infants imposing burdens upon themselves, upholds such as simply confer benefits upon them without imposing burdens, and invalidates or sustains such as contain both benefits and burdens according to the interest of the infant as to which it assumes to judge on principles of equity. It follows that an infant has an imperfect power of self-obligation, but a perfect power of acquisition. That the power of self-obligation is not altogether absent is evidenced by the fact that the interest of the infant may impart validity to a contract in which the exercise of that power occurs, as in the case stated of mixed burdens and benefits. While the obligations assumed by infants can not be enforced on the ground of their inherent binding force, yet with the sanction of the judicial power they may have such efficiency.

Before generalizing these rules of the law it is necessary to examine the relation that the two branches of the judicial administration—the legal and equitable—sustain to each other as bearing on the study of the principles of the law. The distinction between law and equity is administrative merely. In nature the principles of law and equity are the same. As society is a unit, all the influences tending to give it form or vital function must be parts of a unitary system. Those influences are displayed in the tendencies of social actions to group themselves into two classes, the one tending to individualize the parts of which society is composed, and the other to unitize the system as a whole. The principle of individual equality has been pointed out as fundamental to that class of influences that tend to develop individual traits, and the protective principle, derived from the idea of the parental relation, is the source of a tendency to produce homogeneity throughout the aspects of society, which, if unbalanced, would prevent those functional differentiations that constitute a high organic condition. In a word, the protective principle unbalanced tends to produce paternal government and repression of individual energy, while the principle of individual equality, while acting as a modifying influence upon the tendencies of the protective principle, tends to produce free and balanced government. It is clear that the distinction that has been recognized between legal and equitable administration is the result of a relation between the two methods of administration and the fundamental principles just pointed out. The tendency of the spirit of the common law courts has uniformly been to leave the individual to the consequences of his own action, as the arbiter of his own future for good or ill, which is the highest appreciation of the principle of individual equality, as a separate principle. On the other hand, the courts of equity incline to revise the structural forms that individuals give to their rights and obligations, in order to rectify the adjustments from which they spring by the application of standards of right action, generalized from the best tendencies of social habit. The latter is essentially a protective function. As a balanced administration of justice is the result of a proper equilibrium between these two administrative principles, it is obvious that the courts of law and equity that have these opposite tendencies must be regarded as parts of the general function of administering justice amenable to the same general principles.

The principles of the law themselves have the same twofold tendency. They tend on the one hand to the development of form, and on the other to vital action; and it is agreeable to the general laws of the distribution of organic functions that they should be found formulating these separate and distinct aspects in separate functional arrangements. It must not be inferred that the courts of law are not influenced by protective considerations, or that the courts of equity are not conservators of the right of individual equality, but that the dominant tendency of these institutions is in the lines indicated.

This general view of the relative tendencies of the administration of law and of equity would lead to the conclusion that equitable administration is in a peculiar sense the representative of that principle of protection that underlies the structure of government. But in the case of the treatment of infants, as having a peculiar claim on the protective care of government, the relation of the courts of equity to that providential duty is manifest on historical grounds as well as in constant practice. The function of the king as *parens patriæ* over infants passed into the English Court of Chancery and thence to our own, and that jurisdiction has always appertained to those courts; and, where separate courts of equity have been abolished, has followed the jurisdiction derived from those courts.

That an infant may contract so as effectually to bind another results from the fact that he has a perfect power of acquisition. That he can not bind himself by such a contract results from the fact that he has no independent or perfect power of self-obligation. Such a contract, when it contains mutual obligations, is in an anomalous condition. It can not pass into an obligation of the infant without public sanction, and, as its obligations are mutual and dependent, it can not operate in part alone. To confer this sanction does not appertain to ordinary judicial action, because judicial action is based on individual right, and not on the judicial conception of individual interest. The peculiar function of sanctioning an infant's contracts upon the ground of its interests has been conferred on judicial bodies so that its exercise may be harmonized with judicial principles so far as such principles extend, but must be regarded as extrajudicial, and accounted for on the ground of the duty of protection due by the government to the infant. The contract of the infant that confers advantages and imposes burdens not being void in itself, but incapable of creating such an obligation as is essential to its efficacy, must be either sanctioned by public authority or dissolved by judicial action. The power of sanction and dissolution being lodged in the same tribunal, gives rise to a convenience that suggests at once the reason why the power of sanction was transferred to that judicial body.

The power of acquisition which has been found perfect in the infant is an essential element of every obligation as constituting the idea of capacity in part. Every effective obligation operates to transfer some right previously existing in one capable of self-obligation to one having power to acquire such right. This follows from the correlative nature of rights and obligations. It is certainly proper to classify the capacity of acquisition among the civil powers, for, although it is subject to fewer limitations than any other civil right, yet instances occur where it is denied, and others where it is limited and qualified.

Where the contract of an infant is ratified after maturity, the consequences of such act are to be referred to the exercise of mature powers, and need not be considered with imperfect powers. The incidents of guardianship appertain to the general subject of delegated powers.

Idiocy, considered as a case of arrested development, is the indefinite prolongation of the period of immaturity through causes recognized as abnormal. The perpetuity of that condition draws after it the continuous application of the general law of immaturity, as illustrated in the case of infancy.

Insanity, as a genus involving certain species, exemplifies in its treatment by the law another aspect of the question of legal capacity in its bearing on the validity of contracts. In all cases, except infancy, where there is an alleged defect of the power of self-obligation, the question is, whether the natural conditions essential to the exercise of that power exist in a sufficient degree to make it available for social purposes. This is determined by examining the conduct of the subject of the investigation and comparing it with the general habit of man in society. The application of such a standard involves the forming of a conception of the lowest condition of rational development that can subserve the uses of man in his social relations, and the application of such standard to the conduct undergoing investigation. If it falls below that standard, there is a deficiency of natural condition to maintain the power of self-obligation. This standard is gathered from the actual facts of social intercourse, as in the course of this investigation will be found to be the case whenever the standard of judgment is formed through the operation of the principles of the law, and is not imposed arbitrarily by public law. Where the consequences of certain physical defects, or of certain diseased conditions, are recognized as a deprivation of rational power, such a conclusion must be regarded as generalized from instances of individual conduct as affected by such disturbing causes, and accordingly rest ultimately upon a comparison between the conduct of persons so affected and the general habit of man. Such generalizations may be brought to the aid of such an inquiry, but can not displace the actual conduct of the individual as essential to the proper comparison.

The subject of insanity affords a favorable opportunity for

studying the operations of the principles of the law in giving rise to certain presumptions; and, as this view of the principles of the law will constantly recur throughout this investigation, an early opportunity to develop a general view of the subject is desirable.

In the correct use of the term *accidental*, it undoubtedly implies an effect produced from a cause external to that regular sequence of cause and effect that constitutes the ordinary and normal course of nature or events. In this sense insanity is due to an accidental cause. Viewing the events of nature and of social life in a general way in reference to all the possibilities of outcome, the mind, by a process of natural logic, places the regular course of nature and events in the position of a rule or principle, correctly apprehending that the regular element in the course of nature is the ground of unity, and as such is subject to the action of a variable element that produces variety, standing as an exception to the rule or as a modifying principle. The regular method of nature being thus perceived as a universal constant of natural processes, is formulated as a rule, or, more accurately speaking, as a principle, and occasional, or, as we call them, accidental causes being recognized as the means of producing variety in the cases under that principle, a habit of thought is produced that is essentially logical. The mind habitually recurs to its own experience and observation to ascertain what, according to the regular course of nature, would take place in a given case within that experience, while it looks to extrinsic evidence to ascertain the existence of instances of departure from that regular order. The law, being the complex mind of the community, pursues the same method. Its rules of presumption and evidence are the embodiment of these principles. As a general rule, it assumes, on the ground of its own experience, to determine what is the regular course of nature, and of the actions of mankind, and utilizes such experience in the form of presumptions or assumed facts, and demands that all departures from this regular course shall be established by extrinsic evidence. In this sense it is that the presumptions of the law are based upon the habit of nature and society.

Upon these principles the law does not presume the existence of insanity, but gathers that fact from trustworthy evidences, or *indicia*, either direct or indirect. The inquiry, then, as to the existence of insanity, is one of fact based on presumptions derived from the ordinary habit of nature and society, guided by legal rules.

The power of self-obligation may be affected either by loss, to a certain extent, of self-control, or by hallucinations affecting the materials from which a judgment is formed. Insanity presents both of these cases. It is the inability to form a deliberate purpose that is characteristic of all descriptions of insanity. Deliberate purpose is formed by co-ordinating all the motives that momentarily act upon the mind in a general resultant or state of the will. The purpose becomes deliberate through the exercise of judgment, which is the mind's self-consciousness of the value, both as to quantity and quality, of the motives acting upon it. If, then, power to restrain momentary impulses is not possessed, co-ordination among such impulses is impossible. On the other hand, if the mind mistakes its own spontaneous impulses for motives acting upon it from without, judgment is impossible.

Medical observation and experience are admitted to ascertain the existence of morbid physical conditions and their associated mental states, and also to refer the mental phenomena appearing in the case to some known class with recognized consequences, as the means of interpreting aberration of conduct in its relation to the conditions of mind on which the power of self-obligation depends.

From the ground of reason already laid, the reason is obvious why the law validates the acts of a lunatic performed during a lucid interval, and why, the general fact of insanity being shown to exist, it will not presume the existence of lucid intervals for the purpose of supporting a contract, but demands specific proof of such fact. The law of nature operates by constant rules, as well in abnormal as in normal causes, and has, in relation to such causes, a regular course.

While the law will not assume the existence of a cause contrary to the ordinary course of nature, yet, when such cause is shown to exist, it bases its presumptions upon the habit of nature in this new condition, and demands proof of any departure therefrom. In this way whatever is exceptional to the general law of insanity, such as the occurrence of lucid intervals, must be demonstrated by proofs.

The effect generally ascribed by the law to marriage, of depriving a married woman of the capacity of self-obligation, is traceable to the persistence of primitive habit, and not to any actual loss of natural capacity. Such a disqualification has no justification in natural reason. The law of nature furnishes no warrant for such a discrimination, for the faculties requisite for self-obligation are present in the woman as well as in the man, and in the married woman as fully as in the unmarried. It is presumable, on historical grounds, that the same feature of the institution of marriage existed under the natural law before the appearance of civil law, and was derived to the latter from that source.

It is hardly necessary to repeat that natural law as applied to human society is not identical with the law of nature. The term natural law as here used may be regarded as taken in a different sense from that commonly understood. Without discussing this matter from a critical point of view, it is only needful to say that, if any phase of human institutions is entitled to be called natural law, it is that which was the result of formulations under the dominance of such institutions as prevail in a state of nature. A state of nature is something contrasted with what exists under civil institutions. When we use the expression we are looking to a possible condition of things which would exist if civil institutions were unknown; to borrow the language of a kindred science, to a state of things when society was functionally homogeneous, and before separate functions had differentiated. By the very definition of civil law such a state of society must have preceded it. The best historical data lead to the conclusion that some derived form of patriarchal or tribal government, followed by government of a transitional character, such as the militant type, preceded organic government, and this would confirm the deductive conclusion already stated. The law of nature must stand as the fundamental principle of the natural law under this view. The law of nature is itself the principle of the entire material universe, while the principles covered by a still wider generalization are common to that form, and all other forms of existence.

In examining the status of married women under primitive institutions, we must be guided in part by historical data and in part by necessary deduction. That a married woman was under the primitive law more completely under the dominion of her husband than at the present day is a necessary conclusion on both these grounds. Assuming that she did not possess independent power of self-obligation, it does not follow that she was regarded as not possessing the natural requisites of the power of self-obligation. It would be more natural to ascribe it to the precept that married women were bound to yield implicit obedience to their husbands. It would be inconsistent with that duty for her to subject her conduct to an obligation to one who is not her husband. If this was the foundation of her disqualification, then the consent of her husband would remove the reason of such disability. Under such a supposition the ground of her disability would not be incapacity in a personal sense, but the interference of the right of dominion over her by her husband. The dominion of a husband over the wife contains an idea beyond that of property. It is one of the instances where authority and protective duty were associated for protective purposes. As this authority, as it existed in primitive times, was, upon the principles that have been presented, absorbed into the authority of the community, and replaced by a civil authority, of the nature of the pre-existing dominion, but necessarily diminished by the fact that the sovereign power of the nature of which it partook remained lodged in the community, it is obvious that, as some part of the protective duty of the husband had passed into the state, the exercise of that protective duty might lead to the restriction of the wife's power of self-obligation intended to protect her from the undue influence of her husband.

Concluding that the effect of marriage, in depriving the married woman of the capacity of independent self-obligation that she possessed while still unmarried, is due to the operation of the protective principle, an instance is presented illustrating the immense conservative energy of the protective principle. While, as will appear hereafter, there is no natural reason why the principle of individual equality should not have produced the same modifications of primitive habit in favor of woman as in the case of man, the fact still remains that the institution of marriage has been very generally left under the unbalanced control of the protective principle. It is obvious that this is due to an institutional policy, resting on a conception of the nature of marriage, that has afforded no opportunity for the principle of individual equality to assert itself.

Slavery is another instance of the persistence of primitive habit carrying with it the consequence of the deprivation of the independent capacity of self-obligation, notwithstanding the possession of the natural attributes essential to that power.

If domestic servitude is regarded as the primitive type of slavery, as it may well be, both on historical grounds and upon deductive principles, it is not difficult to harmonize its origin with the idea of parental power. Whether the slave was obtained from capture in war or from other sources is not material to the question of his status in the domestic group. It is easy to resolve the idea of the domestic institution, in its primitive state, into that of the co-ordination of the parental and marital law with that of domestic servitude; indeed, it is difficult to conceive of the family as an institution, while the parental power possessed its full significance, without conceiving domestic servitude as part of that system. The remarks that have already been made in reference to the persistence of certain features of the institution of marriage are applicable to the case of slavery, with the qualification that in the latter case the assertion of the force of the principle of individual civil equality, under the stimulus afforded by considerations of utility, has characterized the institutional policy of most of the enlightened states of Christendom within the last century.

There still remains for notice the effect of civil death on the capacity of self-obligation. It is not difficult to trace the origin of the idea that a complete loss of civil function may arise consistently with the fundamental principles of government. To destroy the enemies of society was naturally the first conception of the mode of preserving its existence. This would lead to destroying the lives of those ranked as public enemies, and would equally cover the cases of alien and citizen enemies. Those who were guilty of crimes that in their nature were destructive of the social status would fall under this head. Advancing liberality would naturally preserve the natural life of such public enemies before reflecting on the possibility of preserving their civil rights consistently with the safety of society. The idea of civil death has, no doubt, this origin, and accounts for the fact that a loss of the capacity of self-obligation may result as the consequence of certain crimes against the wellbeing of society.

CHAPTER IX.

CONSIDERATION.

THE next subject in order is that of *consideration* as a necessary element of the force of every executory obligation. While an obligation is in a condition to call for the immediate or future performance of some act, or the omission of some act capable of present or future performance, it is executory. It will be hereafter shown that after an obligation has passed beyond the executory stage, through what the law calls *performance*, it still retains its character and force as an obligation; but that such force solely consists in the protection of the rights created by or under it. As a consideration is material to the legal efficacy of an obligation while it remains in an executory condition, and as the term contract is applied to the statement of the terms and conditions that enter into an obligation while in an executory condition, it is accurate to affirm that a consideration is essential to the efficacious existence of a contract. The idea of consideration is that of a certain equipoise of burdens and benefits which should be present in every interchange of right and obligations which is not based wholly on motives of benevolence. The origin and nature of this idea are traceable in the law of nature when we find that all stable conditions of related bodies depend upon the presence of a compensative principle, while instability is the result of its absence. As our notion of equity, both as a formal system and as a principle inherent in all legal transactions, evidently springs from the idea of equality either as to position or as to benefits and burdens, the nature of the compensative principle is of particular interest.

It must be admitted that the law has a distinct conception of benevolence as embodied in human conduct. It must, then, have a distinct conception of the state of motives in the mind when that particular motive is absent from the transactions of individuals. As it is the existence or non-existence of compensative equivalent that distinguishes acts flowing from these opposite motives, that principle must give rise to important legal consequences. The fact that the law will not enforce a naked promise made upon motives of benevolence alone is fundamental to the doctrine of consideration. This proposition does not exclude the effective creation of civil rights, even where the motives that induced such creation were purely benevolent, for reasons that will be hereafter discussed. A deed, covenant, bond, or release, in form and sealed and delivered, is capable of creating rights, although the actual motive that prompted such act may be purely benevolent; and this is equally true of a perfected gift.

Another circumstance that serves to mark the legal conception of a consideration is the rule of law that gives efficacy to executory promises made upon what are termed moral considerations of a certain character. The proposition that appears to be fundamental to all these cases is that an executory moral duty will not be enforced; but, where a moral duty has been performed by the creation of an independent civil obligation, such obligation will be enforced. It remains, then, to ascertain whether this proposition is actually present in all the cases necessary to be reduced to a class in order to find their common principle.

The mere fact of promising to perform a certain act, from the motive of discharging a merely moral obligation, is not in a moral sense such an act as, irrespective of performance, can satisfy and extinguish such moral obligation. The only ground of obligation is the unperformed moral duty. If, then, the law should assume to enforce such a promise, it would occupy the position of giving efficacy to a purely moral obligation, and obliterate the distinction between legal and moral obligations.

It is true that a moral obligation that has been recognized

by the person morally obliged, and expressed in terms of value that are capable of legal estimation, stands on a better footing as to possible legal enforcement than a general moral duty unascertained and unvalued by the party morally obliged; but both cases have one common feature, and that is: that the idea of right is that of moral right alone. The fact of the ascertainment in terms of value in a legal sense would be of practical value if the law could assume to compel the performance or compensation of an unperformed moral duty; but that it can not do without enforcing moral obligation as such. It is obvious that, if the ground of the promise is not a recognizable moral duty, but an act of voluntary benevolence, the application of what has just been said to such a case is still more clear.

The question then arises why, if the foregoing be true, the law will give efficacy to a deed, covenant, bond, or other instrument, under seal, containing an obligation without other foundation than that of moral duty, or, perhaps, voluntary benevolence. It is commonly said by the law-writers that a seal imports a consideration. This is undoubtedly the language of the law, and force must be given to it, although it is a maxim or precept, and not in form a rule or principle. This should not be read as declaring that a seal evidences a valuable consideration. The seal is here used in a symbolical sense as standing for the whole instrument as to form.

The solution of the question just suggested lies in the distinction between a parol agreement and a specialty. As it regards the means of their proof, there are three kinds of contracts—namely, such as are not specifically evidenced by the common act of the parties, but admit of proof of the entire range of transactions to which the character of an obligation is ascribed, those that are evidenced in writing by a common act of the parties, though not in the form of a specialty, and those that are evidenced in the last-named form. As it regards the nature of contracts, however, the law recognizes but two classes —namely, parol contracts and specialties. It is not difficult to trace the precise difference that is implied in this classification. In the case of the parol contract, the acts and declarations of the parties in their dealings together on the subject of contract prior to the moment when the obligation was consummated are part of the obligation itself, while in the case of a specialty they form no part of the resulting obligation. In those limited cases where resort is had to the transactions out of which a specialty has arisen, it is as to something extrinsic to the obligation itself, as for the purpose of ascertaining some such fact as fraud or duress bearing upon the validity of the obligation, but not entering its terms as an element of its construction. This distinction is apparent as between specialties and unevidenced parol contracts, but requires consideration as it regards written contracts not in form specialties. It will be manifest, on examination, that the difference between specialties and parol contracts, written and unwritten, arises from their respective natures, and that the difference between written and unwritten parol contracts results wholly from their several relations to the rules of evidence. That there is a difference in nature between specialties and written parol contracts, as it regards the connection of the obligation assumed with the acts and declarations of the parties in their mutual dealing that led to it, is evidenced by the fact that the law will not, in the case of specialties, resort to those acts and declarations for the purpose of making clear the intentions of the parties in the consideration they had in view, while in the case of written contracts not under seal such resort is allowed, where necessary, to ascertain the nature of the consideration they had in view. This evidences the fact that there is no difference in nature between parol contracts written and unwritten.

The idea that the parties may agree upon a certain specific proof of that which the facts and circumstances prior to the contract tended to exhibit, is not inconsistent with the general proposition that, in the case of all parol contracts, the transactions out of which they arose are part of the contract. The nature of the evidence is the same whether, as agreed upon, it details these facts and circumstances at large, or merely gives their effect in the form usual to contracts. The nature of the contract is not changed by the fact that the parties have placed themselves under the operation of a rule of evidence in such manner as to shut out more or less of those transactions from the observation of the law.

It is not possible, without undue prolixity, to trace the consequences of the view just stated in the mode of treatment to which the law subjects the two classes of contracts, but it is enough for the present purpose to ascertain that, as it regards specialties, the acts and declarations of the parties that preceded the embodiment of their purpose constitute no part of the resulting obligation. The result of this view is that, according to the legal idea of a specialty, it is, as it regards the actual considerations that prompted it, an independent obligation, such considerations being merged and lost in its forms. The law necessarily presumes, from the general habit, that a consideration existed for such a specialty, and, as the parties have, by the selection of a form for their transaction, shut out the inquiry into the fact, that presumption must remain unrebutted. Hence it is that a seal may be properly said to imply a consideration, on the ground of those presumptions, from general habit, that form the basis of legal inquiry.

The obligation in the case of a specialty, according to the view just presented, does not consist of the considerations, tenders, and acceptances of the parties, though it is produced from them; it differs from them in *species*, entitling it to the name of a specialty. Assuming, then, that a merely moral obligation induced the creation of the specialty, as, according to this view of the effect of a specialty, the moral duty was performed, and passed entirely out of existence, and an independent legal obligation took its place, it is an instance of an independent legal obligation based upon an executed or performed moral duty.

The next inquiry in order is, whether the legal enforcement of a parol promise to pay a debt barred by the statute of limitations is reconcilable with the proposition that the law enforces obligations resting on moral duty only, where such duty has been performed by the very act of assuming the obligation, which, as has been seen, can only take place where the new promise is in the form of a specialty. The reason for enforcing a parol promise to pay a debt barred by the statute of limitations does not rest wholly on the ground of moral obligation. The effect of the bar of the statute of limitations upon a legal demand is simply to deprive it of the capacity of enforcement, and thus to reduce it to the condition of an imperfect obligation. The nature of this imperfection, as defined by the object of the statute of limitations, is such as to leave unaffected all the elements of the original obligation that are necessary to combine with the new promise in order to form a new obligation, so that the new promise fulfills all the conditions essential to a new obligation. As the legal effect given to a promise to pay a debt barred by the statute of limitations is not dependent on power to enforce a purely moral obligation, it is not inconsistent with the proposition under consideration.

Gifts of personal property, accompanied by actual delivery, being held valid, though based on moral duty or benevolence alone, it becomes necessary to consider what relation they bear to the general proposition that enforces obligations resting on moral duty only, where such obligation is independent, and the moral duty is performed. Whether a gift, accompanied by delivery, should be ascribed to motives of moral duty or benevolence, the delivery certainly terminated the moral conditions that induced it. In this case the delivery of the property is the equivalent of the delivery of the specialty in the case of a deed or other sealed instrument, as it regards the termination of the antecedent moral conditions. In the one case the previous conditions are merged in the ownership of property in a strict sense, while in the latter case they are merged in an obligatory instrument assimilated by the law to property for many purposes.

Moral obligation and benevolence have been referred to as if ideas incapable of interchange, but, strictly speaking, such does not appear to be the case. In order to enforce this idea, purely moral obligations must be discriminated from such as have mixed moral and legal elements. There are certain obligations that are usually termed moral, although possessing, beyond that character, the qualities of a general and imperfect legal obligation. Of such a nature is the duty of a father to support his child during infancy, and a husband to supply his wife with the necessaries of life. From these two instances the class will be recognized. It is clear that the father or husband, in these cases, is under a clear legal obligation, though general in its nature and imperfect, at least in the sense that within an undefined limit it may be violated with impunity, as it concerns legal interference, and yet, within that limit, such duty may be a good consideration to support a promise. This should be regarded as a case illustrating the manner in which imperfect legal duties may be transformed into such as are perfect, rather than the case of a promise based on moral duty.

In a legal sense, an act imparting benefits is benevolent when it does not spring from an antecedent compensated obligation. In a moral sense, all duties are compensated, even that of benevolence. An act entitled to be called benevolent, in a legal sense, may proceed from a sense of moral duty, so that it is impossible, on legal principles, to discriminate the motives on which such a distinction depends; and, as the purest benevolence arises from a sense of moral duty, the moral quality of all acts performed of a meritorious character must be referred to moral duty.

It must be concluded, from what has gone before, that the law will enforce an imperfect legal obligation when fortified by a promise without other consideration, yet that it will not enforce a purely moral duty as such, but that a moral duty, ascertained as such by the person morally obliged, and actually performed by the creation of an independent executory obligation, or perfected right, supplies all the elements, either practically or theoretically, essential to the creation of civil right. The case of benevolence, as has been seen, must be referred to the class of moral duties. No distinction is suggested by the principles of the law between the two cases of moral duty and benevolence, which is in harmony with their identity, as it is the foundation of moral principle on which they rest.

This general doctrine, as ascribed to the law, is in harmony with the principles of the law in its dealings with questions of morals. Where the welfare of the community is concerned in the performance of moral duties, the law clothes such duties with the force and sanction of legal obligations, either general or special, perfect or imperfect, leaving all others to the forum of individual conscience. The law could not be regarded as having attained the full ends of civil association unless it recognized the legal capacity of individuals to fulfill their moral duties. It must, therefore, recognize the power of the individual to create civil rights when in his estimation the creation of such rights is demanded by some moral duty, general or special. This is all that it does, and less it could not do without some degree of responsibility for the neglect of individual moral duty. If the civil right is not brought into effective existence, this principle could afford no justification for legal interference with the voluntary character of that power, which, while it should be competent to convert moral obligations into perfected rights, or independent civil obligations, should not be coerced in that direction when such moral obligation does not sufficiently concern the welfare of the community to have civil recognition.

A mere promise, or, as the law terms it, a naked promise, is not recognized as the origin of civil right, and therefore a promise to perform what is regarded as demanded by moral duty alone does not present the case of a civil right created in discharge of a moral duty. A promise is not an obligation in any sense, but becomes such when it is part of an interchange of rights and duties, or when embodied in an instrument which, in virtue of its forms and attributes, is recognized as possessing all the essentials of an obligation. These distinctions, as dependent on form, doubtless had their origin in primitive customs which, as we may conclude on historic grounds, distinguished between an ordinary promise and a solemn promise, the latter taking the form of a covenant or oath, attended with symbolical acts. The distinction between a promise with and one without an accompanying duty is inherent in the nature of the mind. That the law should recognize this distinction appears clearly from its principles.

The object for which society exists can not be attained except by co-operation between the individuals that compose such society. They must co-operate in what concerns the common interest, and in what is essential to secure, as among individuals, the benefits intended by civil association. If the members of a community refused to co-operate with each other for the pursuit of individual ends, the most important object of civil association would be defeated, even though they united in everything essential to the maintenance of the public authority. Co-operation for the accomplishment of individual ends, that sustains this important relation to the social state, must have some sanction in the obligation in which that structure rests. This reasoning would imply a general obligation affecting all members of the community to co-operate with others in the pursuit of proper ends. That there is such a moral obligation none will deny; and, as it concerns the effective existence of civil society, it must be regarded as having some degree of civil sanction. It is certainly an imperfect obligation, for the time and manner of its performance can be fixed by no principle of law; hence no measures can be applied to it for the purpose of enforcement, unless afforded by public law.

It can readily be deduced, from the propositions just stated, that there is an underlying principle of the law that is fundamental to all co-operative relations among individuals, and this principle would naturally be distinguished as the principle of co-operation, or the co-operative principle. It has an analogy in nature in the principle that underlies the composition of forces. We may, then, complete the statement of the fundamental principles that are the centers around which society integrates itself by adding the principle of co-operation to the protective principle and that of individual equality. The possibility of equilibrium between the protective principle and that of equal individual right lies in the normal operation of the principle of co-operation.

A mere promise contains no element of co-operation, while mutual promises are a distinct co-operative act. The one is within the sanction of the imperfect general duty of co-operation, while the other is not. Hence it is, on the principles already stated, that, in the case of mutual promises, an imperfect obligation is converted into a perfect one, while in the case of a naked promise it is incapable of being linked to any antecedent obligation either of perfect or imperfect character, and hence there is nothing from which an obligation can grow.

It will be hereafter shown that all cases of a valuable consideration can be referred to the principle of cases of mutual promises.

In concluding the discussion of the inferences to be drawn from the rules of law as to the necessity for and the general nature of a consideration, the results of what has been said may be summed up in a few propositions. The existence of a consideration is only essential to executory obligations. In the case of an executory obligation under seal, such consideration is assumed as a necessary presumption. In the case of obligations not under seal, usually termed contracts, in order to render them obligatory, the existence of a consideration must appear either by the written or unwritten declarations of the parties, or by what is disclosed in the course of their dealings. The necessity for a consideration arises from the fact that an operative contract is an interchange of burdens and benefits between two or more parties, a burden assumed in respect to a person, not a party to the contract, being a proper subject of such interchange.

The benefits and burdens thus interchanged must have civil recognition as such. A mere promise may make a general obligation of a perfect character obligatory in a specific sense, for although a mere promise is not in itself an interchange of benefits and burdens, and therefore not a contract, yet the general obligation necessarily possessing this character, by the union of the promise with it, all the elements that are requisite will be supplied. For the same reason an imperfect general obligation may supply the necessary elements to a promise of a certain character. As the law does not recognize moral duty as equivalent to civil obligation, it does not contain the elements that are due to the nature of contracts as interchanges of burdens and benefits, and accordingly it can not with a promise constitute a contract.

By comparing together the two great classes of express and implied contracts, we shall find important points of unity and diversity that mark their common and particular principles. The exact difference between the two classes is that, in the case of express obligations, the form of the obligation is determined and evidenced by the volitions of the parties, while in the case of the implied obligation the promise is formulated by the law from the conduct and relative situation of the parties, and from the nature and condition of the subject-matter of the contract.

The common law of England recognizes the right of the individual possessing full power of self-obligation to bind himself by any terms that are in their nature capable of legal enforcement or compensation. The Roman law acted upon this general recognition, but allowed a certain disproportion between a promise and its consideration, in a contract of sale, to conclusively evidence *mala fides* in the contract itself. The precise difference between the two systems was that one ascertained the fact of *mala fides* in the case stated from the terms of the contract alone, while the other sought for such evidences in the circumstances surrounding the contract at its inception. Both agreed as to the fundamental principles that an obligation assumed in the absence of bad faith was valid, whatever might be its terms, if capable of legal enforcement or compensation, and that the presence of bad faith in the inception of a contract destroyed its binding force as against the action of such bad faith. Their difference consisted in the fact that one allowed one of these principles to encroach upon the other and displace it under certain conditions, while the other gave indefinite operation to each. The spirit of the common law of England, where unrestricted by the influences that supported the institutions of feudalism, was that of individual liberty, while that of the Roman law largely conceived the ancient idea of paternal government. That which in general distinguishes the common law of England from the Roman law is the great influence the principle of equal individual right had in determining its forms and methods, while the persistent force of the protective principle dominates throughout the law that emanated from Rome. This difference of policy expressed itself in the divergences that have just been pointed out, both systems acting from the same fundamental principles. The common law, equally with the Roman law, recognized the principle that an equipoise of burdens and benefits constituted the reason that underlies the doctrine of consideration, but the Roman law demanded that that reason should not be violated beyond a certain arbitrary limit, while the common law made no such demand.

While the mode in which the law treats express contracts is reconcilable with the idea that equality of benefit and burden is involved in the true conception of consideration, that idea appears clearly in its method of raising implied contracts. As has been said, the promise in an implied contract is formulated by the law itself upon the ascertained intentions of the parties. Where one has parted with some legal right on the reasonable expectation, derived from the conduct of another, that such transferred right will be compensated in a particular manner by the latter, the law implies an obligation on the part of the latter to perform that which was virtually promised by his conduct. The question in such a case is, What was the promise which the party parting with value had reasonable ground to assume as made by the opposite party? His actual expectation is not the test, for it might rest on insufficient grounds. To allow the operations of the mind of one of the parties to give form to an obligation to bind the other would be inconsistent with the nature of the right of self-obligation.

Three elements enter into the question of the implication of a contract: namely, the position of the parties, their acts and declarations relative to it, and the nature and value of the benefits interchanged. The object of noticing, in this connection, this subject, which in its broadest aspect exhibits the operation of most of the principles of the law, only requires attention to a particular feature of all processes for the implication of contracts—namely, the principle of equality considered as an essential ingredient of the idea of a consideration. The idea of equality attaches alike to the position and to the rights and interests of parties. As applied to the relative position of parties dealing together, it implies that each party has performed toward the other all that is enforced by his legal duty, particular or general, that could be material to the advantage of the other in such dealing. If the communication of any fact is demanded by such duty, and that duty is not performed, inequality in point of relative position appears. In a word, the legal idea of good faith in mutual dealings resolves itself into one of equality of position. The correctness of this conclusion can be made evident through the fact that fraudulent conduct of a party to a contract, in the course of the dealings out of which such contract originated, can not vitiate such contract in any degree unless of such a nature as to be capable of prejudicially affecting the contract rights of the opposite party, or, in other words, unless such party has lost through it some advantage in contracting. The advantage so lost would be precisely that which such party would have possessed had the other fulfilled all his obligations. The proper position of the party was that which was intended to be secured by the general obligation binding the opposite party to good faith, and it is manifest that the deprivation of this right caused inequality of position. Whatever other consequences may flow from an act of fraud, its effect in vitiating a contract must be ascribed to its bearing on the relative positions of the parties.

This conception of equality, as involved in the relative positions of parties dealing together, is fundamental to the idea of equity both as a quality of all transactions and as a formal system of administering justice. It is presumable that the want of attention to this aspect of the sense of the term equality has led some to deny that there is any connection between the ideas of equity and equality.

To trace the consequences of this fundamental principle, derived from the relation between the common obligations and the power of self-obligation, belongs to a consideration of the various classes and kinds of obligations, their origin, particular nature, and incidents. The present inquiry is concerned only with the qualities that are common to all obligations, and it can only be considered to the extent that it enters into the idea of consideration.

It may be urged that this conception of equality of position should be considered in connection with the subject of the voluntary character of obligations, inasmuch as a determination of the will, brought about by an act of wrong, is, in effect, coerced. It is certainly true that an obligation imposed on one by some misrepresentation, improper concealment, or other artifice in violation of legal duty, is, in an indirect sense, involuntary; but, if taken as true, in a strict sense it would place the idea of volition in such a position as to confuse the operation of the mind with the materials upon which it acts. It is also true, as said in another place, that, in their relation to the fundamental principle, the external control of the mind through a wrong done to the intellectual faculty and an improper control through the physical and emotional natures are identical. Though thus connected in principle, the cases have distinct features.

If it be true that, when the judgment is perverted through a wrong, there is no volition, then it must be equally so where the perversion is attributable to accidental causes. Volition is capable of being exercised, although the judgment is defective, and its exercise is independent of the nature of the cause that may have produced such defect. The law does not invalidate or dissolve the contracts of parties on the ground that one of the parties has acted on a false assumption of fact, independently of the fault of the other. This shows that it is not a defective action of the power of volition that is acted upon in such cases, but the want of equality of position as affecting the consideration or equivalence of benefits.

It was observed, while discussing the subject of the voluntary character of the power of self-obligation, that the principle fundamental to that doctrine is common throughout the whole class of cases where the contract rights of a party are impaired by misconduct connected with the origin of such contract. It was then seen that such misconduct was a violation of the common obligations, imposed by the nature of civil association, commensurate with and giving effect to the right of self-obligation. As such, it may become the subject of direct redress or compensation, as in the case of an action of deceit, willful misrepresentation, or concealment, and the various legal and equitable remedies in cases of fraud predicated on such common obligations. But when such misconduct enters as an element into a contract at its origin, although it does not necessarily destroy such contract, it necessarily modifies the state of rights under it. If the effect of such misconduct was to invalidate wholly every contract which it affected, it might, with much reason, be said that its true effect was the destruction of the voluntary character of the power of self-obligation, on which the validity of the contract depended, but such is not the case. The law, where it is enabled to look into the consideration of a contract, does not necessarily invalidate it wherever it finds any degree of misconduct incident to its origin, and prejudicially affecting a party to it. It is true that, when the misconduct vitiates the whole design and purpose of the contract, it has an invalidating effect upon the whole; but where it affects only some subordinate incident or matter, and the rights of the parties are capable of readjustment and compensation, in harmony with the principles of the contract, the contract is upheld, and compensative redress afforded. To destroy the voluntary character of the power of self-obligation is to destroy all that is claimed as produced from its exercise; hence the necessity of a distinct classification that shall group on the one hand the causes that necessarily destroy the contract as a whole, and those on the other that only have the effect to disturb the equilibrium of the rights and obligations of the parties under a contract in a manner admitting ordinarily of readjustment or compensation, though, possibly, inability to make such adjustment complete may lead to the rejection of the contract as a whole.

The propriety of referring to the idea of consideration all those agencies that disturb the equilibrium of rights and obligations under contracts calling for readjustment or compensation, even though they may indirectly, through the inadequacy of readjustment, destroy such contracts, is suggested by both convenience and accuracy of classification. As consideration has been defined as the idea of a certain equipoise of burdens and benefits, it may not appear obvious at first sight that inequality in the position of the contracting parties at the moment of forming the contract can be referred to that principle. The value that attaches to equality of position arises from its relation to the equal balance of benefits and burdens produced by the contract. If that equality is disturbed, an inequality of the resulting benefits and burdens must ensue; hence the relation that the idea of equality of position sustains to that of consideration.

The idea of consideration here presented, as involving that of the equality of position as between contracting parties, contains elements that are common to the administration of both the courts of law and equity, reducing all modes of dealing with contract relations to a common root of principle. In fact, it may be affirmed that equity as a formal system is in its chief constituent a product of this conception of consideration.

As it regards the rights and interests of parties as distinguished from their relative position, the legal conception of equality has both a qualitative and a quantitative expression. The term rights is here used to express those legal powers of control over the conduct of persons, derived from obligations that are the means of control over the material objects, that are the subject-matter of the contract. The term interest covers that of value, both as to quality and quantity, in the material property or other valuable right acquired or lost through the contract. That the law does in fact weigh together, for certain purposes, the various rights and interests entering into contracts, needs no illustration. That in so doing it must take into consideration equalities and inequalities, is consistent with the nature of reason. The general consequences flowing from these sources are so familiar that they need not be developed for the present purpose.

Summarizing the foregoing, the reason of the following propositions is obvious. The law demands for every contract, as essential to its entire efficiency, that the relative position of the contracting parties should have been equal at its inception. If inequality appears in this respect, there is a defect in the consideration of the contract. If the case is one in which it is enabled to look into the elements of the consideration, and to readjust or compensate them, it does not declare the contract invalid as a whole, though it recognizes in certain cases a right of rescission, given as an alternate remedy, enabling the party injured to determine whether compensatory remedies would be adequate to his protection. If the law can not separate the infected element from the other elements of the consideration without defeating the general purpose of the contract, it rejects it as vicious. As between parties capable of full self-obligation, the application of the rule of equality as between the rights and interest interchanged is left wholly with the parties, and their judgment as to what is equal is conclusive. When called upon to imply terms of contract either to supply a want of express terms or to adjust or compensate some defect in consideration of the contract, it applies the principle of equality as between the rights and interests of the parties.

It is not to be assumed, from what has just been stated, that whenever the law undertakes to imply a contract it purposes to formulate one perfectly equal, according to its own judgment of equality. The result of an implication may be to find that the parties had, in terms or effect, valued the rights and interests to which these dealings related. The primary source from which to gather what was reasonably understood by a contracting party as the intention of another, is the acts and declarations of the parties. If what was intended is clear, though clothed in acts and partial declarations instead of words properly expressing terms of contract, the consideration of the effect of such intention upon the equality of rights and obligations resulting does not arise. It is clear that the law would not construe the acts and declarations of parties admitting of any doubt so as to accomplish gross inequality. On the other hand, the greater the uncertainty that attaches to the acts and declarations of the parties, the greater is the influence exerted by the fundamental conception of equality of interest, while in compensating wrong the law uses its own judgment of what is equal.

The idea of equality of burdens and benefits, as involved in the comparison of the rights and interests interchanged for the purposes of a contract, necessarily implies some standard of estimation. Value, in a legal sense, is the estimation of the means necessary to accomplish a certain end or to compensate its absence. This standard is ascertained by the universal habit of mankind, and is represented by money; and the existence of that habit determines the legal sense of the term value. It follows that comparison, for the purpose of ascertaining whether equality exists between certain rights or interests, implies that such rights and interests are capable of being reduced to comparison with a money equivalent. This general subject will be more fully considered in another place, it being sufficient for the present purpose to observe that the word valuable as prefixed to that of consideration is intended to exclude from the idea of consideration purely moral or ideal conceptions of value that are not reducible to pecuniary equivalents.

The rules of law determining what subjects of contract or promise are capable of forming a valuable consideration will materially aid the ascertainment of the principles fundamental to all obligations. As has been already said, the typical contract is that containing mutual promises to which all others are reducible. The subject of a promise is an act to be performed or omitted. It follows, from the fact of the necessity for a valuable consideration to give efficacy to an executory contract, that the promise or omission of a given act must be capable of having value ascribed to it in order to become the subject of a promise suitable for the purposes of consideration. Where there are mutual promises, the acts that are the subjects of such mutual promises must necessarily have, respectively, the same quality in this respect. It would follow that, in the case of mutual promises to perform future acts, the rules governing the character of such acts as are capable of becoming the subjects of contract, govern, equally, the character of such acts as are proper elements of a consideration. As the subjects proper to contracts will be considered as a separate feature of the law of contracts, the discussion of this subject will be deferred to that place.

It is not essential to the idea of mutual promises that they should be made concurrently in point of time. A promise, when made, may be conditional or purely voluntary, and yet, if responded to by a suitable counter-promise, while outstanding and unrecalled, the two promises may assume the relation of mutuality and a contract result, as commonly takes place in contracts formed by correspondence. So it is not essential that concurrent performance should be called for. A contract of sale is frequently one in which the promise on the part of the vendor and its fulfillment by the act of delivery are practically concurrent, and yet the promise of payment by the purchaser may by its terms call for a future act; but this fact evidently does not change the character of the contract as one essentially of mutual promises.

There are cases, where a promise is made subsequent to and based upon an act performed previous to the making of such promise, that need consideration. These cases are reducible to two classes, already noticed, in one of which classes a promise is made based on an antecedent perfect obligation, and in the other such promise is based on an imperfect legal obligation. It will be necessary to consider the propriety and the effect of this classification.

As it regards the operation of a promise based on an antecedent perfect legal obligation, no particular discussion is necessary. Both the novation and partial transformation of a contract is within the power of the parties to it. There is no reason in the nature of contracts why their essential elements or terms may not be found in part contained in some antecedent obligation, and in part in some new act performed in reference to such obligation. As the antecedent obligation must, if perfect, have contained mutual promises, or what is equivalent to them, the new obligation must possess that character.

The case of an imperfect legal obligation, giving rise to a contract through the operation of a subsequent accepted promise, needs more full examination. It brings to light two classes of cases of common occurrence that are representatives of a very large and diversified class. A common feature in these two classes is the existence of a benefit voluntarily conferred by one, and the enjoyment of that benefit by another. Where one performs an act advantageous to another without the promise of compensation or request which implies such a promise, the act is a voluntary act that gives rise to no perfect legal obligation. If one, without promise or request, purchases, in behalf of another, an article, and the latter, knowing the circumstances, and that it was not intended as a gift, accepts the benefit of such transaction, he is under an obligation to pay for it. But, on the other hand, if one, without promise or request, imparts value to the property of another, as in the instance of building upon his land, the fact that the latter gains thereby a benefit in the use of his property does not subject him to any obligation to compensate such benefit. It is obvious that the difference between the two cases is, that in one the fact of acceptance is capable of demonstration, while in the other it is not. When the benefit conferred consists in obtaining possession of some specific object, the acceptance of such object is an act demonstrative of specific acceptance; but when value is imparted to that which one has an existing right to use, the fact that, in using that to which the benefit has been attached, he enjoys the benefit, is fully accounted for by his previously possessed dominion, and therefore there is nothing from which to imply specific acceptance of such benefit. The difference between the two cases stated being formal, merely, is consistent with a common principle uniting the two. The specific acceptance of a benefit under circumstances that exclude the idea of benevolence or moral duty as inducing it, is clearly a ground of obligation, the situation of the parties being the same as if mutual promises existed at the time the benefit was conferred. As it regards the applicability of this principle, it can make no difference whether such benefit consists in property transferred, or in value imparted to property already in the ownership of the one who gets the benefit. Without the ascertained fact of acceptance, it is true that a perfect obligation can not exist, but where the benefit is actually enjoyed, although acceptance may be impossible of proof, it can not be said that none of the legal elements of an obligation are present. If part of those elements are present, as beyond doubt they are in the case supposed, then an imperfect legal obligation exists which may be made perfect through the addition of the wanting element by a common act of the parties, such as either an express promise, or one implied in an act of acceptance.

It is obvious that an imperfect obligation may give rise to a perfect obligation through the instrumentality of a subsequent promise, from the consideration of the general nature of obligations. An obligation must of necessity be considered as capable of existing in an imperfect state, for what is capable of being perfect is also capable of being imperfect. To say that the elements of an obligation have no existence as such until all are present that are essential to a perfect obligation, contradicts both the theory and practice of the law, and would tend to deprive it of the power of giving relief in the case of imperfect contract relations.

The same result can be reached from a broader synthesis of the principles of the law. Recurring to the proposition that the specific acceptance of a benefit, under circumstances that exclude the idea of benevolence or moral duty as inducing it, is clearly a ground of obligation, it is only necessary to observe the ground on which the law allows a remedy in such cases to trace that proposition to its fundamental principle. The law ascribes the origin of such remedies to the principle of good faith. As has been already seen, each member of society is bound by a common obligation to observe good faith in his dealings with others. Independent of the existence of relations between the parties of a fiduciary nature, this common obligation calls for the performance of no positive act; all that it demands in such cases is the absence of conduct proceeding from bad faith. This common obligation can not, then, in the absence of an act of bad faith, impose any positive duty, such as compensating a benefit received; but it is obvious that, when good faith, as an abstract principle, demands that an act should be performed, and the party abstractly bound to such performance promises to perform the act, the general obligation to good faith is capable of giving rise to a specific obligation induced by such promise, and that, consistently with its nature as a general obligation, it must have that effect. The moment that a benefit of such a nature is conferred, an imperfect obligation arises out of the common obligation to good faith that lacks only the element of a promise to give it legal efficacy, and when that promise is made its efficacy is perfect.

The subject of consideration is so interwoven with principles that pervade the whole system of contracts that some attention is required to the principles that are the causes of diversity among the various kinds of contracts. This inquiry must, for reasons of convenience, be limited to a very cursory generalization. It is necessary, then, to state the relation that exists between contracts that establish mutual interests alone and such as establish a common interest of the contracting parties. An illustration of a contract establishing mutual relations exists where an interchange takes place between rights of property, money, and labor, or some of these subjects of interchange, as where one having property exchanges it for money (which is property in a particular sense) with one desiring to exchange money for such property. Contracts creating a common interest are such as are intended to unite property, money, and labor so as to form a common fund for the common benefit of the contracting parties with the ultimate intention of their obtaining individual advantages from the existence or administration of such common interest, as in the case of contracts of partnerships, part ownerships, and the large and diversified class of contracts in which the idea of community is present but under restricted forms.

It is material to inquire whether there is a common principle uniting these classes, and on what particular principle that diversity of character depends. The statement that has already been made—that all contracts are reducible in principle to contracts of mutual promises—implies that there is such a connecting link or bond of principle, and, moreover, that the contract of mutual promises is the simplest illustration of that principle. It remains to see whether this proposition finds adequate support.

As the idea of mutual promises is that of the interchange of obligations, it necessarily includes that of the interchange of the rights corresponding to such obligations; and by the same necessity an interchange of rights implies an interchange of obligations. Such an interchange of rights and obligations is essential to the creation of a common fund, for the existence of such a fund implies that two or more individuals have transferred individual rights to a collective body. But the administration of such common fund calls for powers that are a necessary part of such a contract, and, if not expressly provided for, the law implies a suitable obligation as inherent in such contract from the general habit of the community in reference to such dealings and relationships. The existence of an obligation, whether express or implied, providing for some administration of the common fund, necessarily involves that of the existence of mutual promises as part of the original contract. In addition to this, as has been said, every contract creating a common fund implies, if it does not express, an intention of ultimate division of its common fund arising as a necessity of the intention to create a common fund, where such fund is not created as a perpetuity, and is the foundation of the authority by which equity separates the interests of such common proprietors.

It is, then, manifest that all the properties of a contract of mutual promises are present in every contract creating a common fund or interest in any form. On the same principle, when mutual promises are made by two or more persons, jointly obliging themselves either on one side of the contract or on both sides, as between such joint contracting parties, the elements of a common interest, or, what is equivalent, a common duty, are present, either arising directly from such contract in which they have joined themselves in a dealing with third parties, or from some prior contract as between themselves.

It is, then, the community of interest that characterizes the class of contracts creating a common fund or right. The principle that underlies all communities of right and interest here appears as a particular principle associated with the principle of co-operation, that gives efficacy to mutual promises common to all contracts. It belongs to a different part of this discussion to examine those institutions that embody and illustrate this principle that is central to all community interests, but the general relation of such institutions to contracts may be briefly stated.

Every institution embodying the principle of community consists of the individuals composing it, a common good which is its end or purpose, and a law or obligation which is the means of attaining that end. That which is essential to all such institutions is the means of combining the conduct of its individual components so as to effect by co-operation that which is embraced within its common good—a purpose of being. Governmental institutions, having the additional function to perform of regulating the relative conduct of the persons composing it as it regards their individual interests, demand the presence of an additional principle which is supplied by the idea of sovereignty. All such institutions rest primarily on an obligation voluntarily assumed by the individuals composing them, and when such obligation contains a specification of terms and conditions, whether expressed or understood, it possesses all the qualities incident to contracts.

Among institutions we recognize those that possess a specific organization or distribution of the various functions essential to their existence or efficiency among distinct agencies, and others that are destitute of such organic elements. A contract in which two or more persons unite their property or labor to accomplish an end of common advantage, embodies the principle that has been stated as fundamental to formal as well as inorganic institutions, and contains the same elements. The idea of a community of good becomes more and more obscure as we pass in review the various kinds of contracts when common interests exist, but under forms more and more restricted.

The fact that a principle tends, under certain conditions, to embody itself in certain forms, and in the absence of such conditions exhibits no tendency to produce such forms, does not contradict its unity. The principle that underlies the existence of a common good and common duty is thus at once the source from which all the complicated mechanism of civil government arises, and that from which the administration of purely private rights of that nature spring. Without anticipating the further development of this subject at this time, it may be suggested that the characteristic of the obligation that supports a common good or interest is that it gives rise to a delegation of powers molded to their proper uses, and thus becoming either public or private powers, which, when not defined by the terms of such obligation, are defined by the nature of such powers and of the conditions under which their exercise is evoked.

The essential and fundamental character of the protective principle is that of an obligation, on the part of one to whom power is delegated, to use such power for the purpose for which it was so delegated. Where the powers delegated are of a governmental nature, as where delegated in order to constitute the authority of a sovereign community, the resulting obligation, imposed upon such community by the acceptance of such powers, though imperfect for the want of the means of enforcement, assures to individuals the protection afforded by laws and the means of their enforcement. In the case of private powers, where authority is delegated to an agent to perform some duty in the interest of the author of the power, the obligation imposes the exercise of active good faith and is the basis of fiduciary duty. Where, then, a common interest has been created by the act of private persons, and the means of its administration as a common fund granted, whether expressly or as an implication, from the necessity of such administration, a delegation of power necessarily exists, giving rise to the correlative, protective obligation. The duty of administration draws after it all those arrangements and instrumentalities that are incident to its nature, and thus the protection duly becomes an organic principle or source of form. The propositions that have just been sketched will be developed more fully in treating of the nature and development of the functions of communities and institutional organisms.

Such a delegation rests for its reason in all cases upon the existence and exercise of the individual power of self-obligation; and, where it exists as a delegation of private power, it rests upon the actual exercise of the powers of self-obligation through the force of a contract. The sanction of that contract rests in turn upon the principles that confer stability on the determinations of the individual will—that is, upon the co-operative principle, as embodied in mutual promises. The ultimate sanction is the private right of the members of the society.

It might seem to be inferable, from what has just been stated, that in historical order the right of the individual, as recognized from the principles of the law, must have existed in a perfect condition for exercise before civil society could be called into existence. This inference may be thought to arise from the idea that cause must pre-exist effect, and that, as the authority of government is derived from the exercise of the right of the individual, such individual right must be first perfected in the order of time. But, although individual right is the sanction of public authority in organized civil societies, it is not, in an historical sense, its cause. Were we dealing with mechanical principles, we should be able to distinguish between the causes that produced a certain mechanism and the causes that produce its action as a machine. It does not follow that because the mainspring is the motor of a watch that it was the first part that was manufactured. It is the peculiar property of all organic systems that they pass through a period of immaturity before attaining a perfect stage of development. The period of imperfect development is characterized by the dominance of a principle that at maturity must surrender such dominance to a principle not altogether absent in the first period of growth, but relatively weak during that period. There is a distinctive law of infancy, and another of maturity. The law of infancy, or immaturity, is dominated by those causes that tend to unify the conditions of the new growth with those that determined the character of the parent source from which it sprang. The tendency of these influences is to cause the offspring to repeat the characteristics of its parent. Culture is brought to the aid of heredity to preserve the unity of the product and its producing cause. Maturity is the consequence of the development of the principle of individuality. Under the operation of this secondary principle, a development characteristic of the individual takes place. Ancestral tendencies lose relative influence, and a process ensues by which the individual is distinctly differentiated from any individual that existed among his ancestry. If the primitive principle ceased to operate altogether when the secondary principle came into a condition of dominance, the result would be that the individual would diverge from his ancestral type to an extent that would destroy the fundamental unity characteristic of species; on the other hand, if, during the dominance of the primitive principle, there should be no action of the individual principle, the moment of maturity could not arrive, or, if it occurred, it must come as a sudden and spontaneous change of equilibrium that never takes place in organic development. The true conception is that both principles coexisted from the first moment of organic being; but that which has been termed the primary principle, from the fact that it stands first in influence in the historic order of development, has its maximum force at the first moment of organic existence, but gradually loses its dominant character, and at the moment of maturity is, theoretically, in a state of equilibrium with the secondary principle, from which point of time, in the course of normal development, the relative force of the secondary principle rises to a final maximum.

In the case of the development of society these laws are operative. That which has been termed the protective principle, as embodying the essential characteristics of the parental relation, is the primitive principle that dominates social immaturity with a force that, in the normal order of social development, undergoes gradual diminution. The secondary principle, which is termed that of equal individual right, while at the early period destitute of any large degree of force, should, in the normal course of social development, arrive at some time in such a condition as to cancel the dominant force of the protective principle, and from that point forward assume dominant and increasing force.

According to the view of civil government that has been propounded, treating it as an organic system of differentiated functions, it would seem necessary to place the period when society should be regarded as under the law of maturity, in the sense of the distinction between mature and immature powers, at the time when civil functions were effectively differentiated. The very idea of civil institutions embraces that of a certain individual autonomy. The citizen is the subject endowed with functions that enter the aggregate called civil forces. When the subject becomes a source of authority to the state seems to be the fitting time for him to attain the civil distinction of being called a citizen. The fact that, historically, the habilitation of the subject with civil function, not as an agent of the community, but as an individual, commenced in cities, accounts for the connection between the idea of individual civil function and residence in a municipality. Certainly the individual has a distinct function as an element of civil government. Theoretically that must be conceded, but practically it is demonstrable.

It is inconceivable that, while the functions of making laws, administering justice, and the proprietary rights of the community resided in the person of the sovereign, he should, as his voluntary and benevolent act, separate such functions from his person and place them in the hands of agencies in some degree independent of his will. Such a voluntary functional distribution is contrary to the tendencies of those clothed with authority, and would stand as a social effect without an adequate social cause, and therefore must, in the nature of things, be ascribed to the operation of the principle of individual liberty. The moment this secondary principle obtained force sufficient to balance the opposite principle that tended to identify authority with personal right, was the earliest moment when the functional distribution of the powers of government could be expected to take place. This proposition completes the deduction that the origin of civil function must be regarded as coexisting in point of time with the occurrence of that stage of maturity that immediately succeeds the final stage of immaturity.

In another sense of the term, maturity of social power is the product of long development after the influence of the secondary principle has afforded the means of an individualizing growth, but the period of maturity is here indicated rather than any maximum of maturity attained during such period.

It is possible to deduce a conclusion from the foregoing that would exhibit the relation between civil law and the condition of law which is here termed the natural law. The natural law under this view would represent the law of social immaturity, and its characteristic would be the unbalanced dominance of the protective or paternal principle.

It is evident, from what has been premised, in what sense civil authority may be said to rest on the exercise of the individual power of self-obligation. The difficulty that many have found in accepting the idea that there is anything in the nature of a compact or contract of society that determines the authority of the sovereign power, or the duty of the subject, in part at least, arises from giving that conception a character that is technical rather than vital. It is repulsive to the ideas of many, and may well be of all, that a body of men should have agreed among themselves, at a certain period of time, upon a certain mode of governing mankind that should be final in all ages to come. Such is not the intended or the true conception, for it ignores any natural and progressive relation between the state and the individual. The conception that has already been in part developed depends on natural conditions, and not upon any arbitrary assumption. It assumes that the sanction of public authority is something momentarily proceeding from the individual, the unit of the system, to the system itself as a compound unit, as the power of all organisms proceeds from the separate units of which they are composed, and are merely aggregated and directed through the general functional arrangements. So long as the individual maintains a proper connection with the civil society of which he is a member, this ministration of power from the individual to the many takes place, and public authority is momentarily renewed from its original sources. The legal conception of a contract as applied to the relation of the individual to the community is merely the expression of certain necessary conditions that must exist where that relationship is normal—that is to say, where its character is in harmony with what is essential to the existence and efficacy of the community as a means of promoting the welfare of the individual. As it is obvious that the individual must perform certain actions and abstain from others as a necessary condition of the maintenance of a proper relation between himself and organized society, the performance or omission of such acts is stated, in principle, as an imperative necessity or obligation arising out of the relation between himself and the community, and this is the idea common to the ideas of law and obligation. When, then, the various rules and doctrines of the law have been examined, and certain principles are found that must in the nature of things enter into every obligation, the application of their principles to fill out the intention to be inferred from the fact of association to form civil society will give an aspect of such transactions that is not distinguishable from a compact or contract.

It is important to ascertain whether the proposition, that the existence of mutual promises of a certain character is the essential idea of a contract or obligation capable of being enforced while executory, is a universal truth; that is to say, that it is the law of all obligations that are in an executory condition. As it regards the common obligations, it is obviously true, for they are the results of mutual promises ascribed to the transaction implied as existing between the members of a community regarding its existence and maintenance. It must, then, be equally true of all obligations of which the common obligations are a component part. The common obligations are general obligations—that is to say, they are of such a nature that it is possible for an indefinite number of varied states of circumstances to occur each giving rise under the general obligation to a specific duty or liability. The obligatory force of all these derived specific duties depends upon the presence in the general obligation of all the elements essential to obligatory force.

Those obligations that are imposed by public authority, independently of any exercise of the individual power of self-obligation, are produced through the exercise of the public powers delegated by means of the common obligations, and have their obligatory force from the common obligations from which they spring.

All the obligations that affect the individual that are not created through his own voluntary act are derived from the common obligations, either directly or indirectly, through the medium of the public authority. This includes the obligation to compensate every wrong done to the right of person or property of another, for, as will appear hereafter, general wrongs are reducible to violations of the common obligations.

When an obligation arises in consequence of a promise, expressed or implied, based upon a pre-existing obligation, either perfect or imperfect, the common obligations supply that which may be essential to constitute the elements of mutual promise.

If, then, all the various obligations that are the structural features of the civil fabric within which civilized man has his dwelling and sphere of action are capable of being reduced by analysis to the simple typical case of mutual promises of a certain character, or to that which is their equivalent, the means are afforded for studying the nature of obligations in their simplest and most rudimentary form.

The idea of mutual promises is that of concerted conduct. The executory contract is the private law of future conduct between the parties. It takes just so much from the actual liberty of the individual as it imperatively demands to be done or omitted. As this actual liberty is given by law, it must be taken away by law, and, as the contract has the capacity to take it away, it must have the quality of law. Law is necessarily bilateral. It may be said that man is a law to himself, but the word law is here taken in an elliptical sense. It is the quality of law to displace voluntariness by necessity. A person can not divest himself of that which is in its nature voluntary or undetermined by necessity, except through his relation to persons or things outside of himself. He may fasten himself to a physical object by a tie that he can neither undo nor break, and in that case his voluntary power may be to some extent limited. So he may bind himself to another person with like effect upon his voluntary power. If he binds himself to a physical object, that object must be bound to him, and the law, which is a tie between persons, is of such a nature that, if he binds himself to another, that other must be bound to him. There is at least analogy in nature for this fundamental peculiarity of the law. It is very evident that a law is a common property of two or more persons, and can not be conceived of as something affecting an individual by himself apart from relations with others. If the law of a contract is a common property of all the parties to a contract that originates in their volitions, it must be their common creation. An individual can impose an obligation upon himself, but has no original power to impose one on another. As the law of a contract must have obligatory force as it regards all the parties to it, it must proceed from the power of self-obligation of each of the parties; or, in other words, there must exist a case of mutual promises to afford all the elements of an obligation common to all the parties to the contract.

The necessity of a state of mutual promises to the existence of an executory obligation being thus demonstrated from the nature of obligations, there remains something still equally essential to the idea of obligation. The conduct of each of the parties must have a relation to the other, either directly or indirectly. If one agrees to walk up this hill, and another responds by agreeing to walk up that hill, no contract arises out of these barren promises, for the act of each has relation only to himself. It may be said that their mutual conduct is concerted, but a quality of such conduct essential to obligation is lacking. If each one is capable of having a beneficial use of that which the other promises, and that benefit is of such a nature as to be estimable for the purposes of pecuniary compensation, then, in addition to a case of mutual promises, it possesses the character of one of mutual benefits; or, in other words, it is a mutual engagement of benefits and burdens. A benefit for a third person may be stipulated for without destroying the character as an interchange of benefits and burdens. The benefit to be received by such third person may be a mere charity as it regards the person stipulating in his behalf, but this does not preclude the idea that the promise to give to such third person is a benefit to the one to whom the promise is made. The discharge of a moral obligation, or even a duty of benevolence, though incapable of being compelled as such by law, is, as we have seen, a recognizable benefit to the person under such moral duty. If one loans money to another to expend in charity, the loan has all the elements of benefit to the borrower; so, if the money is directly applied to the needs of one at the request of another, the latter is benefited in the same degree as if he had borrowed the money and applied it to the charity himself.

It is clear, then, that if there are mutual promises, and each party has a valuable interest in the aggregate of what is called for by the contract, it is quite immaterial whether that interest assumes the form of a common or mutual interest. It is true that, where there is a common fund created, something is brought into existence that demands administration for the common good, and that, in that case, each having an interest in the common good, has, unless restricted by specific engagements or the nature of the administrative duty, a power of administration over the whole, that can only be accounted for by the fact that each has delegated such power of control to the other. This new element, superadded to the simple idea of a contract, is perfectly consistent with the nature of that simpler form. The idea of an interest of a certain character in the concerted conduct of the parties conferring the quality of obligation is as well satisfied by that of a mutual as by that of a common interest.

CHAPTER X.

PROPER SUBJECTS OF CONTRACTS.

An executory contract calls for the performance or omission of acts on the part of one or more of the contracting parties; and as the law of the contract must be capable of uniting with the law in its larger sense, so as to form an harmonious whole, it is apparent that there are acts and omissions to act that are not capable of being performed or omitted at the will of the individual, but are of an imperative legal character, and hence it might be inferred that there must exist a principle tending to limit the power of self-obligation. The proposition embodied in the statement just made is, that a contract considered as private law must, in order to be effective, be of such a nature that its provisions can harmonize with the general law, so that the union of the two may form a coherent system. It is obvious that if this union can not take place, which must occur when the one is contradictory of the other, the contract must either take effective civil force independently of the law, or fail altogether of effect. The former of these conditions is impossible, and therefore such a contract is without legal efficacy.

This general view must be submitted to a close scrutiny in order to ascertain what is the precise relation between the law, as a general system, and private obligations. The general law, as has been already stated, is composed of common and public obligations. While all public obligations, such as the requirements of statutes, are referable for the ground of their obligacy to the common obligations, yet the last-named obligations produce certain obligatory consequences independently of any specific exercise of the public ·legislative authority. These obligatory consequences result as the effect of the operation of the habit of the community upon these general obligations, for the standards by which the force and effect of these general obligations are measured are those afforded by the habit of the community. By applying the common obligations to the customs, usages, and practices of the community that have attained actual permanency, and are recognized as imperative in the community, that body of obligations is produced that is generally understood as common law. The status of particular customs, usages, and practices, as imperative or otherwise, is ascertained in the course of judicial action by the courts of justice, and decisions resting on these sources of authority are said to arise from the principles of the law.

Those obligations that are here termed public, to distinguish them from the common obligations that are implied from the necessities of the civil state, constitute the other branch of that aggregate called the law, in its general sense. The enactments of the legislative authority of the state, the conditions of the grants of public authority, and the obligations imposed by the judicial authority, are classed together as public obligations. It is obvious that the principles of the law, that are the means of stating the common obligations, are the proper means of interpreting the declarations of the public authority that have the force of law in their constructive relation with the common obligations, while the habit of the community is the means of interpreting their language.

It would seem to follow that whenever a contract calls for conduct that is not strictly conformable to the ends and methods of the law, such contract would be inoperative, but, owing to the operation of the principle of individual liberty, embodied in that of equal individual right, this is not the case, as will be hereafter illustrated. There is a limit to the operation of the principle that would condemn all obligations, that are not strictly conformable to the purpose of the law, imposed by the principle of equal individual right, that renders it possible for an individual to engage in an effective manner to do that which is not within his legal or actual liberty. An attempt will be made to ascertain the nature of those principles as a means of comprehending the general system under which contracts are allowed or disallowed legal force, according to the character of their subjects.

As an important class of cases exists where the ground of the invalidity of contracts is referred to the policy of the law, it is important that the relation that the governmental policy of the state bears to the common good of the community, as a part of the fundamental obligations incident to the civil state, should be considered. The common good and purpose of an institution, as established by its fundamental law, are clearly recognized as distinct from its policy. The former has chief regard to ends, and the latter to means. The proper idea attached to policy as a definition of legislative purpose is that of some special purpose within the general scope of what is propounded by the common good or purpose inherent in its fundamental compact.

What appertains to the common good is to be ascertained from the nature of government, and of the ends and means rendered necessary by that nature.

The maintenance of order, the regulation of intercourse, and the administration of the property and resources of the community, considered as a collective individual, must be regarded as the particular purpose in view in establishing civil government. The class of secondary powers is large, but appears to be reducible to these governmental principles. If it were possible that habit, as the product of a social function, could be perfectly formulated and universally observed, without the aid of government, so that the intercourse of each individual with all others would subserve all his purposes, as to one of its important functions, government would be unnecessary. A social aggregation thus conditioned could exhibit orderly conditions, but its purposes and achievements could rise no higher than the level of the purpose and achievement of its individual components. To attain higher ends, co-operation must be secured, that implies the co-ordination of individual purposes to constitute a common purpose, and the means of regulating the conduct of individuals to the extent necessary for the accomplishment of such common purpose. When the community has purposes of its own to accomplish, some of its members are necessarily diverted from the pursuit of their individual purposes to accomplish those that concern the interests of the community, and, as they are thus compelled to contribute to the common good, their efforts must be compensated by all who participate in that common good. Such a condition calls for the means of regulating the relative conduct of the members of the community so that the due distribution of burdens and benefits may take place.

Common experience has demonstrated that mere social aggregation has no self-regulating power, but that the agency of government is indispensable, both to define in certain cases the conditions of individual intercourse, and to enforce such conditions, and the principles that should govern the relative conduct of the members of society. These ends are accomplished by laws and the means for their enforcement.

The direct object of the association of individuals for the purpose of forming or maintaining civil society must be considered to be the endowment of that society with the conditions essential to the maintenance of government capable of maintaining order, regulating the intercourse of individuals, and administering the property and resources of the community.

The rules of implication do not admit of the inference that any specific end of governmental policy formed part of the intent in such a general act, or that any selection of particular means was made where there was a possible choice of means to accomplish the contemplated end. That the community as a collective individual was intended to be endowed with the same powers in kind, though supreme in degree, that are properly attributable to individuals according to natural ideas, can not be doubted. The endowment of such a community with unlimited power to make laws to govern the conduct of individuals, and to enforce those laws by force applied to person and property, is the creation of what may be called universal means as comprehending all modes of attaining the end, and is inconsistent with the idea that certain means were selected in preference to others. In such cases it is only where particular means are in their nature indispensable to that end that they can, on the principles of implication, be ascribed to the direct intention of the act of forming civil society. The maintenance of order sustains this relation, as a means necessary to the accomplishment of the purpose in view, for without order, maintained to a certain degree, the agencies of government can not perform their functions. It is only when a considerable body of citizens unite upon the means of preserving order that government has any efficiency whatever. This principle has been utilized by despotic governments by creating powerful privileged classes interested to maintain that degree of order essential to governmental function. The existence of disorder is a consequence of individual action, and, therefore, the intention of the fundamental obligation must be interpreted as pledging the members of society, each to the other, to maintain the conditions essential to the efficiency of government by proper individual conduct.

Order once established so that government can perform its functions, the selection of particular ends and means for promoting the common and public welfare may well be regarded as committed to the discretion of that government. The common good directly contemplated by the act of forming, as well as by that of maintaining, society, would then consist in the state of public order, and in the due condition of the functions of society as a governmental institution, for the maintenance of which each has an individual interest, as essential to the security of all his other individual interests.

Superficially considered, order, in a legal sense, means obedience to the laws, but, in its relation to the preservation of social conditions, it has a more profound significance. The primary source of disorder in society is the violation of moral obligation or duty. There may be, indeed there are, instances where, notwithstanding a scrupulous regard is paid to moral duty, violations of law may occur. The general rule is well founded in common experience, that a strict conformity to moral duty leads to conformity to legal duty. The exceptions arise at points where the law has a technical or arbitrary character not corresponding to the conditions attached to moral duty.

Infractions of moral duty are not very clearly classified according to the language of the law. The graver class are generally designated as such as involve moral turpitude and gross moral delinquency, while the lighter class are simply regarded as disorderly in a moral sense. The distinction very evidently lies in the direct tendency of certain moral delinquencies to destroy the foundations of social order, while others, having, perhaps, a remote tendency of that character, do not immediately threaten public security. We distinguish among physical diseases those that threaten life directly, and separate them in thought from such as, though capable of inducing causes destructive of life, do not ordinarily produce this effect. This is an instance of basing a distinction on the habit of nature as operating through distinct classes of causes in a different manner, and is in harmony with legal methods of thought. The same ground of distinction must inevitably appertain to causes of moral disorder, although the experience of the effect of moral causes is not so exact as to render possible a perfect distribution of all cases under these classes.

Moral delinquency becomes a social fact when involved in relative conduct. Offenses against morals, however destructive their individual tendencies, while confined to the conduct and knowledge of single individuals, are, like contagious diseases affecting persons isolated from the community, a matter in which the public interests are not directly concerned. It is the contaminative capacity, coupled with the existence of conditions favoring contaminative propagation, that is of public concern.

That certain violations of moral obligation, affecting gravely the well-being and order of the community, are recognized as violations of civil obligations, inherent in the nature of society, is apparent from the common law jurisdiction of public wrongs. Indictments for gross immoralities have this character. To these punishable offenses many have been added by statute. The principles that control criminal administrations do not admit of the recognition as crimes of all acts violative of morals and destructive to the well-being of society. According to that system, crimes are defined by certain acts, or classes of acts, either usually or necessarily associated with such offenses. The necessity for such definition arising from the nature of individual liberty, leaves many possibilities of injuriously affecting society beyond the limits of such definitions. It is obviously impossible that, in all cases, all acts violative of moral duty, of such a nature as to demand condemnation for the protection of society, should be punishable as crimes.

Another circumstance connected with the criminal law that gives rise to legal distinctions as to the qualities of acts of wrong, is the fact that all public wrongs to which punitive consequences are attached are not cases of the legalization of an antecedent moral duty, but regulations of public law dictated by public convenience alone.

Recurring to the class of cases where moral delinquencies exist that are destructive to the fundamental interests of society, if certain acts, assumed to represent such delinquencies, are prohibited, with or without penalties, it is clear, upon the principles already discussed as to consideration, that the law can not, consistently with its own principles, regard the doing of that which it has prohibited as destructive of the social integrity as possessing the capacity of legal valuation for the purposes of compensative redress. This principle equally applies to recognized crimes representing lesser grades of moral delinquency, for it is equally at variance with the conception of legal value to attach it to an act the lawfulness of which is denied as contravening morality, and which is therefore capable of producing no good, for there must be a recognition of good before value can be recognized.

In the cases that have just been mentioned of punishable public wrongs, a definite act constituted the offense when accompanied by a certain motive. If, then, the act itself—that is, the subject of contract—discloses the motive, as an act of homicide is presumably one of illegal motive, then all difficulty disappears, for the subject of the contract is capable of being identified with the subject of the criminal offense, and the engagement to perform such an act is on its face an engagement to do that which the law considers as wanting in the element of good, of which value alone is predicable.

The gravity of the present question presents itself when the case is considered of an act engaged to be performed which by its nature may or may not produce a violation of law or morals, but when accompanied by certain circumstances may become an offense or gross moral wrong. In morals it is the intention and tendency of an act that confer upon it its moral quality. It is possible that that tendency may be conclusively demonstrated by the act itself, so that an agreement to perform a certain act may carry upon its face evidence of a moral delinquency sustaining a close relation to destructive civil causes.

Assuming, then, that an act is of such a nature that it is a demonstration of an attempt to violate moral obligation of a kind and to a degree destructive to the interests of society, it is clear that, with or without its criminal recognition, such an act can not contain the elements of value in any direct sense. Such an act may indirectly afford profit in its results, but that circumstance may or may not affect the estimation of value. If an act has in itself any appreciable value, however small, its legal value for compensative purposes may be estimated by the results reasonably to be expected from it. The condemnation of the act on legal or moral grounds of that high character does not merely reduce the conception of its value quantitatively, but destroys its capacity for any ascription of value whatever, by denying it the quality of good in any degree.

On the other hand, if the tendency of the act, in its legal or moral aspect, does not appear in the nature of the act itself, or in anything disclosed in the dealings of the parties evidencing the contract, it is difficult to see how such an illegal or immoral tendency could be ascertained consistently with the rules governing legal inquiry in such cases.

The attempt that has just been made to refer the insufficiency of certain subjects of contract to a defective quality of such subjects, under the general principles demanding a valuable character for such subjects, needs further examination. If such insufficiency does not proceed from some defect of their general qualities, it must be accounted for on the idea that such denial of efficacy is a punitive act. It remains for examination whether the principles that control punitive remedies admit of so general an application of that peculiar remedy.

The preservation of the liberty of the individual, a necessary outgrowth from the principle of equal individual right, considered as a social tendency, is a fundamental tendency of the law, and one especially embodied in the common law of England, that may be regarded as the specializing feature of that system of law. This principle, or, more exactly speaking, tendency, leads to the general rule of compensating wrongs wherever such compensation can be adequately applied, instead of encroaching upon the liberty of the individual by either constraining his personal action to conform to his engagements, or by denying civil validity to his action. This gives to the individual, in a certain sense, civil capacity to do that which the law does not sanction, but leaves him to the consequences imposed by criminal law, or to make the compensations demanded on the principles of the civil law. It must be understood here that criminal law is a department of civil law taking a special name, while the term civil remains both as the general designation of the whole system and as the particular name, collectively, of the departments other than the criminal law. It would follow, from the principle that prefers compensative to invalidative remedies, that the rule of invalidation should not necessarily extend to all acts or contracts contrary to the policy of the law, whether that policy rests on moral, political, or economic grounds.

It is necessary to form a more exact idea than has been stated of the compensative principle of the law before its limits in opposite directions can be fully ascertained. The idea of punishment is embraced within that of compensation. Compensation is here taken in a sense defined by its opposite, specific enforcement. When the law requires an act to be performed as imposed either by public authority or by individual self-obligation, and such act is wrongfully left unperformed, it applies force to the person of the wrong-doer, or to his property, preferably to the latter, to compel the performance of such act specifically, or of some other act or acts adjudged by the law as compensative of that left unperformed. The cases in which specific enforcement is permitted constitute a small class, while compensatory redress is the general rule. It is obvious that the same general principle and policy that limit the extent to which the law goes in compelling the specific performance of acts that ought rightfully to be performed, apply to the cases where, by destroying the civil competency of certain acts, they in effect destroy, in a certain legal sense, the capacity to do wrong. Both act upon the liberty of the individual in the exercise of his power of self-exertion, in the one case by putting restraint upon that power, and in the other by impairing its capacity, and both are under the influence of the tendency that leads to a preference for compensative remedies. The reason of the law of specific enforcement is developed in the class of cases in which such enforcement is allowed both in legal and equitable principles.

The idea that is always prominent in cases of specific enforcement—that the propriety of that form of remedy depends upon the insufficiency of compensating modes—is clearly fundamental, and may be accepted as fully disclosing the policy of not allowing specific enforcement where compensative remedies will produce competent results. It is obvious, as in harmony with the spirit of the law, that the limit thus imposed to interference with the liberty of the individual is not capable of yielding to the exigencies of particular cases, but is determined with reference to classes of cases according to their common nature, and is not affected by the actual sufficiency or insufficiency of compensative remedies in particular cases.

The conception of individual liberty that is thus involved in the preference for compensative remedies over specific enforcement has a response, in our conception of the status of man, in the general moral system. His acts, though contrary to moral duty, are capable of entailing both natural and moral consequences that become part of the natural and moral order of things, more or less persistent and productive of future consequences. If the legal system is in harmony with the moral system, which it must be in order to be subservient to it, civil law must recognize a certain capacity to do wrong as moral law does. Such an administration of the law as would eliminate the power of man to do wrong would arrest his development as a social being, in the direction indicated by the principles of equal individual right, and could only characterize a polity dominated by the unbalanced protective principle, producing a state of arrested development that has its analogy in another department of nature in the instances of idiocy and imbecility.

In view of the circumstances that punitive remedies are essentially compensative, and exclude the idea of specific enforcement, it is obvious that, if the punitive principle is invoked for the purpose of invalidating contracts, it possesses no such power.

The question then remains whether there is any ground on which the principle of specific enforcement can be employed for the purpose of invalidating a contract on the ground of the illegality of the conduct called for by it. That to declare a contract void on such grounds is essentially an act of specific enforcement, will readily appear. To deny force to an obligation, on the ground that it is a violation of some other obligation, is, in part at least, to specifically enforce the obligation thus impaired. As, then, the invalidity in such a case can only proceed from a violated antecedent obligation, it is apparent that the case under consideration is that of specific enforcement. As specific enforcement is not allowable when there is any other adequate remedy, and as the want of value in an act engaged to be performed destroys the legal idea of consideration or equivalence between mutual promises, and thus avoids the contract, a complete remedy in principle exists without applying to means the tendency of which is hostile to individual liberty.

Having ascertained the fundamental principles of the law as it regards the invalidating of contracts on the ground that the subject of contract is incapable of sustaining the idea of legal value, it is not appropriate to the present stage of the discussion to go beyond this point in the analysis of the different classes of cases that are its specific applications, inasmuch as we are at present concerned only with those principles that are fundamental to all obligations.

CHAPTER XI.

TERMS AND CONDITIONS OF CONTRACTS.

In addition to the requirement of a subject of contract to which the legal idea of value may be ascribed, it is necessary to an executory contract that it should contain terms and conditions that are enforceable elements of such contract. The word *terms*, signifying boundary, is of a general descriptive character, including that of conditions. Conditions are either precedent, attendant, or subsequent. As the expression *conditions attendant* is not employed by the language of the law, it is necessary to show the propriety of its use. To do this it is necessary to examine the nature of conditions as attached to rights transferred, and of such a character that they become limitations of the right acquired by the transfer. Every condition annexed to a grant is a limitation of the quantity of right passing to the grantee. This is equally true of grants of material substance, of labor, and of executory right. The term quantity, as used by the law, includes that of duration, for the reason that the subject of grant is some quantity of legal right, of which duration in point of time is a means of measure as well as of amplitude of authority over the subject-matter of the right. In the strict sense, the right or power is the subject of the contract, and that over which the right is established is the subject-matter, and in that sense these words will be used. As matter has length and breadth, so rights have duration and amplitude. Conditions precedent and subsequent affect the quantity of a right in respect of duration, while those to which the term *conditions attendant* is applied, and, in the language of the law, are described by the general expression *terms*, affect the amplitude of the right. The imposition of terms is, in a proper sense, a restriction of the fullness of right transferred. Terms of grant are frequently used as a means of describing the right, or subject-matter conveyed, rather than to subject it to any limitation in favor of the grantor; but this circumstance does not change their nature. When the grant of lands is subjected to an *easement*, the amplitude of the right acquired by the grantee is restricted by what is in substance a condition. It may neither have the operation of a condition precedent or subsequent, but is none the less a condition, and, obviously, may be termed a condition attendant. All other limitations of the right transferred are of the same nature with the particular limitation just mentioned, the difference among them being that of form, not of substance. It may be affirmed, as in harmony with legal ideas and language, that, whenever a right is transferred by one to another subject to terms or conditions that confer on the latter a less quantity of right or interest than that possessed by the former, whatever right may remain in the hands of the grantor is to be regarded as an undisposed part of his original right. When the subject-matter of a contract is labor or materials of a certain description to be applied by one to the use of another, whatever may be prescribed, effectively, as to the kind, quantity, or mode of use of such subject-matter, is a limitation of the right of the party furnishing such subject-matter to the compensations prescribed by the contract, and it is immaterial, as it regards the conditional nature of the limitation, whether the language expressing it is conditional or descriptive. From the case just stated, the intimate relation between a condition precedent and a condition attendant may be discerned; for, if the contract is for a gross stipulated sum to be paid in compensation for the labor and materials, only when applied in the exact manner prescribed, then the mode of applying such labor and materials is a condition precedent to the right to claim the agreed compensation; but, on the other hand, if the contract calls for the payment of the reasonable value of the labor and materials furnished, then the condition is neither precedent nor subsequent, but attends the right so as to become one of the means of measuring the quantity of the compensation.

Reducing the idea of a contract to that of an obligation consisting of mutual promises, and a promise to that of something demanding, permitting, or refusing the exercise of certain powers, the nature of conditions will appear in a manner not only identifying in nature the three kinds of conditions just indicated, but suggesting the common principles that underlie all conditions affecting rights. Starting from the proposition already advanced, that every civil right is a derivative from some obligation, general or particular, its actual strength being that of the civil force available to enforce such obligation, it follows that, where one transfers a right subject to, or diminished by, any condition that continues in him any part of his original right, such continuance of right is the result of an obligation assumed by the opposite party to respect the same by doing, or abstaining from, some act appropriate to such condition. This may be illustrated by an instance from each of the three classes into which obligations are practically divisible—namely, where the subject-matter is either material substance, labor, or an executory right.

Where one conveys to another land or personal property, subject in the one case to a servitude, or in the other to a right of particular user, the contract being executed by a delivery competent to make an actual transfer of such subject-matter, the one who has parted with the general right or possession of the subject-matter stands bound by an obligation, either expressed or implied, to respect the right of property thus transferred, in virtue of which he is not only a trespasser in common with all others, if he violates such right of property, but is, by the operation of his contract, estopped from any assertion of an independent right in respect thereof that would be contradictory of the proper force and effect of such act of transfer; on the other hand, the party who has thus acquired the general right of property under such transfer is bound by an obligation to respect the right remaining in, or resulting to, the opposite party through the conditions annexed to the transfer. These conditions may be either precedent, attendant, or subsequent. If there is a condition precedent, the party standing as grantee is bound to respect the property of the grantor in the subject-matter of the transfer until such condition takes place. If, as in the case under immediate consideration, a servitude or right of particular user is reserved after the grant has become effective, the obligation assumed by the party taking title is to respect the particular right thus reserved. If there is a condition subsequent, the obligation is to respect the right of the grantor as owner of the property, conveyed from and after the happening of such condition subsequent.

If the contract be one by which a party hires his labor to another, subject to terms imposing any limitation as to the time or mode in which such labor should be used or applied, it is manifest that the same reason as that applied in the case immediately preceding the present must lead to the same conclusion.

If one makes a general engagement, by which he gives his labor to the service of another for a particular consideration, with the condition that, for particular purposes, or on the happening of particular events, he shall have the use and benefit of his own labor, or that such engagement shall cease upon the happening of some contingency, such reserved right of labor can only be harmonized with the general obligation by regarding it as arising out of the contract, and not from the natural control of one over his own labor, and, in that case, it must arise from an obligation binding the party against whom it is asserted.

If, finally, the subject of a contract is an executory right, or what the law terms a right of action, any right reserved or arising from any condition, expressed or implied, must consist of the obligation of the opposite party, for rights of that nature are the creation of obligations, in legal understanding.

Under the foregoing view it would appear that every acquisition of right is on the foundation of a corresponding obligation, and every diminution of the duration or amplitude of that right is based on a counter-obligation, thus placing conditions precedent, attendant, and subsequent on a common principle.

The subject of a condition is either an act that may be performed or omitted by one or more parties to the contract, or an event presumably beyond the control of all the parties. When the subject of the condition is some act that is capable of being performed or omitted at will by a party to the contract, or, what is equivalent, where the performance of the condition is within the power of a party to the contract, it is manifest that the sufficiency of such act to form the subject of an effective condition must depend on the same rules as those that govern all other subjects of promise. When the subject of the condition is some event independent of the will of the parties, according to familiar rules of the law, the happening of such event must be a natural possibility. This brings to view a principle that equally applies, whether the question is as to the validity of a subject of promise or a condition, and thus is a fundamental principle of obligations.

From premises that have already been stated from the nature of obligations at large, the proposition may be advanced that where there is no natural power to act in a particular manner there is no civil power to bind one's self to act in that particular manner. This follows from the fundamental proposition that rights and obligations are commensurate with civil powers, and that natural powers are the basis of civil powers, as there can be no civil powers unless corresponding natural powers exist. There is a natural power to disturb the order of nature, and there is a civil power to violate the law, so that the question of the possession of natural or civil power in a given case is not identical with that of the rightful use that may be made of such power.

The law will not enforce a contract to do that which, from its knowledge of the laws of nature, it knows to be impossible, nor will it allow such an obligation to stand in the place of either consideration or condition. In such a case the power of performance is not existent in the order of nature. But it does not follow that, if an individual is deprived of some natural means of performing an act common to mankind, he may not bind himself to do that which, as a general fact, implies the necessity for such wanting faculty, as when a blind man should engage to do that which demands the use of eyes, that such obligation is void. The act in itself, if possible according to the laws of nature assuming the possession of faculties common to mankind, is a proper subject of obligation. As a question of capacity, it is the infirmity of the individual alone that interferes with the usual mode of executing the contract, and that is not in itself a reason why it should not be performed so long as others have power to perform it in aid of the party engaging performance. As it regards the class of cases where, ordinarily, the personal act of a party making an engagement is demanded, if the one to whom such promise is made is aware of such natural defect, such a contract could not be construed as intended to be personal. If, on the other hand, the defect is concealed, in the case of a contract of that class, such concealment would have to be regarded as fraudulent, and the question of enforcement would depend on the principles of fraud.

For the same general reason just stated, it does not follow that an agreement to sell the property of a third person to another is an agreement to do an impossible act, for it is not out of the natural power of a party so contracting to acquire the qualifications necessary to the performance of such a contract. Even if his means are known to be inadequate to procure that which he has engaged to transfer, the case would not be one of natural impossibility, for it is possible that the means of performing his contract may be conferred upon him as a gift.

The test, then, is whether the act is in its nature impossible, and not whether it is beyond the capacity of the party engaging to perform it. While thus an attempt to bind one's self to the performance of an act, that, according to the course of nature, is impossible, is nugatory, yet, if the act is possible, an obligation assumed to perform it, when the party has no present power to perform it, is in effect an engagement that he has the capacity to acquire the means of performing it, and that he will use such means to that end, and in this light is clearly distinguishable from the case of an agreement to do an act naturally impossible.

The proposition that one can not effectively engage to do that which is naturally impossible may be resolved into the proposition that, when an act is of such a kind that it is contrary to the order of nature to such a degree that the assumption of its existence would imply the subversion of that order, the law will not regard its existence as possible. That to which the law looks is its experience of a certain regularity in the recurrence of the phenomena of nature, or what is equivalent, and serves to connect the theory of natural with that of social events, the habit of nature.

The fact that the sufficiency of a promise is determined by what is possible to mankind, and not to the particular individual making such promise, is agreeable to the nature of law, and in harmony with the practical solution of the same question that lies in the fact that it is the proper province of man to act by agencies both delegative and associative. In view of such capacity of re-enforcing his powers by the aid of others, there is a natural possibility that any individual may be able to accomplish whatever is possible to mankind in a natural sense.

A close relationship in principle can be traced between the rule just stated and that in virtue of which value must be capable of being predicated of a promise in order that it may form part of an engagement of mutual promises. A promise to do that which is naturally impossible is a valueless promise, and therefore it can not admit of compensation or supply a consideration or condition. Considered as a means of initiating, terminating, or qualifying a right as a condition, it must also be regarded as non-existent. In the case of the absence of the element of value in a promise, owing to the fact that the act that is the subject of the promise is one subversive of moral order, the proposition involved may be stated in terms admitting of comparison with the principle just stated. That proposition is that, when an act is of such a nature that its occurrence would be contradictory of the order of society to such a degree as to imply the subversion of that order, it is not capable of useful or valuable existence. It is obvious, comparing the two propositions, that the method of reasoning is the same in both cases, the difference being that, in the one case, the reasoning is applied to the order of nature, and, in the other, to the order of society, leading, in the one case, to a question of possible existence, and, in the other, to one of useful existence, both conclusions depending on the reconcilability of an act or event with the ordinary course of events. The general view resulting from this comparison is that an event, to take any part by way of anticipation in the modification of rights, must be one consistent with the habit of nature, and, to become the basis of an obligation, must also have useful existence consistently with the habit of society.

That, in a legal sense, a question of morals is one of the habits of society, will readily appear from the nature of law, as founded in its experience of the habit of mankind. The standards of morals must either be ethical or such as are afforded by the habit of the community. The law derives its standards, habitually, from the last-named source. Questions of moral policy, as well as of political and economic policy, reach the law only through the legislative or political power, and are not propounded by the nature of its principles any further than as embodied in social habits. In considering the law as derived from its original sources, it is necessary to consider it apart from those modifying influences that are due to public law, and to confine attention to the effects produced upon the habit of the community, and to the reflexion of such habit upon the institutional system of the law, and from these sources to study the principles that are fundamental to them. This method must be equally applied when a question of legal standard is presented, whether political, economic, or moral considerations are involved.

The cases where contracts are invalidated through the operation of public law do not belong to the present discussion, as such results do not directly flow from the principles of the law, but sustain only an indirect relation to such principles.

CHAPTER XII.

OBLIGATION TO GOOD FAITH.

AMONG the essentials to the validity of contracts has already been enumerated that they should be free from fraud on the part of one seeking their enforcement. It is not strictly accurate to say that fraud prevents the agreements of parties from ripening into obligations, for the obligation comes into existence as such, though vitiated from its inception. A vitiated contract is one that does not possess the immunities that protect the voluntary power of self-obligation, and the rights springing from the exercise of that power. The principles that lead to the result just indicated may be strictly termed universal, and, being fundamental to all obligations, are entitled to consideration in this place.

Fraud must be referred to its most general principle, which is bad faith. It is desirable that the terms used to express our legal ideas should appertain to our own language, and that Latin terms, as well as those derived from all other languages, should be reserved to express the exact shade of meaning they carry with them in the language to which they belong. The use of the terms *bona fides* and *mala fides* has become inveterate, and it is difficult to avoid their use. As those terms describe that which on examination will appear to be universal to all law, they do not differ in the sense they yield to the English mind from what they conveyed to the Roman mind, in this respect differing from most of the technical terms imported into our law from the Roman law. The terms good faith and bad faith, employed in a legal sense, have no perceptible shade of sense differing from their Latin equivalents, and, therefore, there is no good reason why they should not be preserved in legal English.

The law regards the exercise of good faith as implied in every dealing, and, consequently, in every obligation. The exercise of good faith is, then, an implied obligation incident to the relation existing among the members of civil society, and, therefore, in its nature, a common obligation fundamental to civil society and law, and a condition attached to every right that emerges from the common obligations through the exercise of the power of self-obligation. The existence of bad faith must then be considered as an element capable of affecting the force of every obligation, and a cause of impairing every right capable of being enjoyed.

Good faith exists in a twofold form, as active and passive. Those relations that demand the exercise of active good faith depend upon a principle that has its fullest expression in the fiduciary relations. Where this principle is inoperative, passive good faith is all that is required. Good faith contains a moral idea embodied in the natural law of society, and incapable of being absent from the conception of civil society. As a moral idea, it is based on a duty binding every rational being to afford some measure of protection to all other beings and objects. This fundamental idea branches out into a general duty, as between those possessing equal endowment, and a particular duty, as between superiors and dependents. It thus contains within itself united elements, that, when separately examined, yield the conception of those principles that are here respectively termed the protective principle and that of equal individual right, while the duty of co-operation essential to that end is the sanction of all which rests upon the co-operative principle. Within this moral idea are thus contained, as in a seed, all the germs that in their development constitute the expanded system of the law.

As a legal idea, good faith has a more restricted sense. The rule of passive good faith, as prevailing between those standing in independent and equal right, demands that nothing shall be done by parties dealing together to destroy equality of position between them. The expression equality of position is used in the sense ascribed to it when treating the ideas fundamental to the doctrine of consideration.

The rule of good faith, as excluding active bad faith, equally binds persons who have the means of prejudicing the rights of others, although no dealings or contract relations may exist between them. The common obligation which is its sanction is sufficient ground for redress. When bad faith is an incident of contract relations, it may be redressed through proceedings instituted to enforce such contract relations.

Wherever personal confidence is involved in the relations of parties, the rule applicable is that of active good faith. A confidence exists when a trust is reposed in another, the acceptance of such trust implying an obligation to the exercise of active good faith. Investing one with the ownership of property to be used for the benefit of another is a trust in a technical sense; but there are many other dispositions that have the nature of trusts. When one authorizes another as his agent to buy, sell, or exchange property, to make obligations in his name, or to modify or discharge obligations due to him, a trust is reposed, and a confidence exists. It is the fact that one's rights are placed by him in such a position that another may exercise them that is the controlling circumstance in cases of trust or confidence. As it appears that all changes in the state of one's rights, produced by any cause other than that of a voluntary gift to him, must be attended by the exercise of his power of self-obligation, for the reason that for all that he receives he parts with an equivalent, and the transfer of that equivalent is an act of self-obligation, it follows that the essence of confidence is the conferring upon another authority to put in exercise one's power of self-obligation. Such a communication of authority is a delegation of civil power. Where civil powers are delegated to be used for the benefit of the author of such power, a confidence or trust exists, and the exercise of active good faith in the administration of such trust is covered by an obligation implied from its acceptance. Powers of this kind, when clothed with a certain administrative function, are technically termed fiduciary powers. They sometimes exist as common or mutual powers, as in the case of partnership and joint ownership.

Active good faith is also demanded where authority is granted to another to perform some act affecting the condition or value of material property, as when an artificer, servant, or laborer is employed to produce some change in the condition of such property, or to protect or preserve it. The authority to exercise any control over property is exclusively in the owner, and when conferred on another it is clearly a delegation of that authority that implies personal trust or confidence in some degree in the one thus authorized, to which confidence an obligation to use a certain degree of active good faith responds.

In all the cases that have been enumerated, the rules of law are the necessary result of the nature of the principle of good faith as a social element, and are universally, among all men and in all times, embodied in the habit of dealing conformable to social sanction.

When confidence is an element of any relation, the rule of active good faith demands that some variable degree of care, skill, and diligence shall be exerted, measured on the one hand by the nature of the duty imposed, and on the other hand by the character of the means applicable to the discharge of such duty.

The precise idea of an obligation to passive good faith is only indirectly recognized by the law. Its existence and principles are to be gathered from the treatment of cases of fraud, deceit, and negligence, as it is under these positive aspects of wrong that force is given to these principles. It is necessary that, when a wrong exists, a right corresponding to that wrong should also exist, and hence the necessity of interpreting the rules of law in the case of wrongs of this description, so as to give rise to the conception of a positive obligation, the breach of which constitutes wrongs of that nature.

The common obligation to good faith exacts the presence of a certain quality in relative conduct. As it regards declarations capable of affecting civil rights, it demands truthfulness as to action, faithfulness in the discharge of duties, special or general.

This demand is made not only when one is using powers delegated to him upon a personal confidence, but when he is using his own powers in dealings with the rights of others, in certain cases that will be presently indicated.

Truth, in its largest sense, is the attribute of all conduct that conforms to the motives that actually influence it, and, indeed, is descriptive of the conformity of natural form with the laws of nature and use that it represents. In the ordinary sense, as applied to conduct, truth is the attribute of representations, whether signified by word or action, that conform to the realities represented. In this last sense truth is necessarily, from the terms in which it is described, a fundamental element of good faith, and its opposite, falsehood, characterizes those phases of bad faith termed by the law deceit, misrepresentation, and fraudulent concealment.

The second element of good faith is embodied in the general idea of faithfulness in the discharge of duty. It assumes the existence of a positive duty, and requires that the ends and purposes in view, in its discharge, shall conform to those that caused the imposition of such duty. This is the element that characterizes relations involving confidence.

The third element of good faith has relation to the means proper to the discharge of certain duties, and is embodied in the general proposition that one who assumes to perform an act in behalf of another is bound to apply to it the requisite means; and, when the duty is imposed upon him without its voluntary assumption, he is bound to use the best means available for the purpose. These means are both material and personal, including the personal qualities of care, skill, and diligence, in appropriate degrees.

The features that have been described as the elements of the legal idea of good faith are operative in different degrees in both varieties of good faith, active and passive. In the former they determine the conduct appropriate to the discharge of duty, while in the latter they condemn conduct containing the attributes opposite to these elements.

When one in the control of property uses it in a manner

RULE OF PASSIVE GOOD FAITH. 127

tending, according to the laws of nature, to inflict injury upon the person or property of another, the law exacts of him an adequate degree of care, skill, and diligence in its use; and if damage results to the other, in consequence of the neglect of this requirement, an injury is done that must be compensated. The nature of this injury is that of the violation of a general obligation to use such precautions in such cases. This doctrine is clearly an outgrowth of the principles of good faith embodied in the common obligation.

The natural objects that are the subject of property are part of a systematic whole that we call nature. Although some of these objects appear to be entirely detached from that system, as in the instance of what is called movable property, yet this apparent independence of the general system is not real. The very existence and position of some bodies entail modifying changes upon other bodies having no other definite relation to these than that of position, and all bodies that are called independent bodies have a tendency, in undergoing change of condition or place, to affect the condition of surrounding bodies. It is obvious, then, that, in order to adjust a system by which the various natural objects may pass under the control of different individuals, it is necessary that such a legal system should be adjusted to the circumstances that, to some extent, connect all material objects together as parts of an interdependent system. The rule that requires the exercise of care, skill, and diligence in dealing with natural agencies is reducible to such an adaptation of the law to the natural conditions with which it is connected. It in effect demands that in dealing with material substances that mode of using them that admits of the least tendency to disturb or impair the condition of surrounding objects, subject to a different control, shall be adopted. It is evident that it is essential to both the individual or common use of natural objects that there should be a limitation of right of that character. Upon the principles of implying obligations, the necessity of such a limitation creates a corresponding obligation. In referring that particular obligation to the general principle of good faith, the force of this principle of implication is not destroyed, for all that appertains to the legal idea of good faith may, in the same manner, be shown to be an inherent necessity of man's social condition, and therefore a social law. The idea of good faith, in its broad sense, generalizes a diversified class of necessary conditions affecting both natural and moral order, and refers them to a principle that has its interpretation in common experience without the aid of technical researches.

From the view that has just been presented, the reason is obvious why rights other than such as relate to the control of material substance are not affected by this limitation. Subjects of property made such by law give rise to artificial rights, and have no such relation to other subjects of property such as that which obtains among the various parts of a natural order of things. Hence it is that a creditor may use his legal powers of coercion over his debtor in an unnecessary and uselessly oppressive manner without fear of redress, while, in certain cases, he can not use his own property so situated as to endanger the property of another without a certain effort to prevent that result.

The owner of land immediately adjoining the building of another is not, upon the principles of the law, precluded from digging upon his land, even should the consequences follow of undermining his neighbor's building, but he is required to perform certain acts, and to permit certain to be performed, on his land, and to use care, skill, and diligence in performing the work; and, if any damage results in consequence of the neglect of duty, an injury is done demanding compensation.

The rules of law as to the commission of waste, as between persons entitled to successive estates in the same land, and the corresponding doctrine affecting the use of personal property in like cases, must be traced to the same general principle. The existence of a right of that nature does not depend upon the existence between the parties of any contract relation whatever.

CHAPTER XIII.

EFFECT OF EXECUTED CONTRACTS.

To complete the present outline of the nature of obligations, it is necessary to notice that contracts exist in two states: namely, as executory and as executed. The general principles on which the law enforces executory obligations have already been stated, and it has been noticed that obligations exist in the executed stage. It is necessary to make this proposition more distinct, and to show that it is necessary as an interpretation of the actual determinations of the law. For remedial purposes, as a general rule, an obligation ceases to exist the moment it is performed. While there is no such a distinct recognition of efficacy in an executed contract as would exist if it was capable of supporting an ordinary action at law, there is yet ground for such conclusion in the mode on which parties to executed contracts are, in certain cases, held to the effects and consequences of such contracts after execution.

The doctrine of estoppel has given rise to rules the principles of which certainly point in the direction of the proposition under discussion. To stop a party is to hold him bound to the terms of an executed obligation, which implies that such an obligation may have binding force. If one sells property without title, and afterward purchases the actual title that was outstanding in a third person at the time he sold, why is he excluded from claiming the property under a good title against one who has no lawful title, as all others may do? The law says that his executed contract of sale prevents it. An executed obligation is not only a link that binds its immediate parties to certain consequences that continue after it has passed into execution, but it binds as well others who are in certain relations of privity with those parties. The deed that is the link in such case must have some inherent force. It is certainly more than evidence of a fact in the past; it is evidence of the existence of an obligation, and, as such, it could not evidence it unless it contained it. The law certainly considers that when one agrees to sell land or personal property there is an obligation to respect the title conveyed, as part of the agreement. It is a necessary implication from such an agreement, because the idea of a sale would be incomplete without it. The doctrine of estoppel demands such an implication. If a necessary implication, then it is a part of the contract of sale. Performance is completed when the sale is consummated by delivery, but that is not an act in its nature fulfilling the obligation to respect the title conveyed. If, then, there is such an obligation, a fixed legal incident of the contract of sale, and performance, so far from weakening it, actually brings it into efficacy, it may be clearly affirmed that such obligation may exist, as such, in what has been termed the executed stage, but which is really, in relation to all the incidents of the contract implied as well as expressed, a stage of execution only in part.

The doctrine of estoppel, applied on legal principles as due to the effect of an executed deed, can not be explained on the general principle of good faith. Circumstances may exist showing that, on the general ground of good faith, as applied to the dealings of the parties, the grantor ought not to be debarred from any technical advantage that he may possess, and yet he is held to his implied engagement against all the force of the principle of good faith.

The covenants accompanying deeds, and which retain force after the deed to which they are accessories has passed into execution, embody, though in a more expanded and effective form, that which, unexpressed, would still be impliedly present. The existence of force in the conditions of a deed after it has become executed by the transfer of possession is irresistible evidence that a deed is to be regarded as an obligation retaining force indefinitely. A condition subsequent or attendant can only be regarded as an accessory of a deed without independent existence or force as an obligation. If, then, the principal obligation passes out of existence at the moment of delivery, the accessory would follow the condition of its principal and become inoperative. But such is not the case, as the condition, if once effectively interposed, remains so indefinitely. It must, then, be regarded as a characteristic feature of obligations that they are in their nature perpetual, never losing force until some new change in the relative rights of the parties has obliterated the state of rights produced by such obligation.

The conclusion reached, that any effective transfer of a right implies an obligation to respect the right thus transferred, would lead to the further conclusion that such a common obligation exists. The fact that the common obligations are conceived as the basis of all right renders it necessary that they should be interpreted as containing in themselves all that reappears in particular transactions, which would embrace the implication under consideration. The common obligations to respect rights that one has created must be distinguished from that which requires all to respect the individual right of each. The grantor of rights is subjected to a different and more stringent rule, as it regards interference with the rights created by him, than that which affects strangers to such transaction. He can not take advantage of any defect in the title transferred by him, nor avail himself of a subsequent purchase of good title. Strangers to the transaction are not thus affected, but may acquire a better title, and dispossess a purchaser in good faith of a defective title. The difference between the two rules is, that one involves the principle that when one brings a right into existence he is bound to afford it protection, at least as against any attempt on his own part to destroy it, while the other is simply a recognition of the inviolability of individual right. Both rules clearly originate in the idea of good faith, and it is impossible for the mind to disassociate the idea of good faith from any act that intentionally violates either of these rules. It is easy to recognize the principle of protection operative in the one rule and that of equal individual right dominant in the other. In the case of the transfer of a right, the principle of good faith gives rise to an obligation determining the effect of the act of transfer, and this obligation attaches itself and becomes part of any such act. This explains what is meant by the implication of an obligation as part of an express obligation. It is the recognition of the fact that the specific or express obligation has become embodied with the common obligations, and so much of such common obligations as must take effect with such express obligation has become part of such express obligation on what are called the principles of implication.

CHAPTER XIV.

SUMMARY OF THE ORIGIN AND NATURE OF OBLIGATIONS.

From the view that has been taken of obligations, it appears that they are the means by which man acquires a permanent control over such of the objects of nature as are subject to individual control, and an assured use of those elements of nature that admit only of a common use among men, as against his fellow-man. By them he forms about himself the material sphere within which he enjoys a large liberty of control over the products of nature, and can largely propound and pursue his own ends. Through their instrumentality the family is compacted to its head and domestic and social order, and consequent happiness rendered possible. The state, itself the largest social means of enlarging the liberty of man, by controlling the agencies that oppose his proper liberty, is the creature of obligations. Every line of action is marked out by obligations, and every possession secured by them.

If it be true that the social life of man in its developed condition is the product of the system of obligations that surrounds him from the cradle to the grave, it is necessarily equally true that obligations are the foundation of his moral nature. A system of morals that presupposes a state of balanced and perfected individual motive, so complete as to render the ideas of obligation and duty unnecessary, is, to say the least, an idea that can not be illustrated from any experience. It is supposing the results of co-ordination present where co-ordination does not exist, or the existence of effect without its proper cause. It is replacing co-ordination, as a relation to a common purpose and common means, by the idea of an equilibrium of individual accidents, as it may well be called. The idea is inconceivable. The idea of goodness that is to take the place of duty can have no definition except by contrast with disobedience of duty, and hence must pass out of existence with that of duty. The moment that intention or purpose takes a persistent form, the foundation of the idea of duty exists in the mind. As society must consist of relative movements of individuals adjusted to each other, persistence in certain lines of movement is indispensable to the performance of its functions. It does not follow that repressive and punitive mechanism is essential to the idea of duty and law. If all mankind observed their various obligations, such mechanism would be unnecessary, but the idea of law and duty would still remain. Among the causes that produce adjustment among the forces of nature, there is nothing to correspond with the penal motives that are essential to preserve the adjustment of man's social relations; but, nevertheless, the idea of law is as definitely presented in the system of nature as in the civil state.

All attempts to base the civil law upon any other ground than that of obligation must result in placing the consequence before the cause. If rights are taken as the basis, and obligations are conceived as a consequence derivable from an antecedent idea of right, then no account is given of the origin and nature of rights consistent with what we know of the operations of nature or of moral relationship. The idea of right is inconceivable apart from that of a consequence of law, and law is in its form and essence obligation.

The law, considered as a system of obligations, must, then, be regarded as the frame-work of civil society. The very act of mankind in consenting to live together in social relations evidences an intention to subject themselves to such obligations as in their nature are indispensable to the social state. In the foregoing pages an attempt has been made to put an interpretation on the simple act of forming the social state in order to state the character of the obligations that sustain such a necessary relation to social existence. There are two modes in which such an inquiry may be pursued, one of these methods consisting in testing, by the individual experience of the investigator, what obligations are inseparable from the existence of society. The other consists in utilizing the collective experience of mankind in regard to that subject. Obviously, the view of the subject that is found embodied in the conduct of communities of men is of more value, as an embodiment of collective experience, than any individual experience can be. This collective experience is the source constituting the basis of this investigation.

Questions of individual right and wrong have been adjudicated, in the most formal and deliberate manner, upon grounds that embody a view of the character of the obligations necessarily incident to all social relations. These decisions express what collective bodies of men, through long and continuous periods of time, have thought upon the subject with sufficient strength of conviction to base the practical disposition of questions of life, liberty, and property upon them.

The conception that man, as a member of civil society, parts with some part of his natural liberty, is a consequence of this natural view. That which remains, as transformed in its quality, may properly be called civil right, and is that which composes what we call his civil liberty. Civil liberty is usually spoken of as an idea containing no constant quantity, but no reason appears why it should not be regarded as one of exact measure. By the use of the expression legal liberty, an opportunity is afforded of expressing the idea in its variable character as dependent upon the laws of different countries. One great advantage in the use of these terms to express different conditions of liberty is that it affords the means of conveniently contrasting the amount of actual liberty enjoyed under the various governments with a fixed standard representing the maximum of liberty capable of being enjoyed under any form of government. It will be observed that, while the attempt that has been made embraces the recognition of the principles of the law, as their nature and various aspects are illustrated throughout the body of the law, it also strives to state, with as much accuracy as possible, the state of obligations that constitute, as right, that quantity of right intended to be expressed by the term civil liberty. To accomplish this it is necessary to recognize the powers of man in their unlimited state, and the limitations of them due to the existence of civil society.

As has been previously remarked, the statutes of a state are inadequate to account for the large body of rules that constitute the law of such state. This fact is necessarily so, for the vast and diversified body of cases that arise in every community are incapable of being anticipated, and therefore of being provided for in any system of statutes. The source of the rules that are thus left unaccounted for must be traced in order to give a complete account of the principles of the law. It is a common remark that custom makes law, and within certain limits is actually true. Custom is in this sense used in this common remark, the equivalent of habit, as used in this inquiry, for the purpose of getting rid of a technical sense attached to the word custom. That habit is divisible into custom, usage, and practice, is obvious. Customs, in the legal sense as well as in the general import of the term, imply methods of acting employed by communities or bodies of individuals in certain cases. Usages have particular relation to the foundation of rights of person or property that originate in customs. Practice expresses the peculiar force allowed to certain symbols or modes of expressing ideas giving them intelligibility. Custom is thus the generic idea from which the ideas of usage and practice are particular derivates, and habit is a generalized expression that embraces this compound idea.

It is admissible to transpose the common remark that custom makes law into the proposition that law consists of the persistent habit of the community, persistence expressing the difference between those habits that make law and those that do not. The persistence of a habit is a question of fact in its nature, though general customs do not require specific proof of their existence, and therefore, for legal purposes, it is classed among questions of law. If, then, one entering into any given society, previously constituted, promises to conform to all the habits of the community that are recognized as persistent habits, he in effect obliges himself to obedience to that part of the law to which the term common law has here been applied. This would subject him to all that is established by proper public authority, for the reason that obedience to public law is part of that persistent habit. That a person could become a member of civil society and entitled to its privileges on any narrower ground of obligation than that just stated, is not reconcilable with the nature of civil society; that he should oblige himself to more than that, is unnecessary for the purpose in view.

If a stranger, entering a community with the intention of becoming a member of such community, complies with the necessary requirements for that purpose, his rights and obligations take the character that is prevalent in that community. If such community habitually holds property in common, his proprietary right assumes that form. If the habit is that of individual holding, that becomes the character of his right in that respect, although no statute may exist enforcing an obligation of that character. What he may or may not do in the control of his person, his property, or of those subjected to his authority, constitutes his legal liberty. If the habit of such community, including its public laws, admits of the largest amount of liberty reconcilable with the existence of the social state, then such legal liberty is precisely equivalent to what is termed his civil liberty, as distinguished from legal liberty. It may be that no country exists in which can be found that amount of legal liberty which is expressed by the word civil liberty, still it is not proper to call that conception a theoretical conception, because the actual determinations of the law are based upon it. It can only be called theoretical in the sense that one may call the idea of a straight line theoretical, because no man has it in his power to draw a line absolutely straight. It then appears that the conception of civil liberty is an actual factor in the determinations of the law, and its value to the lawyer, at least, is not to be disputed.

The principles of the law as here presented are propositions that contain the exact quantum of natural right that is relinquished on entering civil society, as a necessary consequence of such association, and which is not returned in the form of civil rights. That which is thus relinquished is expressed in the terms of an obligation, and that obligation, being the foundation of law, must contain all the elements that the law contains in its most expanded form.

It is not essential to the legal idea of a principle that it should be incapable of being resolved into elements. The principles of the law that have the most universal character are doubtless traceable to broader generalizations that lie beyond their form of statement; but that process of analysis that can resolve them further is not strictly a legal process, and can only be completed with the aid of research in other departments of research. For legal purposes a principle must have the character of a proposition, formulated as an obligation, although it is possible in many cases, and probably in all, to recognize a substratum in man's moral nature, and in the laws of nature at large, that accounts for such principle.

As the effect of obligations is to negative something that had a prior existence, whatever is not thus negatived stands admitted by the nature of obligation. This is the relation of the obligations imposed by law to the natural state of man's capacities. His powers as they exist in a state of nature are, as a member of civil society, converted into civil rights, except so far as they are taken away by either the habit or public law of the community. So the proposition remains that man can exercise in the form of civil rights every natural power that is not restrained by some social obligation. It follows that, where the exercise of a given power does not appear to be prohibited or qualified by the public law, or the recognized customs, usages, and practices of the community, the question of the rightfulness of its exercise must depend upon its relation to those obligations that are inherent in society, and are here termed the common obligations. Cases arise in practice that are governed by no precedent—that is to say, that can not be determined from antecedent legal action, which is the proper evidence of common habit, and which can not be determined by statute law; and in such cases their decision is based on the principles of the law—that is to say, the inquiry is, in effect, made whether there is anything in the fundamental obligations that is decisive of them. This mode of inquiry is a necessity, for a judgment must either enforce an obligation or deny the existence of one. A principle of the law can only affect the character of a judgment by having the force of an obligation, showing that the idea of a principle of law and that of an obligation are identical. As, then, all that appertains to natural powers may be enjoyed as a right that has not been taken away by the fundamental obligations, the habit of the community, or its public laws, the inquiry in such a case must relate to the nature of those obligations that are fundamental to society, and which are here termed the common obligations. It is clear, then, that the subject of the present inquiry and the method of its development are within the practical treatment applied by the law to actual cases of right and wrong.

The principles of the law, so far as they have been examined, have been found generalized in the obligation to good faith. It is to be anticipated that as principles are traced toward their common origin they lose their exact definition, but, on the other hand, they disclose their nature. The principle of good faith is important as a link between the moral and the legal systems. The implications from this principle have brought to light the fundamental tendencies of society in the opposite directions of subordinating the individual to the judgment of the community as to what concerns his individual interest, and, on the other hand, to leave him largely to the consequences of his own choice in his action, and also a means of equilibrating these antagonizing tendencies through certain co-operative principles. By these principles of co-operation, individuals are enabled to mass their forces, and thus compensate the advantages that government possesses in enforcing that view of their proper balance that is natural to institutional interests.

It remains further to examine these conclusions, through the medium of an inquiry into the nature and character of rights and powers, where more ample means of verification are to be anticipated. Unless the principles that have thus far been found to be fundamental to all obligations explain the system of rights propounded by the law, they are not entitled to that value which they appear to possess.

CHAPTER XV.

GENERAL VIEW OF RIGHTS AND POWERS.

HAVING attained a conception of the fundamental character of obligations, by being enabled to state those of their attributes that must be present in all obligations, either actually or potentially, we have the means of understanding the fundamental character of rights, for, as we have seen, civil rights result from corresponding obligations, and, of course, have the nature and the measure of the obligations by means of which they are constituted.

As obligations of all classes and kinds have a common nature, so each particular class or kind has a nature peculiar to all the members of such class or kind, and different from that of any other class or kind. It is only by the knowledge of the features of likeness and unlikeness that appear among individuals having a common nature that scientific knowledge is advanced; and this principle is applicable to the science of the law.

The division of obligations into classes results from the different natures of the powers that are the subjects of such obligations. The general subject of obligations, as has already been seen, is the conduct of individuals. The conduct of an individual is the mode of exercising his powers; thus, as conduct is the subject of obligations, powers, the matter of which conduct is the mode, are equally the proper subjects of such obligations.

It is necessary to distinguish accurately between civil powers and their mode of exercise. To illustrate the importance of this distinction, the power of control over material property may be instanced, to which the law attaches the idea of dominion. The owner of such property is not at all times and in all places entitled to exercise his right of dominion in the same manner and with like consequences. In a thickly-inhabited vicinity he is bound to use many precautions to prevent the exercise of his dominion from becoming detrimental to the community, or individuals, which amounts to restriction in the mode of exercising such dominion. In a wilderness such restrictions would not be imposed, and, therefore, a larger exercise of his right of dominion is capable of being there enjoyed. It is evident that the nature of his dominion has undergone no change in these different situations, but that its exercise as it existed in the one case is modified in the other. This instance is the type of a class of modifications affecting the fundamental nature of powers which result from the fact that each member of a community is more or less limited in the exercise of his rights by conditions inherent in the nature of communities. The nature of a power is that which it is, independent of and under all modifications. The study of the conditions that produce modification, and of the consequences of such varied conditions, serves both as a means of ascertaining the constant qualities that, appearing under all modifications, constitute the nature of the subject, and the additional purpose of bringing to light the tendency to and limit of variation of which that nature is susceptible. We have, then, to study the varied natures of civil powers, as well as that nature which is common to all, and the causes and conditions of the modifications they undergo.

Individual obligations of a voluntary character—that is, such as may be made or omitted at the pleasure of the self-obliging party—as has been seen, result from a contract or agreement of mutual promises, which determines the character of the civil powers concerned and the mode of their exercise in the particular case, and also the uses and purposes of such exercise of powers contemplated by the parties unitedly, thus defining the subject and object of the contract, and the private law of the conduct of the parties, to which the general obligations of the law supply the remaining element necessary to form the law of the contract to which the private purpose of the parties is molded upon the principles of interpretation or construction, as the case may require.

As the natures of powers are not changed by the obligations to which they are subjected, but remain constant throughout the entire range of obligations, and as their modes of exercise are dependent upon their natures, the fact that obligations are modifications of such exercises of power would seem to suggest that the nature of powers constituting the subjects of contracts would be the basis of their classification. Practical classification frequently makes some rule of form, such as the required mode of evidencing certain contracts, or some rule affecting the legal capacity of the class of persons to which the parties, or one of them, belongs, or the purpose intended by the contract, the basis of classification; but it remains to be seen whether a strictly analytic method would not reduce all modes of classification to a single mode having its basis in the nature of powers.

It is essential to a full conception of powers to expand more fully the distinction between natural and civil powers, and between powers in themselves and their mode of exercise. The basis of civil power is the natural power of man, consisting in the exercise of certain faculties conferred by nature. That which limits any given power arises either from its nature or the operation of other powers with which it is associated.

The nature of the change that has been effected in what may be called the quantity of a natural power, by converting it into a civil power, may be exhibited by the proposition that that which limits the operation of a power is the operation of some other power of equal or superior force. As both can not in the nature of things operate together to their full capacity, either one must give way or both must be restricted in some degree. In a state of nature, independent of mutual obligation, this limitation of powers is *actual*, while in the civil state it is *legal*. Independent of mutual obligation, or law, every action that can overcome the resistance that is opposed to it carries the idea of right under the adage that might makes right. Under the operation of law the exercise of a force may be wrongful, independently of its capacity to overcome resistance. It is obvious, then, that society compels an adjustment among powers, which consists in clothing civil powers with the quality of enforcibility, by the whole power of the community, which has the effect to make individual powers equal as it regards their ability to overcome resistance. In a word, civil association establishes a balance among the powers of men that eliminates natural force as the dominant element, and substitutes for it the power of ideas. Civil habilitation does not, then, change the nature of powers, but, strictly speaking, acts upon the liberty attached to such powers.

CHAPTER XVI.

CIVIL POWERS.

CIVIL powers are either original or delegated. They are original when accompanied by the right to enforce the obligations, general or special, on which their civil efficacy depends. They are delegated when the power is in the hand of one for exercise, and the right attending the power is in the hand of another. So long as the right to exercise a particular power is united in the same person, with the right to enjoy the benefits derivable from the exercise of such power, rights and powers are indistinguishable; but the capability of a severance between the two, so that one person may hold the right of exercising the power and another may rightfully claim the benefit to be derived therefrom, illustrates the distinction between the two, and the necessity of treating them as distinct elements of civil action. Every perfect right of an individual, or group, or community of individuals, is necessarily accompanied by a power commensurate with such right, but upon the principles of self-obligation the possessor of the power may oblige himself to abide the consequences of the exercise of such power by a third person. This indicates the general origin of all delegated powers as connected with those that are original in their nature. Political powers belong to the class of delegated powers, whether lodged in the hands of an individual as an individual political right, such as the power of an elector to express choice in the selection of public agents or public measures, or whether belonging to the class of public or official powers. All political powers are exercised for the benefit of the community, and subsist as delegations of the sovereign authority; hence, they can not exist as perfect individual rights, nor can such powers be regarded as original. The electors of any community, whether numerous or few in number, are a body or class of persons clothed by law with power to perform certain political functions, and the effect of such power lodged in their hands is the same in either case, and would be unchanged if placed in the hands of a single person.

A power is capacity to perform or omit certain actions that may be the subject of a right or obligation which the law will protect, enforce, or compensate. Delegated powers differ from original powers in being subject to peculiar limitation. The nature of the power, the conditions attached to its delegation, and the object or end of the delegation, constitute the law of delegated powers, giving them a narrower scope than that of original powers. Convenience will be subserved, as well as natural order followed, by treating the subjects of original and delegated powers separately. The subject of original powers will be examined somewhat in detail before taking up that of delegated powers.

To distribute original powers into classes, it is necessary to examine the subjects of such powers, for, being molded to certain subjects, or subservient to the proper uses of such subjects, they are impressed with the character of that which they serve and to which they are molded. This is, of course, the classification of both delegated and original powers, but the former take an additional quality that conforms them also to the will of the author of the power in whom subsists such power as original.

The actions that in this manner receive civil energy concern the person of the possessor of such powers, material objects other than persons, and the persons and actions of others. The idea that the omission to act in given cases is a power, embraces that of resistance to external force tending to compel the performance of such act, and thus contains a positive as well as a negative idea. The subject of powers will be considered in the order just stated. As rights and obligations are the civil measures of powers, and as rights contain the most positive idea, the various subjects will be treated under the head of rights, but will necessarily involve the consideration of the obligations that give being and character to such rights. They may, then, be classified as personal, proprietary, and associative rights.

The exact idea of the classification is that all the powers of an individual that do not affect objects external to himself have a certain character that distinguishes them from such as affect external objects, and that, as among such as affect external objects, there are characteristic differences between those that affect other persons and their actions and those that affect merely material bodies. Under each of these classes there is a peculiar principle, originating in the nature of the subject of the power, and the object in view is to obtain a clear comprehension of their principles. An absolute division of actions to correspond with these classes is not possible, in consequence of the constant interlacing of rights of different qualities and kind, forming complex relations; but, by studying from the subject of the power, a sufficiently complete grouping can be attained.

CHAPTER XVII.

COMMON RIGHT TO THE USE OF NATURAL ELEMENTS.

THE various rights that have direct relation to the physical, mental, and moral qualities of the individual will be next considered, apart from the modifications produced by public or private law, and as we must suppose them to stand upon the principles of the law as embodied in the general habit of civil communities. The inquiry may be stated in this manner: What are the rights of the individual as it regards the preservation of his body, organs, and their functions, and the exertion of his natural faculties for the accomplishment of his own gratification, independently of statute law and any special obligations by which he may be bound? This statement presupposes that such individual is surrounded by others of like endowment with himself, and with relative duties springing out of that fact, and therefore must take in view the obligations necessarily due to others; but it seeks to group various rights, individual and relative, in their relation to the principle common to acts of self-preservation, of self-exertion, and of self-gratification.

It is obvious that in this grouping especial prominence is given to the primary principle of equal individual right, which must be regarded as the basis of that individualization that separates the idea of common right into parts, and confers upon the individual peculiar rights derived therefrom.

The idea of self-preservation must be here taken, in its largest sense, as covering not only that of the preservation of life and health, but of all the organs, functions, and faculties of both body and mind. But, as the power to do that which is essential to that end would be barren without the appropriate means, the power of self-preservation carries with it, as a necessary implication, power over the requisite means; and, as self-exertion is a means to that end, the right of self-preservation assumes the form of the right of self-exertion. The right of self-exertion is not, as a legal right, limited to the purpose it subserves to self-preservation; for, as will be seen, the right to pursue those lawful objects that afford gratification to the individual is equally recognized and protected by the law, and becomes a ground on which the exertion of the faculties of body and mind receives the respect due to rights.

The first legal right that appears in the order of this classification is that which is always considered as the first in obligation—namely, that of the preservation of life. The law accredits to the instinct and desire for life the force of a right of a pre-eminent character. The life is imperiled through want of sustenance, through disease, and through external violence. As all of these causes may operate through long periods of time, and thus affect the health as a preliminary to the destruction of life, it is obvious that common principles underlie both classes of cases as threatening either immediate or ultimate danger to life. But an act done to avert the immediate destruction of life has certain legal qualities that do not extend to an act done to prevent disease or other destructive causes that do not immediately or directly threaten the destruction of life. The two cases are specifically different, though dependent on common principles.

It is only necessary, at the present time, to indicate the existence of a distinction, fundamental to the exercise of the right of self-preservation, between those cases that involve an impending destructive cause and others of a less threatening aspect. The law draws a marked distinction between actions that are prompted by a desire or instinct for the preservation of the life in the presence of actual or threatened danger to life and such as are prompted by the desire or instinct of preserving the health, or the members and organs of the body, from causes threatening less than loss of life, an instance of which is incident to the right of self-defense. Where the life is immediately endangered by the violent act of another, the necessity for so doing as a means of preserving the life may, under certain circumstances, justify the taking the life of the person offering such violence. This special principle clearly depends upon other principles than that of the right to do that which is essential to the protection of life, and is dependent upon the unlawful character of such violence, as is evident from the following considerations. The law would not justify the taking of a human life in order to prevent the loss of life when threatened by accidental causes merely, for one has no right to cast upon another his own misfortunes. It can not be doubted that the fact, that the form of violence that justifies defense to the extent of taking life is a crime, is material to its justification, as well as the fact of its necessity to self-preservation. It will be seen hereafter that self-defense contains, to some extent, the principles that appertain to the administration of justice, and may be called an act of private justice containing no punitive element, but merely a preventive quality.

The first elements of that which is necessary to the sustenance of life and health to be noticed are the common elements, air and water. It is the necessity of these elements to life and health that is fundamental to the legal idea of individual right connected with them. Their ministration to life and health is secured by treating them, in a sense, as property, or, more strictly, as assimilated to property. Water being capable of maintaining its qualities, to a large extent, without communicating with those natural bodies of water that are incapable of such subdivision as is essential to the full idea of property, has, for certain purposes and under certain conditions, the character of property. Considered as property, it is such only in a peculiar sense, the idea of property attaching rather to the continent than to the content. As water passes continually into the air by evaporation, and into the earth by absorption, in a manner that prevents it from being identified specifically in the various forms it assumes, it lacks the quality of specific identification essential to the full idea of property. Hence it is that the law regards land under water as the proper subject of property rather than the water itself; but, in the estimate of the qualities and value of land so situated, treats the water itself as, in a sense, property. This element is now being considered in its relation to the sustenance of life and health; its uses as property in a more special sense appertain to the subject of proprietary rights.

The law recognizes a common right to the use of the natural stores of air and water, limited, in the case of water, by certain proprietary rights that may be asserted in it. The difference, in the laws of their distribution, between air and water is recognized in their legal treatment. Air being universally present, the question of the entire deprivation of that element as the result of the exercise of proprietary right can not arise. Structures erected upon the land of one person may obstruct the natural flow of the atmosphere in a manner that may more or less affect indirectly the health of others, but the law does not regard them as a violation of the common right to air from the natural sources, for the reason that all lands have access to the atmospheric stores above them, and such structures do not necessarily tend to diminish the quantity, or destroy the useful quality, of the air in the neighborhood of such structures. It is otherwise with obstructions to the natural flow of water. Water in motion is distributed according to the configuration of the surface over which it flows. Its use as a sustenant of life, as well as a means of industry, is recognized by the rules of law that prevent one person from obstructing a natural water-course so as to divert its water from the land of another. This rule is not based on the nature of water in the abstract, but upon the idea that natural water-courses are a natural means of distributing water, and as such subserve a purpose to an entire region, as roads do to a community, and it is the natural quality of the region that is considered the direct subject of common property.

That access to the natural atmosphere is regarded as a civil right is evidenced by the fact that it is capable of forming the foundation of a wrong. The existence of a remediable wrong implies the existence of an obligation, and consequently of a right commensurate with such obligation. Every judgment at law that enforces or compensates a right contains elements consisting of an obligation, a wrong, and a mode of enforcement or compensation. The exact character of the right vindicated must be ascertained by the examination and comparison of the nature of the obligation, the wrong to such right, and the compensations that represent it by means of an equivalence in some other right or rights. It will be found, on the further prosecution of the general subject, that the implication from the measure of damages, as appropriate to cases, is of great importance in this respect. It is evident that the existence of a wrong, capable of redress, implies the existence of a right capable of being defined by that wrong.

Communicating noxious or offensive gases to the atmosphere, and contaminating natural bodies of water so as to produce injury to life or health, are nuisances or injuries to common rights. These cases illustrate the existence of an obligation to respect individual right as it regards the use of the elements air and water as sustenants of life and health. But they have a wider import than this, for the interference with the right to air and water as a means of enjoying life, as well as of sustaining its functions, is recognized and protected. It is true that an individual who sustains no peculiar or appreciable personal damage from impurities improperly communicated to air or water, affecting alike the inhabitants of a community or region, must resort to a remedy that belongs to the community or class of persons similarly affected as a whole, but that results from a remedial policy of preventing a multiplicity of suits; but he has the right, as a member of such community, or of the region inhabited by such class, to institute a suitable proceeding for the purpose of prevention or redress, without special authorization by the other members of such community or region, and may maintain such proceeding to judgment as the representative of the body of persons injuriously affected, subject to the right of others similarly situated to take part in its maintenance and control. For any special injury, however, he may have his independent action.

But this right to have the air and the water in common use kept from impurity is subject to limitations resulting from the general proposition that all persons may make the natural use of these elements. One of these natural uses is the discharge of gaseous, fluid, soluble, and, in some instances, insoluble substances that are the waste products of animal and vegetable life, the waste of the soil and its contents, and of human industry. All common rights are subject to the rule that their exercise must be reasonable. This question of reasonableness affects generally both the mode and degree of use of common rights, and varies with conditions of locality, population, and the prevalent habit of the community. Thus a factory, emitting noxious or offensive gases, may lawfully exist in certain localities, and yet be unlawful in others. Such a factory, in a sparsely-inhabited region, may have a lawful use of this common right where the same mode of use would be unlawful in a populous community.

The right to the common use of air and water is thus accounted for by the obligation that affects the use of individual rights having a tendency to impair the rights of others through the laws and operations of nature. This rule requires the exercise of a certain degree of care, skill, and diligence in dealing with natural qualities and forces of a distributable character, and liable to be the means of impairing the rights of others. The degree of care is that measured by the expression ordinary prudence, and the measure of that degree of prudence is the standard afforded by the habit of the community. It will be convenient and sufficiently accurate to speak of this rule as demanding prudent care. If one, in dealing with his individual property, is bound to the exercise of prudent care to avoid certain injuries to others, he is as distinctly bound to the use of such measure of care, at least when dealing with those elements of nature that are incapable of being reduced to the condition of individual property, but are for the use and enjoyment of all. It is evident that this rule is a consequence of the laws of nature, and involves the general proposition that, in dealing with the qualities and forces of nature, one must deal with prudent care to prevent unnecessary injury to others, and that for its application it must be referred to the standards existing in the habit of the community.

Light and heat are means of sustaining life and health, in part derived from natural sources, and in part from artificial means. Natural light and heat, in one respect, have the same relation to each other as air and water; heat is indefinitely distributed like air and light, both in lines of definite direction and diffusively. The relation of man to natural heat is, for physical reasons, not defined by actual cases. A person may lawfully erect structures on his own land, although diminishing thereby the diffusive light, and cutting off its direct radiation in a certain direction to his neighbor's premises. Such power may, of course, be limited by public law or voluntary obligation, and sometimes from usage derived from the fact of long continued and exclusive use. As such results are a necessary tendency of the use of one's property, the rule that excludes unnecessary injury is inapplicable, and no obligation appears to support a right to prevent such use. Every owner of land has the lawful use of an open sky above his land, and therefore an abundant supply of reflected or diffusive light; if, then, he deprives himself of access to this source of light by the form of the structure he puts upon his land, no reason exists for imposing upon his neighbor the necessity of conforming his structures to compensate for the obstruction of light occasioned by his own act.

CHAPTER XVIII.

PRINCIPLES OF INDIVIDUAL SUSTENANCE.

As the human body is composed of elements that are derived from the lower animal, vegetable, and mineral kingdoms, and as it wastes by exertion, it needs constant renewal from the sources from which those elements are obtainable, and that process of renewal is nutrition. Apart from the sources of food which are common to all, such as birds, animals, and fishes of a wild nature, and are controlled by any claimant, and the product of waste and unclaimed and common lands and waters, the law considers every person having full natural powers as able and bound to procure the means of his nutrition by his industry. For young infants, for the destitute needing temporary relief, for the physically and mentally incapable, and for the infirm and aged—when such persons are without the means of support, it recognizes an exception to that rule. The general rule has its origin, no doubt, in a moral as well as an economic principle, based on the worth of industry. For the destitute who need temporary relief, governments generally recognize the duty of affording aid in the form of public charity. The fact that no person need die for want of nutrition through the intervention of public charity is the justification of the rule of law that the necessity of maintaining life can not justify a theft of food. The policy of the law in this respect is indisputable, but it imposes upon the government the moral necessity of extending public charity to the cases embraced by such policy.

As an abstract question, it may appear difficult to recognize the justice of the proposition that, as between two persons, the one having the right to life and the other having property of inconsiderable value needed to support that life, the law will protect the property of the one, even at the sacrifice of the life of the other. The sense of injustice that is awakened by this naked statement has at least a moral foundation. A policy resting on moral and economic grounds, intended to strengthen the motives that lead to industry, may well be embodied in the law, and need not be run out into that intermeddling which has been justly charged against what are called paternal governments. If the government offers suitable aid to the destitute, it justly and wisely prohibits a resort to the violation of the laws of property for the means of preserving life.

If the master of a ship should deny food to his sailors at a point where other supplies could not be had, and the sailors, having a clear right to demand their food, should be threatened with starvation, it is not to be assumed that, if they should seize the necessary food with violence, they would be guilty of even a technical crime. It is true that the case supposed is not decisive of the existence of a general principle that would justify the taking of the property from a person, amenable to no blame in the matter, for the support of life. The question is similar to that already mentioned of the nature of the right of self-defense by the taking of life. In the case supposed, as in that previously mentioned, the doing of an act of wrong threatening life is an element of the question, and it may be necessary to regard the act as one of private justice compelled by necessity.

It may be difficult for a case to arise without being complicated with other circumstances obscuring the question of the existence or non-existence of such a principle; it can not, however, be safely affirmed that the law ignores all idea of superiority of right in the conflict between the right of self-preservation and that of property. Certainly the case of punishing as an act of theft, the taking of the property of another to save life, is accounted for without the assumption in question.

The principle upon which public charities are administered has a much wider scope than that just described. The policy of government very generally recognizes a more enlarged protective duty than that implied in relieving temporary destitution. Those who are bodily or mentally incapable—young infants, the aged and infirm who are in destitute circumstances, as well as those receiving injury in the public service—are, under a just administration, to a greater or less degree, assisted in the sustenance and protection of life. These charities are a distinct recognition that government exists for the protection of the individual as well as for that of the community, and as definitely for protective purposes as for the purpose of regulating intercourse and administering public interests. The idea of divesting government of the function of individual protection has no sanction in the facts of social life. Scientific investigation demands that the existence of the fact should be appreciated, and narrows the controversy down to a question of equilibrium between that and other social forces. It is eminently unscientific to consider the possibility of harmony among forces if an existing force should be annihilated.

From a legal stand-point—that is, from the consideration of existing social facts—it is impossible to disassociate the idea of sovereign authority from that of protective duty. That association existed in the idea of paternal authority, and is therefore present in all systems derived from that system.

A conservative faculty is an essential part of every organic system. Society can only perpetuate itself through its capacity to reproduce the parts of which it is composed. This involves the care of the immature members of society. Ordinarily, this function will be performed by the parental instinct and moral impulses acting on individuals; but when unperformed or unprovided for, as it regards individual sources, the interest of society that it should be performed suggests the existence of a duty of performance resting on society itself. There can be no difference of opinion on the point that society should regulate the performance of this duty on the ground of a direct social interest in its performance. This view could not only cover coercion to compel individuals to perform such duties, but, when neglected or unprovided for, to perform that function itself. A still broader principle covers at once the duty of society as it regards infants, the aged, and incapables generally. The object of public authority being protective as well as regulative, the duty of protection must be measured by its necessity, and that would extend the duty of government to protect and assist all such persons in all cases where due assistance can not be obtained from individual sources. This would not indicate a replacement of private duty by public charity as inconsistent with the principles of government. The duty of government to afford public charity is an imperfect duty, as the individual duty that preceded it was also.

CHAPTER XIX.

NURTURE.

It is necessary to examine the nature of the principle that lies at the basis of the ideas of self-preservation in a more general aspect than that hitherto discussed. It is the means of explaining many of the complicated phenomena presented by social organization and action. It not only tends to make clear the basis of individual relationships in society, but the relationship of the individual to society, and discloses the purpose and end of government, as well as the character of the means it may rightfully employ to accomplish its ends, in many cases of the greatest complexity and delicacy.

When the importance of the life of the individual to society and that of society to the individual are considered, it becomes manifest that each must be considered as charged with a duty of self-preservation, thus placing that idea in its social aspect on the ground of obligation. This inquiry becomes of special interest as illuminating the duties that are incident to the relations of society and the individual to the dependent members of the social body, a subject that has already been noticed in some of its features, but demanding more full consideration. As all the principles of the law culminate in that principle that conserves and perpetuates the vital conditions of society, its discussion must call in review much that has already been said; but is of so much significance as to demand the construction of its relations to a larger systematic whole.

As the law exists as well for the moral and intellectual as for the physical well-being of man, his right to perform certain actions, and to demand that certain should be performed for him, with a view to his occupying a position favorable for the accomplishment of the higher as well as the lower objects of life, is obvious. The idea of sustenance, which, in its relation to corporal existence, has a limited scope, derives an enlarged signification in its application to man's mental organism. To bring this subject into a light that displays all its bearings, the individual must be regarded as standing in three distinct attitudes to society—that of immaturity, maturity, and decadence. Hitherto the principle of self-preservation has been treated as applied principally to man in his maturity; it remains to consider whether that principle underlies the rules of law defining the relations of government and individuals to infancy and infirmity. To solve this question we must examine the exact status of the liberty of the mature individual as the means of discovering the ground of the difference in the treatment of those that are of imperfect civil right.

In entering this discussion, we must get rid of the impression that the principles of the law are identical with the political principles on which government is administered. The necessity for this distinction becomes apparent when it is considered that in the historic development of the highest liberty, civil and political, that is embodied in the most advanced of existing systems, we find that paternal government preceded individual liberty, and that the acquisition of individual liberty was accomplished by the abandonment by government of certain claims essential to the idea of paternal government, as previously entertained and actually realized. It would seem to be inferable that sovereign authority was the primary fact and individual liberty a concession made by it, and, accordingly, that the principles of sovereign authority were the first principles of individual liberty. It is a misnomer to call a government that practically denies that the liberty of the individual is the first principle of society and government a paternal government. Such a government lacks the instincts and feelings that are normal to the parental relation, and without which that relation is, in name and fact, a mere absolutism. The parental relation is based upon the idea of duty to the future manhood and womanhood of the child. The historic governments, or what is called the paternal type, have never thought of recognizing the proper civil and political liberty of the individual as a right incident to the matured powers of mankind, and the concessions that have been made in that direction have all been concessions to force external to the regular operations of government. If, then, the action of governments were the source to which we should properly look for the solution of the status of infancy, we should be compelled to concede that that class of rights which we group under the term liberty of the individual has no inception until arrival at maturity, is a legally recognized fact, and at that period of time is acquired as a benevolence. It would also have to be concluded from that source that the duty of protection and nurture, when imposed upon an individual, was due wholly to the state, and in no respect to the subject of such care.

It is proper to observe, as a preliminary to the inquiry suggested, that the principles of the law are not restricted to an adjustment with any particular form of government or principle of administration. While the law originates in a single source, that has been pointed out, its particular form is a development from the power of absolute sovereignty. The principles of the law are the causes of fundamental harmony between systems molded by different policies, while the policy that molds it is a variable force, giving rise to variety of form.

A normal government is one where the exercise of sovereign power is harmonized to the principles of the law; where their proper force is denied, the product is a political monstrosity, to which we may look with interest as disclosing possibilities of variation from the normal, but not as a typical expression of the constant principles that vitalize government. The law is the formulated conscience of society, and the laws of nature and the standards of right and wrong, in the highest sense, exist until silenced in political and civil death.

The law recognizes all the rights and powers that belong to maturity as existing in the infant, except the power of self-obligation in its perfect condition, but subject to an obligation to render service and obedience to its parent. These powers are of the same nature as those exercised by adults. The loss to the right of self-obligation is compensated by another right— namely, the right to protection during immaturity. The protection and care of a parent are compensated by a right to the services of the infant during infancy. The property of the infant is protected as against his parents and guardian equally as against all other persons, and both his property and person secured by remedies independent of the control of his natural or legal custodian.

The capacity in virtue of which one delegates his powers to another for exercise arises directly from the nature of rights and powers. It is clear that the power of self-protection is capable of delegation. If a person overpowered by violence calls to his aid a stranger, the law clothes that stranger with so much of the powers of the person he undertakes to protect as such defense may demand. That an infant has this power of delegation as a means of self-defense, and may call upon a stranger for help against unlawful force, and may confer his legal powers upon such stranger for that purpose, is so obvious as not to need illustration.

It can not be doubted that the law regards the right of self-preservation as existing and active in the infant as well as in the adult. The doctrine of parental and governmental protection of infants is readily harmonized to this view. If sovereign authority is properly regarded as a delegation of individual power, as it regards the class of persons who enjoy mature civil rights, it is equally so in its relation to immature persons. By the law of nature, that delegated power over offspring passes into the hands of the parent, who exercises it under the same sanction as if it were the result of a competent act of volition on the part of the infant. Upon the constitution of civil society that natural function passes to the community, and is, in a modified form, created as an individual civil right.

The general duty of care for all individuals, existing as an imperfect obligation on the part of the community, molds itself to the condition of the infant. The infant possessing the right of self-preservation, but inadequate power for that purpose, government recognizes the necessity for an individual guardian, and accredits that authority in the first instance to the parent, the person who exercises that authority under the law of nature. If a parent is wanting, a guardian is supplied under legal authority. It is obvious that, if the infant had unlimited power and capacity to delegate his power of self-protection, and should actually delegate it in the form characteristic of the parental power, the resulting right of exercising such power would have the same nature as that embodied in the existing parental relation as recognized by law. The reason why the parental power, though in its nature delegated power, is treated practically as an original and not as a delegated power, is, that the father has a legal interest in its exercise as entitled to the services of his child, and thus unites the character of master with that of parent. The union of this interest with the paternal power is, according to the definition of original powers, an original power that confers a general character on the relation, without altering the character, of that portion of the parental authority which is due to the right of the infant, and not to the interest of the parent. It is unquestionably true that part of the elements that enter into the idea of paternal authority are to be treated as delegated powers, and are affected by the principle of those powers. It must be concluded, then, that the law regards the right of self-preservation as incident to the condition of individuals in a state of immaturity, and that parental interposition and guardianship are modes of the exercise of the civil powers co-ordinate with such right. The applicability of this view to all incapables of all classes is so apparent as to need no particular elucidation.

The right of self-preservation in the case of the infant looks not only to the preservation of his powers as existing in a realized condition, but to the existence of such conditions as render development and maturity possible to both the physical and mental systems. The very idea of preservation to that which is undergoing organic growth is the furnishing of the conditions requisite to maintain such growth. As the infant can not accomplish this wholly by his natural powers, government is bound, under its general protective duty, to make good such defect of power, and to designate instrumentalities for that purpose.

The conditions demanded for the development of the infant, both physically and mentally, are covered by the duty of nurture, instruction, and discipline.

To view such systems as the domestic institutions and the educational system, including apprenticeship in the industrial arts, from the stand-point of the right of the infant to demand nurture, instruction, and discipline, may be regarded as novel, as until late years it was novel to examine the principles of government from the stand-point of the right of the citizen to be governed; but, at all events, the view taken from this stand-point can not fail to aid the observations made from other stand-points. All that is appropriate in the present place is to ascertain the existence of a relation between the individual right of self-preservation of immature persons and the duties of those having authority over them, for the purpose of showing the sanction on which such duties rest. The expansion of these duties belongs to the consideration of delegated powers of a protective nature.

Idiocy and imbecility in the nature of idiocy may be regarded as cases of immaturity without the power of attaining maturity. That persons in that condition are accredited with the right of self-preservation is evident, though the natural powers to which the idea of right attaches are inadequate for that purpose. In this case, as in that of infants, with natural power to attain maturity, the right of self-preservation, considered as a right to certain external aids to that end, arises in part from obligations affecting the community, and in part from obligations affecting individuals. As that right is an imperfect one, as resting on the obligation of the community, both classes are dependent on the policy of the administration for the realization of that implied by their imperfect right. The difference between the cases of infants and idiots is that, the latter lacking the power of attaining maturity, the right of protection is divested of those incidents that grow out of the possibility of attaining maturity, as in the ordinary case of infants. It is proper to observe that the idea of maturity, as understood by the law, is not that of physical maturity alone, but takes into account the periods appertaining to intellectual and moral development.

All other persons lacking the natural powers for their protection may be classed together as affected by decadence of power. To the extent that their natural powers are inadequate to support the right of self-preservation, such powers are supplemented in the same imperfect way expressed in regard to infants and idiots. The administrative policy of the government converts this into a perfect one to the extent that the care of such persons is imposed either upon public officers or private individuals. These duties are available as a protection to property as well as person, but in the last-named respect only are at present under consideration. Bad faith implies the violation of a trust or confidence. That trust may be either general or special. The conception of a general trust is that which should exist among all individuals in their mutual dealings. A special trust implies the existence of some delegation of power either by public or private authority. When there is a breach of good faith in the exercise of delegated powers, the wrong consists in the violation of the obligations as implied by the acceptance of such delegation, and may arise by either non-use or misuse of such powers. That which distinguishes such wrong from ordinary violations of obligations is the wrong done to the faith that induced such delegation of power.

When the obligation to good faith is general, as it is between parties dealing together each in his own interest, it is manifest that, bad faith occurring, its essential idea is that of deception. The wrong done in such a case is, to the judgment of a party in its exercise, in his own behalf. That wrong may control the conduct of a party dealing with the author of the wrong, or with a third person, either connected with or disconnected from that party. In either case the law judges it a violation of civil duty, and compensates any damage received through it. For the same reason, by an act of bad faith, which is described under the general term misrepresentation, one may be prevented from exercising the precautions necessary to the preservation of his life or health, and a wrong consummated. It is evident that through all these instances a common principle runs, contained in the proposition that every individual is bound by an obligation to afford to every other individual some measure of protection, both as it regards the preservation of his personal and proprietary rights, and this conclusion enables us to enumerate the right corresponding to such obligation among the incidents to personal protection. As it is not essential to this proposition that any special obligation, either created by public or private authority, should exist between the parties, it is obvious that upon the principles of construction it must be referred to the fundamental or common obligations as one of their qualities.

The general obligation to good faith is independent of a relation of confidence calling for active good faith, inasmuch as the existence of a delegation of power is essential to the idea of a relation of confidence; the general duty of good faith simply demands passive good faith. Hence it is that failure to disclose a fact, material to the interests of a party connected by a confidential relation, is a wrong, while it would not constitute a wrong in its effect upon the dealings of parties unaffected by such a relation. In the latter case, active bad faith is that which is necessary to constitute a wrong.

It is of interest to inquire whether the protective duty that is due, in some measure, from each member of society to every other is identical with the obligation to good faith. For the purpose of such inquiry, certain familiar instances of the particular duty may be stated. The duty of the owner of property, in its use to exercise prudent care to prevent unnecessary injury to others, has clearly a protective character. The obligation to make a reasonable use of the common rights, whether derived from nature or public license, and prudent care in the use of such rights, to prevent unnecessary injury to others, clearly impose a certain protective duty on each individual.

The same protective principle pertains to the relation of principal and agent, and was borrowed, beyond doubt, from the primitive relation of master and servant. The agent, or servant, is universally bound to exercise reasonable care and a variable measure of skill in his principal's or master's service. In all such cases there is a delegation of power, and a consequent obligation, the duty of using a reasonable care and skill being present as an incident of every act required to be performed by one on the property or person of another.

One who delegates some portion of his powers to another to exercise in his behalf is prompted more or less by faith or confidence in the agent, and the obligation that arises from the acceptance of such an obligation is molded upon the motive that induced such delegation. This would subject the agent to an obligation to exercise good faith. This principle runs through all the grades of agency, from the simplest form in which the agent acts as a mere implement in the hands of his principal, to the cases in which he is clothed with discretion, and to the highest grade in which he is called upon to exercise a determinate judgment of the highest fiduciary character. The measure of care and skill differs in all these cases, but the principle remains constant.

It is apparent that, taken in its general sense, good faith is the fundamental idea of all these cases, but it is important to see whether the instances cited can be found within the definition of good faith that has been attempted.

Little more will be necessary than to ascertain whether the obligation to employ certain precautions to prevent injury to others can be brought within the idea of good faith. Where such precautions are demanded of one exercising some sort of agency over the property, or affecting the person of another, the relation of such agency to the principles of good faith is obvious; but, when one is called to exercise such prudent care in the management of his own affairs, the connection is not so obvious. In the latter case the duty is clearly an active one, for it demands certain efforts to be put forth in certain cases. If, then, such case comes under the rule of good faith, the kind of good faith involved is that of active good faith, implying a confidence. If anything in the nature of a delegated power exists in such cases, then it is obvious that active good faith is an element of such relation. The definition that has been given of delegated powers is, that they exist where power is exercised by one in which another has the interest. When, then, one is bound to perform certain acts to prevent injury to another, while the power is in the one bound by such obligation, the interest is in the one for whose benefit they are required to be performed, and thus, as it regards the precautionary acts to be performed, the definition of delegated powers is satisfied.

There is no difficulty in understanding the application of this rule to those that use common rights, for in that case the existence of community of interest implies a certain duty and agency in each to maintain the common interest, obviously involving the idea of a duty founded on good faith. The principle of community of interest would embrace the common elements of nature that are incapable of becoming individual property, so far as there may be a possibility that the use by one may be prejudicial to others, for in such case there is a common interest that the natural condition of these elements shall not be impaired. The forces of nature and the elements of nature sustain the same relation in this respect to the action of man. Every act sets these forces in motion with consequences in some degree affecting others. No natural force is strictly limited in its action to any particular subject of property, but is, in a general way, propagated from object to object, affecting more or less the condition of all objects within its sphere. Man can not, in the nature of things, exercise absolute control over the general forces of nature so as to limit the sphere within which their influence is exerted, but, by observing certain methods and establishing certain conditions, he may, within certain limits, circumscribe the sphere of their injurious action to others. Upon this idea the rule of prudent care is based, and it is reducible to the idea that he sustains to the forces of nature a relation that he sustains to the natural elements, by which all use of these forces is in the nature of common use. One who uses the common rights, to the extent that such use may be attended by any conditions for the preservation of the common interest, acts as the agent of all that participate in that common interest for the purpose of maintaining conditions tending to conserve such common interest, and, as the relation of man to the general forces of nature has that character, the individual is, to the extent that he may set in motion trains of natural causes entailing injury upon others, bound with such a duty in dealing with that which is of common concern to all. It follows that not only is the technical agency present arising from the fact that the power is in one and the interest in another, but the relation of man to nature renders it necessary that, in dealing with the general forces of nature, he should deal as one bound in good faith under the obligations that apply in the use of common rights.

It may be asked why the obligation to good faith exacts only passive good faith, as between persons dealing together in their individual interest, and yet demands active good faith in the mode of using property where there is natural tendency to the injury of another. The nature of the confidence exercised in the one case differs from that exercised in the other in the same measure that the rule differs. The idea of agency is not present where two are dealing together in their several interests. The right that is the subject of such dealing is that of self-obligation. In the absence of an actual delegation of power to create obligations, no one can exercise that power in any degree but its rightful owner. Parties contracting together have no semblance of a delegated power over each other exacting active good faith. Each acts for himself, and exclusively in his own interest. If deception is used, its injurious character can not depend on the idea of delegated power. The effect of deception upon the rights of the parties implies the existence of a confidence that nothing will be done of an injurious character in the representations made, but is not of the nature involved in delegations of power.

It is, for the foregoing reasons, to be concluded that the idea of protection, as afforded either by the community to individuals, or by individuals to the community, or to each other, is of the essence of good faith, and that the rule of good faith is the formulation and embodiment of that principle in a manner that gives efficiency to the distinction between the general protective duty and a specific duty of that character. It would thus follow that the duty involved in the relation both of the community and of individuals to immature and incapable persons rests upon the obligation to good faith of an active character. From the nature of sovereignty, this duty, on the part of the community, is of an imperfect character; but that circumstance does not change its nature. As the parental relation is of the same nature as that between the state and the citizen—a fact that is essential to the idea that sovereign power was derived out of paternal power—and as the relation of parent and child, as it concerns the personal care of the child, is similar to that which exists between the state and its citizens, the obligation of the parent to the child is an imperfect obligation, and is only rendered perfect to the extent that the administrative policy of the state gives it that character.

CHAPTER XX.

INDIVIDUAL REDRESS AND PROTECTION.

The nature of the right of self-preservation is illustrated, as to certain of its features that escape ordinary attention, by the powers that are capable of being exercised to prevent injury to life from disease. The first case to be noticed is that of one exercising some degree of control over the person of another for his own protection. The second case is where one exercises control over the person of another through motives of humanity in order to prevent injury to such person. In both of these cases, acts that, under ordinary circumstances, would be invasions of individual right, become, in the presence of danger of a certain character to life, rightful acts. With these two classes another is intimately connected, proper to be incidentally noticed. This is where some duty is modified by the fact that its performance in the usual mode may involve the exposure of one's health, or that of persons committed to his care, to injury threatening life. A few observations on the last-named case will dispose of all that is proper to be said in this connection, and clear the way for the consideration of the classes principally concerned.

Under ordinary circumstances an innkeeper and a common carrier are bound to entertain, or convey, certain classes of persons; but, if any such person is affected by a disease of a character dangerous to the lives of others in the same dwelling or vehicle, such duty either ceases, or is greatly modified. It is unnecessary to trace the actual modifications of this ordinary duty in view of such danger at this time, as it is sufficient, for the immediate purpose, to ascertain that such causes have a tendency to modify ordinary obligations.

Acts that would, under ordinary circumstances, amount to an assault, may be performed, in certain cases, toward others affected by maladies threatening danger to life, without any such legal consequence. Such interferences with the liberty of others are authorized to be performed in proper cases, not only by public agents, but by private individuals, whether professionally devoted to the care and cure of disease or otherwise. The rule that permits persons affected by such diseases to be isolated and confined, both by public and private authority, as in public or private hospitals, has its origin in the principles under consideration.

The sanitary laws and institutions of government are a recognition that it is part of the duty of government to protect the lives and health of the individuals that compose the community against pestilence. Such an obligation has already been shown to exist as an imperfect obligation. It becomes a perfect duty only through public law.

It is in the case where private persons may exercise powers over persons, under the sanctions of the right of self-preservation, that, under ordinary circumstances, would amount to wrongs, that a necessity exists to find the origin of such power, as it must derive its force from the common obligations, and is, therefore, a means of stating the nature of those common obligations. The right of government to interfere with the liberty of individuals in such cases rests upon a delegation of authority, in a general form, and it is presumable that, if individuals may exercise such powers, a delegation must exist in some form to warrant it.

In order to examine the question, the character of which has been suggested, a case may be stated containing all its elements. A person finds another sick of a disease of a pestilential character, lying in the highway near his dwelling in such a position as to expose the lives of those occupying such dwelling, and seeking egress from it or ingress to it. The term *pestilential* is here used, as a general term, to include all contagious or infectious diseases that propagate their conditions through proximity to a suitable subject, which is the legal idea connected with the term. The person supposed is, through the effect of the disease, disabled from removing himself from such place, and is unwilling that the owner of the dwelling should remove him. The latter, against his will, removes him to a proper place, such as his own dwelling or a hospital. In this case, an interference with the person of the sick man, which, under ordinary circumstances, would constitute a wrong, has occurred. Under the circumstances stated, the act performed by the owner of the dwelling was clearly justified. Upon what principle can this conclusion be supported?

To analyze the relations of the parties, it is necessary to consider the relation of the conduct of the sick man to his common obligations. Upon the principles governing the use of common rights, the use of each individual must be reconcilable with that of all others having the same title to such use, or, in other words, it must be reasonable, as that term is defined by the habit of the community. To expose a person, sick of a disease threatening danger to the lives of those coming in close contact with the person affected by it, in a highway, in such manner that, according to the usual habit of using such highway, would be likely to produce that effect upon such persons, is a wrong of the class called nuisances. To make a highway a place of deposit for persons in such condition is clearly an unreasonable use, as it would be to convey persons so affected upon a highway in a manner unnecessarily imperiling the lives of others. It is obviously immaterial whether one places himself in such a position, or is placed there by another, as it regards the nature of the act. If, then, one affected by such a disease occupies such a position, without regard to the causes that have placed him there, if, unable to remove himself, he refuses proffered assistance in removing him, he is clearly in the position of a wrong-doer.

Instances have already been encountered that point to the existence of a right of individual redress where the preservation of life creates a necessity for immediate redress. Such a right is present in the case of self-defense, and in other instances that have already been suggested; and it has been observed, with regard to such a remedy, that it is merely preventive, and never either punitive or compensative. It remains to consider whether the instance under consideration is referable to that principle. The nature and value of a preventive remedy in cases involving danger to life will be hereafter considered, but it is evident that such a remedy must exist; for all other remedies presuppose the possibility of adequate compensation, while the taking of human life admits of no redress, except as it regards the wrong done to the community and to surviving persons. It would not, on known principles, be possible to construe the act of surrendering the right of individual redress to the community, where, in the nature of things, such surrender would be the entire destruction of the remedy, for the most important purpose for which it is applicable. The occasion that warrants the use of such preventive remedies as would, under ordinary circumstances, amount to an encroachment upon the rights of others, presupposes the inefficiency of public remedies. In the class of cases where such contingencies are likely to happen, it would be reasonable to find some form of preventive remedy existing in the hands of the individual for the protection of life, and such is the case.

The application of this principle to the case in hand is obvious. The danger to life from pestilential disease is a sufficient occasion for the exercise of that preventive act of private justice, and when the person, being incapable of self-exertion, is removed to a place proper, according to general habit, the reasonableness of its exercise is apparent.

The modification of the ordinary duty of the innkeeper and the common carrier, where the accepting of a guest or passenger would tend to place the lives of those under his care in jeopardy, is a necessary result of the principle just stated.

The second case, noticed above, was that of one subjecting the person of another to control through motives of humanity. A person finds another in a state of insensibility, and removes him to a proper place of safety. This is a justifiable interference with the person of another, which the law would place on the ground of an implied assent to such act, on the part of the person removed, arising from the necessity of the case. It is evident that implied assent does not here mean actual assent inferred from facts and circumstances disclosing an assenting mind, for the assumed state of insensibility precludes the idea of an assenting mind. That the idea of assent is present, however, in some form, is evident, for if the person in question, instead of being insensible, were conscious, but incapable of movement, and should refuse such aid, the person proffering it could not properly act against the will of the other. The elements of the case are, then, a certain power of control over the person of another, to be exercised in the interest and for the benefit of the subject of such control, either derived from the consent of the party or from his incapability of will, under the necessity that an act should be performed by another for his safety. Such power of control would be a delegated power as performed by one in the right and for the benefit of another. Upon what principle, then, does an individual obtain delegated authority to exercise control over the person of one not subjected to his authority? The fact that such power is attributable to an inference created by the nature of the circumstances surrounding the parties, points to its origin in an obligation either perfect or imperfect. It is not enough that such duty should exist in the form of a moral duty or a duty of humanity, for no right of control over another can possibly flow from a merely moral obligation. It can not be said that interference in such a case is a mere voluntary act, not attended by any legal relationship between the parties. The unwarranted interference of one with another in a state of unconsciousness is a wrong of the same quality as if committed toward a conscious person, and is, in some degree, aggravated by the existence of unconsciousness. It must, then, be warranted; that is, in harmony with some legal relation between the parties. Then, again, one, who has charged himself with the care of another incapable of self-protection, has the legal right of protecting such person, as against third persons, that would exist in the case of one committed to his care by the assent of the protected party.

It has been seen that a person incapable of self-protection has an imperfect right to call aid in his protection, and the community is under an imperfect obligation to afford such aid. It is evident, from the case under consideration, that individuals, as well as the community, are affected by such imperfect obligation, and owe a certain undefined protective duty to such as are incapable of self-protection. The existence of such an obligation as a passive duty is sufficiently evidenced by the fact that an advantage taken, in dealing, of the incapability of another, is a breach of good faith amounting to a wrong. That the voluntary assumption of an agency is sufficient to convert this passive duty into an active one is clear. The only point of difficulty is, how the assumption of such an agency can produce any change in the legal relations of the parties independently of the acceptance of such agency. The case in hand is not that of the ordinary case of an assumed agency validated by subsequent ratification, for the unconscious person, though subsequently repudiating the assistance offered from the first moment of consciousness, could not convert the interference with his person into a wrong.

It is evident that the peculiar relationship between individuals, instanced, in the cases alluded to, depends on fundamental principles, and evidences some peculiar feature of the relationship of members of society. It is also evident that there is a duty of mutual protection that affects individuals as a common duty as well as the community as a public duty. The fundamental idea and purpose of all civil association is mutual protection, as among individuals of a community.

The creation of a public agency to carry that purpose into effect is the adoption of means to that end. If the creation of civil government were to be considered as the end rather than the means of civil association, such association would cease to have the character of a stable obligation, as among individuals; for, as government is a means of creating as well as enforcing obligations, it would be assumable that the intention of the act of association was to leave all dispositions as it regards individual obligations to the positive will of the government. No such a theory of government can be reconciled with the existence of common law, and the only test of obligation would be public law. No such system of legal ideas has ever prevailed in any society entitled to the name civil or civilized; on the contrary, the civil relation between the members of society has always been regarded as a source of obligations and rights apart from all legislative interposition.

Considering, then, mutual protection as an end, and government as a means, that which could not, in the nature of things, be as perfectly performed by government as by individuals, must continue to rest upon individual duty even after the larger instrumentality has been put in operation. There must be, then, among the individual members of a common society, a common protective duty, for there are, and must be, occasions when, in the course of events, and especially in the presence of calamity suddenly befallen, the aid of government is impractical, and mutual individual aid is the natural and indispensable means of protection. If an individual suffering from a sudden deprivation of natural power, when some act material to the preservation of life is to be immediately performed, were dependent for such aid on public authority alone, the purposes of life could not at times be fulfilled. Hence, the necessities of self-preservation call for mutual individual assistance as a necessary incident of civil association.

The existence of a duty of mutual assistance implies a delegation of power commensurate with such duty. And, as the duty is imperfect, that power must have the same character. The voluntary assumption of a specific duty of that protective character renders the imperfect duty perfect, and the existence of a state of suspended will on the part of the person assisted renders the power perfect. It is self-evident that the duty of assistance can not give any power to antagonize the will of the subject of assistance, for in that case the act would be one of authority rather than of assistance.

It remains to be seen whether the view of the fundamental

obligations, involved in the explanation that has been given, sufficiently accounts for all the instances in which an individual interposes as a volunteer in the affairs of another with proper legal sanctions.

The value of a clear conception of the degree of obligation that binds the members of society to mutual protection, and of the amount of interference with the affairs of others that may be justified under such duty, is likely to be underestimated. Not only those striking features of the relationships of individuals that give rise to controversies involving practical interests, but the lesser features of these relations, must be studied to reach a complete understanding of such relationships. Natural science is advanced by the study of microscopic objects, as well as of those which, by their magnitude and direct relation to the uses of life, attract interest. In the same way legal science must be attentive to the causes producing modifications, however slight and seemingly unimportant in legal relationships.

The legal doctrines of presumption and implication have a philosophic foundation, entitled to more consideration than they have received, and without the examination of which it is impossible to construct the actual theory of the law. The propositions that contain the principles on which presumptions and implications are drawn, cover much that is important to the question of the exact amount of protective duty due by each member of society to each other. For practical purposes, it is assumed that each individual is perfectly independent of any other, independently of specific-obligation; but, while this may be stated as a useful formula, it is not the accurate statement of the fact. The consequences of the protective principle, as well as those of the principle of equal individual right, are present in every legal relationship; it is only when their balance has been disturbed that attention is drawn to the former, which, considered as a principle subservient to individual right, ordinarily sustains a subjective relation to that right and does not press itself upon consideration. As legal right, is equilibrium between certain elements, the nature and conditions of that equilibrium can not be fully understood until all the elements that enter into it are separately appreciated as well as conjointly recognized.

Every change produced in the relations of individuals by the imposition of a specific obligation is a modification of a preexisting relationship to be determined by the nature of society, and the modification can not be perfectly understood until that which is modified is clearly comprehended. The protective duty of man to man constitutes the side of the law that is nearest in nature to morals, and appreciates most accurately moral ends and means. It is, necessarily, vaguely defined in the practical operations of the law, but its solution is, nevertheless, to be sought and found in these practical operations. Until the exact position in which man is placed, in accordance with legal ideas to his associates, is understood, much that exists in the practical action of the law must be dismissed from a rationalizing effort as merely arbitrary, while, in fact, the expression arbitrary merely signifies that the causes of a phenomenon are occult and undetermined, as in nature things are called accidental that can not be foreseen in advance of their happening.

CHAPTER XXI.

NUISANCE.

It is necessary, in connection with the subject of self-preservation, to notice more particularly the legal doctrine of nuisance. The term nuisance has received a technical signification by which it describes, in a general way, a varied class of indirect injuries. The idea of a private nuisance is not very clearly defined, and embraces cases of wrong that have specific technical designations. The idea associated with common or public nuisances is more accurately defined, as wrongs of this class are not generally reducible to distinct classes with specific names. The idea of a common nuisance is that of an injury to common right. Under this class of rights are included the common right to the use of the natural elements, light, air, and water, the use of public highways both by land and water, and other common rights.

The common rights that subserve the uses of life and health derive their chief value from their relation to the right of self-preservation. Those that concern the power of passing from place to place, as the right to the use of highways both by land and water, directly concern the right of self-exertion, which is intimately connected with that of self-preservation, as the former is the essential means to the end of self-preservation. The doctrine of nuisance also rests on the idea that individuals are entitled to comfortable and agreeable enjoyments of life as well as to the means of subsistence, and thus illustrates the existence of the right which has been termed the right of self-gratification.

Instances of wrongs of this class are: Emitting noxious and offensive gases, vapors, and effluvia into the air in situations affecting the health and comfort and the value of the property of others; polluting waters subject to common use, and unfitting them for such common use; placing obstructions in highways by land or water, and to the flowage of water in certain cases. As against such acts individuals who sustain any special damage have their action, but, where the damage done is general alone, the remedy must be that of the public or of the class of individuals whose common right has been invaded. The damages awarded to individuals in such cases may be such as are sustained to the person or to property. When the damage sustained is to life and health, it is obvious that such actions have a deeper foundation than that of the value of the common property thus withheld from one entitled to use it in common right, for such damage embraces injuries done to the person by reason of such want of rightful common use. That the right to the conditions necessary to the maintenance of life and health is involved is apparent, for the damages are measured by that right.

The character of the common rights to the use of the natural elements is exhibited by that which has just been stated as not of an independent or proprietary nature, but as that of accessories to the rights of person. Where the subject of a common right admits of proprietorship, the use of such common right tends to give rise to individual right in that which is appropriated under the common right. The nature of the common elements, apart from their being subjected to artificial conditions, does not admit of this proprietary conception in a full sense. Injury to rights of this kind is not capable of being estimated on the basis of a valuation of the subject of the right. As an accessory right, intended to fortify that which it subserves, an injury to such right would carry the consequence that the wrong would be measured by the injury done to the right of person to which it is accessory, which is the case in the instances under immediate consideration. The rule of damages may in this way often become useful to an inquiry whether a right undergoing redress is to be regarded as an independent or an accessory right.

A noticeable feature of the action of the law in cases of common nuisance, that demonstrates the relation of such cases to the rights of person, and especially to the right of self-preservation, is the right of abatement by public authority, and sometimes by individuals aggrieved. Abatement must be regarded as a specific remedy of a preventive character, whether employed by the public authority or by individuals. The relation of preventive remedies to cases involving injury to life has already been noticed. Abatement consists in the destruction or removal of the cause of a common nuisance, and may involve the destruction of the property, the condition of which occasions such nuisance. The reason of the allowance of such a specific preventive remedy has been already sufficiently developed, and furnishes additional evidence of the accessory character of the common rights that derive their value from their ministrations to life and health.

The nature of the conditions that attend this remedy will be readily apprehended from the reason that justifies its use. It is obvious that the destruction of property for the purpose of abating a nuisance would only be justified, in harmony with the principles of the law, where essential to the abatement of the nuisance. If the wrong arises from the condition of the property, and that condition can conveniently be changed so as to remove the cause of injury, the destruction of the property would appear to be at variance with the reason fundamental to preventive redress. If destruction in such cases is warranted by public law, it must be ascribed to a punitive intention.

One of the objects embraced within the law of nuisance is to prevent infectious and contagious diseases from being disseminated through the atmosphere and natural waters, and, in a more specific manner, through the use of highways and public places and the conditions to which populous neighborhoods are subjected.

One of the common uses that the atmosphere and the waters, resting upon and absorbed into the earth, subserve, is to distribute through great areas substances of a volatile or soluble character; and through such medium impressions made upon the air and water may be propagated to an indefinite extent. This diffusive tendency of air and water constitutes at once an element of great utility to life and a possibility of injury to life. But for this diffusive quality, the atmosphere and water in the neighborhood of populous localities might, in the absence of the motions of these elements that constitute winds and currents, become unfit to maintain life. On the other hand, the diffusion of the contents of such gases and fluids is the means of carrying deleterious influences to great distances from the places of their introduction. Manifestly, this habit of nature represents a force in which the community have a common interest.

As has been already seen in another place, those who deal with the forces of nature, that have a general range of action, are limited to a reasonable and prudent use in order to prevent the unnecessary liberation of destructive forces. As it regards the communication of substances in their action deleterious to the atmosphere and natural waters, such an interference with the natural conditions of the elements is at the same time a dealing with the destructive forces of nature. When, however, a substance thus imparted is in itself innocuous, but renders the atmosphere or water unfit for their proper uses, the wrong is distinctly to the purity of the conditions of these elements, and is not within the principle that applies to the liberation of destructive forces.

The infectious qualities of certain diseases are regarded as capable of dissemination and propagation through the diffusive property of air and water. Where injury is caused by the dissemination of the germs, or other causes of disease, such injury is necessarily indirect; and, therefore, the character of the injury, being that of an indirect injury to an indefinite number of persons, is properly treated as appertaining to the class of common nuisances. It is obvious that such injuries must be regarded as sustained to the right of self-preservation, through the accessory right that governs the use of the common elements, so as to prevent the unnecessary liberation of destructive natural forces.

The principle inherent in the quality ascribed to the forces of nature, in their disseminative tendency to give currency to destructive influences, applies to the doctrine of the propagation of diseases through the public use that is made of highways and public places where people assemble and pass and repass. The effect of the movements of individuals has a relation to the propagation of disease similar to that instanced in the case of the natural elements and forces as it regards the distribution of infection. The habit of the community must be regarded as possessing a tendency to disseminate causes of injury to life and health. This habit represents a social force similar in its consequences to the natural forces that have been commented upon, and necessarily affected by the same general principles. Hence it is that exposing persons in public highways and in public places to the effects of diseases that may be communicated from person to person, or from persons to the places they frequent, and thence, through infection, to others, is a case of dealing with a social distributive force, so as to impart to it a destructive character, and is subject to the same law that has been demonstrated in its relation to dealing with natural forces of a like injurious character.

The same general principle is illustrated in another and distinct class of cases, which, though not recognized as cases of common nuisance, in a direct sense, yet depend upon the general principles that have been illustrated as fundamental to the doctrine of nuisance. These cases will be briefly described.

Among the various acts that are affected by considerations growing out of the right of self-preservation may be enumerated the furnishing or selling of deleterious substances liable to uses detrimental to health, such as articles of food, drugs, and dyes liable to contact with the body. That the wrong done by one who knowingly sells or gives to another, ignorant of its qualities, that which is prejudical to health, for a use liable to be dangerous, and, when damage results, is referable to a violation of the obligation that looks to the preservation of life and health, is obvious, from the fact that the personal injury produced by the use of such substance is the measure of damage in such cases. If a merchant, who buys to sell again, is deceived in any such respect, his remedy is based upon the commercial value of the article he intended to purchase, and not of the spurious article deceptively substituted for it. The consumer of such commodities is not limited to any consideration of commercial values, but may base his claim to compensation on the assumed value of life or health.

The manufacturers of such articles as have just been mentioned are liable to the injured consumer, although his wares may have passed through the hands of third persons, and no contract relationship may exist between him and such consumer. This circumstance shows that the wrong consists in the violation of a general obligation, and not in the specific dealing by which the property passed out of the manufacturers' hands. The general obligation being violated the moment that a deceptive and injurious article is put in currency in the channels of trade, with the expectation that it will be used, all that remained to complete the wrong, as an individual injury, was that the causes, set in motion, and placed beyond the control of their author, should produce individual damage. In all these cases there may be an element of deception in the causes of liability, but the foundation of the action is exhibited by the nature of the damage, for the measure of the damage is the measure of the right of which the damage is the representative, as it regards pecuniary estimation.

The development of the principle of the rule of law just noticed brings to light certain important social functions that are performed by commerce, trade, and general intercourse. The interchanges between persons, property, and place that are expressed by the terms commerce, trade, and general intercourse, are vital to the corporate integrity of the community. These social operations perform functions similar to those that are performed by the circulation of the materials for nutrition in the animal body. The term trade contains a larger idea than that of commerce, for it expresses a relation to each other that all the individuals of the community sustain, while commerce, though implying the movement of larger values, involves the co-operation of a much more limited number of persons. General intercourse is an indefinite term, intended to embrace such interchanges as do not fall under the heads of trade and commerce.

The consideration of this subject will be materially assisted by examining it in its relation to trade, and the principles thus reached will apply themselves readily to the other classes. In its largest sense, trade embraces all interchanges of labor and material property that take place in a community, including the work of artisans and professional persons. In a more restricted sense, it applies to the interchange of vendible commodities. Such interchanges imply and demand individual movements from place to place, in which nearly all the members of the community may be assumed to take part in some measure, great or small. The concourse of individuals at certain places, and passage and repassage on the public highways, occasion the contact, or close proximity, of persons belonging to the various separated families and social groups. The personal consequences of this distributive movement, as a means of propagating disease, have already been noticed, but other aspects of the same idea demand that the whole subject should receive connected attention.

Another phenomenon of trade is the distribution of those commodities that constitute the food and clothing of the individuals of the community, and the various articles that are applied to the body, or brought in close contact with it, and thus may sustain a relation to health. Trade flows in definite channels, those channels being marked by the customs of the community. The method of the distribution of such things as are demanded by the individual wants is as definite as the courses marked by geographical features along which the water-courses flow. In virtue of the habit of the community, the commodities dealt in flow through these channels, not only in an ideal sense, but in a physical sense. The custom of trade prevailing in any community, taking the word custom as including the habit of individuals in purchasing and consuming, as well as the habit of dealers in purchasing and selling, constitutes a social function that is the means of directing an important social force. If the energies that are put forth by the instinct of gain, co-operating with the desire for the use of commodities, be regarded as a social force, as they clearly must, the fact that the customs of trade give direction to social force will be apparent.

Commodities placed in the channels of trade are thus brought into direct relation to some or all of the members of the community. The fact that dealers in commodities give currency to a particular article is found, in practice, to do much to insure the distribution of such article and its use for the purpose for which it was communicated to the channels of trade. There exists a certain degree of confidence on the part of the members of a community in the qualities asserted for commodities, by the mere fact that they are publicly dealt in. This confidence is absolutely necessary to enable trade to perform its proper functions to the community. It is obvious, then, that one who abuses this confidence, by placing in the course of distribution spurious articles deleterious to health, commits a wrong to that confidence that is a clear violation of the obligation to good faith. Viewing the same transaction from another standpoint, it appears equally clear that one who uses the facilities that arise from the habit of trade makes use of an important social force capable of becoming the means of transmitting destructive force. As such, the same principles that demand that natural forces of that character shall be used with reasonable and prudent care have a clear application to these cases.

In the case of placing dangerous commodities in the channels of trade, it has been seen that both the law of the use of dangerous forces and the common obligation to good faith lead to the same conclusion. The connection between the two is perfect in this instance. In the case of the use of dangerous force, the relation of an abuse of that force to the obligation to good faith is not so obviously manifest. The social force capable of being abused would have no existence but for the public and individual faith, while the natural force exists independently of individual will, and therefore it is that the connection of such cases with the rule of good faith is more apparent in the former instance. The general laws and forces of nature exist for all in common precisely as do the social forces that constitute functions of society, and he who uses them must exercise reasonable and prudent care, as exacted by the rule of good faith.

CHAPTER XXII.

INJURIES TO THE PERSON BY FORCE.

THE legal treatment of wrongs affords the means of estimating the exact qualities of the obligations that define rights. A wrong being a violated obligation, the nature of the obligation is represented by that of the wrong. The nature of the right of self-preservation will next be considered from the standpoint of the wrongs that may be committed against it.

The term violence undoubtedly was derived from the qualities of certain actions, by which they were violations of some form of obligation or duty. In this sense all acts of a positive character in violation of duty are acts of violence. But, in common use, that word has become a means of expressing the degree or quantity of a force, rather than its character, as violative of duty. In its technical sense, this term sometimes conveys a qualitative, and sometimes a quantitative force, but does not exclude the idea that the smallest amount of physical force of a certain character may be termed violence. The term force, though a very general one, is here employed to designate the agencies that may be used as means of injury to the person in preference to the word violence, as the latter term admits of a possible sense that would not be in harmony with its use for that purpose.

Among physical causes that may thus be employed to consummate a wrong to the right of self-preservation may be enumerated those that act externally to the human system, destroying, deforming, or deranging the functions of that system, either wholly or in part depriving it of its functional capacity, and such as act internally to the system, as poisonous substances introduced into the body. The first class named comprises what are called physical injuries, while those of the latter class are recognized as injuries to the health. The operation of mental causes to produce injury to life and health may be generally illustrated by the effects of fright or sudden alarm. Social forces may be brought to bear so as to produce injuries of that character in a variety of ways. Loss of reputation may react upon the conditions of health, and persecution, through the forms of law, may become an indirect means of destroying health, and even life. The particular subject at present to be considered has special relation to the wrongs resulting from physical forces operating to produce injurious consequences affecting the body, its organs and functions.

The extent to which an individual may be charged with the consequences produced by the agency of physical force is determinable in part by the nature of such agencies. To produce such responsibility, either the existence and direction of such force, or the exposure of the subject of such force to its influence, must be capable of being traced to the act of a person done in violation of some common obligation, or of some public law. That an individual may be responsible for the existence of a particular form of force is reconcilable with the physical idea that the quantity of force existing at any moment of time is equal to that existing at all other times. Man is not a creator of force, but is capable of originating it in some particular form of force. The forces contained in the chemical condition of the elements composing gunpowder may be liberated, in the form of an elastic gas, by human agency applied to produce the conditions under which such a chemical transformation takes place. So the energy involved in the position of a body, heavier than the same volume of the atmosphere, may be converted into the active force of gravity by force applied to change the position of such body. In these, and many familiar instances, man may, with propriety, be said to originate force, though incapable of producing it otherwise than by inducing a transformation of one form of force into another.

The idea of the direction of force is more complex. The

origination of force at a particular time and place, where natural conditions exist tending to direct it to the accomplishment of a particular end, is equivalent to a direction of the force itself. Taking advantage of the directions in which bodies naturally fall, or of circumstances tending to give a particular direction to such fall, and using currents of air and water flowing in determinate directions to produce a certain effect through the operation of natural laws, is in effect giving direction to natural force, as it is a control over one or more of the conditions giving such direction. The vehicle of the destructive force may in such cases act independently of any human agency, but the harmful substance conveyed may represent destructive force, directed by means of the selection of its vehicle. Artificial means may also constitute the cause of the direction of natural force, as the form of the bore of firearms determines the character of the flight of the missile.

When the force is incapable of taking direction from any human agency, still the position of one injured by it may be the direct consequence of a wrong. The contact between the force and its subject of injury is that for which legal responsibility exists, when such contact is the consequence of the violation of an obligation accessory to the right of self-preservation.

The primary form in which man is capable of producing force is, by means of muscular motion, set up within his own organism, which is uniformly presumed to be voluntary. When a wrong consists in the performance of an act, the ground of responsibility is the use of muscular power—either that of the author of the wrong, or of some animal agent under his control. All the modes in which the volitions act beyond the sphere of the animal body group themselves under the general designation of agency. These agencies are again grouped into those that employ direct muscular force and those that bring into operation some new form of force as the result of conditions instituted by some exercise of muscular force.

It is proper to notice, in this general outline, the fact that the creation or direction of a force in an injurious relation to an individual may be either a voluntary or intentional act, or an unintentional one. In a physical sense, such an act is a voluntary one where its author was conscious of the effort that put such force in motion. In a physical sense, all acts that are performed without intention are accidental. The legal idea of what is voluntary takes into account the relation of the force to the subject on which it may be expended. The throwing of a stone may, in a physical sense, be a voluntary act, while in a legal sense it may lack a voluntary character in two ways. In the first place, it may be performed under mental constraint, and, even if voluntary in that respect, it may be purely accidental as it regards its personal consequences; that is, a person may be struck by it who could not have been supposed to be within its influence. The idea of legal negligence requires that the acts that are, in a physical sense, accidental should be divided into such as are negligent and such as are, in a legal sense, accidental.

As a preliminary to the investigation, it is necessary to recur to what has already been said, that obligations are either executory or executed; executory, where they call for the performance of some act; executed, where nothing remains but to respect the rights perfected under them. An executory obligation thus imposes an active duty, while an executed one imposes merely a passive duty. As obligations and rights are correlative, it would follow that rights exist in the same twofold condition of a right in possession and one in expectation, or, as the law phrases it, in action. A contract for the sale of land confers the right to demand, at some time, and on certain conditions, the dominion of land. The actual transfer of such land by means of a deed following the contract represents the same obligation in its executed form; the act called for being performed, all that remains of the obligation is that the dominion thus acquired shall be respected. Actions brought to compel the performance, or compensate violated executory obligations, are denominated actions upon contract, while such as are founded on the common obligations are termed actions *ex delicto*, or actions of *tort*.

Every right implies the possibility of the exercise of certain legal powers. If the right is executory, these powers are in their nature remedial, as they look wholly to the enforcement of the obligation out of which such right arises. If the right is wholly executed, the powers possessed are such as are appropriate to the nature of such perfected right. As, for instance, under a contract for the sale of land the right of the purchaser implies power to perform toward the seller the conditions of the contract, to demand performance, and to compel, by legal agency, either specific enforcement or compensation, in lieu of that. If the contract is executed, then the right of the purchaser implies the powers that the owner of land possesses, as it regards the possession, use, and enjoyment of such land. The powers appertaining to an executory obligation include certain of a contingent nature. These contingent powers are only brought into exercise in the event that such obligation is violated, and are remedial in their nature.

In considering the right of self-preservation from the standpoint of the consequences of the wrongs to which it is liable, we look at it through the medium of the contingent or remedial powers annexed to it. Without looking at a right through both the nature of the powers that are active under it and those that are dormant, it can not be seen on all sides.

Having premised thus much, with a view to accuracy of method, we pass to the consideration of the different forms of wrongs which the right of self-preservation is liable to sustain.

CHAPTER XXIII.

WRONGS TO RIGHT OF PERSON.

ALTHOUGH the power of contracting obligations is subservient to the right of person in an indirect sense, yet, when one engages to perform an act for the benefit of another, the mere fact that the performance of such act will tend to make more available or secure some right immediately connected with the person does not render such an obligation accessory to the right of person, so that its violation would be measured by the loss of the advantage in the exercise of such personal right that was intended to be acquired. The principle of proprietary rights is, that such rights are compensated according to the estimation of the value of the subject-matter of the right, measured by the standards of value prevailing in dealings according to the habit of the community. All dealings in regard to material property are subject to this rule, including the obligation to pay money. Contracts for labor sometimes give rise to proprietary rights, and sometimes are accessory to the right of person. The case of a surgeon or physician employed to perform some act affecting the person is an instance of the latter class, and will be considered in a later place. In this respect property has a certain independent character and recognition by which it is regarded as a direct object of dealing, and in rare instances is treated as an adjunct of personal right.

Wrongs that consist in violations of executory obligations do not, therefore, belong to the class that illustrates the nature of the rights of person. On the other hand, the common obligations are in their nature accessories both to the right of person and to the proprietary rights, and the compensations for the violations of such obligations are estimated from the effect produced upon the right of person or property to which they are accessory. In this respect the common obligations partake of the same general nature as those obligations called conditions, and as collateral obligations.

The fact that the law prohibits all persons from dealing in the rights of person and property of others, evidences the existence of a common obligation of that character. The universality of the obligation and of the right that it supports, and the fact that a rule of conduct common as among individuals, and in which society has an interest as one of the essentials to its maintenance, establishes the claim of that obligation to be classed as a common obligation. As all individuals are equally under this obligation, equality of right is its necessary consequence, for the expression equal right means that all of whom it can be predicated are under the same law in respect to all that is equal between them. This obligation manifestly brings into civil existence individual right, or, as expressed in a relative sense, equal individual right. As the formulation of principles is, according to the nature of the law, in the form of obligations, it would follow that the obligation to respect the rights of others, or, what is the same, to refrain from dealing in the rights of person and property of others, must be regarded as, in a legal sense, the principle of equal individual right. Beyond this formulation, that principle has a substantial existence and appropriate form, the consideration of which belongs to general philosophy rather than to law.

The object of the common obligation that has just been recognized being the conservation of equal right in all individuals as it regards control over the person and property, it is manifest that such obligation is accessory to such rights, as constituting the barrier set up for their defense, and the violation of such obligation must of necessity be equivalent to injury done to such rights of person and property; and the redress of wrongs of that nature must be based upon the value lost thereby to such rights as it regards the application of the rule of compensation. This view develops the nature of *actions of tort*.

The various modes in which an individual may exercise his powers, that are incident to the right of self-preservation in the presence of justly apprehended or actual danger to the person, embrace acts of prevention, resistance, and redress. The various wrongs that affect the conditions of existence material to the faculties of body and mind, the power of performing the various actions that appertain to individual life, and the capacity of the comfortable enjoyment of life, are intimately connected together by a common nature, and by many formal characteristics which they have in common. The general classification that is here adopted to bring all these features of personal right into review distributes the various wrongs into such as affect the right of self-preservation, the right of self-exertion, and that of self-gratification. These specific rights, considered as elements of the more general idea of personal right, represent that feature of personal right that consists in the independent control of the body and mind, apart from any necessary relationship with objects or persons exterior to self, and yet recognizes the possible interference of external forces with that right. Those necessary relations that connect individuals with the material substances that are aids to individual life will be considered under the general title of proprietary rights, and those that connect individuals for co-operative purposes will be treated under the head of associative rights.

Personal rights can not have any complete independent existence, apart from their relation to and interaction with proprietary and associative rights. These three classes have a common nature, but, as they have separate characteristics, the separate treatment of each, for the purpose of ascertaining what is peculiar to it, is essential to the possession of the full means of stating both their common and individual natures. In the same way, personal rights must not only have a mold fitting them to conserve the integrity of the individual powers, considered by themselves, but, in addition to that, to assure to the individual that capacity through which alone he can accommodate himself to the use of the means of developing the purposes of life afforded by the possibility of proprietary and associative right.

The first concern of the law is to define and conserve the individuality of persons, and its next concern to afford them a capacity and field for the exertion of the powers and the pursuit of such gratifications as they may desire consistently with the common good. The function of the personal rights may then be regarded as the individuation of persons in a civil sense, and their endowment with the capacity of social integration, while associative right gives the law of that integration and proprietary right the law of the controlling means to that end.

In a natural order, then, the individual must be considered, in a passive sense, as an object of protection before attempting to define the place which he occupies, according to legal recognition, in the scheme of proprietorship and associative activity. This narrow subject again has its starting-point in the preservation of the body and the mind, and in that function of those faculties termed self-exertion in its relation to such purposes as are propounded for individual ends of self-gratification. Foremost in this limited view stands the right of self-preservation, or the consideration of the civil means by which the individual may protect his body, its organs, and their functions, from invasion on the part of other individuals of like powers and rights as his own.

The various injuries that may be sustained to the body, its organs, and functions, are conveniently grouped together as injuries to the body.

The body is a system of organs, so that every injury to the body is necessarily an injury to one or more of its organs; and the reverse of this statement is equally true. The proper conception of health is that of the proper function of the bodily organs, through interaction between the physical system, as a whole, and its several organic parts. It is manifest that to disturb the function of any organ in any degree disturbs the equilibrium of the system, and produces deterioration of that general functional condition called health. In ordinary use, the word health is taken, in a more restricted sense, as the condition opposite to that of disease. Specific diseases are attended by definite sensible phenomena, and are not recognized in insensible deviations from a state of health; and hence the absence of certain defined symptoms is regarded as indicative of health, even where there is an imperfect performance of functional acts.

Wrongs of the class under immediate consideration embrace those that consist in the application of force externally to the body, and those that consist in the establishment of destructive internal conditions. In a physical sense, they may be intentional or unintentional, but, according to legal distinction, they are to be investigated from the inquiry whether they result from an improper dealing with the rights of another or as an incidental consequence of one's dealing with his own rights, with or without the occurrence of negligence, which is equivalent to a want of prudent care.

CHAPTER XXIV.

ASSAULT.

THE characteristic wrong to the person of the class of intentional acts, constituting a dealing with the rights of others, is an assault in its characteristic form, attended by a battery. An assault and battery is a menace and demonstration of force without lawful authority, in personal encounter, to the injury or restraint of the person. An assault consists in conduct declaratory of such purpose, and menacing its immediate execution, and a battery in the execution of such purpose, wholly or in part. The peculiar office of a menace arises from the fact that the mode in which force is applied may not indicate whether the personal contact, or equivalent act, is with or without license, independent of the menacing conduct accompanying it, and hence the existence of a menace may be requisite to qualify the subsequent or attendant act. The ceremonial practices of all communities permit contact with the person of another under certain conditions. Taking the hand of another in virtue of a suitable relation between the parties, at a proper time and place, is within a presumed license, having its warrant in the habit of the community. On the same principle usage confers a presumed license to go upon the property of another on proper occasions. Taking the hand of another involves a certain degree of restraint, that may be lawful or unlawful, according to the intent with which it is done, that intent being manifested either by actions or words. We are now dealing with an assault and battery as an injury to the person, and not to the liberty merely; the latter subject will be considered in another place. Threatening declarations, without contact with the per son, or what is equivalent thereto, is not a battery, nor even an assault, unless the threatening language is accompanied by some corresponding action, when it becomes a menace. At the moment of the commencement of the development of the injurious force, or actual physical restraint begins, the wrong is complete, and what follows from the same motive belongs to the consequences of the wrong. Pointing a loaded firearm at one, in the apparent act of firing, and directing a blow with a weapon, consummate the wrong. The civil injury, consisting in the violation of the common obligation to respect the rights of another, is consummated thus before physical injury is inflicted. The general term of damages embraces the idea of the injurious consequences resulting from a wrong.

It is evident that the idea of assault and battery is that of private warfare. The fact that personal encounter is requisite to complete an assault is decisive of this conception. Personal encounter does not necessarily imply actual contact, or even that degree of proximity of person that would admit of engaging with the natural powers of attack and defense. The conditions of an assault may be such as to admit of the separation of the combatants for a considerable distance, according to the nature of the weapons employed, without destroying the idea of personal encounter. When firearms are used, such a combat may be maintained at a great distance between the combatants. The nature of the weapon determines the distance that may be consistent with the idea of personal encounter. So long as the distance does not exceed that in which the weapons may be employed with effect, the idea of personal encounter may attach to the transaction.

Prior to the institution of civil means of redress, it must be assumed that private warfare was the method employed. It is easy to conceive that the union of combatants on each side, giving support to the members of their family, or clan, or to their friends and allies, would develop this idea of private warfare into one of a more complex character, which, when communities are engaged, would assume the form of public warfare. The distinction between the declaratory acts, that constitute an assault, and the executive act, that constitutes a battery, at once suggests the relation that a declaration of hostilities bears to actual public warfare. The assault and battery must be regarded as the survival of an institution having its origin in the natural relations existing among men, and imperfectly eradicated by substituted civil means of redress.

The duel is a still more distinct survival of the primitive conception of individual warfare. For the class of wrongs that are regarded by many as a justification for personal encounter with deadly weapons, civil society affords either no redress, or only partial redress. Whether some form of redress should be afforded for injuries of this nature, not constituting civil wrongs, is a question that can not properly be connected with the present discussion. It is evident, however, that the practice of terminating such difficulties by a resort to personal encounter with deadly weapons does not give such indications as are afforded by all normal institutional developments. All institutions that have proper relevancy to the advancing stages of civil development show signs of increasing adaptability to their uses. If, on the other hand, they show retrograde tendencies, the inference is inevitable that they have lost vitality, and are undergoing elimination. The modern duel with pistols, which may be regarded as the offshoot of the primitive private war that possesses the most vigor, has lost all power of adaptation for the uses for which personal encounter, as a natural institution, was intended. It affords no measure of retribution proportioned to a wrong done, but renders all offenses against the reputation or person of another capital. The means of redress it affords are as likely to visit its worst consequences upon the innocent as upon the guilty. Moral hardihood and intellectual insensibility are the only qualities it educates, and the kind of physical skill that it calls for is not available for any general purpose. There are marked evidences of retrogression from that state in which personal encounter, in the defense of right, was a school of the most vigorous development, preparing mankind for all that was arduous and sacrificing in the contests of civilization with the forces of nature and barbarism.

The remarks that have just been made in respect to the private duel have a clear application to the development of modern public warfare. The increasingly destructive tendencies of modern warfare, and its increasing want of adaptability as a means of adjusting national differences, point to a conclusion that this means of balancing the interests and the rights of nations is not destined to such a course of development as to adjust it to the wants of civilization. In such cases it is to be expected that, whatever may be the ultimate character of the means adequate to co-ordinate the action of nations, and produce more thoroughly connected and stable national systems, will appear as a reaction from excesses developed by the decline of the primary means.

Following the view that has been presented of an assault and battery as a mode of private warfare, its complex nature may be perceived. The object of an assault may be to punish a real or supposed injury, or to prevent or restrain the performance of some act from which injury is anticipated, to the author of the assault. In such cases the assault is an assumption of an authority that is denied to individuals by the common obligations, and can be exercised by the public authority alone, except under very peculiar circumstances, that can not, at present, be considered. So the assault may be purely malevolent, without any element of vindictive or repressive justice, as when intended, through hatred or envy, to inflict loss of natural power or pain. It may also be intended as a means of depriving the assaulted party of his liberty, or of his property, or to prevent him from performing some act, in the voluntary exercise of his rights, that would be no source of wrong or injury to others. In all such cases it is evident that the assault, though directed against the person, may be in reality means intended to destroy or deny some right other than that to the safety of the person. In this way an assault and battery may, in its real nature, be an aggression on any of the rights that an individual may possess or claim. Considered as a violation of the common obligations to respect the person and rights of others, which are accessory to such rights, it is apparent that, in the compensation of wrongs of this class, inflicted by assault and battery, the value of any right that the assault may have impaired may be brought into consideration as an element of the damage.

It is equally apparent that preventive remedies of the most energetic class, lodged both in the hands of the public authority and of individuals, together with the power of individual resistance to such unlawful aggressions, must exist in a vigorous form. The subject under treatment is most important to a complete understanding of individual relations under civil society, as illustrating an important class of reserved powers, based on those existing in a state of nature, that are not capable of being exercised under ordinary circumstances in civil communities, but, through the importance of their relation to the right of self-preservation, are to be regarded as dormant rather than as non-existent, under the conditions established by civil society. The inadequacy of compensative remedies to meet the exigencies of aggressions of destructive force has already been pointed out, and the necessity for specific preventive remedies in such cases noticed. The inefficiency of preventive remedies, if lodged in the hands of the public authority alone, has also been clearly shown, in relation to some cases of this class, as creating a necessity that power of prevention and resistance should be lodged in the hands of individuals for their own protection. The practical illustration of this subject will appear in treating of the power of self-defense and of that of resistance.

Conceding, then, that no individual has the legal right to resort to that class of means for redress that fall under the description of private warfare, still, when one is placed on the defensive by an antagonist using such prohibited means, his conduct in that relation must be governed by the law of that relation. The demonstration of the principles of self-defense furnishes the means of stating the law of the relation thus wrongfully brought about, and its development and comparison with the principles recognized as governing public warfare are essential to the understanding of the relations that are sustained by parties who are thus brought in a contact from which it is the object of civil institutions to withhold them, but which, when it occurs, involves the nature derived from primitive ideas and institutions.

CHAPTER XXV.

SELF-DEFENSE.

THE means afforded by statute of preventing persons threatening violence to the person from executing such purposes, by placing them under special obligations and surety to preserve the peace, do not belong to the category of original individual rights. These remedies are conferred by public authority, and have for their end the preservation of the peace of the community, while affording, incidentally, public protection to individual right.

Among preventive remedies stands conspicuously the right of self-defense, peculiar to the class of cases under immediate consideration. That it is not a mere right of resistance will be apparent on close scrutiny. Resistance, in a general sense, is a very general term; but, in distinguishing it as a feature of defensive action, it must receive a more restricted sense. To resist physical force is either to change its direction or to exhaust it upon a subject other than that on which it tended to act. A blow or thrust that is parried is diverted from its course, while one that is received upon a portion of the body, or substance foreign to the body, less liable to injury than that against which it was directed, is exhausted. To seize and hold a weapon, or object, so as to restrain its use as against the force of another, is an instance of resistance. All of these acts are obviously acts of prevention as it regards the intention of an assault, and acts of resistance as it regards the means of effecting that intention. It will become evident, on examination, that self-defense implies the idea of prevention in a larger sense than that expressed by resistance. The right of resistance may be exercised for the protection of property as well as of the person. If one seizes your property unlawfully to carry it away, you may neutralize his effort by a corresponding one in the opposite direction. This is physical resistance, but falls short of the idea of self-defense. One may remove another by force from a place over which he has control, and into which the latter has unlawfully intruded, but this exercise of dominion is recognizable as differing essentially from self-defense.

The law allows one engaged properly in self-defense to overcome his adversary to the extent necessary to prevent the accomplishment of the purpose warranting the use of self-defense. This implies positive means of overcoming him, as well as the negative means peculiar to resistance. From this circumstance we may gather the nature of self-defense, and the proper measure of the means appropriate to its exercise. It may, then, be defined to be a right to overcome the physical force of one engaged in the commission of a civil wrong after the wrong is, in a legal sense, consummated, in order to prevent its injurious physical consequences. This resolves itself into a right to arrest a course of action constituting a civil wrong to the right of self-preservation, so as to prevent the consequences of such action. This definition makes the case of self-defense one of preventive remedy. This remedy is to be examined both as to its nature and mode of exercise. Its general nature, as a preventive remedy, is common with other rights than that of self-preservation, but it has in its application to that right a specific and peculiar character, and, as to its mode of exercise, is peculiar to the immediate class of cases under consideration.

Self-defense, regarded as a remedy, has the general nature of all specific remedies. The nature of specific remedies is to compel the performance of an act in specie, called for by some obligation, as to prevent the performance of an act violative of an obligation. The equitable remedy by specific performance and the legal remedies to compel an actual delivery of property from one person to another are instances of the first class, and the ordinary injunction in equity of the other class. All other remedies than specific remedies are either compensative or punitive. As the object of self-defense is to prevent, specifically, the prosecution of an act of wrong, its relation to remedies of a specific and preventive character is obvious.

That which is peculiar to self-defense, considered as a specific remedy, is that it may rightfully be exerted to the extent of depriving an antagonist of all physical power, and even of life itself. In this respect it differs from all other specific remedies, as that result can only be lawfully produced in the course of the administration of public justice through the operation of punitive remedies. As self-defense is a species of war, it has this nature in common with public warfare. Public warfare has the twofold character of a means of protecting the civil life of the community and of enforcing its rights as against communities or combinations of individuals. In both cases of public warfare and justifiable private warfare of a defensive character, the destruction of life may be a possible result consistent with the relations of the combatants. Whatever may be the occasion of entering upon a public war, the nature of the means employed for that purpose threatens, in some degree, the civil life of the state, and thus the instinct of self-preservation and its consequences are always an active element, in some degree, of all contests of that character. The same remark is true, in some degree, of every individual encounter, although means may be employed that do not threaten life.

As has already been said, war should be, and is, regarded as an act of justice of a remedial character, and the analogy between the ends and method of public war and of self-defense, as a private right, justifies the statement that the latter possesses the nature of war and its title to be called an act of private warfare.

As has been stated in another place, the policy of the law prefers compensatory and punitive remedies to specific remedies, where the former classes are sufficiently effectual, out of respect to the liberty of the individual. Liberty, in the broadest sense, is the power of effectual volition in the exertion of the natural powers, as will be hereafter demonstrated, and the power of effective volition is one of those powers covered by the right of self-exertion; while, then, the use of specific remedies is generally avoided, out of respect to the right of self-exertion, it would naturally follow that, when that right, and, indeed, the right of self-preservation, demanded such a remedy, the general objection to their use would be inapplicable. It is the inadequacy of compensative and punitive remedies that has led to the retention of specific remedies, to a certain extent, in advanced systems of law. That such remedies were, in the primitive state of society, the rule rather than the exception is apparent, on historic grounds as well as from the natural sequences of development. Their gradual displacement by compensative and punitive remedies is due to the advancing spirit of liberty, which, rightly appreciated, is the advancing conception of the sanctions of equal individual right.

In a state of nature previous to institutional law, an act of war, public or private, is the only means of redress. This mode of redress persisted, through its intimate relation to the right of self-preservation, after public means of redress had largely replaced private means, and passed in this condition into the customs of civil communities. This typical and historical nature has never been lost by the right of self-defense, but prevails on the same grounds and sanctions on which it rested in the earliest periods of civil society. It is this persistence of early ideas and types that renders the right of self-preservation one of the most fruitful means of investigating the fundamental ideas and principles of the law.

The inadequacy of compensative or punitive remedies to protect and redress the right of self-preservation is obvious. The loss of life or limb can not be made good by any pecuniary compensation, and certainly can not be compensated by any amount of pain or injury that may be imposed on the person causing such injury. It is, then, clear that, by the principles that govern specific remedies, the power of opposing force to prevent the consequences of a wrong consisting in an aggression of physical force, threatening injury to the physical powers of man, must reside somewhere in civil society. As that power, from the earliest times, has resided in the individual under the form of the right of self-defense, having its origin in the idea of an act of private war, it is apparent that, until civil authority provides some adequate means of accomplishing the end proposed by it, it must remain unchanged in its essential nature.

While the right of self-defense exists in all that class of cases where unlawful force is applied in personal encounter threatening injury to the body, or physical restraint of the exertion of its powers, yet it has certain specific characteristics dependent upon the nature, extent, and tendency of the means employed, and the purpose intended. By comparing these characteristics, the limit, as well as the nature of the right, will be brought to light. Assaults with reference to the mode of exercising the right of self-defense are of three kinds—namely, simple assaults, assaults with a dangerous or deadly weapon, and assaults with a deadly weapon and with intent to kill.

A simple assault implies, as its consequence, pain, inconvenience, and mortification, but does not exclude the idea of the possibility of permanent and irremediable injury resulting from it. In its compensation, while it is treated as an injury to the person, it is also treated as an injury to the right of property; and property or labor lost or expended, as its direct consequence, is also compensated. An assault with a dangerous or deadly weapon is of a higher grade, some loss, temporary or permanent, of physical power being implied by the character of the means employed. An assault with intent to kill, and with means appropriate to that end, implies the destruction of life. The idea of an assault in its simplest form becomes complex, as incidents connected with the nature of the means employed and the end pursued become implicated with it. The general idea of a dangerous weapon does not demand that some instrument should be used in addition to the physical organs; the nails in destroying an eye, and the teeth and feet as applied to certain parts of the body, may constitute dangerous weapons for certain purposes. A deadly weapon is one constructed for the purpose of destroying life, or naturally tending as a weapon to produce that result. A weapon may have the effect merely to augment the physical force or increase its natural power of destructiveness, or to introduce a source of force independent of muscular power. A club intended to add the momentum of its weight to the force of a blow, a cutting or penetrating weapon constructed to produce a highly destructive effect with the least physical exertion, and firearms acting from chemical forces, are instances of these various classes.

An assault with intent to kill demands an intention of that character, accompanied by adequate means to that end. These distinctions will be found to have an important bearing on the various forms assumed by the right of self-defense.

When a simple assault is committed, destitute of aggravating circumstances, the law does not justify an attempt to take the life of the assailant, nor to deprive him of any of the important organs of life; while, if life is endangered by such assault, the necessity of such means may justify their use. In this respect the principle of the primitive idea of *an eye for an eye and a tooth for a tooth* so far applies as to demand that the measures adopted for defense shall have a fair relation to that against which they are exerted. Although self-defense implies the right to disable an adversary, in order to prevent the accomplishment of a certain injurious purpose, it does not open to that end all means, under all circumstances, as is apparent from an examination of its nature.

There are two modes of self-defense—one purely defensive, and the other aggressive. Defensive war, public and private, must be distinguished from mere resistance, for it implies the right of attacking an adversary as well as in the case of aggressive war, but it is the purpose for which the attack is made that characterizes the mode employed as either defensive or aggressive. The principle of defensive warfare, as distinguished from mere resistance, is to occupy the attention and efforts of an enemy so that he can not pursue the ends that prompted its institution, by attacking him, and keeping him active in his own defense. The aggressive principle aims to deprive him of the means of prosecuting the conflict, either personal or material. It is obvious that, in the case of public war, as well as in that of individual self-defense, a resort to an aggressive policy is not justifiable by the principles that should govern human conduct where a defensive policy is amply sufficient. In the case of public war, this general proposition is qualified by the fact that punitive means are within the proper scope of public war, while not admissible in the case of individual self-defense. If a public enemy is pursuing a wanton interference with the rights of a community, retaliation, in excess of what is demanded by self-defense, is reconcilable with the principles that should govern the state of warfare. On the other hand, however wanton may be an individual assault, self-defense, to be justifiable, must be confined to defensive objects. If the practice of mankind, when standing in the attitude of belligerents, does not support this conclusion, still, the judgment of impartial criticism fully sustains it. The right of self-defense, unlike that of war, is subject to legal investigation, and, in its treatment of such questions, we have no difficulty in finding the propositions just enunciated taking rank among its principles. They are the clear reason of the distinctions that the law takes as to the proper relation between the form of the right of self-defense and the causes justifying its exercise.

It follows that as an assault, in its simplest form, implies no greater injury to the right of person than is involved in the infliction of pain, inconvenience, and mortification, it justifies only the mildest form of self-defense, and that it can only be met by strictly defensive means, and not by an aggressive attempt to deprive an adversary of those physical powers that constitute the object of self-preservation.

If, on the other hand, the attack is made with intent to destroy life, and with means adequate to that end, the necessities of self-defense may justify the taking of life. The necessity that determines the proper measure of self-defense is not *actual* necessity, but that which is *apparent*. It is that necessity that is demonstrated by the conduct of the attacking party, consisting in his acts, declarations, and choice of means, regard being had to whether the means employed result from voluntary selection or accident. Motive is only provable as involved in conduct, and, although a party may be allowed to testify as to the character of his motives in certain cases, the test of the truth of his assertion is the coherence of the ascribed motive with the conduct attending it. Whether the intention to take life exists, may be gathered either directly or indirectly. The process of ascertaining such fact indirectly is implication or inference. Implication is the more exact expression, for it carries the idea that that which is sought for is present within that in which it is sought. Inference may be based on analogy alone.

In ascertaining the proper mode of self-defense, the tendency of the attack, rather than the actual state of mind of the attacking party, is the leading point of inquiry. This results from the fact that the remedy is in principle preventive. If the remedy were punitive in its character, the question of actual motive would be the leading one. If the declarations of the attacking party show an intent to take life, and the means at hand are adequate for that purpose, nothing is left to implication. In the absence of such declaration, the tendency of the attack must be determined by the character of the weapons, and their mode and reason of use. What is here meant by its reason of use is whether it was selected for the purpose, or was accidentally at hand. If the weapon is one that was designed by art for the purpose of destroying life, and its mode of use is agreeable to its nature and design, and the attack has a hostile character, the inference is irresistible that the intent is of such a nature as to threaten life, as when one in anger points a loaded gun at another, in the apparent act of firing with deadly aim. If the mode of the use of a deadly weapon is indecisive, the fact that it was selected for the purpose, or that it was in the hand of the attacking party as the result of accident, is material to the question of tendency or intent. These elements of the question are summed up in the legal proposition, that the taking of human life by way of self-defense is justified where there is reasonable ground to conclude that life was in jeopardy, and the taking of life was necessary to its protection. It would follow that the apprehension of danger to life, without a sufficient cause, would be insufficient for such justification. The standard of what is reasonable in these, as in all cases, is the habit of the community. It is through such habit that the conduct of individuals is interpreted. The value of conduct as a means of interpreting motive is imparted to it upon the same principles that give to words, and combinations of words, their power of imparting ideas. The common use that is made of certain motions and gestures is the means of interpreting the intent accompanying their use.

The question of necessity, in all cases, under the right of self-defense, depends upon the principles governing the various forms which that defense may assume. Aggressive defense admits of two subordinate forms—namely, that dictated by the policy of disabling an adversary, and that of destroying him. These distinctions are recognized in the case of public war, and are applicable to individual self-defense, for the reason that such defense partakes of the nature of war. Whether the weapon is deadly or merely dangerous, and the motive be that to kill or otherwise, a resort to the means of destroying life is in no case justified unless apparent necessity exists for it. It is the inadequacy of less resolute means, and not the motives and character of the attack, that constitutes a case of necessity. In a word, under all circumstances the least destructive means of defense must be used when adequate for the purpose of self-preservation.

In the case of an assault by force in personal encounter, an intention to destroy the functions of a vital organ is an intent to destroy life itself. Menacing an organ that is not vital is not in itself evidence of an intent to kill. This may be implied from the proposition that a weapon, constructed for the purpose of destroying life, and used in a manner agreeable to its nature and design, gives rise to the implication of a motive to destroy life, for if it is manifestly used for a subordinate purpose, as that of crippling without killing, that implication disappears, as when a firearm is aimed at a point that is not vital, or where such a weapon is used as a club merely.

The principle of the rule that requires that the mode of using the right of self-defense shall be discriminated with reference to the tendency of an attack and the necessities of defense, also produces certain consequences arising from the difference that exists among the cases where the crippling of the power of an adversary is the motive of defense. An adversary may be crippled by disarming him—that is, by separating his instruments of attack from the force with which he wields or directs them, by destroying or rendering useless such instruments, or some organ or organs of the body essential to their use. The principle of using the least destructive force adequate for self-protection places these means, as it regards the propriety of their use, in the order just stated. If the instrument answers the description of a weapon—that is, something actuated or directed by the physical force of the attacking party—the application of these rules is direct and clear. In the first place, the adversary should be disarmed; if that is impossible, his weapon should be rendered impotent, or destroyed, and, when that is not practicable, the organ that wields it becomes the proper object of attack, and, finally, the general power of the attacking party to maintain the contest. But an instrument may be used detached from the person of the attacking party, such as a ferocious animal or a servant, or other agent employed for such purpose. In that case the principle in question would direct the power of self-defense against the agent in the first instance. A human being of sufficient capacity acting voluntarily, as the agent of another to accomplish such a purpose, takes the place of his principal as it regards the personal consequences of such attack. If the instrument of attack, whether animate or inanimate, is a subject of property, whether that of the attacking party or of a third person, its necessary destruction in the course of self-defense is not an unlawful inteference with the property of another. If the use of such an instrument is incidental to a personal encounter, the right of self-defense exists specifically. If the party responsible for the wrong is not present and immediately acting in the matter, while the absence of personal encounter deprives the right of self-defense of that quality, as against the cause of the assault that it derives from the nature of war, it still exists as directed against the instrument itself.

This brings to light the proposition that one may, with legal impunity, destroy the property of another when essential to the preservation of life, and such property is in effect the instrument of danger to life. This proposition is embodied in many cases involving the destruction of property when a means of communicating fire or infection.

The law does not permit the right of self-defense to be used for punitive purposes, or as against one acting with legal authority, such as public officers acting under a competent warrant. This conclusion results from the nature of those principles as already stated. The principles of self-defense extend themselves to the defense of the dwelling-place of the assailed party, and of those under his authority and protective care. According to the quaint expression of the early law, a man's house is his castle—that is to say, a means of personal defense to himself and those under his authority and protective care. An assault delivered upon an instrument of defense is an assault upon a person defending himself with such instrument, so that, as the house is an instrument of defense, its protection is dependent upon the principles of self-defense. The right of protecting property as such by resisting the efforts of those attempting to deprive the owner of his legal control over it, and the power of removing a person from a place where one has dominion, and where such person is unlawfully intruding, rest on a different foundation of principle from that of the right of self-defense. The one class of cases depends upon the nature of the proprietary rights, while the other depends upon the nature of the right of self-preservation.

As in cases of personal encounter it must be anticipated that there will be present, in some degree, greater or less, the passions of hatred, envy, or fear, the law can never form a practicable formula or rule for conducting such controversies while such passions have any considerable degree of force. It is none the less important to recognize the elements of right and wrong that appear in such cases, not only as calculated to produce an organized state of public judgment, more or less affecting individual action, but for the further purpose of defining the proper relations of individuals to each other in society, and the attributes of right and incidents of obligation that individualize persons as members of communities. There is in every community a sense of justice in regard to such cases, precisely as the same sense exists in individuals. It is from this sense of justice that right conduct proceeds, both in the cases of individuals and communities. In the absence of strong impulses, or in the direction of such impulses, man recognizes moral and legal distinctions, and shows much aptitude in placing his conduct upon the line indicated by such distinctions. It is when great interests are involved that legal and moral definitions of right and wrong become obscure, and the only guide to right conduct is persistent habit, formed under the influence of a sense of right. The sense of right, when forming a subject of reflection in calm moments, may give rise to the consciousness of its elements and the law uniting them; but, when it becomes the guide to energetic action, such elemental consciousness is apt to disappear, and the sense of right and justice takes the place of a subjective influence. While, then, the service that the law does to the individual in discriminating the elements of right and wrong does not, in this class of cases, consist in laying down practical rules sufficient as a guide in every emergency, it is nevertheless most important, as tending to form a habit of right-doing that does not necessarily lose its force in the presence of strong motives to a course opposite to such habit.

So far as the law arises from the nature of the common obligations, it is merely the interpretation of that which belongs to all right-minded individual consciousness. When a conception of the demands of good faith is fostered by habitual right action, and even when it is rather an ideal than an actual force in the mind, the means exist of conforming the conduct to the requirements of the law. Indeed, the highest conception of a legal system would be that which would sanction that which a right-minded man would do under the influence of the sense of justice, accepted by the best opinion of the community of which he is a member.

CHAPTER XXVI.

ACTION OF ASSAULT AND BATTERY.

THE right of resisting, as well as preventing, injuries from force in personal encounter having been considered as embodied together in the right of self-defense, it remains to consider the modes of legal action, applicable in such cases, constituting the redress of such rights. The term redress is often used as if a wrong was the proper subject of such redress, while, accurately speaking, the right which has been impaired is that which demands redress. Redress of a right involves a change in its form, as when the right of self-preservation is in part converted into a right to have a certain sum of money, as the measure of damages, awarded in compensation for an injury to such right; or where the right to money or property, resting on a general or special obligation binding another, is converted into a right to seize such money or property specifically, or the money or property of the party obliged generally, under the course of judicial process, and either retain it specifically, or sell it, and apply the whole or a part of the proceeds of such sale to the use of the creditor. As a wrong done to a right brings into existence a specific right to an action at law, so a certain result of that action creates a new form of right evidenced by a judgment. Whatever one may do, or abstain from doing, in virtue of his rights, is part of the powers incident to such right; and, when these powers are either enlarged or modified through any means, it is clear that the right has undergone a change of form. As the proper effect of an action at law is either to render active or specific certain rights that antecedently existed in a contingent or general form only, in the cause of action, or in the right out of which the cause of action arose, or to change one class of active powers into another, the propriety of the expression, *redressing a right*, is manifest.

The proper means of redress is an action at law, or a submission to private arbitration. The nature of an action at law must, according to the method of the present inquiry, be established on constructive principles, from the dealings of the law with such actions; but such an inquiry is materially aided by illustrations drawn from historic sources. The history of the evolution of legal institutions certainly tends to throw important light upon legal discussions, but, to find the principles of the law, its present, as well as its past action, must be considered, for it is in the nature of fundamental principles to subtend equally primitive and derived forms, and their nature and incidents can not be fully known until both of these sources have been exhaustively examined.

The legal conception of the nature of an action at law is ascertained by an examination of the consequences it attributes to such actions, and thus appears most clearly in the view it takes of the force and effect of a judgment in such actions. The present inquiry is confined to civil actions as involving original powers and rights. The effect ascribed to a judgment, apart from the judicial means of enforcing it, is precisely that which would result if all the parties to such judgment should unite in the execution of some instrument, capable of being enforced, containing the dispositions as to rights and obligations established by such judgment. A confession of judgment is, in effect, such an act. The consequences of a judgment are the same whether rendered *in invitum* or by confession. The parties are equally bound as to the matter of right and obligation contained in a judgment as it regards the state of that right or obligation established by such judgment in either case. Persons possessing imperfect power of self-obligation, and made to stand in the relation of parties to it, are not bound unless their powers have been supplemented by a proper representation—that is, where one having power delegated to act in their name and stead has so acted. Third persons not parties to it are unaffected by it, unless they are, in substance and effect, parties to it, though not formally such, or unless they acquire or accept benefits under it, or unless the judgment supplies some condition on which their rights or obligations depend. That a judgment is an obligation is not only the language of the law, but the consequence of its rules and principles. That it proceeds from the power of the parties to oblige themselves is evident from the fact that its effects are limited to those powers, and that the parties must stand toward it in the same light as if it was an obligation voluntarily assumed by parties of full capacity of obligation, and of the proper representatives of such as have not that full capacity. It is evident that, unless a judgment is confessed, it is not in a direct sense the act of the parties to it, for it may not conform to the volitions of some or all of the parties. It is the act of the judicial body or officer that pronounces it. This fact shows that it is produced by delegated authority, for that is the character of all public authority.

It is not according to the nature of judicial authority to create obligations either as affecting individuals or communities. As law is in the nature of obligation, the function of creating obligations appertains to the legislative or law-making power. It is obviously essential to the purposes of society that the community should possess the requisite means for adjusting any disturbances that may occur among the rights of individuals, as well as among those of the community itself and individuals. This power of adjustment is the judicial power of the community, forming part of the sovereignty delegated by the act of constituting civil society. To adjust the rights of parties implies the harmonizing together of their obligations, mutual and common, and therefore excludes the idea of creating obligations. As the right to adjust the mutual and common relations of individuals resides primarily in such individuals, as part of that liberty that is the outgrowth of the principles of the law, it would follow that the judicial function, properly understood, consists in the exercise of rights properly belonging to the individual, and that in the performance of such functions the judicial authority stands in the place and rights of the parties upon whom it is acting. This idea is significant of the exercise of authority delegated by the parties for such purpose. If the judicial authority, in its action on the rights of litigant parties, is to be regarded as acting as the agent of the entire community, in such particular matter its judgment in such case would have, naturally, binding force on all members of the community. The legislative body acts at all times in such a general agency, and hence the authority of the laws is as general as if each individual had communicated express sanction to the exercise of such authority. The force and effect ascribed by the law to judgments show that the judicial power, when acting between parties, is only such as might result from an express delegation of such judicial authority by the parties concerned, and no others. When a controversy of a judicial nature exists between the community and an individual, the judgment pronounced has the same limited force and effect, showing that, in that instance also, the community takes the place of an individual as it regards the application of the idea of a delegation of judicial authority of a limited character.

The general idea of judicial power as a public function is that of authority and adequate means for subjecting persons and property to such conditions as are essential to the investigation of the state of rights and obligations existing between specified parties, for ascertaining and establishing such rights and obligations, and for compelling conformity to the obligations so established. This idea includes a general view of both the nature and incidents of such public judicial authority. It is important to form a clear conception of that nature, apart from all its incidents. The essential feature of the judicial act consists in the establishment, in the form of a specific obligation or judgment, of the relative rights and obligations of the parties. The powers of control over persons and property for the purpose of promoting such an inquiry, and for enforcing its consequences, are, properly speaking, the incidents attendant upon the essential elements of the power; following legal distinctions, they are ministerial functions attendant upon a judicial act.

The powers of arbitrators selected by the parties to a controversy answer to the description just given of that which constitutes the essential feature of judicial authority. While arbitrators, selected and empowered to determine a controversy between parties, are very clearly the agents of the parties to such controversy, it is evident that their agency possesses characteristics that are not common to other classes of agencies. Agents ordinarily represent the interests of those communicating to them their representative authority. Arbitrators, however, represent their principals, not for the purpose of adjusting their relative interests, but their relative duties. The adjustment of interests is the proper sphere of a contract or compromise, and those intrusted with such an agency are negotiators, rather than arbitrators, in a legal sense. Another distinctive feature of the arbitration exhibits the same characteristic of that agency, and is the fact that the power of recalling or revoking authority, communicated for that purpose, ceases at the moment when the parties, having concluded the presentation of their respective cases, submit the matter to the arbitrators for decision. Ordinary agencies may be revoked at any time prior to the complete execution of the agency, either in whole or in part, except in those cases where the agent or a third person has an interest in the agency, and does not unite in such act of revocation. That, in the case of arbitration, the limitation to the power of revocation that has been stated does not arise from any outstanding interest preventing such revocation, is obvious, for, if such an interest existed, the act of delegation would be irrevocable from the moment it was completed, whereas the delegation may be revoked at any time prior to the actual submission for decision. It must, then, be concluded that the irrevocability of the power of an arbitrator, after the case is submitted for decision, arises from the nature of the agency itself. Considering an arbitration as an instance of delegated judicial power, the independent nature of the power of the arbitrator, and the fact that his power can not be terminated, after final submission for decision, by the revocation of his authority, by less than all concerned in such arbitration, is readily understood.

The conception that effective jurisdiction depended upon the actual or assumed delegation of power, by the parties to a controversy, to the judicial body, was reflected in the early practice of the common law of England, both by the rules that required the presence of a defendant, or of his representative selected by him for that purpose, for the regular conduct of litigation, and in the forms of pleading, that were a distinct appeal to the judicial power, as to an agency for the adjustment of right. This subject can not receive full discussion in this place, but enough has already been said to show that the judicial authority, when acting in the controversies of individuals with each other, or with the community, must be regarded as acting in the stead and exercising the powers of the parties subjected to its authority, and the result of its action must receive the same interpretation as if it had been accomplished through the voluntary obligatory act of such parties.

The means by which mankind have in all ages settled questions of practical right and wrong are reducible to three modes— that of an appeal to force, to fate, and to reason. Force is the means natural to the animal man, and one to which man, even in a high state of rational development, may sometimes find himself compelled to resort. When the relations existing among men are not regulated by permanent institutions, differentiating and distributing the various functions that appertain to civil society, and producing an organic system, the necessity for a resort to force, as a means of adjusting difficulties, must frequently arise. This is seen illustrated in the intercourse of nations, and can not fail to impart the impressive lesson that the conception of organized civil society must be so expanded as to link nationalities, as well as individuals, into permanent communities before wars can be dispensed with. The fundamental idea of a complex community, of which lesser communities are the units, is well illustrated by the federative principle in the composition of the United States.

Relatively to our civil stage of legal development, the appeal to force may be regarded as a primitive type; but it is by no means certain, or even probable, that it is entitled to be called primitive in the broadest sense. In the earliest days of our race, when mankind may be supposed to have been thinly scattered over vast regions, yielding more than was demanded by their needs for subsistence, clothing, and shelter, the elements must have constituted the great disturbing influence affecting man's state. Before the conditions of dwelling, clothing, supply, and transportation were adjusted to climatic peculiarities, the powers that were believed to govern the atmospheric conditions naturally exercised a controlling influence over his conduct. Difficulties that might arise between man and man, where realized possessions were small, and the capacity of acquisition almost unlimited, were trifling in comparison with the evils that might be inflicted by flood or tempest. Under such circumstances it is to be expected that, whether the conception of Deity was spiritualistic or naturalistic, reverence, at least of that type that possesses a large element of fear, would be the habitual mood. In such a condition, the appeal to fate would be the natural outcome. In substance or intention it might be an appeal to the Supreme Ruler of the universe, conceived as sustaining a judicial relation to mankind, while in form it might assume the character of a determination by lot, by augury, or by prophetic impulse. The lot has survived to this time, and still has a place among the civil means for adjusting differences. It has lost its relation to religious ideas, and represents in its best use, at the present day, the idea of a determination by accident, excluding selection. In this character, as excluding selection, it is preserved as a means of ascertaining the persons to constitute a jury.

An appeal to reason is an appeal to some competent means of applying to the conduct of antagonists the standards of right and wrong that are accepted and embodied in the intercourse of men. Discussions of speculative morals can not produce such standards. Whether embodying a high or low ideal, it is their acceptance by social man that constitutes their force, and that acceptance can only be ascertained either from what is declared by the law-making power or from what is embodied in the habitual conduct of individuals.

A rational process implies the action and reaction of mind upon mind, and therefore demands the conditions under which it is possible for such action and reaction to produce a stable judgment. Fortunately, it is possible for two minds, without the intervention of a third, to harmonize their practical conclusions; but an appeal to judicial means of adjustment implies that the simpler means are incompetent for such purpose in that particular case. The collective mind of the community is that which supplies the intervening mind in civil communities. That mind may be represented by the person of a judge, or the complex arrangements of a modern court; but, if properly represented, may be as effectually expressed as if no individuality intervened between the common mind and the litigants. That common mind is in part represented by a literature, the essential feature of which is a record of the actual transactions of the legislative and judicial bodies, in part by the unwritten experience of individuals, and in part by phenomena occurring as the result of habit operating on the intercourse of bodies of men.

The necessary conception of a complex or collective mind is that of a totality of mental action of the same nature as that of the units of which it is composed, but having certain characteristics specifically different from any single individual mind. It would result that rational processes, conducted by a collective mind, must repeat in principle those processes that characterize individual minds in like conditions. This would lead to the anticipation that a perfect judicial system would reflect the principles that underlie individual mental processes in a manner highly valuable as an objective embodiment of a process that in the individual is largely subjective. It will be found that, by the examination of judicial systems, this anticipation may be realized.

A practical individual judgment is based upon a concrete generalization. A practical judgment is necessarily a complex judgment, and its excellence depends not only upon its quality, but the degree of its complexity, as embracing all elements possible to enter, directly or indirectly, into its composition. A complex judgment is a whole of which lesser judgments are the parts. It is as natural for man to act promptly from a judgment which, according to his consciousness, is full and complete, as it is for him to hesitate when he does not possess that consciousness. A concrete generalization is the product of observation acting on general experience, and is distinguishable from those speculative generalizations that are useful for the purpose of arranging the ideas in preparation for exact investigation, but can only produce abnormal action when treated as an end rather than as a means. The formation of such a concrete generalization is a rational act, independent of the exercise of the higher rational power. The higher rational effort consists in subjecting such concrete generalization, as produced directly from observation, to an examination of the separate elements of which it is composed and of the laws governing their relationship. The cognition of these laws must be reached from the primary facts elicited by analytic methods through an inductive process, although capable, possibly, of being anticipated in some degree on grounds of analogy. When the law may be stated inductively from the fact, and the fact potentially from the law, by the opposite means of deduction, the process is perfect.

The proper outcome of this analytic method is the restatement of the primary concrete generalization, with the modifications made necessary by the results of the exact method. The genesis of our ideas, as distinguished from our observations, is thus, in the form of a concrete generalization, of a low type, and their development a process of functional differentiation and distribution of the organic type. The process thus embraces observations correlated with antecedent experience, under the influence, greater or less, of ideas of elemental nature and relationship. The modifying process deals with facts and modes of action or laws.

In the constitution of courts, that have the aid of juries, may be found a functional arrangement closely assimilated to that which exists in the individual mind, as just stated. It is necessary, to a full understanding of the various mental reactions that enter into the formation of a legal judgment, that a broad generalization should be made, embracing, not only the influences that have a direct part in the formation of judicial conclusions, but those also that exert only an indirect influence. The difficulty in attaining such a view is the habitual mode of looking at courts of justice as if part of their machinery was designed to advance the development of a sound judgment, and another part designed merely to obstruct that end, or perhaps render it impossible. A trial is the product of interaction between several distinct classes of minds, sustaining each a different functional relation to the proper function of the court. The instance that will be examined in a general way is the court, consisting of judge and jury, as the differentiation of the judicial functions, in such cases, leads conveniently to the principles involved. These different classes are: the judge or judges, the jury, the advocates, and the witnesses. It is the function of the judge to regulate the admission of facts into consideration, both as it regards their relevancy to the question and the mode in which they are sought to be brought into consideration, and also to state and illustrate the bearing of the law on the various classes of facts introduced. The jury are the body to be impressed, and are assumed to represent fairly the average intelligence of the community, and to possess some measure of experience, both as it regards the habit of the community and the general habit that occurs in the sequences of events, both natural and social. In a word, they represent the common mind, possessing a variable amount of experience, or, as the idea is gathered up in a familiar expression, *common sense*. The group of witnesses represent the actual sensible impression made upon observers of the events and objects that are to be transferred by narration in language to the minds of the court and jury. The actual presence of the witnesses leaves nothing interposed between the minds of the jury and the events and objects narrated and described but what concerns the accuracy of the observations and of their memories of the witnesses and their truthfulness. Through the office of the advocates the various observations of different witnesses are compared with themselves and with the observations of other witnesses. Points of agreement and disagreement are ascertained, and that which can be harmonized together is focalized in a single point of view or generalization. The opposite interests of the advocates render this process generally very thorough. It is obvious to any one who is familiar with the course of investigation that prevails in courts of justice, that the impression usually made upon the minds of the jury, assuming them to possess fair intelligence and impartiality, is more reliable than the impression of the same facts on the mind of any single witness, even if the most intelligent and observant, so that the jury get by this means a better impression of the actual facts, narrated and described, than could be anticipated as the result of personal observation upon any single individual mind. The fact that the jury do not have direct sensible perception of the matters narrated and described has a parallel in the fact that the reflex powers of the mind, that are principally concerned in the formation of conclusions from antecedently observed facts, habitually act from the memory of past experiences, arising from impressions made upon other and distinct parts of the mental organism. It is through the medium described that the jury attain impressions as to the objects described, including their identity, qualities, and quantities, and of the events narrated, with their causes and consequences. Through the aid of witnesses, more or less expert in the methods of general or particular transactions, they learn the common standards of value and quality of property, and, through experts of a higher order, the properties of matter and motion in organic and inorganic conditions, being aided by standard works, that by common acceptance are standards of authority as to the matters of which they treat; and of such articles as conveniently may be exhibited to them, such as written papers or documents, they are entitled to the personal inspection.

In view of the facts thus presented, the effect of the body sought to be impressed is naturally to harmonize the matters submitted to them with what experience they have of nature, life, and conduct. This process is attended by one of a different character, conducted by that part of the court that is charged with raising the generalization formed by the jury to a higher rational standard than would be possible without such aid. The facts are analyzed, and conduct, motive, and the tendencies of natural causes stated in their relation to habitual modes of action. The law of conduct and the law of nature are applied to the facts disclosed, both to test their actuality and consequences. This function is performed both by the judges and by the advocates, the former having a passive duty as it regards the initiative in investigation, while the advocates have an active duty to perform. At every step, opposite criticism, induced by opposite interests, brings to light all that can be affirmed for or against any proposition that may fall under discussion. It is impossible to draw a more striking picture of what takes place in an acute individual mind, when pursuing independently and with acumen a similar process, than such as is presented in the course of such judicial action.

The separation of the function of the court into the distinct functions of the judges and juries is, beyond question, the result of such a differentiation as constitutes a step in organic development. There still remains, in existing systems of an advanced type, the remnant of an earlier habit, that left both of these functions united in the legal members of the court, which prevails on obvious grounds of utility. Even in equity, where the division is not so strictly made as in the courts following the course of the common law, the agency of the master as a means of investigating facts preserves the principle of this duality of function. The difference in the mode of applying the principle is very well accounted for by the almost indispensable prolixity and intricate character of the cases that constitute the characteristic feature of the business of the courts of equity, demanding an investigation, ordinarily, intermitted from time to time, and a permanent record of each step of procedure, instead of the naked memory of a dozen unskilled men. In addition to this, special skill is usually required of a master, and at times is so essential, even in law cases, as to require the substitution of experienced referees for the ordinary jury.

A return to the simple forms that brought the litigants and

their witnesses into immediate contact with a judge capable of deciding all questions, and dispensed with the costly aid of advocates, would be the abandonment of those features of the judicial system that make it possible for the law to attain a scientific character, and for the judgments of the courts to express a high order of rational development. The motives that led to the use of this intricate and costly machinery were, beyond doubt, to neutralize the undue influence of public authority in the production of judgments agreeable to the public interests. It is yet a question whether the prevalence of forms of government, that give the highest interpretation to the principle of equal individual liberty, is a sufficient safeguard against abuses of public authority to insure the safety of a return to simple habits, commended chiefly for their cheapness.

It is obvious, from the foregoing, that the rules of pleading and evidence should be counterparts of the methods by which the mind advances along the best lines of thought to its conclusions. This is claimed for them, and with much reason. The fact that these rules have persisted with little change, and that merely in the direction of forms, during the whole period represented by a reliable judicial history, is positive evidence that they are in conformity to the civilized habit of thought; and a proposition to revise habits of individual thought by these great standards would recommend itself as more reasonable than one to reverse that process. The general view that has been taken of the methods of legal investigation places the rules that govern such investigations upon the ground of the universal habit of mankind. While the definition of rights and obligations may, in large part, rest on the habit of particular communities, the method by which the consequences of those rights and obligations are traced is based on the broad foundation of universal acceptance. Having indicated the sources to which attention must be given in order to develop the principles that are fundamental to judicial proceedings, their consequences must be left for consideration, as brought to light by particular subjects of inquiry.

It is desirable to reach a generalization of the subject of

damages as preparatory to the examination of the characteristics of rights and obligations exhibited in their treatment in the course of judicial procedure. Damages are the compensations awarded by judicial procedure for violations of obligations. The nature and the incidents of damages are to be considered for this purpose in a brief, general way. Damages are estimated in pecuniary amounts, and the ascertainment of damage, after the existence of some degree of damage has been established, resolves itself into one of the amount of money that would represent the injury done to a particular right, the measure of damage being the expression employed to describe this part of the operation of fixing the compensations for wrongs. When by a contract the pecuniary value of an obligation is fixed, by the act of the parties, that amount constitutes the compensation for the violation of such obligation. But many specific obligations leave the value of the obligation unascertained, and in these cases, as well as in all cases of the violation of the common obligations alone, the measure of damages is ascertained by a judicial act. It is with the principles involved in the mode of ascertaining damages, in cases arising from violations of the common obligations, that the immediate subject is concerned.

As the common obligations are accessory to large classes of rights, the estimation of the consequences of a wrong, consisting in the violation of such obligations, would naturally extend to all, or so many of the particular recognized rights as may have received injury through such act of wrong—a circumstance that will be verified in a very full manner in the further consideration of the action of assault and battery. It would follow that, whenever any given class of injurious effects is allowed to be shown as the foundation for the allowance of damages, a right must exist of the nature that is inferable from the character of such compensated injurious effects. It is clear that the law would not allow, as an element of damage, that which affected no recognized right; and the reversed statement is equally maintainable, that, when a wrong is compensated, that which has sustained such injury must, of necessity, have the character of a recognized civil right, and, as such, the protection of a common obligation. With these principles in view, a statement of many recognized rights may be made that could not otherwise be made, as many rights are of such a nature that they can only appear for judicial recognition as elements of a question of general damage. It is for this reason that the action of assault and battery is of special interest, as an examination of the elements that may enter into the damages in such cases shows a large range of personal and proprietary, as well as associative, rights.

It is important to ascertain, as exactly as possible, the legal sense of the terms cause and consequence, as these terms are used to trace the relationship between an act of wrong and the injurious effects to which it has given rise. As the violation of an obligation may give rise to injurious consequences, both where such violation consists in an injurious act performed, and where, in neglect to perform an act, the idea of cause in such a case materially differs from the idea of physical cause, for a physical cause is always an active one. It is obvious that conduct, according to common as well as legal understanding, may be the cause of physical consequences in a very different sense from that used to express the relation between a certain physical force and the subject of that force. When the injurious effects are such as can not exist without a physical cause—that is, a physical force acting through certain conditions, in order to link conduct with such injurious effects, as their cause—it is necessary to ascertain that the existence of that force, or of the conditions under which it came to have injurious effects, was due to such conduct. It appears, then, that the idea of physical cause may be contained within that of legal cause, and it is necessary, for the full understanding of the latter, that the nature of the former should be studied.

An injurious effect, as the result of physical force, arises from a change produced by the action of such force upon some material object, either changing its condition, form, or relation to place. The idea of a change of condition contains that of a change of form, but includes also that of a change in the qualities of the substance itself. When a physical force assumes the form of a destructive force, it may become such in virtue of the conditions attending the force itself, or of those appertaining to the subject of force, or of the conditions relating the force and the subject together, or from all these conditions united. The existence of conditions admitting of such destructive effect must have a cause, and hence the expression cause may be applied either to the agent that liberated the force in a particular form, or to that assembling the conditions that rendered its tendencies destructive. In the common use of the expression cause, one or the other of these dual agencies is understood, and usually without confusion as to which is intended. The mode in which such expression is usually interpreted appears to be as follows: Where the force is one that is constantly present, like that of gravity, or where, though acting through intermitting stages, yet, from the habit of its appearance at particular times, or within periods of time, more or less definite, like that of the tides of the sea, or the ordinary atmospheric changes, the agency that produces the conditions under which such force becomes destructive is understood as the cause of injurious effect. Thus, if one allows an object to fall; or releases a boat, permitting it to be carried away by the tide; or if one pierces a vessel so that it sinks in water, or, when it contains a fluid, so that the fluid escapes—in all these cases the force is that of gravity; but the source of whatever effect may be produced by such act is understood to be the agency that produced the conditions under which it came to have that particular effect. If, however, the conditions habitually exist, but the time, place, and mode of the action of the force are not due to the ordinary habit of the force, but to some voluntary agency, then the agent producing such active condition of force is understood as the cause of the effect. Thus, if the outline of a section of inhabited country is such that a body of water, liberated in a certain position, would sweep over a certain space and produce certain injurious consequences, one that should liberate such a force at that point would be understood as the cause of all the effects occasioned by the topographical form of the place. This method of interpretation involves the idea that, when the force, acting in a given case, is a constant force, and the conditions under which it may act are variable, the author of a particular condition is the cause of the consequences flowing from that condition; and, when the conditions are constant and the force variable, the author of the force is the one that is understood as the cause of its effect. The mind, reasoning from the constant element as its basis, looks to the variable element as to a source of modification, thus making the habit of nature its general premises.

When a force passes beyond the control of its creating or governing author, before producing destructive consequences, or before the completion of such consequences, a question arises as to the applicability of the common idea of cause to its author, as it regards injurious consequences produced after the force was beyond his control. So long as the identity of the force and the conditions attending it and connecting it with the subject remain, the consequences resulting are attributable to the same cause. When the force is changed in direction or form by some new intervening condition, if the intervention of such new condition is due to the ordinary sequences of events, the link of cause and consequence remains unchanged. The reason of this is, that such intervening condition forms part of the general class of constant conditions, while the cause, which is the agency controlling the variable conditions, remains unchanged. But if a new force should intervene, not to be anticipated in the ordinary course of events, and not called into existence by the primary force, and such new force dominates the direction or the form of such force, subsequent consequences are not attributable to such primary cause. Again, if the original cause has the tendency and the effect to liberate a new specific force, that becomes an agent producing injurious consequences, such consequences are, according to our ordinary ideas, attributable to the original cause. A still more remote connection between cause and consequence, and yet one that is recognized according to ordinary ideas, arises where, in consequence of injurious effects produced upon some subject, it becomes exposed, at some future time and under circumstances disconnected from the original cause of injury, to be destroyed by causes that, but for the injuries previously done, would not have produced such effect. An instance of this class is a building receiving injury that is the means of its being overthrown by a tempest. It may be that the tempest in that case is one of extraordinary force, not to be anticipated in the ordinary course of events, yet the damage done by the tempest, which would not have occurred but for the injury previously sustained, is readily traced, in common understanding, to the responsibility of the cause of the first injury received. This would appear, at first sight, to be ascribing to an original cause the effect produced by a new variable, but such is not actually the case. The original damage was complete before the tempest struck the house, but the occurrence of the tempest merely disclosed the degree of damage that had been previously done to the house, which, but for the occurrence of such tempest, might not have been ascertainable with any certainty.

To fix the legal sense of the term cause, as applied to an agency producing injurious effects, the fundamental principles already discussed should be considered. Liability results where one, in dealing with the rights of another, produces effects injurious to the latter, whether intentional or otherwise. Such liability also arises where one, in dealing with his own rights, wrongfully neglects the use of prudent care, and, as a result, injures the property of another. The two cases are reducible to a common idea. One who causes an injury through negligence is responsible for the destructive condition of the force that might have been prevented by the exercise of prudent care. The difference between the two cases, then, is that, in the one case, there is a general liability, while, in the other, there is only a specific liability. It would follow that, when injurious consequences are attributable to such specific liability, they would be governed by the same rule that governs the more general liability, as the species partakes of the nature and law of the genus. If this view is correct, then there is no reason for a difference between the legal idea of cause and that which is in ordinary use understood by the same term.

It would be out of place to pursue the question that has just been mooted, to the full extent that its importance demands, at the present time. It may serve a useful purpose, however, in this connection, to show that, both according to common and to legal understanding, the idea of the habit of the community may replace that of the habit of nature in the problems just stated. An action, performed upon a street or in a market-place, that tends to produce injurious consequences, through the fact that large numbers of persons are apt to be assembled in such places, is clearly an injurious one. The habit of the community is one of the conditions classed as constant in such cases, and, according to the principles already stated, the author of the injurious force would stand, both in common and in legal understanding, as the cause of the injurious effects.

The effects of an act of wrong, that find admittance into the legal idea of damage, are thus both direct and consequential. Direct damages are such as appear as the immediate result of a wrong, while consequential damages are such as result from some contingency, or from the capacity of injurious consequences to reproduce themselves under changes of form. If a train of injurious consequences, set in motion by an act of wrong, becomes, at every remove, implicated with external circumstances, introducing an increasing number of causes, mingling their consequences with the primary cause, so long as these intervening causes may be ascribed to the ordinary tendencies of events, they are recognized as conditions of a constant character, such as should be anticipated and guarded against by one responsible for the use of force capable of becoming destructive. If, however, an entirely new agency appears that dominates after consequences, the fact of such dominance precludes it from being placed in the class of conditions subservient to another independent force. The new force must be regarded as the cause of all that ensues, and, so far as the effects of the first cause are interwoven with those of the second cause, they take the place of conditions attendant upon the new force.

The legal proposition that proximate causes are alone to be considered is explained by the view just presented. If the term proximate was translated into dominant, it would undergo no substantial change of meaning; in fact, the expression *proximately dominating* would express the actual force of the legal expression *proximate*, as used in such connections.

It would follow, from the general principles stated, that damages are either necessary or contingent; necessary where they must, according to their nature, follow independent of the operation of any new cause; and contingent when the introduction of a new cause or condition is essential to their existence. Contingencies are either probable or remote; probable when their occurrence may be anticipated, either through constancy of habit or the known law of their recurrence, remote when their happening is not indicated by any habit or law. From the nature of these distinctions, in view of the immense productive energy of producing causes, both according to the laws of material nature and those that govern the conduct of mankind, problems of the greatest complexity must be constantly involved in the ascertainment of the consequences of wrongs.

Only a general attempt will be made to summarize the foregoing principles in their relation to the rule of measuring damages, and that will be confined to damages consisting in physical or physiological injuries. Only injurious damages are estimated as where produced as the result of a violation of a common obligation, through the operation of causes that owe their existence, or injurious character, to such act of violation. The necessary and direct consequences of such injurious force are included. Consequential or contingent damages are also included where the contingency is one that is liable to occur according to the ordinary course of events, whether such events belong to the class of natural or social occurrences. Such contingent damage may arise from causes operating within, or externally upon, the subject of injury. Either chemical, mechanical, or vital forces, operating within such subject, may produce consequences estimable as damage where the injury produced by such causes is due to conditions created by the direct injuries received. So also, where conditions are produced exposing the subject to injury from external causes that are capable of being anticipated, the effect of such causes may be estimable as damages where the injury produced by such causes is due to conditions created by the direct injuries received. So also, where conditions are produced by the direct injuries that expose the subject of injury to extraordinary causes of a destructive character, the consequences of such extraordinary causes enter indirectly into the question of damage, as affording a means of determining the degree of actual deterioration of condition that was produced by the original injury received. In the case of injuries to certain proprietary rights, the damages are estimated upon principles peculiar to proprietary rights—that is, according to standards of value prevailing in reference to marketable articles. But that subject must be considered in another place.

The institution of a jury, as a means of solving such problems in their most complex form, has obviated the necessity of drawing out the principles of the law to that nicety and minuteness that would be necessary if judges were required to give an exact account of the principles on which the extent of damage was to be ascertained, and which would not add to the value of the law as a practical system. While, then, it is not expected or desirable that every actual case of damage should be analyzed to its principles, it is important that these principles should be isolated and studied as part of the general system.

An additional general observation is called for by the nature of the difficulties that surround this particular subject, and that involves the effect, upon the rules of evidence, of certain characteristics of an examination of the extent of injurious consequences flowing from a particular act of wrong. It is obvious that what is called the measure of damages influences the scope of admissible proofs, and yet all damage that is allowable is not directly provable. The ascertainment of damages proceeds upon actual proof and reasonable probability. If the means of ascertainment are simple, proof is admitted as the basis of an actual estimation; if complex, a reasonable probability is put in the place of actual proof. For instance, as there is a market value for manual labor, there is a simple means of ascertaining the value of labor lost; but one whose labor, and his capital and skill, are combined to produce variable profits can not exercise the right of submitting in proof all the facts that would illustrate his probable material losses through time lost. In the last-named case only general circumstances can be submitted in proof as part of the question of damage, and the estimate must be based upon such general circumstances. The introduction of the particular circumstances in such a case would be open to the legal objection to speculative proofs of damage. Whether a conclusion in such a case is based upon general circumstances, or upon particulars of the most minute character, the result, at last, is conjectural merely. The introduction of particulars in such a case could only produce the effect of opening a broad, speculative realm within that of the general conjecture, and thus each particular fact would be as likely to introduce an element of error as of truth. It is upon these principles that the law excludes from proof evidence of facts that have only a speculative relation to the question of damage, both as it regards injuries to person and property.

The principles that have been stated will be found illustrated in the course of the treatment of the law of questions of damage in cases of injuries to the person.

Loss of life is not estimable as a damage resulting from personal injuries, for the reason that the right ceases with the death of its possessor, and is no longer a ground for vindication, except as a violation of public duty; the legal maxim that embodies this proposition being, that *personal actions die with the person*. The loss of a member or organ, not vital, or of general health, does not admit of ascertainment in terms of pecuniary value, in a direct sense, for that which is not vendible in its nature is not strictly estimable in terms of pecuniary value. But such a loss implies physical pain, inconvenience, and mental suffering, as a general personal condition, and loss to the power of exertion and self-gratification. It implies, also, possible loss to the proprietary rights, and to the associative rights, as involving both waste and expenditure of physical means and loss of the power of performing labor, and as diminishing ability to perform those acts that are due to relative interests and duties. As this statement includes the entire range of rights capable of being enjoyed, it is manifest that all the principles of damage are represented in some degree in what may be presented by a case of personal injury, and especially by the action of assault and battery, that may cover a violation of every possible right in a much more direct way than any other form of personal wrong.

Before noticing the particular elements of the legal idea of damage, as illustrated by the class of cases in hand, it is necessary to notice certain general rules applicable to many cases of damage, and to examine the principles on which they are based. Provocation and aggravation are capable of diminishing or increasing the amount of damage in many cases. Provocation consists of an act performed by the assaulted party previous to the assault, tending to produce the state of mind in the aggressor that would induce the assault, such as angry, threatening, or defamatory declarations of a nature calculated to provoke a personal assault. He who provokes an assault is, in a certain sense, the author of its consequences, and the law affirms this proposition in a limited sense when it allows the particular measure of general damages to be affected by circumstances of provocation. On the other hand, the undefinable class of aggravating circumstances that may attend a personal assault is also admitted into the consideration of damages as possible means of swelling the sum of general damage. The idea of provocation may be referred to the general principle, that the product of one's own act can not be ascribed to the wrongful act of another, and the idea of aggravation to that of an injury to the feelings. The first of these two propositions will be next considered. It is a principle of the law that, when a wrong is in part the product of the improper action of the party complaining of injury therefrom, it will either rectify the impaired obligation on both sides or refuse relief when that can not be done. In actions for personal wrongs, the law invariably refuses redress when the injury is produced wholly or in part by the misconduct of the complaining party, yet that principle does not extend so far as to prevent discrimination among the consequences of an act of wrong, in order to separate those that have their origin in the conduct of the aggrieved party from those that are alone due to the conduct of the aggressor. A civil wrong, considered apart from its consequences, is, when it springs out of a general obligation alone, an indivisible thing, while the consequences of a wrong are in their nature divisible. When the wrong itself is a composition of the wrongful action of both parties, that nature affects each incident of its consequences, and therefore no discrimination can be made that would place some of such consequences to the account of one of the parties and some to the other. Where an act of wrong, entailing injury to the person, is capable of being ascribed wholly to the conduct of the aggressor, but its consequences are affected by the action of the aggrieved party in such manner that the injurious consequences are enhanced beyond what would have naturally arisen from the action of the aggressor, the application of this principle needs no illustration. It is where an act like that of provocation, having merely a moral relation as cause to the wrong, is involved, that the application of the rule is not so readily apparent and needs discussion. Provocation may be an act committed previously to the commission of an assault morally inducing it, or it may be an act committed during the assault, affecting only the extent of the injurious consequences. The law does not regard any degree of provocation by means of language as a justification for an assault, for, if it did, then an assault would assume the character of an act of justice of a punitive nature, which it can not have consistently with the common obligations, as already expounded. It follows that one provoking an assault, by acts not amounting in themselves to an assault, so as to justify self-defense, can not be regarded as having produced the consequent assault in a legal sense, and therefore is not regarded by the law as the author of the civil injury resulting therefrom, so as to be incapable of claiming redress; but it will appear, on examination, that he is the author, in a certain sense, of the active condition of at least one of the forces upon which the extent of injury depends. Anger is presumably implicated in a personal assault. In the nature of things, it must be present in an aggressive assault. Theoretically, it may or may not be present in the exercise of the power of self-defense, but, practically, it is always present in some degree. Anger is the brute form of the energy excited by injustice as well as by fear, and exists in man as a brutal tendency, evidently a consequence of the origin of his animal powers. One of the primary objects of society is to suppress this brutal instinct in its primitive form, and replace its lower functions by means consonant with the higher nature of man. The obligation to good faith covers the idea of mutual assistance among men to render unnecessary a resort to brutal revenges. If an obligation of mutual assistance in this respect is not entitled to be enumerated among obligations of a civil character, it is certainly within the spirit of the civil obligations that are the foundation of civil law, and must produce some effect upon the principles of the law. If, then, anger is to be regarded as a brutal tendency in the composite nature of man, that requires all the stress of civil institutions to keep in subjection to higher principles, he who unchains this brutal destroyer has more than a moral responsibility for such conduct, and is at least bound to bear so much of the consequences of such an act as flow from its natural tendencies. It is manifest that the rules of law bear this interpretation, and that the principle of justice must lead to such discriminations. Provocation intended to excite a feeling of brute revenge is thus a wrong against social good faith and the principles of justice, and should not be compensated in its consequences by that justice.

If one uses means adequate to induce, and does, in fact, induce another to commit an assault upon a third party, he is accessory to the assault, and implicated in its consequences. If a person induces an assault upon himself by direct means, as may be done by conceivable means, such as by falsely personating another, evidently the wrong may be his own act, of which he can not allege injury. Provocation can not properly be regarded as a case of direct inducement, but it is manifestly such in an indirect sense. It is not a direct cause of the assault, for the law, on moral grounds, will not connect together the act of provocation and the consequent assault as having the proper relation to each other of cause and effect; but there is no such rule to prevent the consequences flowing from the assault from standing to the provocation in their natural relation of cause and effect resulting from the natural tendency of anger. It is consistent with the nature of indirect cause that it should not appear as cause in an act, and yet appear in that character in the consequences arising from such act. If, then, we suppose that a person has used means of an unlawful character morally certain to produce an assault upon himself, the injurious consequences flowing from such means may be ascribed to the one employing them; in dealing with the social force of anger, he is in like condition with one who has wrongfully liberated any destructive natural force, which, in entailing injurious consequences upon another, would render him responsible for such consequences, and which, if the cause of injury to himself, would stand as the consequence of his own act, though another should stand as the instrument through which such injury was inflicted. The result of this conclusion would be that, while an assault provoked by the means just stated would still be a wrong in legal estimation, and, as such, capable of compensation, the injury inflicted might be wholly due to the fact of provocation, and thus not enter into such compensation, leaving it merely nominal.

As damage consists in part of injury to the feelings and to the character, it is manifest that the direct effect of provocation would be to exclude damage of that nature from computation. The mode in which provocation tends to reduce the amount of compensation for physical injuries, when not actually canceling all right to compensations of that class, is of too complex a nature to be considered in a general view of the principles involved in provocation.

It is clear, then, that the principle that one shall not lay the burden of his own wrong or unfortunate conduct upon another has a particular application to the case of consequences of wrong to the person caused or enhanced by provocation.

Aggravation may result from the character of the means of assault, the ends in view or the circumstances attending it, as evincing a brutal disposition or a desire to degrade the subject of the assault. Aggravation may exist as the consequence of anger, or of the broader destructive instincts of which anger is a specialized form. Brutal desire to destroy life, property, or reputation may prompt malignity, that personal or revengeful quality that distinguishes anger when springing from personal hatred, envy, or fear. The idea of aggravation is a direct consequence of the nature of the rights of persons depending on the fact that an injury to character or feeling is one of the means of violating the obligations that secure those rights. It might be assumed from this, at first view, that the idea of aggravation is that of punitive remedy; but, so long as the possibility of an injury to the sense of manhood, and to the sensibilities that compose the positive right of enjoyment, is admitted, no necessity exists for looking beyond the principles stated for the explanation of the rules of law relative to aggravation in such cases. That the enhancement of compensatory damages under the influence of aggravation has incidentally some of the effect proper to punitive remedies, may be conceded, but that is not equivalent to saying that its foundation is in the punitive principle.

It must be admitted that the language applied by the law to cases of aggravated damage admits of the idea that the intention of such damage is punitive, but it is not necessary to conclude therefrom that it is such in a full sense. The general policy of the law, at this day, is to affix legal limits to the measure of punishment, although in some instances it leaves such measure to the discretion of the courts. To suppose that that which is intended purely as punishment should be left to the discretion of a jury, which must be concluded if the aggravation of damage is a punitive measure merely, is to carry the office of the jury far beyond the principles which govern it in all other cases. If the quantity of damages in any case can be increased on purely punitive principles by the act of a jury, then it is possible for a jury to estimate the amount of pecuniary forfeiture which would serve to deter the future commission of such wrongs, and to award that amount to an aggrieved party in excess of what they believe to be the full compensation for his injuries and deprivations of all kinds. This would certainly amount to confusing together the ideas of public justice and private redress, but would be attended by a still more objectionable feature. As punishment is intended for the protection of the community, and the power of remitting penalties properly accompanies that of imposing them, the community should always be possessed of that power; but if the aggravation of damages is punishment, then the community can not remit such punishment without trespassing on the proprietary right of the party to whom they are awarded; thus the power of imposing penalties has become separated from that of remitting them, contrary to both the principle and practice of administering justice. The only way of escape from this conclusion is to hold that private redress may be extended to pure punishment. This is certainly against the principles of the law in all other cases, and that practice rests, beyond doubt, on principles that are fundamental to justice.

It is easier to find ground for qualifying general language, such as that used by the law in regard to punitive tendencies in the aggravation of damages, than to state an exception to fundamental rules where no ground appears for supporting such an exception. It is the necessity that arises out of the practical administration of the law, and not theoretical accuracy of statement, that compels the conclusion that the language of the law in such cases is satisfied with the idea of the adoption of a liberal measure of damages, having incidentally the effect of deterring persons from inflicting aggravated injuries upon others, in which a larger measure of attention is given to effects upon feeling and character than is appropriate in cases destitute of aggravating circumstances.

A study of the various elements that are recognized as possible grounds of damage in actions of assault and battery will disclose a large number of recognized rights, leading to the conclusion that every power possessed by man as an animal, intellectual, and social being, is the object of civil protection, and has recognition as a right for that purpose. It will lead to useless prolixity to examine into these elements in detail, it being sufficient for the present purpose to generalize them.

Loss of limb is a loss to the system of organs that compose the body, and, therefore, is a loss of health in a general sense. In addition to this, it is a loss of power to perform those various functions that tend to the conservation of the body and the development of its useful energies, and thus, under all its aspects, must be regarded as a loss of convenience, and, according to the importance of such organs, in a vital or active sense, may be equivalent to an entire destruction of the power of self-preservation, self-exertion, and self-gratification; and, as these powers are fortified by rights, it is capable of being a wrong to each of these rights. Such an assault may be a wrong to the rights based upon the mental powers of volition, judgment, and sensibility.

This group of general mental functions will be more particularly noticed in another place; but, that which concerns the present stage of this investigation is, to know whether these mental functions and the powers implied in their existence have distinct legal recognition under the conception of civil rights. That such is the case is manifest from the fact that the damages awarded in actions for personal injuries, and especially in actions of assault and battery, are allowed to compensate injuries done to either of these functions. Sensibility, through which communication is established by man with objects exterior to himself, is certainly a proper object of civil protection. Pleasure and pain; as conditions of the functions of sensibility, are motives of immense force in determining the conduct of mankind, that can not be disregarded by any system that seeks to regulate the conduct of mankind. As the possibility of orderly society depends largely upon the repression of those disorders that arise from emotional causes, and as emotional disorders are largely due to the influence of pleasure and pain on the human mind, it is a matter that concerns the interests of civil society that such conduct as tends to arouse the destructive tendencies in the mind of man, by controlling his states of sensibility, should be subjected to controlling influence. As the conduct of others is capable of producing such results, that conduct must, in a civil sense, have recognition as either conformable to the welfare of society or otherwise, and out of such recognition springs the idea of obligation and its correlative right. Hence it is that, as a result of the protective principle, the law considers the production of pain, either physical or mental, by an unlawful interference with another, as a wrong done to the power and right of sensibility, and considers the state of the sensibilities in estimating compensation therefor. The relation between pecuniary compensation and pain is not logically a consequence of their nature, but is established by the common habit of mankind upon a policy based on utility. Money being the object of most general value, as capable of being exchanged for all objects and conditions that can be procured from another, the policy of pecuniary compensation is to place in the hands of the injured party this general means of obtaining such specific compensations as may suit his desires.

The reasons that have just been assigned for the interference of the law between man and man where only matters of feeling are concerned, and possibly in cases that spring from mere differences of taste, have been drawn from the ideas connected with the protective principle in its special relation to the conservation of the interests of society. Such reasoning is sufficient in itself to satisfy the ideas of paternal government, but the conception of balanced government demands that the idea of such interference should be reconciled with the principle of equal individual right, the liberalizing principle of government.

Viewing the matter in this aspect, it will be made clear that the protection of the sensibilities is equally demanded by the condition of the individual as by that of the community. Freedom of volition is the essential condition of that capacity of self-exertion through which alone the liberty of the individual can be achieved and maintained. The relation of sensibility to volition is such that the power of control over the former implies domination over the latter. The liberty of the individual can only begin to be effective when the conduct of those surrounding man has assumed conditions approaching to an orderly state, for, until then, the motives of pleasure and pain are largely in the control of others, and, the conditions of sensibility being dominated by external influences, volition is imperfect. It is the province of society, and, in a peculiar sense, of government, as the organ of society, to produce such balanced external conditions as render individual volition possible. It is, therefore, as much the interest of the individual as of the community that sensibility should receive direct recognition and protection; and, where the protective principle inspires proper public action for this purpose, it is equally subservient to the individual right as to the common interest, and satisfies the idea of balanced government.

An assault may be the means of restraining the liberty of action incident to the right of self-exertion, or to impair the functions that the organs of the body ought to perform to the mind, thus impairing the mental functions themselves, or it may be exercised to compel the assumption of an obligation, as in certain cases of duress.

An assault may cover an invasion of the liberty of speech or opinion, and thus interfere with the power of determining the relative strength of motives, which is here termed the power of judgment, and is a special form of the power of volition. The faculty of judgment is the link between the intellectual and the emotional powers in their relation to volition, and is recognized and protected as a right, as will fully appear in a different connection.

The incidents of an assault, as affecting the power of sensibility, may produce mortification, humiliation, and the deeper sense of degradation. It may also involve injury to character. The very fact of participating in a brawl may, through uncertain knowledge as to its causes and circumstances, lead to the common opinion that one, entirely innocent in his participation, is either a bad character, or the associate of such characters, and this may entail an injury to the personal estimation in which he is held by the community, and may affect his business credit and power of intercourse with those whose society he might prefer. As reputation is one of the subjects of inquiry in examining charges of crime, it may affect his civil standing by impairing his right to the presumptions in favor of rectitude and innocence. So an assault may be an injury to the pursuits of industry and enjoyment in the sense of diminishing one's capacity to pursue these objects. It may be an injury to the proprietary rights, either directly, as where the assault is made to divest one of his property, or indirectly, by occasioning loss of labor and expense in curing personal injuries received. So, finally, it may, directly or indirectly, prevent the exercise of protective care on those committed to one's protection, and the performance of other relative duties.

From the foregoing, it is apparent that the question of damage, in the case of a personal assault, may embrace injury to every possible original right, and obviously to every power delegated to the aggrieved party, whether of a public or private nature. Thus, while the right to redress rests on the simple fact of an assault, the redress of right may lead to the appreciation of every right that in civil society is capable of being enjoyed.

It must be apparent, from what has gone before, that those forms of rights upon which actions at law are based are not simple, indivisible rights, but generalized rights, made up of many inferior classes. The elements that make up such larger forms of civil rights are not indefinite, but consist of defined rights to which obligations are framed. To confine a classification of civil rights to those generalized forms which, while they are the simplest and primitive form of the idea of rights, are in their composition complex in the highest degree, is to overlook element and give undue weight to form. A scientific development of the law must appreciate the elemental conceptions of rights and obligations, for there is nothing else to which the scientific idea can attach. Considering society as an organic whole, every individual function, as well as every public function, must be regarded as taking part in the complex action of the whole. Each individual act, whether important or unimportant in its relation to its direct consequences, is an element of the composite action, and is, as it regards relative right, either a right or a wrong, in a civil sense. Law is an imperative mode of functional action, that can not, consistently with its principles, be made to stamp upon its subject incapacity for all except certain prescribed actions. A conception of the law that could thus make it a limit of the individual in all directions, and thus produce an artificial uniformity, would have nothing in common with the law of nature, and no applicability to man's needs. The limit that human law properly imposes to liberty of conduct is that which renders possible to the individual the largest liberty consistent with the common good, and that liberty can only be afforded by that measure of protection to the individual that will enable him to exercise all the powers within his legal liberty of action. This implies an office, on the part of the law, that extends to every act capable of being performed by an individual, and, consequently, the applicability of a conception of right and wrong to all possible actions. As the vindication of individual right is generally accomplished through a pecuniary compensation, the relative value of every right is assumed to be capable of ascertainment by relation to a common standard of value. It would, therefore, necessarily follow that there must be, within the means afforded by the law, some mode of stating the nature and incidents of all possible rights. The examination of the law of damages affords these means, as has been seen, from the fact that elemental rights appear there as parts of general rights under the compensations by which they are balanced. While under our jury system the actual conversion of personal rights into a money equivalent is accomplished by means that do not admit of analysis, yet the thing converted must be assumed to be capable of some degree of legal definition.

CHAPTER XXVII.

INJURIES TO THE PERSON BY FORCE OTHER THAN IN PERSONAL ENCOUNTER.

THE next subject is that of the violations of the rights of person, consisting in the application of injurious force to the body or its organs, tending to injure them, or to impair their functions, constituting the legal idea of wrong to the person other than by an assault and battery. The essential features of such a wrong are the application to the body, or to some part of it, of physical force, capable, in the mode in which it is applied, of injuriously affecting the corporal powers, the fact that such application of injurious force is the act, or directly produced by the act, of another, and the actual occurrence of some degree of corporal injury.

The agency of man over the forces of nature consists in the development and direction of force. Independent of the action of animate beings, the various forms of matter, in which potential force or energy exists, stand in more or less unstable relations to each other; every change in such relations, and in the relations that exist among the parts composing any single substance or object, is attended by the activity of some form of force. Such changes are constantly produced as a consequence of the principle on which all physical development depends. An additional cause of change lies in the volitions of animate beings, who are capable of setting up states of motion among the parts of their bodies that tend to propagate themselves in the form of changes in the mutual relations of bodies external to the body. The motions thus set up in the animal body are capable of receiving from the volitions a certain direction or mode of action that, through the harmony that exists between the general laws of nature and the particular laws affecting animal organism, may be imparted to the action of forces external to the body, or liberated through actions commenced within the body. It is in this sense that man is the cause of those consequences that flow from the determinations of his volition, and are yet effected by agencies external to his body. When a form of force of a certain quantity and intensity presents itself to an organ or other mechanism, incapable of harmonizing with the proper action of such organ or mechanism, its tendency is to derange the parts of which such organ or mechanism is composed, and it is termed a destructive force. Man may apply destructive force to the person of another, either directly or indirectly, intentionally or unintentionally. In a physical sense, a direct consequence is the product of a force when it undergoes no specific change of form prior to the contact that produces such consequence. A ball glanced by contact with an object, its force undergoes no specific change of form; it is a mere change of direction, and the form of the force, both before and after the change of direction, is identical. When the ball strikes an elastic body and rebounds, its motion in rebounding is due to a specific change in the form of the force with which it was originally impelled. Striking the elastic body, its momentum is expended in changing the relations of the parts of the body struck to each other, and the elastic force that caused the rebound was that characteristic form of force that makes such body an elastic body—namely, the force by which its parts, when deranged, seek to move back into their proper relations to each other. But if the ball strikes and dislodges a rock, that falls by gravity alone, an entirely new force is brought into action, although the force of the ball was the cause of the change in the conditions liberating the force of gravity. The important difference between the two cases is, that in the case of rebound, although the force is changed in form, its law of direction is still impressed upon it after the change, so that the direction of the rebound is in part governed by the direction imparted by the original flight, while in the latter case the direction of the falling rock may be wholly influenced by the law of gravity. But if the rock struck was capable of being moved while falling by the momentum of the ball in the direction in which the latter was moving, the resulting motion is the product of two independent causes; and to the extent that it moves in the direction of the flight of the ball, the force, both before and after the contact, is identical, though transferred from one object to another, while the operation of gravity is to be ascribed to the conditions produced by the original force. Where a force, originated in one specific form, passes into another specific form before producing a certain result, such result is a consequence of the original form of force, but an indirect consequence. That which produces conditions controlling future consequences is a cause of such consequences in the general sense attributed to the word cause, in common use, as has been shown in another place. We say that the wind caused the destruction of the house by fire. In a physical sense, wind is incapable of producing that effect; but oxygen, one of the constituents of air, which, when in motion from natural causes, is called wind, when supplied to the carbon and hydrogen, elements that entered into the composition of the house, under the condition of a certain temperature, converted the carbon into a gas with the consequence of causing a complete separation between the volatile and non-volatile elements, which caused it to disappear as a house. The difference between cause in a physical sense and, according to the sense of the term, as applied in common use, is apparent from this illustration. An attempt will be made to reach, more accurately, the legal idea of cause, as applied to the production of physical consequences by means of causes acting from volition, after some comment upon the nature of the obligations that govern the mode of using one's own property and forbid the abuse of the property of another.

The rule of law, as has been stated, is that, when a particular use of a right has a natural tendency to produce injury to the person or property of another, one who uses such right in that particular manner must, under the obligation to good faith, exercise care, skill, and diligence in such use, so as to prevent unnecessary injury to such other. The two cases to be examined in this connection are, where a man, in using his own right, incidentally impairs the right of person or property of another, and where such injury flows from an attempt to abuse the right of another. The rule cited applies directly to the first of these cases, and the more general obligation to respect the rights of others covers the latter of the two. The inquiry under the rule governing the use of one's own property is here confined to the case of injuries to the person, but is necessarily noticed in its more general scope.

Where one performs an act the apparent or direct tendency of which is to injure the person of another, and such injury occurs as the result of such act, he must be regarded as abusing the right of another rather than as using his own right. A man has a right to walk directly in a public way, but if he thrusts another out of the way in order that he may continue in a certain direction, he is regarded as abusing the right of the other, rather than as exercising his own. One has the right to shut the door of his house, but, if he sees another standing in such a position that the shutting of the door will cause him personal injury, and he uses force in shutting the door that causes injury to such person, he is in like manner regarded as abusing the right of person of another, rather than as exercising his own proprietary right. In the application of this rule it is material to notice the force of the word apparent in its statement. The apparent tendency of an act is that tendency which is capable of being observed from the stand-point of the actor. Every man is presumed to know the general nature of the forces he intentionally employs, as the agents of his will, and the ordinary consequences following their use, under the conditions capable, practically, of being observed by him. These presumptions arise out of the principles of the rule governing the use of one's rights. Employing an agency tending to the hurt of another, without knowledge of its ordinary attributes, is an instance of negligence; so it is another instance of negligence not to observe the apparent conditions that may attend an act tending to the detriment of others. As the direct means of proving the state of one's knowledge are imperfect, the law frames presumptions on the principles of the rule in question, ascribing knowledge where, according to common habit, it generally exists, and where its absence implies a wrong. Another idea is contained in the word apparent. A party receiving injury from force originating with another may sustain a purely accidental relation to such force, as where his body, by his own act, intervenes in the path of the force after it has passed beyond the control of its author. In such case the injury received might not have been an apparent consequence of the act that caused the injury, and the actor, if innocent of wrongful intention, must be regarded as in the exercise of his own right, and not in the abuse of that of the other; consequently his liability or immunity depends on the presence or absence of negligence. In the case last mentioned the direction of the force may, in a physical sense, be the cause of the injury that followed his act, but in a legal sense he may not be the author of any legal injury. As circumstances, accidental in their relation to the state of things apparent at the stand-point of the author of the force, may change the direction of the force and produce injury as the result wholly of such accidental change of circumstances, where the consequences were not to be anticipated from what was apparent at the position occupied by the physical cause of the injury, its author may be regarded as using his own right, and not as abusing that of another, and thus liable for the injuries only on the ground of negligence.

There is still another way in which accident may intervene to prevent one, who by direct force injures another, from standing in the position of one abusing the right of another, rather than that of using his own right. A misdirection may be given to force exerted by one in the exercise of his own right, due entirely to accidental causes, and producing personal injuries. It is obvious that liability for such injury must proceed on the ground of negligence alone, as no intention to injure another can be ascribed to the circumstances, and such injury was not the direct or probable consequence of the act that such person was consciously performing.

Having eliminated, from the discussion of this subject, the complex case of one who, though in form is merely using his own right, is in substance, and upon the principles of the law, regarded as abusing that of another, there remains for consideration the two distinct classes of cases that involve intentional injury on the one hand and negligence on the other. In other words, as related to the fundamental principles, they involve distinct cases, on the one hand of the abuse of the right of others, and on the other misuse of one's own right, as distinct from each other.

It becomes important to fix, as nearly as possible, the legal idea of cause and effect as existing between an act wrongfully performed and certain physical consequences of an injurious character attributable to such act. In the present state of legal development this can only be accomplished approximately. Advance does not appear to have been made in developing the principles that underlie this subject at all proportionate to the advance made in the development of proprietary rights. Instances of this class are seldom placed in a position for exhaustive judicial examination. They are placed by the law peculiarly within the province of a jury. Judges seldom employ any but very general propositions in instructing juries as to the means of connecting a wrong with the various physical consequences flowing from it. These propositions have become, in process of time, molded into technical forms that appear to be simple and decisive, but are in reality complex.

It is presumable that juries, in dealing with such questions, draw a distinction between that which happens in the usual course of events and what happens out of that course, for the operations of the mind necessitate such distinctions. It is agreeable to the common sense of mankind to hold one responsible for what, in the natural course of events, happens as the result of his actions. That is the way in which men in general act and think, and it is presumable that they do not change that habit when acting as jurors, especially when, in the mode in which they are instructed, they find no attempt on the part of the law to change that habit. It is also presumable that, if the legal idea in this respect differed from the popular idea, such fact would appear in the instruction given to juries. There are other grounds for thinking that this is the idea of the law. It is beyond doubt that the legal idea of cause does not correspond to the physical idea, but is much more comprehensive. If one negligently lays an obstruction in a public way, and another, without negligence, stumbles upon it and is injured, no physical idea of cause and effect can connect together the action in placing the obstruction and the injury occasioned by it; and yet the legal idea, as well as the common idea of cause, as applied to conduct, embraces such a case. Those trains of events that fall under judicial examination are usually either set in operation as a consequence of volition, or modified in their course by such cause, or are affected by both of these considerations. The question of what is likely to happen in a given case resolves itself into two questions—namely, what would take place if the laws of physical nature wholly controlled results, and what if man's volitions were a factor. Habit is law in a general sense, and a source from which law in its particular sense is derived. Every train of events in which the conduct of man participates has two distinct elements—the physical law of nature, and the habit of man as a social being. The physical value of volition consists in its ability to correlate physical causes so as to produce definite results by their co-operation. This is accomplished in one sense by every machine which is a composition of forces acting simultaneously or successively to produce a definite result, and in another sense in organizing those trains of events that constitute the greatest mechanism that man uses for the accomplishment of his purposes. In the construction of a machine, certainty as to what will take place at every stage of a train of movements that constitute the proper action of the machine is attainable. In sailing a ship, forces uncertain in their tendencies have to be anticipated, and probability takes the place that certainty occupies in the case of the machine. In organizing a train of events involving the conduct of men, probability as to their action in given cases is an essential feature. From the nature of society, man is under an obligation, largely imperfect, to act so that his action can be interpreted and harmonized with the action of those around him. Without such a state of things society is impossible, and the incoherence and disorder that pervade the conduct of the insane would be the condition of such society. From this root of general and imperfect duty springs the presumption that every man will act according to the ordinary habit of acting in such cases, and on this principle his purposes and motives are constantly inferred. On the same principle, the presumption arises that the conduct of man is based on the probabilities that that which appears in the ordinary course of physical nature will happen in any given case. This view enables an exposition to be made of what is meant by the expression *natural tendency* as used in the statement of the rule as to the use of one's own property. As applied to physical causes, apart from the volitions of man, it is that sequence of events that, according to the experience of man, usually takes place in the succession of natural phenomena; as applied to affairs or events influenced by human volition, it has reference to what usually occurs under social habits of mankind. The illustration of this principle is much simpler than its application. If a man poisons the water of a stream or pond, he must be deemed to have acted in view of the common habit of drinking from that water. If he poisons it in a way that destroys fish, and renders them dangerous as food, he must be regarded as having acted in view of the habit of taking such fish for food. So the habits of the people in populous communities are distinguished from those in sparsely inhabited regions as within the presumed intent of an act, the tendency of which would be dangerous in one place and harmless in another.

As the present discussion aims rather at outlining the principles of the law than attaining the results of a complete induction from all the materials furnished by the law for the purpose, it is not consistent with its purpose to trace the various applications of the principles that have been stated, or, indeed, to verify, in the most accurate manner possible, the positions assumed. It is necessary, therefore, to leave much unsaid that would tend to make the positions assumed appear free from uncertainty.

Assuming, then, that every man is presumed to know the order in which the general phenomena of nature ordinarily occur, and the general habit of mankind, and that he must be regarded as contemplating in his action those consequences that were to be anticipated, either as certain or probable, according to such knowledge, it would follow, as a correlative truth, that he must not be regarded as contemplating that which, according to the habit of nature and man, is not possible or likely to occur. In determining what is likely to occur in any given case, the principle of the law of probabilities, as applied to what may happen to any particular individual, has no application. The probability that a particular person in a populous community will be in a particular part of a highway at any given moment of time, when ascertained independently of the purposes or habits of such person, is, numerically considered, very small; but that some one of that numerous population will at certain times be in such highway, may be a reasonable certainty. An act that is wrongful in its nature, as likely to produce injury to others, may produce injury only once in every hundred times that it is performed without changing its nature. As the essence of the wrong in such cases is the contravention of common habit, the true question is, Was the act inconsistent with the habit of the community in such a way that injury from it might be brought about by the very exercise of that habit? If, then, an act is wrongful in its initiation, or through negligence in its exercise, what are to be regarded as its proper consequences is determinable on the principle of assuming the person performing it to have intended that which constitutes its tendency, through the operation of nature and the habit of man, and as either having intended or disregarded such consequences. So far, the cases of an intentional and of a negligent act of wrong are assimilated, but it is possible to conceive a case that would illustrate a difference, calling for a particular principle in the one case that would not extend to the other.

If one intending injury to another fires a ball against a rock that overhangs another, and, as a consequence of such act, a portion of the rock becomes detached, and, falling by the force of gravity, inflicts injury, although such a result is, under ordinary circumstances, improbable to follow the act performed, yet as the event showed that circumstances existed that rendered it a possible consequence, and as the case supposed is that of an intentional injury, it is obvious that the one who desired to produce a certain end, and selected such means for accomplishing it, must be presumed to have known the existence of such unusual circumstances. Such an inference is necessary to connect the intention to do injury, which in the proposition is assumed, for illustrative purposes, with the means employed to accomplish that intended, so that the whole act would appear to be a rational one—that is to say, that the act should be conformable to the habit of action of the mind of man. It is, therefore, inferable that the consequences attributed to an act of wrong of an intentional character may be so enlarged as to embrace consequences which would ordinarily be assumed as the intervention of mere accident, where the nature of that conduct is such that knowledge of the circumstances rendering such a consequence certain is possible can be presumed, such a presumption being ultimately based upon the general habit of the mind's action.

The effect of intention upon an act is to make it possible that one controlling a certain physical force may be made responsible, as legal cause, for effects produced by an entirely distinct physical cause capable of dominating its own consequences, where the conditions of the action of the second cause are supplied by the operation of the first, and this is the case, although such relation between the two causes is not suggested by anything that occurs in the ordinary course of events. In inquiring for the legal cause of a particular effect, the question is, whether the physical cause that produced it was within the intention to produce such effect, either as general or particular means of accomplishing it, and whether there is a possible actual connection between the responsible act performed and the physical cause that produced the injury. It is the intention that here connects the two causes, just as in the absence of intention they are to be connected by some habit of nature or society. An act performed with the intention of establishing conditions under which a destructive force may be possibly set in motion fulfills the idea of the legal authorship of such destructive force, where injurious consequences actually follow. The case is resolved simply to that of producing the conditions that determine the action of a constant force in a destructive form, not accidentally, but with intention, using for that purpose an intermediate agency, the instrument, in such cases, being the means of connecting the author of the means with the consequences produced through its use. This conception of the effect of intention on consequences serves to distinguish cases where it is an element from those of negligence and unintentional injury, as will still more clearly appear in the course of this investigation.

It remains to examine more critically the nature of an act to which negligence is imputed, considered as an act of force inflicting injuries upon the person. The term negligence describes wrongs to the right to demand of others prudent care in the exercise of their rights, under certain conditions. As the law expresses it, negligence consists in the absence of due care, skill, and diligence; but the distinction between care and diligence, where care is taken in the sense of carefulness, can not lead to any important analytic result, and the simple expression *care* and *skill* may be used with better convenience without reference to diligence. Where the law predicates negligence of an act, it must be assumed that it is in its general nature lawful, but that its illegal quality lies in some element of its exercise which, with the due exercise of care and skill, would have been omitted or changed. In the language of the law, negligence is habitually spoken of as the cause of injurious consequences, and, therefore, as a positive instead of a negative wrong. In this sense negligence is a doing without care and skill in some degree where demanded by some obligation. Negligence may exist relatively to some special obligation, as in the case of the duty of a servant or artisan; but it is as demanded by the common obligations, as an incident attached to all rights of a certain nature and tendency, that the present stage of this discussion is concerned. According to the definition that has been given of the common obligations, the duty of using care and skill in the use of one's own rights is dependent on the tendency of those rights in their general nature, or in some particular use or mode of use, to cause injuries to the rights of others, that view being confined, at present, to the right of personal security from injurious force.

As it regards the class of rights under immediate consideration—namely, those that concern the preservation of the bodily powers from dangerous force—it is apparent that the obligation attaches to every right which, in any of the modes of its exercise, would involve the use of physical force that might become dangerous. That natural tendency to the injury of others, that brings the obligation to prudent care into activity, may reside in the nature of the actions appropriate to such right, or in the circumstances by which some particular act is surrounded. Reference has already been made to what is meant by a natural tendency, as embracing not only the direct consequences appropriate to the nature of an act, but to which it may give rise in virtue of its relation to surrounding objects under the ordinary course of nature and of human conduct. With this broad definition in view, it may be assumed that every right that is held is affected by the obligation that what is done under it shall be done with care and skill, in order to prevent its exercise from becoming unnecessarily the cause of injury to the person of another; it may therefore be denominated, not only a fundamental, but a universal obligation.

It thus becomes necessary to inquire, What is implied by care and skill? and, What is the mode of graduating their degrees and the tests of their adequacy? Care contains the ideas of industry, intelligence, and prudence, while skill has relation to the proper means of exercising care in certain cases. Care, in the general sense, sometimes expresses solicitude and anxiety; but it also expresses what is contained in the more specific expression carefulness as a mode of doing, and thus approaches the legal sense of the term. Industry, in the sense indicated by its association with intelligence and prudence, implies a faithful application of the faculties and available means, under a sense of responsibility, for the accomplishment of a certain end, which, in the case under consideration, is to prevent the exercise of one's rights from becoming unnecessarily a source of injury to the person of another. Intelligence is an adequate knowledge of means and ends and their relation, while prudence contains the general idea of watchfulness and foresight. All that the law exacts of one who does not stand in a peculiar relation to the duty he has in hand is ordinary care and skill. The law defines ordinary care and skill as that which is expected of a prudent man in the conduct of his own affairs. This is a variable measure in two senses. No two individuals are likely to form the same exact conception of what is comprehended in this measure, and the standard itself changes as the condition of society changes. This rule is not only a standard of the personal attributes and exertions demanded, but of the means that are requisite. Ordinary skill is measured by the same standard as ordinary care. In inquiring what it is that must be assumed as that which a prudent man would do in a given case, distinctions of an important character arise to view. If that which is to be done in its nature demands special experience or skill, it must be assumed that a prudent man would employ such experience and skill. A difficult operation would call for an enhanced measure of care and skill, and a dangerous one a still higher. If, then, a man undertakes, by himself or his servants, to do that which, by reason of difficulty or danger, demands special skill, without that qualification, it is manifest that he is not acting as should be expected of a prudent man. It will, therefore, be observed that the requirement of ordinary care and skill means more than that acts shall be performed in order to render them innocuous to others, with the personal attention and means that are employed in the ordinary concerns of life, but accommodates itself to every degree of skill and means that good practice may call for, according to the nature of the thing to be done. The rule of ordinary care must be contrasted with that which demands extraordinary care, in order to be properly understood. Much obscurity exists as to what is implied by this distinction between the rule of ordinary and extraordinary care, and the authority of the law is by no means clear as it regards their respective definitions. The view that appears to reconcile the grounds of difference will be stated. Ordinary care and skill imply the customary means employed by prudent men; extraordinary, that of the best means known in the community. The idea of means as here used embraces both personal skill and experience and material means and aids. The consequence of this definition would be, that when ordinary prudence demanded that work should be performed by skilled labor, or under the guidance of professional skill, the neglect of such means would be a violation of the duty in question; not only would the failure in the use of the proper degree of care and skill, on the part of the employee, constitute negligence, but also the failure to exercise the degree of skill proportionate to the nature of the work, on the part of those to whom the construction or superintendence is intrusted. It is apparent that this would cover the case of the construction and operation of machinery dangerous to life and person in its use, such as locomotive-engines used at high speed, for the prudence that implies a skilled engineer to a task attended with difficulty and danger is identical with that which employs an ordinary laborer to perform mere manual labor. Prudence consists in foreseeing difficulties, and adopting means to ends, and this is all that is needed to meet the emergencies of either a simple or difficult operation. On the other hand, if a higher degree of care and skill is demanded, it must, in the nature of things, consist in the employment of means of a higher grade than those usually employed in the community. The limit in the last-mentioned case clearly must be, with reference to the best means, known in the community, for to go beyond that point would place the proper discharge of the duty beyond the power of those who are unfamiliar with the general state of scientific and industrial improvement throughout the world, for better means might be known and used in foreign countries than in the particular community, to obtain which would presuppose knowledge of the state of the arts in foreign countries.

It is reasonable and natural to look to the nature of the subject of a rule in order to find the distinctions that appertain to the rules. In what sense, then, are the ideas of good and bad predicable of care and skill? As it regards skill, it is clear that the distinction is that which lies between general and special skill. As skill consists of experience and knowledge, and as these elements exist in the two states of general and special in economic use, they are applicable to the composite idea of skill. It is equally clear that the kinds of care are properly indicated by the terms general and special. If the degrees and shades of degrees of care are to be enumerated, they, of course, are incalculable, and no exact classification can be based upon them with exhaustive effect. The general fact appears here, that differences in kind, generally of a simple and intelligible character, produce, by the interaction of one kind upon another, innumerable and complex differences in degree. The two kinds of care, the one general and the other special, are constantly recognized in the transactions of life.

General care implies the direction of attention to general results, while special attention implies, in addition to this, attention to particular results and details. The existence of general attention is implied in special attention, but the opposite is not necessarily the case. If a careful analysis of the actual determinations of the law could be made at this time, it would, beyond doubt, appear that the distinctions pointed out are fundamental to the action of the law, though not always obvious from the language used by judicial bodies.

Assuming, then, in the absence of a full induction, that can not be made at the present time, that the kinds of care and skill intended by the distinctions between ordinary and extraordinary care are such as have been pointed out, the rule in question can be readily understood in its application to cases in which the exercise of one's rights has a natural tendency to injure others. In that case the operation may be such as to be dangerous in the highest sense, and in that case the corresponding duty, as commended by common prudence, would be to employ such special means to prevent such injury as is approved by the best general practice of the community. This would include the employment of experienced and skilled labor and superintendence in proper cases, and a neglect of these precautions would be a violation of the general obligation.

Such would be the result of the application of the rule of ordinary care and skill as the test of the existence of negligence when charged under the common obligations, while in such cases as may demand extraordinary care, not only in degree, but in kind, the best means known by the best informed members of the community would be demanded rather than that approved by general acceptance.

This subject is so intimately connected with the general subject of discriminating degrees of excellence under the standards supplied by common use, that its discussion is of general importance. To make the whole subject clear, the difference between the best common standard and the best possible means must be drawn. In the one case the state of practical art in the community is the source to which attention must be paid; in the other, the state of knowledge as to the best possible means must be considered. In the development of practical skill, sometimes the practice is in advance of exact knowledge of the principles, and even of the conditions, on which that practice depends for its success, and sometimes the knowledge of what is needed to be accomplished, and the general means to be employed for that purpose, precedes any successful application of such means. In the early stages of industrial progress, historically considered, the art is apt to precede the science, but, as science advances, the dominant tendency is in the opposite direction, the conception of possibilities of invention before actual realization being common in an advanced stage of scientific knowledge, while in earlier days practical art grew up by what we call accident, or intuitive knowledge, another name for which is generalized experience.

As has been stated in another place, the first form of our practical ideas is that of generalized experience, and that is equally true of those ideas that are connected practically with the arts. This generalized experience has, relatively, more of that quality termed intuition than appears in the after stages, characterized by particular investigation and exact knowledge.

VARIABILITY OF STANDARDS. 265

What is meant by the practice of the community, as it regards any art, concerns the state of practical art, and not necessarily the state of knowledge incident to that art. A practical standard is necessarily one that has its sanction in practice, while a standard that is not the result of practical use, but is derived from the knowledge of principles and general laws, must be regarded as theoretical or experimental. It is clear that the law demands conformity to practical standards alone as the test of compliance with the common obligations, and never judges one to be negligent in the exercise of his rights, as it regards the rights of others, who conforms to the best habit of the community, even though knowledge may be obtained in the community disclosing the possibility of better means. This method of measuring conduct by common habit is the foundation of the reason of the law in its interpretations of the qualities of objects and of conduct.

But in every community there is a variable tendency in habit. It is common to find large classes of persons adopting standards of one degree of excellence, and other large classes a higher degree. If society is supposed to have any possibility of progress in its practical methods, there must be some means of developing a tendency toward the best means of attaining ends. This duality of standards exists in the same way in the individual mind, where there are classes of tendencies that draw in the direction of the inferior standard, and classes that draw in the opposite direction toward the highest standard. In the individual, ideas of legal and moral duty are implicated with the tendencies that draw in the direction of the best practice and vigorously re-enforce them. If, then, society is assimilated to the individual in this respect, as must be deductively concluded, the standards of legal duty should be found based on the best practice of the community, producing that tendency that renders progress possible.

According to the view that has just been stated, the obligation to prudent care must be regarded as calling for the best practice accepted in the community, which is that described by the law as conformable to the conduct of a prudent man, and as making no demand beyond that which is practically known in the community, as, for that which could only be supplied from theoretical knowledge or by experimental means.

While thus there are but two kinds or species of care and skill, there are many degrees that are recognized by the law. As the degrees in which difficulty and danger may present themselves are innumerable, so the different corresponding degrees of care and skill are incapable of exhaustive definition. The question of the degree of care demanded in any given case is often confused with the question of how much negligence is excusable in such a case. Negligence, when it exists, is never excusable, but it is a question what degree of inattention to some particular consequence of an act performed amounts to negligence in any particular case. The kind of care and skill demanded in a particular case is ascertained by legal standards, and is, therefore, usually termed a question of law, while the ascertainment of the degree of care demanded in a particular case necessarily depends on a variable standard involved in the habit of the community, and from this fact of variability questions of that class are regarded as questions of fact.

Negligence is, both directly and indirectly, proved and inferred. It may be proved by showing some fact of inattention, or the misapplication or neglect of means, to which damage is traceable. It may be shown indirectly by results that are inconsistent with the idea that due care and skill were used. It may be inferred from the nature of its results, but that may be repelled by circumstances showing excusable accident. From the propositions advanced in another place, that the presumptions of the law arise out of the observation of what are the natural consequences in the course of nature and the actions of men, it would follow that accidents which are departures from that customary order must be established, by those who aver their existence, by competent proofs, while in the absence of such proofs the law will assume that the customary course of events has occurred. The laws of a community are its formulated habits, and therefore sustain a close relation to those general habits that have not yet attained the uniformity and persistence that are requisite to legal formulation; it is natural, therefore, that the general habit of the community should form the premises from which legal reasonings start. This indicates the origin and nature of that class of legal presumptions that may be termed natural, in contradistinction to such as are technical and derived from a particular legal policy, such as the presumption of payment after the lapse of time.

The damage ascribed to an act of negligence must be actual damage, for although a wrong is accomplished, in a general sense, the moment that a neglect occurs threatening damage, yet that wrong can only be predicated of the right of some particular person where damaging effect has been realized. The damage must also be connected affirmatively with the act of negligence, but that connection may be established by means of proof or inference on the principles already indicated. The general principles governing the measure of damage have already been sufficiently stated.

In addition to the remedy in the nature of compensative redress, there is a preventive remedy where the act of a party threatening damage is in the nature of a common nuisance. That remedy is by equitable injunction, which may be adopted to prevent the act altogether or in a mode dangerous to that portion of the community exposed to its consequences.

The cases of injuries to the right of person that have just been considered—namely, those in which unlawful force is applied to the person, affecting life, organ, or health—are characterized by the common circumstances that the person aggrieved by the wrong must not have participated voluntarily in the acts causing such injury, but have stood as the passive recipient of consequences resulting wholly from the act of another. The aspect of this rule that is most usually presented is in cases of contributory negligence. The reason of the rule is not fully developed in the judicial treatment it has received, but is worthy of consideration. The idea of contributory negligence is that where one, claiming to have been injured through the negligent act of another, appears to have been negligent in a way that tended to occasion such injury. In such cases the law affords no redress.

It is clear that this rule does not arise from any legal inability to separate the consequences arising from a common or mutual act of two or more in such a way that the consequences due to each may be discriminated. This process is constantly performed where two or more persons unite their labor or means to attain some end to their common or mutual benefit, where no conception of wrong is present. In such cases the law will either consider, on general principles, that each has produced an equally beneficial result, or will actually discriminate the consequences according to the amount or quality of the labor or means contributed by each. In the case of damages resulting from negligence, where there is mutual participation in such negligence by both parties, no such equal division nor actual discrimination of individual effects will be made.

A definition of contributory negligence may be given that will make the reason of such rule apparent, but whether that definition has the sanction of judicial recognition may admit of differences of opinion. Conceiving that contributory negligence exists only where the nature of the negligent act imputed to the injured party is such that but for such negligence no damage would have occurred, and it is manifest that the reason of the rule is clear. In the case supposed, the whole damage is as much the consequence of the act of the injured party as it is of that of the opposite party, and it would follow that to allow compensation in such a case would be to throw the consequences of the fault or misfortune of one upon another, contrary to fundamental legal principles. The case stated may be illustrated by supposing that one has negligently placed an obstruction in a highway, and another has, through negligence, fallen upon it and received injury. In this case he who caused the obstruction is, in a general sense, the cause of all that tended to ensue from his act; but although he is chargeable with the commission of a wrong before any individual damage has arisen, so individual right to redress can only follow such individual damage. If, then, individual damage should at any time arise, it must be in virtue of some action of the injured party coming in contact with such obstruction. All persons rightfully using a highway have a right to assume that such highway is free from obstruction, and negligence can not be imputed from the mere fact of having acted on that assumption. But independently of the question of what is sufficient to constitute negligence in such a case, assuming it to exist as an actual fault of the injured party, then his negligence must stand as the cause of the particular damage received, for but for its existence such particular damage would not have occurred. So if one occupies a dangerous part of a vehicle, that is overturned or injured by the fault of the person in charge of it, and some of the passengers in their proper places are injured and some are not, the fact that such exposed person received injury is not decisive in itself that the fault of the manager of the vehicle was the cause of such injury, a fact that the party claiming compensation is bound to establish. But if the vehicle is thrown down a precipice in such a manner as to imply destruction to the passengers without regard to their position on the vehicle, then, as the damage must be regarded as the certain consequence, to each individual threatened, of the negligence of the person in charge, the position of a passenger in a dangerous part of the vehicle would not appear to have any relation or cause to the consequent damage.

A question then arises whether the definition that has just been given to contributory negligence is too narrow to explain the action of the law in such cases. A case may be stated in strong contrast to those that have just been given, illustrating the definition propounded for contributory negligence by assuming that the negligence of one has rendered certain the happening of damage to another, independently of any participating negligence, but the extent of that damage has been increased by some negligent act, performed after the damage had been in part realized, but before it was completed. Certainly there would be a right to some compensation in such a case, and yet it is manifest that whatever damage was produced as a direct consequence of the negligence of the injured party could not be compensated. This would imply two conclusions: first, that the mutual participation of negligence on both sides in the actual damage, considered as a whole, does not in itself give to that negligence that contributory character that destroys all right to compensation, and, second, that it is possible for the law to distinguish general consequences so as to attribute part to a wrong-doer and part to the negligent act of the party wronged.

If, then, it is possible for the law to separate an aggregate consisting of mixed consequences of the negligent acts of the parties, some other reason for the rule of contributory negligence, as destroying all right to compensation, must be sought than that afforded by the fact that two negligent causes enter into a common result. The only reason that can be assigned for that rule is that made clear by assuming that its proper application is to cases where the whole damage may stand in the relation of a consequence of the act of negligence on the part of the injured party.

It is necessary to notice a distinction between a particular duty of care and skill and a general duty applicable to cases at large. The general rule of care and skill has been already stated as measured by the standard prevailing according to common habit. If an obstruction is placed in a highway where no one is present at the time or place to be affected specially by such obstruction, the wrong done is measured by the habit of user of the place where it is committed; but suppose that an obstruction is placed in a part of a highway not usually traveled upon, but where it is manifest that some particular person will be injured by means of it, as where an obstruction is placed in the way of an approaching vehicle, though not in the usual traveled way, in that case the rule would not apply through the presumption arising from common habit, but as a quality of the actual relative conduct of the parties. In that case the conduct of the party placing the obstruction would be interpreted by its direct tendencies, and not through the habit of the community, thus illustrating the proper relation of the habit of the community to the common obligations as constituting the means of interpreting the conduct of individuals where the direct tendencies of such conduct do not appear independently of such interpretation, or, in other words, as defining social tendencies as distinguished from natural tendencies.

In the classes of cases already considered, the person causing the injury has been supposed to have acted either in the use of his own right, or in the abuse of that of the injured party. In order to complete a view of all the classes of cases affected by the principle of the common obligation to care and skill, it would be necessary to notice cases in which the author of wrong is acting in the right of the injured party, as in the case of injury done to one by the negligence of his servant, employed and acting in his business. This class embraces persons having a license to perform some act in the right of another, and would include persons having a license to do certain acts affecting the person or health of another which could not be lawfully performed except under such license, such as physicians, surgeons, and nurses; common carriers, who exercise a certain control over the persons of their passengers; artisans, laborers, and servants performing duties to the person directly. It also includes persons having a license to use, or operate, upon the property of another, as possibly causing danger to life or health. In the order of this work such cases will be examined under the subject of delegated powers, as peculiarly affected by the principles peculiar to delegations of power. But it may be observed that the negligence of persons standing in such special relations may constitute a breach of the common obligations, and therefore it is that one injured by the negligent act of his servant or employee can pursue the same remedy by an action of tort as a stranger, and is not bound to seek a remedy through the special obligation incident to their particular relation.

The next class of cases requiring examination is, where the distinguishing feature is, that the person aggrieved has cooperated with the wrong-doer as it regards the physical causes of the injury, though either unconsciously or in ignorance of the tendency of such act. This class is illustrated sufficiently by the case of one who eats poisoned food and receives injury therefrom. Although, in a certain sense, poison is a destructive force, and one who communicates it directly to another, to the injury of his person or health, must be regarded as, in a general sense, a wrong-doer in the application of force injurious to the person, yet, when the actual application of the cause of injury is the act of the aggrieved party himself, it is obvious that the nature of the act of wrong must receive a corresponding interpretation. This is obvious, for, if the person injured by such a cause knowingly and voluntarily applies the physical cause of injury to his own system, the wrong disappears in the character in which it is now being considered; indeed, it disappears altogether as a personal injury. It is the fact, however, that the act is voluntary and with proper knowledge that makes it the act of the injured party; for, if his act is constrained by coercion, deception, or concealment, he has no agency in the injury, but that responsibility rests upon the author of the coercion, deception, or concealment, as well as upon the person who actually controlled the physical cause of injury.

The general principle that what one does by his own act can not be ascribed to the wrong of another is constantly acted upon by the law, and results from the principles of reason itself. One of its applications is in the rule that contributory negligence on the part of one charging negligence against another destroys his right to compensation. According to the principles of contributory negligence, already discussed, one who voluntarily applies a poison furnished by another is the cause of all the consequences that follow in the natural order of events, as, but for his act, no injury could have resulted; if, then, such voluntary act was with knowledge of the probable results, either voluntary self-injury or contributory negligence must be imputed to him.

Whether the act of infusing a poisonous substance into an article of food, of such a nature that its presence can not be detected by the use of ordinary care and skill, is the result of intention or of negligence, the wrong consists in the presence of the concealed injurious quality, and, so long as the person injured thereby is not chargeable with knowledge of the presence of such injurious quality, he can not be considered as having voluntarily applied the poison to his system, although it was in fact contained in food that he did voluntarily apply.

Upon the principles stated, one is liable who either intentionally or negligently supplies to another an article having a concealed quality rendering it dangerous to person or health, in its customary use, where such person is likely to use it so as to produce injury, the question whether such injurious use is likely to occur being determinable by the common habit in such cases, or some known particular habit or intention of the individual. It is not material to such liability that such an article should be supplied for compensation. Where one undertakes to perform an act, voluntarily and without compensation, he is liable for the consequences of neglect in such performance. This proposition is the inevitable deduction from the propositions that one, in using his own rights, tending to the injury of another, must use prudent care, and that one exercising delegated powers must comply with the same conditions. A voluntary agent acts either in his own right or in that of his principal, or in both rights, and, in either case, is bound by the common obligations to prudent care, as it regards possible danger to person or property. So a person who presents to another an article of food assumes the position that would be occupied by an agent chosen to make a proper selection of food, and if, by his negligence, it contains a concealed quality, rendering it injurious, or if containing such quality, and knowing it to exist, through his negligence the other is induced to apply it with resulting injury, his liability is that of an agent failing to use due care and skill.

As it regards the nature and proper effect of such concealed quality, the wrong-doer is directly liable to one who is injured thereby, although the article may have become the property of third persons before reaching the consumer. This rule will be found embodied in cases where manufacturers of goods, selling their goods to dealers, and they again to consumers, have been held liable directly to such consumers for the injury produced by their intentional wrong or negligence in such manufacture. Upon the principles already stated in another place, the reason of this direct liability is obvious. The manufacturer must be regarded as performing the wrongful act in view of the habit of the community that consumers should purchase of dealers, and dealers of manufacturers, which gives to the original act the character of a wrong to the community prior to the happening of any individual damage, thus illustrating the principles of common nuisance. If, then, in the course of that which is to be reasonably expected as the consequence of the habit of society, such injury actually results to an individual, the legal idea of cause and effect is present, and the wrong, that was general from the moment the original act was performed, was consummated as an individual wrong by the damage done to the consumer.

So the concealed injurious quality may be the consequence of deterioration and decay, as in the case of unwholesome articles of food, rendering it dangerous to life or health, in which case the same principles apply. Again, such quality may be occasioned through negligent contact with deleterious substances, with the same effect as it regards the principles of liability.

It is obvious, upon the principles stated, that merchants and dealers generally are bound in this respect to use the kind and degree of prudent care proportioned to the nature of their business, as related to the habit of the community, with consequences, in the case of failure to do so, such as have been described. This liability must be distinguished from that specific duty that springs out of a contract of sale, being founded upon the common obligations conferring like duties on all persons in like cases. The degree of care and skill due by such persons is affected by the circumstance that their calling presupposes special means of judging of the qualities of the articles in which they deal, giving rise to a habit of confidence in that in which they deal. As this measure of care and skill is variable in its application to different classes of dealers in the same commodities, and to dealers in different classes of commodities, it is apparent that the custom of a particular branch of trade is one of the elements to be considered in ascertaining it in its effect upon such branch of trade, that custom being the habit of those dealing in that branch of the trade.

This concealed quality may be considered as consisting in the condition of a substance, as well as in its characteristic or permanent qualities, and thus may affect any article which, according to the habit of the community, is likely to be used in modes involving danger, as in drugs, dyes, clothing, paper, or the like. So it may consist in unsuitable materials or workmanship in a mechanical structure or construction, having a tendency through the common habit, or a known individual habit of use, to produce injury to the person, as in a household utensil, or carriage of dangerous construction. In cases of this character, liabilities resulting from the breach of special obligations must be distinguished from those that result from violations of the common obligations, remedies being adapted to both, so that they may be exercised in the alternative.

From the same common principle follows the liability of those who intentionally or negligently cause the infection of the atmosphere or common waters with dangerous qualities, so as to render them injurious to health in the course of the common or of some known individual habit of using them. It is obvious that, if one poisons the atmosphere in an inclosed space, and another voluntarily and knowingly enters such place, and is injured by breathing the air within it, the injury done thereby is his own act. Breathing such atmosphere might not be regarded as a voluntary act, though a possibility might exist of avoiding it, as where the infection is within one's own dwelling, which circumstances might not permit him to leave, or in some place where duty requires him to be. In such cases the relative force of opposing duties would have to be considered before the existence of intentional self-injury or negligence could be imputed.

The cases that have been enumerated embrace the principles that are applicable where, through intentional wrong or negligence, injury is caused by the communication of infectious or contagious disease. In these cases, either the atmosphere, or some substance containing the concealed injurious quality, including the body and its clothing, may be the means of injury. The discussion of these, as further instances, will not materially aid the presentation of the principles involved.

In all cases of injuries to the person, as has been seen, the wrong may operate directly against the individual, or indirectly through some common right impaired. The wrong is direct, not only where its tendency is to affect a particular individual, as apparent from the stand-point of the aggressor, but where it is indicated by some known habit of the injured party, or of the community. It can not admit of question that performing an act, lawful in itself, but that might be injurious to another occupying a certain position at the time of its performance, would become a wrongful act if performed at a time and place when, according to the known habit of some person, he should be present, so as to receive such injury, even though no habit of the community warranted the expectation that any person would be exposed to injury thereby.

It must be concluded that the common obligations to respect the rights of others and to use prudent care in the exercise of one's own rights give rise to particular duties through both the habit of the individual and that of the community. The effect of the known habit of the individual is to establish a personal relation between the parties as the basis of an individual wrong, while the habit of the community operates to bring into existence a wrong to common right, which, according to its nature, becomes an individual wrong whenever individual damage appears. The mode in which the common obligations mold themselves to the exigencies of society is thus ascribable to the influence of habit in rendering presumable certain states of fact upon which the law bases its inferences and reasonings.

The remedies, preventive and redressive, in the case of common nuisances, as appropriate to certain of the cases enumerated, have been sufficiently discussed for the present purpose, as also the remedies that the law affords under the name of actions of *tort*. The remedies that arise out of such special obligations as may be violated in such cases concurrently with the general obligations belong in another place.

CHAPTER XXVIII.

VOLITION CONSIDERED AS A RIGHT.

Thus far the rights of person have been considered with special reference to their relation to the means by which the body, its organs, and functions, may be protected, and injuries to them prevented, or redressed, other rights being noticed incidentally for the purpose of a more clear definition of the nature and incidents of those rights. These rights are now to be considered with reference to the means they afford for protecting and preserving certain functions that depend upon the nature of the mind of man, through its connection with his body. It has been observed that the rights of person are capable of being resolved into the specific rights of self-preservation, self-exertion, and self-gratification. Each of these objects, taking the form of rights, is, more or less, involved in every case of injury to the right of person. In discussing the effect of the nature of man's bodily endowment of organs and functions upon the common obligations, the right of self-preservation occupies a conspicuous place, for the reason that the preservation of the physical conditions is one of the first interests of the law, as all faculties that enter into the constitution of man depend, for their social value to him, upon the conservation of his physical powers. In entering upon the discussion of the higher faculties, the right of self-exertion will take a prominent place, as the chief one of these faculties is to direct the exertions of man as an active being.

The general faculties here brought to attention are those of volition, judgment, and sensibility. Volition, considered as the subject of legal protection, is the power of accommodating the actions of the body to the state of the mind. There is, undoubtedly, an exercise of volition that is a pure mental process; but, as this use of the faculty is only indirectly affected by external relationships, its consideration belongs to mental, rather than to social science, of which the law is a fundamental department. With that expression of volition that consists in actions performed the law is concerned through the fact that such determinations of volition may be detrimental to social interests on the one hand, or, on the other, if rightful, may be impeded by external causes of a social nature. Volition, then, in a legal sense, must stand for that stage of the entire function that affects and concerns relative conduct and duties, and hence arises the propriety of the definition that has been given to express that aspect of volition that is within the direct sphere of legal protection and repression. Although, potentially, the body may be assumed capable of taking any attitude demanded by the state of the mind, yet, actually, it is restricted within comparatively narrow limits by many agencies with a seeming loss of liberty, but, in general, with a consequent gain from the concentration of its forces induced by that fact. Not only the forces of nature, acting both externally and internally, oppose absolute freedom of action, but the conditions of the social state do not admit of it. In the midst of orderly conditions—that is, where the actions of all bodies external to himself are harmoniously constituted—the body is capable of expressing the largest measure of energy, and such expression may be actualized when the internal state of man is properly correlated with the agencies acting external to himself. This is the tendency in well-organized society. As one finds his locomotion impeded in a room where there is much furniture in a state of disorder, so in chaotic or unformed communities a corresponding impediment is opposed to his freedom of action. The liberty of the individual expresses his relation to the sphere within which his potential energy of united body and mind is capable of becoming actual. So far as that liberty is dependent on social conditions, it is recognizable in the form termed natural, civil, and legal liberty. On the principles that have already been considered, his natural liberty was surrendered to civil society upon the consideration of the enhancement of the social energy of those powers which resulted to him under the name of civil powers. That civil liberty we have now to deal with; and it is to be considered as if remaining, as to its substantial character, in the condition in which it emerged at the formation of the civil state, and from which condition it is only diminished through the exercise of sovereignty, delegated by the community or through voluntary concession.

That civil liberty is circumscribed to the measure of civil rights is apparent, for it expresses the state of civil rights. Not only is it circumscribed by the nature of such rights, but by the fundamental conditions attached to them, intended to prevent unnecessary collision with the liberty enjoyed by others under their rights, as already elsewhere exhibited. It is further circumscribed by the constantly developing habit of society formulated as common law, and in a sense that has been explained by habits that have not attained such formulated condition.

The limitations induced by the habit of society are obviously one of form rather than of substance. The common obligations represent the real difference between the measures of natural and civil liberty, for they are in effect the negation of something that was contained in natural liberty, on the ground of its inconsistency with the social status. It is the nature of the common obligations to give rise to specific duties through the operation of the habit of the community. When, then, it is said that the conception of civil liberty is circumscribed by what is contained in the common obligations, it is implied that actual or available liberty of the individual will, from time to time, undergo change as the habit of the community changes, as that habit is contemplated by such obligations as the measure of actual liberty. Thus it is that customs ripening into common law impose new conditions of form to such liberty, but do not change its substantial character, which is determined by the principles of the law embodied in the common obligations.

But, as has already been said in another place, the whole measure of such liberty, available under the principles of the law, is never realized practically in any organized community, as considerations of common interest lead to restrictions. To the civil liberty of the individual that remains after the interdictions made by public authority the name of legal liberty is here applied. As the means by which this further limitation is effected are contemplated by the common obligations, legal liberty may also be regarded as a form of civil liberty, though existing as an abnormal form where not in harmony with the principles upon which civil liberty depends.

Another source from which further limitation arises is the exercise of the power of self-obligation, by which one is bound to respect the right that he has created, and to perform or omit the acts that he has effectually engaged to perform or omit, or make the compensations that correspond to injuries caused to others by the violations of such obligations. It is the nature and the means of using and protecting that measure of liberty that is termed legal liberty, as to certain subjects, that is the immediate subject of consideration.

The volitions of the individual are expressed, within the sphere of which the law has cognizance, in actions and words, words being actions in a particular or specific sense. This subject resolves itself into the consideration of the nature and limitations of the liberty of action, speech, and choice that result from the principles of the law, and embraces liberties that are recognized rights with definite remedies attached to them, and others that are recognized in the sense that injuries done to them are allowed to form elements of the measure of damages in cases where the infractions of rights of a more general character, and accessory to them, are compensated. Thus, a personal assault may tend to prevent an individual from exercising some liberty of action, speech, or choice that the law permits. The wrong committed in such a case consists in the nature of the means employed, independently of the legal character of the ultimate object in view, but, in compensating for such act of wrong, its motive and tendency are elements of computation; and, when that motive or tendency discloses an attempt to deprive one of any portion of that liberty that the law recognizes, it allows that fact to have weight in the adjustment of damages. It is obvious that that which the law values for compensative purposes has the legal nature of a right, though it may not be defined by the adaptation to it of a characteristic remedy.

In order to have a complete self-consciousness of our powers of any class, we must be conscious of their limits, and therefore must have had the experience of having those powers resisted. The history of the efforts of government to deny or encroach upon the liberties of the individual is such a recorded consciousness. It is, accordingly, only those features of the liberty of the individual that have been drawn into discussion, by being at some time denied by states or individuals, that are in a state for complete discussion.

The fact that the liberty of the individual that we conceive necessary to be preserved, in order to carry out the purposes implied in the creation and endowment of man and society, has been at any time denied or restrained by the law, needs to be reconciled with the proposition that such liberty results from the principles of the law. To present this seeming paradox in the strongest light, what has already been said may be repeated —namely; that all that we know, in a legal sense, of the principles of the law is what we gather from its action. The case needs to be stated in still stronger terms. Our present conception of what properly constitutes the liberty of the individual is of very recent origin. The practice of government, which is the action of the law, until of late years has denied to the liberty of the individual many elements of our present conception of that liberty. If, then, the law, in the hands of despotic power, wielded by princes for self-aggrandizement, has been the convenient instrument for accomplishing such purposes, as it undoubtedly has, and the principles of the law are only disclosed by its action, how can the principles of liberty be deduced from the means of destroying liberty? If the law had its origin in a definite purpose to accomplish certain defined objects by prescribed means, it would be impossible to reconcile these apparent inconsistencies; but such is not the case. Its source is the action of mankind in their social relations, and therefore all the motives and springs of action in the human breast are fundamental to it. The action of government, as dictated by its policy, as distinguished from that of individuals and society at large, is only part of that general subject that must be studied to arrive at a knowledge of the principles of the law. If the immense volume of transactions adjusted upon the principles of the law is compared with the cases depending on the public or statutory law, it will be found that the part that the action of the law-making power takes in the action of the law is relatively small. The action of the government, to which reference is here made, is that action which springs from its policy, and excludes that which is done by governmental agencies in the general administration of justice.

As in the breast of man the principle of right lays side by side with the sources of all evil inclinations, so the same conditions would be anticipated in society, which has the nature of man, and, accordingly, in the law, which is the formulated consciousness, memory, and reason of society, as it regards liberty of action and the modes of its exercise. This is indeed the case. In the structural basis of society we find embedded together the germs of liberty and despotism.

The structure given to individual right as it emerges in the form of civil right, prior to its receiving any impress from the delegated sovereign power, that is capable of changing or subverting it, implies the existence of a certain individual liberty of action, and of limits to that liberty definable by the nature of that liberty itself. But with individual right also appears the act of absolute self-surrender to a supreme power. That power is absolute sovereignty, originating in individual right, but capable of annihilating that right. The principles of the law are certain logical consequences deduced from the condition that individual liberty and common right are assumed as the direct and necessary result of the formation of civil society. The sovereign will may modify, or even destroy, their effectiveness, but can not change their nature. These principles of individual liberty constitute and define the nature of society, while the delegated sovereignty determines in part its modes and conditions. Governmental power was created to subserve individual liberty, and stands in the relation of means to that end. Abuses of governmental power tending to the destruction of civil liberty, as it is conceived in the structural principles of society, can do no more than interfere with the effectiveness of principles, but can not change their nature. Fortunately, the mode in which the function of administering justice has been organized has tended to conserve the memory of these principles, so that, in the darkest night of despotism, their light has not been extinguished. Judicial history in all ages is illuminated by these principles.

In order to place the nature and mode of deriving legal principles in a simple light, an illustration may be useful. A question of individual right is presented to a judicial body. The first question is, whether its solution can be effected by means of the positive enactments of the law-making power. Statutes, modern and ancient, are examined to find the means of such solution. Where these statutes are extant, their text is consulted; where they are only known by their recorded consequences on certain rights, these consequences are examined to find evidence that the solution has been given by the law-making power. If this source fails to afford the solution, it is then sought for in the principles of the law. These principles exist only in an embodied form, as involved in the action of the judicial authority in like or analogous cases. They are reached inductively from these sources by a process that begins with the phenomena and ends with the causes of such phenomena. If, on the other hand, the process was a deductive one, it would commence with an attempt to form a conception of the nature and structure of rights in their simplest form, and thence would be made the required deduction. Such a conception must be either an actual or an ideal one. For lack of historic materials, if for no other reason, an actual conception can not be formed. An ideal conception may be true to the state of mind of the person conceiving it, but can not by any possibility be accurately true to the state of any other mind, and, therefore, can not be true as a social conception, that is, a complex of individual minds. There is but one legal conception possible, and that is disclosed by the past and present action of the law, and is attained inductively. That the law must form or involve a conception of rights in their simplest form, in order to reason up to their principles, is demanded by the nature of reason itself. To call this conception the primitive form of individual right is to use the word primitive in its proper sense, as distinguished from the actual in an historic sense. In the search for legal principles, what the law is looking for is, that state of things that arises out of the state of society unaffected by its particular modes and conditions—that is to say, for the immediate consequences of that state of obligations that constitutes society. To say that the law conceives a state of rights as the direct result of the existence of the social state, anterior to any exercise of sovereign power, is simply clothing the same idea in a form that, without diminishing or obscuring its truth, adapts it to be used as a feature in legal discussion. From the foregoing, it is easy to see that individual liberty was potentially present in the very structure of society and law, from their civil inception, although not actual until a late period in the history of government.

Having found the principles of liberty existent in the first form assumed by civil society, it is not difficult to understand the causes that tended to deny development to this principle. The creation of sovereign power implies the possibility of such a tendency. The historical fact that sovereignty invariably is made subservient to dynastic interests tends to make that possibility a certainty, for dynastic interest means the acquisition of means by which the authority of an agent may be made independent of that of his principal. The difficulty arises where the question is asked, How was the knowledge of this principle and its normal tendencies preserved through the *régime* of despotic power? The answer is, that the peculiar nature of the judicial function kept them alive. In the adjudication of individual right, where no governmental interests are present, the public conscience is in equilibrium, and its monitions are tendencies of the best underlying principles. It is so in the mind of man, and, therefore, should be so in the complex mind. Men are habitually performing two classes of actions, one class springing from personal affections and interest, and the other from a reflective judgment. The better nature manifests itself in the latter class, and affords the possibility of his recognizing the true principles that should govern his life. As acts of conscience are never lacking in some degree while conscience is an active principle, there is always something in the breast of man in ordinary conditions to remind him of the best laws of his nature. In the same way the judicial system conceives the higher consciousness or conscience of the community in a sense of public function, and through its best action the principles of society may always be discerned.

CHAPTER XXIX.

RESIDENCE AND CHANGE OF PLACE.

THE most general right or liberty of the class under immediate consideration is that of exercising choice in residence and change of place; that, in a general sense, is the right of self-determining the relation of the individual to place, and may be conveniently termed the right of residence and locomotion. Man destitute of the power of locomotion would be unable, without dependence upon the help of others, to accomplish the purposes propounded by his nature and his will; it must, therefore, be regarded as a general condition attached to every other right, which in its nature may involve a change of place, and, as no right is conceivable that may not, at some time, demand the exercise of this natural faculty, it may be stated as a general condition of all rights. Complementary to this right is that of residence, or remaining at will in any particular place for an indefinite or fixed period—that is, of permanent or temporary residence. The liberty of action of the individual in this respect is of the broadest character, both as a consequence of the principles of the law and as a general legal fact. No restraint whatever is put upon this general right of the individual by the principles of the law. When actually restricted by legal authority, for any purpose, such restriction must be ascribed either to public law or to some exigency of the administration of justice. One possessed of full civil right may select his residence where he will, at home or abroad, and change it when, and as often as, he may please. So, on the other hand, he may go from place to place in his own country, or to foreign countries. If any restraint is laid upon this liberty of action, it must, except in a very restricted class of cases, proceed from public law determined by the policy of the government, or as the consequence of some specific obligation by which one has bound himself, where such obligation admits of a specific remedy. The only way in which the largest liberty in the use of the right of changing place and selecting residence can prejudice one's civil rights, through the operation of the principles of the law, is an indirect one, and that is through the effect upon his character or reputation of inferences, deducible from the manifestation of a roving and unsettled disposition, that may react to the prejudice of his civil rights.

Limitations of these rights by public authority, denying the force of the principles of the law conserving them, need not be particularly considered. Arbitrary governments—denying the right of expatriation or immigration, forbidding residence in particular places, or change of residence, and in designating the place of residence of a citizen or stranger, in forbidding or obstructing intercourse between places, or demanding the special authority of government for travel or change of residence, or obstructing the movements of individuals by the instrumentality of spies and informers—unless acting upon occasions that warrant the use of extraordinary means, according to the principles of the law, occupy the position, considered as phenomena of social monstrosities, unsuitable to aid the studies of general laws. It is only when governmental action is in harmony with the principles of the law that it can become the means of illustrating these principles.

The proper occasions for interference with the liberty of changing place and selecting residence, on the part of government, arise out of either disturbed domestic conditions or external relations. The domestic conditions that warrant such extraordinary means, consistently with the principles of the law, are such as concern the maintenance of the public peace, the public health, and the administration of justice. Under the general head of police regulations are embraced provisions to prevent and suppress violence, to secure an orderly performance of the functions of government, and of the community at large, and to prevent and detect commissions of crime. The ordinary police regulations are a part of the ordinary action of the government, while the apprehension or existence of special causes of disorder give rise to special provisions that should be proportioned to the nature and extent of the danger involved. Health regulations, both of a general and special character, are of the same general nature as police regulations, specialized to meet the peculiar character of the causes sought to be guarded against.

The right of self-preservation, as applied to the maintenance of conditions essential to the orderly conduct of government, is a warrant, derived from the principles of the law, for interference with the liberty of the subject to the extent that may be rendered necessary by the existence of public dangers, without referring such provisions to the arbitrary power of government. Indeed, there are many instances where, without the sanction of legislative authority for that purpose, public officers may, with impunity, encroach upon the liberty of the citizen under the promptings of the necessity for public preservation.

In creating society as a legal person, and endowing it with the right of self-preservation, each individual must be regarded as having conferred the necessary means to that end; and, as the state must be regarded as capable of protection and defense, through the property and personal aid of individual citizens, the duty to society itself must be regarded as imposing a general obligation of that character, independent of any specific obligation imposed for that purpose by public enactment. This distinction will materially assist the solution of a problem that frequently is presented. The police of a city, as conservators of the peace, generally will, in the presence of public danger, assume the responsibility of doing acts that are not authorized by their duty in ordinary times, and that without special warrant of authority. It may be that such an act interferes with the use of the streets, or prevents a person from entering or leaving his house, or going to the house of another, for a lawful purpose. Such interference, however great the public necessity, could not be justified in the absence of legislative authority, unless a general obligation existed to give it sanction. Assuming the existence of such a general obligation, the rightfulness of the act would depend on the question whether the occasion was one to which the obligation applied, and whether the interference with individual right in the case was reasonable, for how could that of which one is deprived by a general obligation become the subject of a wrong? If to abstain from using the particular right in question was a duty under the general obligation, its loss is not an injury under the circumstances contemplated by the obligation. The question as to what is reasonable resolves itself into the question of what is the habit of the community in like or analogous cases.

It may justly be doubted whether any case is possible in which an individual, in virtue alone of the general protective obligation due to the preservation of the community, could be compelled to render a personal service to the community without some requirement of public law. In time of war or insurrection, one may be compelled to perform military service, but such an interference with the liberty of individuals demands positive governmental authority for such purpose, and government has, undoubtedly, the right to convert the general obligation to afford protection to the state into a specific obligation to perform a certain service, at a certain time, consistently with the principles of the law. In monarchic governments, where the whole sovereign function resides primarily in the monarch, and parliamentary authority is regarded as a derivation from that source, the power of exercising the full sovereign functions in time of war might be expected to be left, to a greater or less degree, in the head of the state, and a royal command might be regarded as in itself a proper exercise of the sovereignty of the state. In republican governments, where the only institution in which public authority assumes an original character is the constitution, and both legislative and executive powers are delegated specifically to the bodies or persons exercising them, the rightfulness of the exercise of any particular power, either legislative or executive, is a question of the effect of the act of delegation, and not of the ultimate potency of the community. It follows that a command of the executive, affecting the rights of an individual, in constitutional governments, would not represent the whole original power of the community, but merely that delegated, and this would be effectual only in virtue of the extent of power thus delegated. Certainly no officer subordinate to the executive head of the state could rightfully assume by his command to represent the whole sovereign capacity of the state, or more of that capacity than is embraced in that delegation—that is, his commission of authority. If in the extreme cases of public danger, represented by a state of war or insurrection, nothing short of public law can impose upon the individual specific duties of public service, lesser degrees of danger could not call into exercise such executive authority.

It is clear that the individual may be deprived, temporarily, of the use of his property under circumstances of public danger, without the warrant of direct legislative authority. The necessities of riot, insurrection, and civil war, as well as of foreign war, may justify the occupation of his house and lands for military purposes, both offensive and defensive, and his personal property may be taken to subsist the military force, to aid military operations, and to prevent its falling into the hands of the enemy; but this consequence is inferable from the nature of military authority, and belongs to another part of the general discussion. So the danger from conflagration in compact communities may justify the occupation of houses and lands for the purpose of extinguishing the flames or preventing their extension; and movable property may be placed in positions of safety, against the will of the owner, and in extreme cases houses and personal property may be destroyed where they have become mere vehicles of dangerous forces. The same principles apply to cases of contagious and infectious diseases; to arrest and prevent the spread of pestilence, the interference with the right of property in such cases may be justified on grounds peculiar to proprietary rights (hereafter to be considered), but are distinguishable from those that arise in the case of a demand upon the service of individuals, implying a limitation of their civil liberty. It is readily conceivable that authority to interfere with the freedom of movement from place to place of an individual might be implied, from the general obligation he is under to the community, under circumstances of danger to the community, while that of demanding a particular service could only exist where the law-making power had given authority for that purpose, for the interference arises wholly from local conditions, while a demand for personal service implies selective authority.

The interferences that may result to the liberty of residence and locomotion from the relations of the community to foreign communities depend upon the same general principles. The requirements of war, the regulation of commerce with a view to general convenience, or to the fiscal or economic policy of the government, and the necessities of diplomatic intercourse, clearly justify a certain interference with the right of transit and residence. Laws preventing intercourse with an alien or domestic public enemy, the removal of a citizen or his property to the territory occupied by a hostile belligerent, or power anticipating belligerency, and that circumscribe the residence, movements, and conduct of a citizen of a belligerent state resident, or present for any reason, are not necessarily out of harmony with the general principles of the law that are influenced by the nature of public authority, as well as by that of individual liberty.

These exertions of public authority may be justified as incidents of a state of war, either realized or anticipated; and, as war tends to put in jeopardy the existence of the community, the principle of self-preservation operates in the behalf of the community as it operates in behalf of the individual in analogous cases. It admits of a temporary equilibrium in which the protective principle, acting in behalf of the community, is dominant in its relations with that of equal individual rights. Such temporary dominance has, however, its law, that is defined by the nature of the forces militating against the common interest.

It is conceivable that more than a single state of equilibrium should exist in relative rights. The law of nature illustrates such a possibility; indeed, wherever there is motion from natural causes, that motion is constantly adjusting itself to both a constant and a variable change of equilibrium among the objects, or parts of objects, participating together in such movement. This constant change of equilibrium results from the fact that there are always, for physical relationships, two opposite states of equilibrium that succeed each other in rhythmic order. We very commonly see this alternation of states of equilibrium brought about by different extremes of temperature, and upon this principle depends the succession of the seasons. Between these extreme points there is a gradual passage from the conditions incident to one state to those characteristic of the other. The variable element of what may be called a dynamic state of equilibrium consists in an indefinite number of causes, termed accidental, that are constantly in play.

The same general laws affect the conditions of communities, and hence it is that any attempt to adjust government to a single and unalterable state of equilibrium among its powers, public and private, is an attempt against the course of nature that must fail. An elastic political system has, in common with other elastic bodies, the power of self-adjustment which is the condition of durability, and is at its maximum in the composition of mind and body that we call man; and, as society has the nature of man, it is the proper attribute of political systems. Although such a system appears to imply assent to the existence of causes of change, it is only an assent to a natural fact, and not an invitation to unnecessary changes. For every condition of equilibrium that may occur in the experiences of communities, the principles of the law, as applied to action, and habits of action, contain expositions of the proper state of relations, although such a full development of these principles can not reasonably be anticipated until their nature, separate and combined, have been more carefully studied, and are better understood.

On the other hand, laws that originate in the jealousy of the power or prosperity of other states; that prevent expatriation, except as a measure for averting present public danger, or interfere with immigration except for such reasons; that allow less liberty to the resident citizens of foreign states than to its own citizens, or surround them, while passing from place to place, with restrictions and obstacles, such as passports and governmental supervision—must be referred to the exercise of arbitrary authority inconsistent with the principles of the law. That authority, whether reasonable or unreasonable in its exercise, is within the idea of sovereign authority as delegated to government, when viewed from a legal stand-point; but its abuses, through the exercise of power that is not harmonious with the principles of the law, are of practical rather than of scientific interest. The science of the law deals mainly with the operations of constant principles that determine the nature of law, and these are the principles of the law. The variable elements that give rise to many special, and often abnormal, conditions of public authority, are within the policy of the government, and their proper scientific study is politics. Practical or institutional law takes account of both of these elements, but the scientific basis of the law must be found in the constantly recurring tendencies that are the causes of unity and limits of individuality.

Having reviewed briefly the general operation of the principles of the law, as imposing, under extraordinary but possible conditions, a certain limitation upon the general personal liberty of the individual, and as having lodged a certain power and duty in government, in virtue of which it may, consistently with these principles, extend the sphere of such limitation, it is proper to notice the effect upon the liberty of person of certain means afforded by the law for exercising the power of establishing and changing a residence, and for passage from place to place. The rights involved in the inquiry appertain to the common right of way. The first branch of this subject noticed will be that of the common rights incident to residence and passage upon highways, and allied modes of communication.

A highway is a modification of the more primitive idea of a common way. The idea of a common way is that of the existence of a common right to journey or pass by a certain place in going from place to place. The idea of a highway is that of a certain public or governmental right to exercise control of a proprietary character over places that are subject to such common right of way. The principles that govern the common right of way are best discerned in the primitive form of that right, which still very commonly exists. We are not compelled to resort to history to ascertain what that primitive idea was, for the earliest and simplest methods are still in operation.

Where it has been the habit of the people of a community to come and go at will upon a certain way, either in a particular or general mode of use, for a definite period of time, fixed by public law, or by the presumptions of the law in the absence of public regulations, the law recognizes the existence of a common right in all individuals to use such way, in accordance with the character of such general usage. Such an inferred right presupposes a habit of user, its maintenance for a certain period of time, and a relation between such common use and the common right of all individuals. The fact that one who uses such a way for the first time is benefited by the fact that other members of the community have at a prior time used the same privilege, shows that it is in the nature of the habits and usages of the people of a community to create rights for the benefit of all persons using the privileges of such community. Assuming that such habits and usages are capable of creating rights, when the individuals whose conduct evidences such right do not appear to have acted on the assertion of any individual proprietary right, their conduct is interpreted as an assertion of right in behalf of the whole community. An individual may acquire, as an individual right, such right of way by means of persistent use. When such user is in the assertion of individual right, it is acquired upon the same principles through which the common right of way is created by similar means. So a limited number of persons may, by their common action, call into existence rights common to them as a class; but, should it appear that an indefinite number of disconnected individuals, undefinable as a class, had used such a privilege, such user must, in the nature of things, be referred to a habit of the community.

The creation of a right of way by user presupposes that the proprietorship of the place used as a way belongs to one, while the right of way is claimed by others, either by the whole community, or by an individual, or class of individuals; it is, therefore, an instance where proprietary right is modified by the fact of a persistent habit, either individual or common. The mode in which this habit operates to produce such an effect will be considered when other instances dependent upon the same principle are brought to notice.

All that need be said of the period of time required to give permanency to such habit is, that it is, necessarily, arbitrarily selected, although certain analogies may have dictated the period that has passed into general use, as, for instance, the idea of the life of a generation of men may have suggested the period of thirty years for the required duration of such a habit. The more important question is, the relation that the habit of the community sustains to the idea of common right according to the principles of the law.

The influence of habit in giving rise to particular presumptions has already been noticed, but here habit is observed as ripening into individual right. It is proper to observe that common rights are in their nature identical with individual rights, while public rights, when found in the hands of an individual for exercise, are there by some actual or assumed delegation from the community. Rights are common in the sense that all individuals in a certain community have equal interests in them. That the habit of the community can not directly create a right is demonstrable from the principles of the law, but that it gives rise to presumptions, and that presumptions may exist in a form in which they can not be rebutted or disproved, must be admitted, and such means are clearly sufficient to produce either common or individual rights. As it regards the capacity of common habit or usage to create rights, the difficulty lies in the fact that a right, created wholly as the result of usage for a certain period of time, does not come into existence as a right until that period of time is fully complete. Prior to that moment of completion, such user, as affecting an existing proprietary right in another, is an act of wrong. It is possible to conceive of rights existing in an imperfect form, and attaining their full characteristics by persistent user, but the same act can not at the same moment of time, and for the same purpose, be regarded as both an act of wrong and an immature right. The law does not appear to furnish any principle, or even analogy, for thus confusing together the idea of a wrong and that of an imperfect right, but it does furnish the means of ascribing the effect of habit in creating title to presumptions capable of producing such effect.

The right of one may become transferred to another by two classes of presumptions: on the one hand by a presumption of the actual transfer of that right, and on the other hand by a presumption that the former owner has abandoned his claim of right in favor of one who has wrongfully obtained possession. If the owner of property stands by, making no claim as against one using his property in a certain way, he may be presumed to have consented to such use; and in that case the person using his rights may be regarded as having the authority of the proprietor of the place. That authority being presumed, it is open to question whether it is intended to be temporary or permanent until a sufficient time has elapsed to characterize that purpose. If the right is cut off before the period arrives that evidences a permanent intention, it is presumably a mere license; but, where the duration of enjoyment points to an intention that it shall be permanent, the effect of presumption changes, and the inferable authority becomes a permanent right the moment that authority is evidenced in that form. A license to use the lands of another can in no sense be regarded as an immature right of property, for the two have different natures.

But a right of user may be ripened under conditions of an opposite character to those just stated. The owner of land upon which another is using a privilege may assert his ownership to such an extent as to preclude the inference that he has ever consented to such use, and yet if he allows the use to go on for the full period without effectually asserting it so as to bring the use to an end, either by reclaiming the place, and actually excluding the use of the other, or by instituting means of legal redress, the use may, by lapse of time, ripen into a right, even against the protest of the proprietor of the place. This is the principle that is at the foundation of the idea of acquiring land by adverse possession, and of the allied doctrine as to personal property.

It is also the fundamental principle of statutes limiting the time for bringing actions; in the last-mentioned case this principle acting upon executory rights, while in the case of adverse possession it acts upon the title of a possessor. The principle of abandonment, fundamental to the law, is the correlative of the principle of title acquired by occupation. One who abandons property exercises his power of self-obligation, for he inferentially obliges himself to respect the title of the occupant who gets possession of the abandoned property. It does not differ in principle from an executed gift to an individual, as it is in effect a gift to any individual who may become the next occupant. If, then, the habit of the community may properly give rise to presumptions, it may give rise to the particular presumptions, either of a permanent license of a right of way, or, of what is equivalent in effect, an abandonment of such right of way in favor of the community at large—that is, to the individuals who compose the community, or use its privileges in common.

It is desirable at this point to look a little more closely for the principles that underlie the efficacy of habit, and, for this purpose, the consequences of habit in the instance of the community must be compared with the consequences that flow from individual habit, and their points of agreement and difference noted. It is beyond question that, in the case of individual habits, their legal efficacy depends upon their power of expressing intention. Aside from the obligations that may be directly imposed by public authority, without the consent of the individual, all specific obligations binding any individual must proceed from an expressed determination of his own will. Specific obligations, as here used, must be distinguished from specific duties arising under the common obligations, which may be regarded as specific forms of such common obligations, for such duties may arise independently of any determination of the will of the party bound by them. If one sees another using his own right in a particular manner, his duty under the common obligations is modified by that fact. He must both desist from any act that would tend to the abuse of the other's right and he must so use his own right as not unnecessarily to cause injury to such intended use. It is therefore obvious that that which creates a special duty out of the common obligations is some evidence of intention on the part of one toward whom such duty arises. On the other hand, as has been said, in order to create a specific obligation independently of the exercise of positive public authority, there must be an evidenced intention of a certain character on the part of the person bound by such specific obligation. The conditions, then, which, uniting with the common obligations, created common law, and the various individual duties that spring up under them, are determinations of the will of individuals. To render this statement clear in its application, it may be stated that the visible possession of property is in itself a declaration of an intent to use such property according to the ordinary habit of use. Taking the idea of a declaration of intent in this broad sense, it becomes necessary to inquire into the relation that habit of action sustains to such a declaration of intent.

Habit is merely persistent conduct, and, as conduct is the means of interpreting intention (for it embraces both the idea of action and declaration), it follows that the effect of habit is to ascribe permanence to that intention, and thus discloses a stable state of the intentions by which others not only have the right to adjust their conduct and interests, but, according to the nature of society, are compelled so to do.

The application of these principles to the interpretation of individual habit is obvious; but, as applied to the habit of the community, some examination is needed. It has just been said that possession of property implies an intention to use it according to the habit of the commuity, but this proposition may be extended to interpret a like intention as it regards the use of all other rights. There must be a reason why such an implication arises, and an attempt will be made to discern that reason. It will be readily conceded that a common habit evidences a common intention. If an intention is capable of being ascribed to a number of persons in common, it is necessarily capable of being ascribed to each one of that number in particular, for what is common to all is equal to each. Then each individual in the community must be regarded as declaring his individual intention in what is habitually done by the community as such. This contains the essential nature of all declarative law, common or public. The declared intention of the community is the individual intention of each member of that community, and, when evidenced in certain forms of law, in a perfect sense. The modes of promulgation are either by legislative enactment or persistent habit; just as in the case of the individual, he may declare his intention either by his formal obligation or by his persistent habit. The relation between common and statute law is thus made clear; they are different forms of the same substance, and that substance is the will of the community.

It is apparent that the foregoing conclusions are verified by the rules of the law. Common law is constantly referred to as having its origin in the customs and usages of communities, and statutes themselves are the matured product of habit. Statutes, to a large extent, certainly represent what was more or less present in the habit of the community antecedent to the statute, and such as are out of relation to that habit, and contrary to its tendencies, tend to become obsolete. The ultimate object of the law is to render it possible that the action of an individual, in the exercise of his various rights, may be harmonized with the action of all others, that the degree of liberty possible for one may be possible for each and for all. To reach this possible harmony, some freedom of inaction must be sacrificed; but, more than this, there must be some concerted method of action, so that the relations of the members of society may have some systematic tendency. It is a necessity, not only of law, but of society, that the prevalence of a common method should give a key to its action, and necessarily to the action of the individuals that compose it. When this method appears in a particular custom, usage, or practice—that is, as a habit of the community of a fixed character—it is recognized as law. But, before that full recognition, an obligation of an imperfect character binds the individual to conform his conduct to that method which is a structural principle of the society of which he is a member; and if his conduct is such that he appears to have given his sanction to a particular habit of the community, though not having the general force of law, he is in the position of having given a special form to that indefinite obligation. Upon this principle, the intention implied in the habit of the community is ascribed to the individual, in the absence of the declaration of a different intent, through the operation of legal presumptions. It is upon this same foundation that customs of trade and general habits of dealing become active elements in the interpretation of contracts, for, in contracting with another, and using the language and methods of commerce in general, or of a particular branch of traffic, one appears to give consent to the efficacy of such habits in such particular dealing. All that is essential in substance to the transfer of general or particular proprietary right of a transferable nature is an intention to transfer, accompanied by the permission of actual possession in the transferer. All else is form, however essential such forms may be made by technical rules. Ordinarily, a deed of land is the proper evidence that the requisite intention exists, but a persistent habit of use is equivalent to formal evidence of intention.

On the principles stated, the habit of the community in using a particular way, apparently assented to, or opposition to which is abandoned by the proprietor of the place, is, through the operation of time, an evidence of the assent of the proprietor; for, if the principle may affect general habits of dealing, it may equally affect particular transactions, and that which can evidence an intent to act in a particular way can also evidence an intent to abandon a particular line of action.

The common right of way must be regarded as a personal right, inasmuch as it is subservient to purely personal right, that of locomotion, or change of place. It is a right to use the highways, and all roads or ways, that are subject to use by the community, in a manner conformable to that habitual use. The mode of common use established by usage is the law of the particular way, in the absence of regulations proceeding from the public laws. Therefore, if one employs a way for any other purpose than as a means of passage, according to the established mode of its use, if he causes, by so doing, interruption to the proper use of others, it is a wrong, as it regards their right of way. If he assumes any authority over the soil, or the appurtenances of the way, he violates the right of the proprietor of the place, whether that proprietor is the community or an individual, in addition to subjecting himself to the punitive consequences of violating regulations established for governing the use of highways. The law of the road requires that his use must be a reasonable use, and what is reasonable, where not fixed by public law, is ascertainable by reference to the common habit in such cases. It does not follow that no new or unusual mode of use can be permitted, and that one must continue to do that which his ancestors have done before him, and that which his neighbors do, as it regards the modes and means of locomotion, whether natural or mechanical; but the standards for determining what is reasonable must be the principles embodied in the public habit, for there is in habit, as in laws, a variable element, as well as a constant element, and that constant element is that which affords the standard derivable from habit. Hence it is that, as the idea of a common road became developed into that of a public highway, street, or turnpike, and railroad, the principles that are characteristic of the primitive form extended themselves to these new methods, and assimilated them more or less to common roads, while the law of the common way was modified by the special conditions attending such developed forms. Bridges are but parts of the highway, and follow the law of its use, while from their distinct nature imposing further conditions upon the mode of user. Ferries are, in a certain sense, parts of a highway or road, where they serve to connect its parts, or to connect it with other roads; but here the traveler employs a vehicle of which another has the proprietary right. The right to use the vehicle is a public right, as distinguished from a common right, for it is derived from the public authority attached to a grant, express or implied, of the right to take toll upon such ferry; but such public right is intended to subserve the same general purpose as that embraced in the common right of way, and contains its incidents so far as consistent with the other rights that go to constitute a right of ferry. The law of the proper use of the ferry-boat is superadded to the law of the way itself, consisting, in addition to what is established by public law and general custom, of such reasonable rules as may be published by the owner of the boat, such reasonableness being tested by their relation to the habit of the community, interpreted and applied in the manner already stated in regard to the use of roads. The right to navigate navigable waters depends upon the same principles, and is also a common right; and, as it regards navigation by one owning his own vessel, a new principle is peculiar to their use.

The rules of law respecting common ways lead to the conclusion that the common way by water is the natural highway—that is to say, is such by virtue of natural conditions alone, and without regard to public law, grant, or habit of use. No instance appears where the law designates any portion of the land as a highway on the ground of its natural importance for that purpose. The only sources from which a right of way by land can be procured are either the consent, express or implied, of the proprietor of the place, or through the action of the public authority, however much a way may be rendered necessary by natural conditions.

It is otherwise with navigable bodies and streams of water which have recognition as common ways on the ground of natural conditions alone. The tendency of this fact is to point out the principles governing the use of navigable waters as fundamental to the whole system of the law, as it regards the means of passage from place to place. This fact becomes of particular interest in its relation to the more general fact that the common right to use the great bodies of water—the oceans and seas—is, beyond dispute, the fundamental idea of international law. The common right to use the high seas is an international conception, the earliest of that train of ideas that tend to develop into permanent international society of an organic type. This fact is in harmony with what has already appeared—that the legal idea of common right is, in its broadest sense, a consequence of the relation of man to the elements of nature. The idea of common right distinctly contains that of individual proprietorship as its contrast, and also in the sense that it is intended to subserve exclusive individual enjoyment in a form consistent with the principle of equality, which is the ultimate conception of proprietorship. As proprietorship commences with the idea of an exclusive occupancy, or possession of that which was previously common to all, its relation to the idea of common right is manifest. These two principles may thus be regarded as impressed on man by the elemental condition by which he is surrounded, and as the first lesson given by nature in the school of law.

The next class of cases to be examined, as involving a common right to the means of exercising the right of locomotion, embraces the cases of common carriers and innkeepers. At present we have only to do with common carriers of persons and their personal baggage. Carriers of goods will be considered in another connection. The character of a common carrier is obtained by holding himself out to the community as undertaking to convey passengers for hire from one certain place to another. The terms of the obligation, implied by the fact of becoming a passenger, are interpreted by the law on the basis of a common custom. The common carrier supplies a mode of conveyance, and takes the person of his passenger into his care and his baggage into his custody. The hire for transportation is fixed by the terms of a special contract, and, in the absence of that, by the habit of such particular carrier; and, where no such means exist of determining it, by what is reasonable, as measured by the general habit of the community. Incident to the proprietorship of the vehicle, the carrier may make reasonable rules as to its use. All persons, on tendering the price of carriage and complying with such reasonable rules, have a right to demand carriage upon the route of the carrier whenever, at the time of such demand, the accommodations afforded are sufficient for that purpose. A violation of the right is compensated by the law. It is evident that this right is to be regarded as a common right, based on the assumption by the carrier of a general obligation to carry all passengers duly presenting themselves, which is made a special duty wherever there is a compliance with what is implied by such general obligation. Common obligations tend naturally to produce common rights, for, as the idea of a common obligation is that of an obligation of all to all, the corresponding right would be that of all as against all, each individual having an interest in what is common to all. A general obligation does not, on the other hand, naturally serve to produce common rights, for, unless it is common as well as general, it is not an obligation of all to all, but its natural tendency is to resolve itself into individual right. In the case of the common carrier, the obligation to convey does not bind all, but is peculiar to the class of common carriers, and therefore, while it is a general, it is not a common obligation. The circumstance that, in the present instance, it produces a common right, shows that the obligation of the common carrier is accessory to the common right of using the highway for the purpose of passage from place to place, and, having the nature of that to which it is accessory, may produce rights agreeable to that nature—that is to say, a common right of carriage. That the right to demand carriage by a common carrier is to be regarded as a common right, on certain conditions, is obvious, from the fact that it is primarily due to all.

The common obligation to exercise prudent care is, of course, attached to this relation, as it is to all that may tend to the detriment of person or property. The kind of care and skill required is that termed ordinary. The degree of care and skill is that which results from the degree of danger implied to person or property by the means of carriage employed. The ordinary carrier who employs the power of domestic animals for the purposes of conveyance is bound to a less degree of care than one who employs means and speed of locomotion of a specially dangerous character, the degrees of care being adjusted to the degrees of danger.

The rights and liabilities of the common carrier and his passengers may be modified by special contract, as other private rights, but the mere fact that a passenger has claimed and exercised the right of being carried is not evidence that he has accepted special terms of carriage, offered by a general notice or tender; but any special intention of the carrier must appear to have been brought to the mind of the passenger to produce such an effect.

The right of common carriers to fix the compensation for carriage, independently of what would be a reasonable compensation for such service, has been much discussed, but is not authoritatively settled, and can hardly arise for ultimate settlement until a case is presented in which a person has tendered a reasonable compensation, less than the amount claimed by the carrier, and has been refused carriage. But the right of the carrier to fix the amount of compensation for carriage must be distinguished from the right to change the ordinary legal incidents attached to his contract, such as his liability for injury to the person of a passenger, or loss or injury to his baggage. The terms of his liability are the constant element of the contract of the carrier, the same for all times and places, while the price of carriage varies with all changes of circumstances; it is, therefore, clear that that which tends to change the nature of his contract is not as fully within the control of the carrier as that which brings his general contract into relation to the conditions and circumstances attending the carriage of a particular person. The features of the law that remain unsettled are not serviceable to the present inquiry, which starts from known legal rules to find the principles of the law.

The language of our law is, that this right is derived from the *custom of the realm*. A custom is a habit of dealing so generally prevalent that all are deemed to have dealt with reference to it. This habit of dealing, or custom, is applied to the common carrier by his act of holding himself out as such, and interprets it into a general obligation of the character already mentioned. This circumstance not existing in the case of a special carrier, the same consequences are not applicable to that case.

The right that exists at common law to demand entertainment at a wayside inn possesses the same general nature as that affecting the common carrier. Such inns, according to early modes of travel, were accommodations tendered to travelers, and, through the operation of the habit of the community, formulated into a definite custom. The tender of such accommodations was interpreted as a general obligation which any person, in the position of a traveler, could, of common right, convert into a special duty by paying, or tendering the sum usually demanded, for entertainment at such inn, and complying with the reasonable regulations which the landlord, as proprietor, might make. The custom embraced also a lien on the baggage of the guest for the payment of his dues. This lien evidenced the fact that the innkeeper had a special property as the custodian of such baggage until the guest discharged his obligations to him. As an incident of this idea of a special property, the innkeeper could make reasonable regulations as to where property of certain kinds carried as baggage should be placed for safe-keeping, upon which his liability as custodian depended. Non-compliance with these regulations as to the mode of deposit and safe-keeping did not defeat the right of special property, for the lien existed, although the guest retained his baggage improperly under his personal care, instead of placing it where it would be under the personal custody of the innkeeper. The origin of this special property was evidently a bailment for the mutual benefit of bailer and bailee—that is, for the security of the property of the guest, and of the landlord's demand under the custom.

It is to be anticipated that change in the habit of the community, as it regards modes of travel and entertainment, would induce changes in the interpretation of the general obligation, implied by the opening of a house for the entertainment of guests; and this we observe at the present day, as a consequence of the change in the habit of travel induced by the use of railroads. Where the circumstances under which a house is opened for entertainment, interpreted by the habit of the immediate vicinity, repel the idea that entertainment is offered for all, indiscriminately, as in cities, where hotels are numerous and specialized for particular classes of persons, that feature of the general obligation that gives a common right would naturally cease to operate, while equal reason does not exist for the disappearance of that common right where primitive habits still obtain. It is an ordinary circumstance for the effect of general customs to be modified by the influence of local customs and the customs of particular trades, as might be anticipated from the fact that such customs operate as evidences of intention, for the expression of a particular intent qualifies the force of that evidencing a general intention. A local custom, or custom of a particular trade, operates upon what is done within its sphere, precisely as a general custom operates in a larger sphere, and hence it would follow that the true interpretation of intention would result from the modification of the general custom by what is implied by the more limited custom.

A modification of the general custom that controls the general law of the innkeeper might then leave those elements of the general custom operative that are not affected by the local modification, and thus it might happen that a common right to demand entertainment at a city hotel may not exist as a consequence of local custom, and yet such features of the general law as that which gives the landlord a lien on the goods of his guest may remain unchanged.

The rights and obligations attending carriage of the person by inland waters depend on the same principles as those of carriage by land, without presenting any modification of these principles of special interest. Carriage of persons by sea depends on the customs of commerce at large, as distinguished from the local customs of particular countries engaged in commercial intercourse. The contract for the carriage of goods by inland waters, and by sea and by land, exhibits marked peculiarities, the discussion of which belongs to another place. The making of regular trips between certain specified places that is the characteristic of carriage by land, is, as it regards carriage by sea, a habit of comparatively recent origin. It is easy to conceive that when a regular intercourse, by definite modes of conveyance, should exist between place and place, the habits of the community would become adjusted to such means of communication, and would become a regular feature of it, while chance voyages, such as constituted the means of making journeys by sea in early days, would not give rise to precisely similar habits and customs.

The next class of individual rights intended to afford means of locomotion are derived out of public right, and are in the nature of common rights. The case referred to is that of railroads, as legalized at the present day. It is very clear that a railroad is not a highway at common law, for the right of transit upon it is wholly controlled by the owner of the place where the road exists. The only right of others is to demand transit by the vehicles of the owner of the railroad. In this respect the ferry and the railroad differ, for any person may use the same waters that the ferryman uses, for the transfer of himself in his own vehicle; that which the exclusive right of the ferryman displaces, when he has an exclusive right, is the right of other persons to carry persons, at such place, for hire, while the owner of the railroad may exclude all persons from the land he holds for the purposes of his road, except when they use his vehicles.

As all persons have a right to demand conveyance by railroad, upon compliance with the requirement to pay the proper passage-money and comply with the reasonable regulations of the railroad proprietor, it is proper to class these rights among common rights, having their origin in general obligations, and not in common obligations. In this respect, the case of the railroad is identical with that of the ordinary common carrier, but there is a difference between the two. The general obligation, in the case of the ordinary common carrier, is the product of custom or the habit of the community, which gives to it that character that enables it to give rise to a common right of carriage. In the case of the railroad, the same grounds exist for creating such a general obligation, for the railroad proprietor is presumed to offer himself to the community as a common carrier, according to general custom, subject to such modifications as arise from the nature of the means of carriage; but, in addition to this, the railroad carrier is usually more or less limited in his duty and right as a common carrier by public law, that fact introducing a new element into the contract of carriage. The existence of legal regulations, of a positive character, in the case of the carrier by railroad, that do not exist in the case of the ordinary carrier, depends upon the facts—first, that the railroad carrier usually exercises the functions of a corporation that are derived from a grant of public authority, which is subject to conditions that may extend themselves to qualify the contract of carriage with individuals, and, second, the railroad, for the purpose of its construction, requires, generally, the acquisition by its proprietor of the lands of others, and usually compulsory means of acquiring such lands; and, as these compulsory means must be obtained from a legislative authority, conditions may be attached to such a grant affecting individual contracts of carriage.

It is certainly not essential to the idea of a common carrier that he should assume to carry by a common highway, although there is generally such a practical necessity in the case of the ordinary carrier. It is the fact of the custom of carriage, and the assumption, under that custom, of a duty to the community, that are the distinguishing features of the common contract of carriage, and these elements appear in the contract of the railroad, although associated with the fact that the carrier is the proprietor of the place where the carriage takes place. It is very clear, then, that the character of a common carrier, as applied to a railroad, does not depend on the fact that the railroad is a highway, but upon the same incidents that have been stated as characterizing the contract of the ordinary common carrier, except as modified by public law. It would follow, that the community has no right of way upon a railroad of the nature of the common right enjoyed in places where a common way exists, but that they have the common right that appertains to the duty of the common carrier, although, as has been said, that common right of carriage is assimilated to the common right of way. While it may well be assumed that, if the carriage of persons and property had not involved the use of the common highways, the contract of the ordinary common carrier might have assumed a different form from that it has at present, yet it does not follow that the idea of the use of a common highway is essential to the force of that contract. The obligacy of the contract is the existence of the custom, and, although the particular conveniences that gave to the custom its primitive mold should pass out of use, that would not of itself defeat the persistence of the custom, although it might introduce a tendency to modification of that contract. This fact, of the persistence of custom as the support of obligation, after that which gave it its primitive form has passed away, has been already noticed in the relation that the common law of innkeeper sustains to the city hotel keeper.

But, although the railroad is not a common highway, it is a substitute for the common highway, in general acceptance and use, and hence the reasons that were afforded by the nature of common highways, as interpreting the duty of the common carrier, extend to railroads as to a substituted agency; and, as the reason that controls the ordinary common carrier is that which controls, at least in part, the contract of the railroad carrier, it is proper to say that the contract of the railroad is in the nature of the common right of way, without implying that the existence of a common way is at all essential to it.

It then appears that the contract of the railroad carrier with his passenger is based upon the custom of common carriage, through the assumption of a duty to the community, and modified by the nature of the means of conveyance, and the terms of public law. It is certainly not based upon the fact that the railroad carrier is a corporation, for corporations exist for private as well as public purposes, and, therefore, the corporate character, in itself, contains no such implication. It is not based on the fact that the railroad gets its right to acquire land, by compulsory means, from a grant of public authority, for the laws might be so framed that land could be compulsorily acquired for purely private purposes, such as for the location of a mill or storehouse, so that such a grant does not necessarily imply a public agency, but is consistent with purely individual right.

It is true that railroad corporations are regarded, for certain purposes, as public corporations, but this has regard to their office to the public as common carriers, and not to the nature of their proprietary powers. The public duty of a common carrier is imposed upon a private person, in such cases, in the same sense that any other public duty may be imposed upon a private individual, who may have complete proprietary control over the material means of performing such duty.

Railroad carriers, considered as carriers of persons, independently of public law, have the same obligations as ordinary common carriers, but the consequences of these obligations are modified by the nature of the mode and means of conveyance.

The circumstances, that the nature of the road is such as to admit of carriages of a particular construction only ; that the road must be in a certain condition to be used, and is exposed to a loss of that condition from wear and the action of the elements ; that carriage can only take place between definite points, and along a definite line joining them, when the condition of the road will admit of it; that a force is generally used for the purpose of propulsion that is liable to produce destruction to life and injury to person and property when not controlled through the exercise of great care and skill both in construction and management—affect the rights and obligations of the carrier and his passenger as it regards the terms of contract, the question of what are reasonable regulations, the degree of care and skill due on the part of the carrier and his servants, and the degree of prudent care that the passenger should exercise to avoid injury.

Regulations as to the time when a journey shall commence, its duration, continuity, and stoppages, are in general subject to the control of the carrier, and the right of the passenger to be conveyed is subject to these regulations. So the establishment of rates of charge is the right of the carrier, unless modified by public law, and the individual right of carriage is based on such charges, at all events, if reasonable. All persons paying the proper charges, and complying with the regulations of the road, have a license to enter the carriages, and such buildings, or places of the road, as are opened for the reception of passengers, and it is a trespass on the right of person to attempt to remove one so licensed therefrom by force, the ordinary proprietary right of control in such cases being modified by the existence of such license, which shows that the license is in the nature of a common right.

There is a noticeable feature of the license that distinguishes it from licenses in general, that will be presently considered. If one attempts to enter a store against the will of the proprietor, he is a trespasser, although, in general, all persons have a license to enter such places for the purposes of trade; but if one, having paid his passage and complied with the regulations of the carrier, should attempt to enter the proper place for carriage, at the proper time, he would certainly not be regarded as a trespasser, even though forbidden so to do by the proprietor of the place. It is assumed here that the order forbidding such entrance was a violation of the right of the passenger. It is manifest from this that the license in such cases implies more than assent on the part of the proprietor of the place, and is in effect a right on the part of the passenger as against such proprietary right. It must then be concluded that the license is part of the obligation of the common carrier, and is not revocable at the pleasure of the carrier. Such a license may be regarded as part of the common right that the community enjoys under the obligations imposed on the carrier by reason of the nature of his calling. Another consequence would follow from this view, that if a passenger is unlawfully ordered to leave a carriage or other proper place, he is not bound to obey, and look to his action for a violation of his contract for redress, but may lawfully refuse to obey such order, and resist force employed for its enforcement.

Regulations as to the position of passengers in vehicles, that are a reasonable precaution against particular danger incident to such mode of travel, are conditions of the rights that the passenger enjoys under his contract. The fact that a regulation intended to impose restriction on a passenger is a precaution against danger is not in itself sufficient to justify its imposition; it must also appear that it has a proper relation to the habit of the community in traveling. The consequence of disregarding regulations intended to prevent violence and preserve proper order may be the loss of right as a passenger and liability to eviction.

The authority of a common carrier to exercise a certain degree of control, in the nature of police power, is evidently allied in principle to that which the head of a household may exercise, and, indeed, to a power existing in some degree wherever there is proprietorship over place. The full consideration of this subject belongs to another place. The foundation of the right evidently lies in the nature of proprietary power, but the extent to which it may be exercised is dependent upon a principle illustrated by the law of associated relationships. Where a protective duty is due from one to another, and to some extent where it is voluntarily assumed, the nature of the protective principle produces modifications of ordinary relationships. This is most forcibly illustrated in the case of the family, the internal powers of which are most closely assimilated to the powers of government. The proprietary powers of the owner of land, in part, but not altogether, account for this as affecting strangers to the household. It can not be questioned that, when the legal duty of protection exists, the person bound to protect another may, within proper limits, exercise the powers of those he is bound to protect in their defense. If, for instance, one that is under the protection of another is assaulted, the legal protector may exercise the right of self-defense, that properly belongs to the assaulted party, in the defense of such person.

It may be presumed that the same principle applies when voluntary protection is afforded by one and accepted by another. The protector must then be regarded as having a certain amount of delegated power belonging originally to the protected person, capable of being exercised in the defense of such party. It is equally clear that the principles here illustrated are natural principles, as would be presumed from their civil recognition, independently of public law. It is not necessary to demonstrate so obvious a proposition as that such ideas have acceptance by man in all conditions, civilized and savage, for their recognition is the necessary consequence of the action of the mind, and is manifested in the conduct as well of children and brute animals. The principle that has been termed the protective principle is the outgrowth of this natural condition. Government itself is a product of similar causes, operating upon a large scale, and the delegation of individual power to the community, for the purposes of governmental protection, is an exercise of the same protective idea, modified by the principle of equal individual right. That this is the modifying principle in question will be evident from the fact that a purely natural delegation is from the weaker to the stronger, and the conception of the idea of placing the community in the position of the strongest, in a natural sense, is an idea that could not be reached until the conception of the individual units, brought about no doubt by the idea of equal individual right, has produced a modification of the protective instinct as it exists in a state of nature.

The existence of such a delegation of power from the protected is readily accounted for upon grounds of legal presumption. The imposition of a duty implies the concession of the means of performing such duty within the power of the one imposing such duty. Where the law imposes the duty, the proper legal means are presumably authorized, and where an individual, by the acceptance of protection, converts a voluntary proffer into a duty, he must be presumed to transfer so much of his own power to his protector as may be necessary for the purposes included in the duty. This presumption expresses what is habitual in the operation of the mind, and what may be regarded as a general law of the nature of mind.

The application of the principle that has just been developed to the case of the common carrier is obvious. He is not only clothed with proprietary right over the place, capable of being exercised over all that are not rightfully there, but he is charged by the law with the protection of his passengers against violence and disorder that he may have the means to prevent; and in person, or by his agent, he may exercise, for the protection of his passengers, reasonable power of restraint and ejection. The power of making regulations suitable for such a purpose is merely giving such authority a stable and regular character; and, if such regulations are in proper relation to the habit of the community, they become conditions of the right and license of the passenger, and their violation places in operation the protective right of restraint or the proprietary right of ejection.

The violation of regulations tending to prevent injury to individual passengers affects the right of the passenger to claim damages for injuries, through the operation of the rule as to contributory negligence. A passenger is bound to use ordinary prudent care in avoiding danger, and, if injury is caused through the contributory negligence of the passenger, the carrier is without liability; if the consequences of an injury, through the negligence of the carrier, are aggravated by the negligence of the passenger, such aggravation is not chargeable to the carrier. The baggage of the passenger is in the personal custody of the carrier, with a special property for his indemnity, and he is bound to use care and skill in its carriage and delivery, on reasonable demand, to its proper owner.

Among the particular rights that define the general right of going from place to place is a license, derived from public authority, to enter and use public buildings, parks, and places, for the purposes for which they were designed. The right is not a common right, but a license in the nature of a common right, conditioned upon the particular use to which such building or place is dedicated. Thus one has the right to enter places where legislative bodies or courts of justice are sitting, but subject to the authority of such bodies to exclude the license or subject it to conditions. Legislative bodies are independent in the exercise of this right. Courts of justice are generally required by law and custom to be open to the public; but no individual can claim to enforce this obligation as a right to himself individually. Public offices are usually open to all who have business to transact in them; and it is the right of all having business with the public authority to enter the customary places where, and at times when, such business is transacted, for the purpose of its transaction. Public parks and places are assimilated to highways as it regards the conduct of persons using them toward others enjoying the same use. No individual has the right to appropriate or use public property unless possessing power delegated for that purpose. Such licenses, when implied, rest on the same grounds as private licenses, next to be considered.

It remains only to consider private licenses in the nature of common rights, and particular licenses as affecting the right of entering upon the lands or places of a private proprietor and performing certain acts there. No one, of common right, can go upon the lands of another for any purpose without an express or implied license, except in an emergency involving the right of self-preservation in view of impending danger.

A license to go upon the lands, and approach and enter a building, belonging to another, is implied under certain circumstances. The ground of this implication is the habit of the community. One, on a proper occasion, may go to the dwelling of another, and upon his land, for that purpose, and seek admission to such dwelling, when it is the habit of the community so to do, and upon occasions recognized by that habit. Places of business, such as shops and offices, are professedly opened for public access, and the act of opening them for such a purpose implies such a license, the general nature and limit of such license being presumably fixed by the general habit in such cases. Such license may be excluded at the will of the proprietor of the place, or subjected to conditions, but is presumed to exist, according to general usage, until that will is exercised, so as to give notice to the person affected by it of a contrary intention.

The classes of cases that have been noticed as affecting the exercise of the general right of passing from place to place, and into other places than those over which one has a proprietary right, illustrate very clearly the relation that general or common habit sustains to the principles of the law. Such habits, where they affect relative rights as to the use of property, constitute usages giving rise to a presumed intention of a transfer of some permanent or temporary use of property. Those habits that concern the modes and forms of transactions or dealings are customs, and become part of the means of interpreting the intention of parties dealing together. Those habits that concern personal conduct merely, without that special character that relates usages and customs to dealings with property, or in trade, are here given the general name of practices. Among habits of this class an illustration may be taken from what is called the law of the road, or the duty of avoiding collision with the person or property of another on a road by turning in a particular customary direction. Many others are too familiar to need particularization.

CHAPTER XXX.

RESIDENCE.

CERTAIN principles of the law are illustrated in particular cases connected with the right of residence, which will be briefly noticed. Residence implies more than a certain relation to place, being a definite relation to the community occupying the place where such residence exists, and in this respect has the aspect of a social and civil right. Residence in a community is membership, either temporary or permanent, of that community, and, as has been seen, is an expression of an intention to stand in the particular social relation that characterizes such community with its members. If one is free to choose his permanent or temporary residence, then, whatever may have been the cause of his occupying a particular place as his residence, his remaining resident at such place signifies his will to remain a member of that local community. The law must be regarded as constructing the idea of the civil compact on the principles applied to all contracts. The element of volition must be active wherever such an obligation as that which has been stated exists. It would follow that, by the principles of the law, one must have the capacity of expatriation, otherwise he would be an involuntary party to an obligation that can only subsist in virtue of actual or assumed exercise of volition. If this is a fair inference from the nature of the principles of the law, then laws forbidding expatriation, independent of some ground of special obligation, must be referred to the exercise of arbitrary or despotic power, out of harmony with the principles of the law. The fact that the prevalence of a higher conception of civil liberty has, to a large extent, led to the abrogation of such legislation, points to the same general inference, for the very conservation of the idea of civil liberty is naturally accounted for by the circumstance that it has, in all ages, and even under the most despotic rule, been embodied in that portion of judicial action that has sprung from these pure fountains, which has, fortunately, been relatively large.

The right of withdrawing the person from a community to which it has been subjected was recognized long before that of casting off allegiance to that community was recognized and the correlative right to assume allegiance to a foreign power assented to. At the present time the existence of such a right is recognized, but it is not yet fully realized as a permanent civil right. That the principles of the law demand, in order that the relation of man to society shall be voluntary, that he shall have the general right to sever his connection with a particular community, and unite himself to another, as well as to remove his person from subjection to such community, is obvious. The full recognition of this principle remains to be realized, and until it is realized a hindrance must exist to the clear recognition of the nature of the civil bond that unites man to the society of which he forms a part.

The possibility of the limitation of this right rests on obvious principles. Where voluntary removal or expatriation would amount to a violation of existing obligations detrimental to the community, or to individuals, it could not be claimed as within the proper legal liberty attached to the right, under the principles of the law. The degree of obligation that would justify the refusal of the right of removal or expatriation would demand too prolonged consideration to be entered upon in this investigation; but it may be affirmed that considerations growing out of the duty of self-preservation imposed upon the state, and what is due to the administration of justice, would spring from sources competent to produce a proper limitation of this general right.

The right to change one's residence within the same domain stands on different principles from those already considered in connection with expatriation. It is a common right that arises out of the essential nature of society rather than one that may be exercised against society, but proceeds from the same conception of liberty. It is very clear that, independently of some particular exercise of public authority, or some act of individual self-obligation, the fact of removal from one part of the same general community to another, for either a permanent or temporary residence, is neither a wrong to any individual nor to that portion of the community that has thus lost a member. The only semblance of a right, as between different communities of the same general community, growing out of individual change of residence, that appears in legal action, is in regard to the support of paupers migrating from one county to another; but the right transferring the support of paupers in such cases to the counties of their former residence is the result of legislative action. As no wrong arises from the mere fact of a change of residence, upon the principles of the law it may be affirmed that the power to change, at will, the residence, is a right at common law, only subject to what may be done in the exercise of public authority, or under the individual right of self-obligation, as all other rights are.

As the fact of residence is the ground on which civil obligations rest, it is material to form a more full conception of the idea of residence, both of a permanent and temporary character. That the idea of residence is not consummate by the mere fact of personal presence at a particular place, is a legal conception, and it becomes often an important question whether the presence of the person in a particular place is, under the circumstances attending it and the force of presumptions, significant of the assumption of residence in that place. This is manifestly a question of intention, and, as such, may be presumed from past conduct in its relation to future conduct, but yielding to manifest evidence of a change of intention in that respect, carried fully, or in part, into execution. The ground of presumption in such cases is the habit of the individual, or his particular conduct in its relation to the general habit of the community. Habit is a course of action persistent, as it regards the pursuit of a certain end, or the use of a certain mode in the pursuit of different ends. It is like the tendency of matter set in motion to proceed in a straight line until deflected from it by resisting or co-operating forces. As the tendency of matter in motion is to persist in a straight line must be the basis of all reasoning that attempts to trace the effect of various forces upon it, acting in different directions, so the tendency of a course of action, set up and persistently sustained for some appreciable period of time, must be the basis of legal argument, which takes account of the various social forces under which conduct is modified. Thus it is that the law is continually working from what may be called a base line, indicated by the habit of the community or of individuals, using for that purpose rules embodying assumptions of facts that are based on the general idea that has just been advanced. It appearing that one has habitually resided at a particular place, the intention involved in such habit is assumed to continue until something appears competent to change it, or until consequences appear attributable to such a change. The proof of change is a course of conduct irreconcilable with the former intention, and manifesting a new intention. Declarations accompanying actions forming parts of such course of action are means of interpreting such actions, where the character of the actions is such that both the actions and declarations may spring from the same motive. If the declarations have an independent motive, such as to conceal the true tendency of the actions, they are rejected as means of interpreting the act as bearing on the question of intention. A change of residence involves an executed intention, and, therefore, must be accompanied by the presence of the person in the place indicated by such change of intention. A stranger present in a community may sustain three distinct relations to such community, each of which is capable of producing certain effects upon his civil and political rights. He may be a traveler passing from place to place without attaching himself to any local community; or he may be a resident, temporary or permanent; or he may, when the laws permit, by an act renouncing his allegiance to his former state, and assuming allegiance toward that acquired, assume all the duties of citizenship, and become clothed with full civil powers as a citizen, and such measure of political power as the laws of the country permit in such cases.

In order to show the relation that the actual state of rights produced by the presence of a stranger in a community sustains to the principles of the law, it is necessary to understand that what is called international law is a product of the same principles in which all other branches of the law originate. The principle of comity, as it is called among nations, covers the idea merely of the existence, as between nations, of a social bond, based upon the same principles that underlie all the forms of human societies, embracing the relations of individuals, and societies of individuals, to each other. These principles are necessarily specialized, according to the nature of governmental societies, as affecting such societies. Comity, as the word in its origin implies, contains the idea of companionship, which is a modification of the general social idea involving the recognition of a certain duty among those related together, according to its expression. These duties, though representing an imperfect obligation, are to respect the property and right of each other, to exercise good faith in their dealings, and to afford some measure of protection to each other. The assertion that the principles of the law are such as to demand the existence of a bond of that nature among independent states, is, in view of the many instances of the persistent denial of force to these principles in the practical relations of states, a proposition that demands that its grounds should be made apparent.

It has already been said, in regard to the conduct of individual states, prompted by the policy of government, that the nature of the principles of the law is not to be directly discerned from acts of arbitrary authority that are a denial of fundamental principles of right. The nature of these principles of right will be found better represented in the popular reactions against such despotic power, where the proper means of popular resistance are employed. But, as has been said, a more exact means of pointing out the principles of the law lies in the course of the administration of justice where not disturbed by the intervention of governmental policy. Such a body of adjudications we have, in which private rights are considered as affected by the circumstance that a portion of the acts entering into the constitution of such rights has been performed under one sovereignty, and another part under a different sovereignty, or by the circumstance that acts performed within the realm of one sovereign were so performed by one who was a subject of another sovereignty, or, finally, by the circumstance that acts performed under one sovereignty were intended to affect property within another sovereignty. It remains to be seen whether the basis of that class of decisions that are said to rest on international law, or the comity of states, may not be found in the general principles of the law.

If that which is done under the name of comity is to be regarded as a mere act of grace or courtesy, and not as the recognition of any fundamental obligation, perfect or imperfect, then the exhibition of such grace or courtesy appertains to the political functions of the government. It will not be disputed that the action of the law, in appreciating and enforcing rights matured under the laws of a foreign state, can not be accounted for on the idea of the existence of a diplomatic policy, or of fraternal sentiments from which such judicial action is a necessary consequence. The general principles upon which the judicial power administers what are called the principles of international law are not found in treaties or statutes, and can, therefore, have no other origin than that in the principles of the law. The principles of international law must be, as they are, derivations from the general principles of the law, taking their peculiar forms from the nature of the subject to which they are applied. This proposition will appear quite clear when we look more closely into the general elements of questions of international law.

It is universally recognized that the laws of a community have no force beyond the territory occupied by such community, except in a limited class of cases, resting on exceptional conditions, as, for instance, acts performed on the high seas under the flag of the nation. This is simply applying to the conditions of states a principle of universal application as between individuals.

No argument is needed to show that public law has no power to control the conduct of individuals unless the relation of sovereign and subject exists between its source and such individuals. It is in itself the consequence of a certain relation, and, if that relation has no existence, the power can not exist. This conclusion arises from the general nature of law, and holds good throughout nature. To say, however, that the law has no force outside of the relation of sovereign and subject is not exactly equivalent to saying that public law has no extra-territorial force. If at any time all the subjects of a particular state were within its territories, it would be self-evident, of that particular state, that its laws could have no extra-territorial force. On the other hand, if the subject of a state is within the territory of a different sovereignty, as that circumstance does not, in itself, dissolve the obligation that binds him to his proper sovereign, it would follow, from what has been said, that the vigor of the laws of that sovereign would continue to act upon him within the territories of a different sovereign. Another principle here supervenes, for one who is present, for even a temporary purpose, in a state foreign to that of his allegiance, is, during such temporary presence, a subject of such foreign state. He may not have the recognition of citizenship, but his conduct for the time being is as completely subject to the control of such foreign state as if he were its citizen. The temporary sovereignty does not release such an individual from his duty to his proper sovereign, but operates as an irresistible force, preventing the full consequences of what is due to that relation. It follows that one temporarily within a foreign state is at liberty to conform to the demands of his proper sovereign only to the extent permitted by his duty to the state of his temporary residence. If, then, in such a case, the laws of a foreign state have any vigor within the realm of another independent state, it is only such as is permitted by the laws of the latter state. It may, then, be said that, if the laws of a state have any of the vigor proper to them beyond the territories of such state, such effect as such laws may have upon the obligations or conduct of its subjects within a foreign state, through the permissive authority of the latter, must be ascribed wholly to the state of the laws of such foreign state.

It is necessary to look at the question of the status of a stranger in the light of the various classes of obligations by which a member of the community is bound. As it regards the common obligations, there is no fundamental difference between the duty of the stranger and that of the citizen, the former being bound to obedience to the public authority, and to respect the rights of individuals precisely as all members of the community are bound. He is affected by public obligations such as those imposed by statutes, treaties, and judgments, whatever difference may exist in the actual duties thus imposed depending on the expressed will of the public authority. His right to exercise the power of self-obligation, and, accordingly, of acquiring civil rights, is subject to the same limitations and forms as those that affect the similar powers of others who are citizens, but may be more narrowly limited by public laws or treaties.

In order to fix the status of a stranger under the principles of the law, it is material to ascertain his relations to the common obligations, for, as has been seen, these obligations result from the principles of the law, operated upon by the nature of civil society, and giving rise to specific duties through the operation of the habit of the community. If, then, obligations are characteristic of the existence of sovereignty, then, as a stranger is bound equally with a citizen by these common obligations, it must be concluded that, in the contemplation of the principles of the law, the stranger is a subject of the laws of any country to which his person may be subjected.

But, although the stranger may be properly regarded as a subject, yet the consequences of that relation may be materially affected by the circumstance that his presence may be for a temporary purpose, and recognized and permitted as such. His presence may be due to a license to travel accorded by the laws of the state generally or by the executive authority of the state; and, in that case, it is easy to infer that he would be regarded as a subject of the laws of the country in which his license was permitted, only in the most limited sense. That such a discrimination may result from the principles of the law solely, without the aid of statutes or treaties, results from the nature of these principles, as abundantly and familiarly illustrated in many cases. A guest in a household or a passenger in the vehicle of a common carrier is subject to the law of the place; but his duty in that respect is affected by the purpose for which he is present. In a word, it is accordant with the nature of the principles of the law that subjection to the law of a place should give duties modified to accord with the character of the objects mutually contemplated by such subjection.

The nature of the right of self-obligation gives rise to another fundamental principle of what is called international law, and tends to show that that law is the result of the principles of the law operated upon by the nature of international society. The voluntary obligations of individuals are, in their substance, the products of the will of the individual. The relation that the law of the place, where the obligation is contracted, bears to the voluntary individual obligation is twofold—first, in giving recognition and efficacy to the right with which the obligation assumes to deal, and, second, in imposing some element of limitation or form upon the exercise of such right of self-obligation.

A valid voluntary obligation contracted by individuals is the law of the parties making it, within the liberty of their legal right, according to the law of the place where it is made. It is commonly said that the law of the place enters into the contract and forms part of it. This is true, but not in the sense that the law of the place is the cause of the obligatory consequences flowing from the contract. The law of the place is a constant element of the contract, while, as has been elsewhere seen, the idea of cause is attached to that which controls the variable elements. While the will of the parties may not subsist at all in an effective form, unless in accord with the law of the place, yet, if it takes proper force, the existence of whatever obligation results must be ascribed to that will as its producing cause, and not to the law of the place, which merely supplies the materials out of which the parties are enabled to construct their own mind and purpose.

Again, it is very commonly said that the law is the obligation of the contract. Effective obligation certainly depends upon the law of the place, or of the forum in which it is sought to be enforced. If the law of the place of the contract is, in an exclusive sense, the obligation of the contract, then such contract could not be enforced extra-territorially to that law, for it can not operate beyond the limits of its own territorial sphere. Within the place of the contract the law of such place may be, with propriety, called the effective obligation of the contract, for without it such obligation would depend solely on the voluntary performance of it by the parties. On the other hand, when a foreign contract is sought to be enforced in a domestic tribunal, the law of the place of the contract can not, with any propriety, be called the ground of its effective obligacy, for that would be according such law extra-territorial force, which it can not have. It is obvious that the expression, *the obligation of contracts*, as used in the clause of the Constitution of the United States forbidding the states to pass laws impairing the obligation of contracts, implies more than what is meant by the law of the place of the contract, for, as it applies to foreign-made contracts, it was intended clearly to conserve the private law of the contract, and not the efficacy of a law of 'a foreign state.

Where, then, the law is spoken of as constituting the obligation of contracts, as applied to the inherent force of the obligation as distinct from the means of its legal enforcement, the term law must be understood as embracing the private law of the parties to the contract. It does not follow that, because the public laws of a community have no extra-territorial force, the private law of the parties to a contract is limited by territorial bounds. The proper sphere of the individual will is that of the right subjected to it, and it is only subject to territorial restrictions through the nature of some subject upon which it may act. As the individual will, relatively to individual rights, may embody in itself consequences derived from the law of the place where it is exercised, it would follow that the law of the place, thus embodied in the private law of the contract, would have efficacy as part of the private law, wherever the rights may exist that may be affected by such contract, without regard to the territorial lines of sovereignties. This deductive conclusion is fully verified by the practical rules of international law, so that a contract, valid by the law of the place where made, is, in general, valid everywhere, and is entitled to that constructive effect that is due to the law of the place where made.

The rule just stated is confined to rights that are not objectionable under the laws of the country where the contract is sought to be enforced, for there are many acts valid by the laws of one state that are contrary to the policy of others, who will not therefore enforce them.

The rule of international law, just considered, illustrates the relation of the individual to governmental society in an important aspect. His acts and obligations have current value beyond the limits that circumscribe the efficacy of the laws of the community of which he is a member. The general qualities that the law ascribes to the acts of individuals, in the exercise of their power of self-obligation, are not ascribed to them as members of any particular communities. The principles of civil law are an appreciation of elements that existed in human nature prior to the formation of civil government, and which would bind together individuals if the existence of communities were unknown. When the separation of community and individual interests occurred, it was to further the ends contemplated in the nature of man, and not to subvert their foundations. Civil recognition and form are like the coinage that gives currency to gold without changing its essential qualities. The law is, then, under the necessity, arising from the nature of its principles, of conceiving that rights may be acquired and obligations created by individuals, with all the general qualities ascribed to them under all governments and forms of government, and even where no government may exist.

Taking the two rules that have been mentioned as rules of international law, as here explained, and familiar legal results are readily accounted for. It is obvious that delegated powers of a public nature, as derived from the authority of the laws and obligations binding individuals, created by the public authority in one state, can not, while executory, be enforced in another, while, on the other hand, proprietary rights appertaining to states may, on the principles of the law, be enforced in the manner permitted to like individual rights. The authority of an administrator is an instance of the first class. His power, though individual in its nature, is delegated by the public authority, under which he derives his authority ; hence, when he attempts to enforce those rights, in the character of administrator, in a foreign state, he must be regarded as calling upon such foreign state to establish consequences under the laws of another sovereign, which is in effect giving operation to those laws beyond the territory to which they relate. But if the administrator has reduced property of his intestate to possession, and comes into a foreign state to vindicate that possession, it is the proprietary right of the administrator, and not any duty under the law of a foreign state, that is the subject of the controversy, and it will be entertained. So, if one acquires title to property under an administrator, he may vindicate that title in any forum, as he stands upon an executed and not an executory power. Obligations created by public authority alone, and imposed upon individuals, have no other force than such as the laws of the community may impart to them. To enforce such obligations beyond the territory of the state under which they exist, as such, is to give efficacy to the laws of a state beyond its territorial limits, which, as has been seen, can not, on the principles of the law, be done. But obligations consummated in the exercise of private right, whether by individuals or communities, are based upon individual right, so that their enforcement by a foreign state is merely the recognition of the private right of self-obligation. The act of a community in binding itself by a contract, although consummated by the exercise of public authority, is a private act, and the law of a contract, even where a sovereign state is a party to it, is to be regarded as private, and not as public law, for the state in binding itself acts as an individual.

The expression international law covers an important idea,

if it does not suggest an independent source of law. When we examine what is meant by international law, we find that it consists of certain consequences, resulting from the application to the principles of the law of the habits of intercourse and dealing among independent sovereignties and the individuals that compose them. Just as the principles of the law accommodate themselves to the habits of dealing among those engaged in commerce throughout the world, bringing into existence the departments of maritime commercial law, so these principles, under the influence of the habits that characterize the relative conduct of communities, formulate the department of international law. It is in this sense that customs, usages, and practices of nations, as affecting their mutual conduct, enter into the law and form parts of it. It is obvious, from what has already been said as to the tendencies of the habits of individuals, that it must be equally true of the habits of communities in relation to the common interest and duty of mankind at large, for the idea that the sphere of man's social duty is co-extensive with humanity is inseparable from that of a general community in which all mankind participates, whether that community is regarded as ideal or real, as incipient or realized.

Passing from this broad subject, which is entitled to consideration under other than the present points of view, we have only to notice some of the consequences arising from the presence of individuals in communities upon rights there created. When a stranger voluntarily enters the territory of a civil community he evidently expresses an intention to use, to some extent, the liberties and common rights and common licenses that appertain to the members of that community, for he could not otherwise use its highways and enter places of entertainment. Without extending this assumption, it is manifest that, according to the ordinary operation of the principles of the law, he would become, to some extent, bound by the law of the place. Taking benefits from these conveniences, he would subject himself to whatever constituted the conditions upon which such rights are enjoyed in that particular community. These rights, regarded as civil rights, having their origin and sanction in the common obligations, constituting the government and society of such community, his conduct would be interpreted in no other light than as a voluntary assumption of the obligations attached to such rights. The obligation that constitutes society is necessarily a unit, as civil society is a unit, and indivisible in its nature, though composed as an organic whole of subordinate obligations; and, therefore, each right and obligation contained in it must depend on every other. The consequence is, that a stranger under such circumstances would, independent of some modifying agency, according to the ordinary action of the principles of the law, be subjected to the law of the place in every particular as fully as any citizen of the community while remaining in the use of such liberties, common rights, and licenses. He could, of course, terminate this obligation, as it regards future consequences, by removing from such territory. This modifying agency is the habit of civilized peoples and governments. Upon the same principles that give rise to implications from the habit of the people of single communities, universal habits, disclosed in part by the law of other countries, and in part by more general means, lead to inferences having an important bearing on the interpretation of the conduct of a stranger. The habits of travel for the pursuit of particular business, for the pursuit of studies, and for general observation and entertainment, that generally prevail, would, on these principles, as applied to appropriate conduct, establish such presumptions as would rebut the general inference that a stranger intended, by his presence in a community, to use all its rights and fall under all its obligations. The presumption of an intention, according to the habit of travel, to make only a partial and definite use of certain liberties and rights, in view of the absence of any action of the political power tending to prevent the ordinary use of the habit of travel, or imposing special obligations on such persons, would, on the principles on which licenses are inferred, lead to placing the liberty of such persons on the footing of a peculiar license. This view must rest mainly on deductive grounds, for no exact determinations as to the basis of the right possessed by travelers in foreign countries are available as the means of establishing it inductively. Liberties of this character, in common with other liberties of the citizen, have been developed slowly against the practices and tendencies of arbitrary authority of an unsocial tendency, doubtless having their origin in the weaknesses of infant societies, and the formidable character of the external antagonisms that they encountered, but have been prolonged beyond the occasions that could justify them by dynastic and national fears and jealousies.

Assuming the conception, that the right of travel enjoyed by strangers stands on the basis of a license, it remains to examine the general characteristics of such license, for the double purpose of examining the truth of that conception and of conveniently arranging the matter bearing on the general discussion.

As a fact, strangers exercising the right of travel have an unlimited power of dealing; indeed, without the power of making contracts, the simplest purposes of travel could not be accomplished. Whether we adopt the view that a stranger in travel is bound in a complete sense by all that the laws of such community imposes upon its own citizens, or only to the extent contemplated by a particular license, his liberty of using the power of self-obligation must be ascribed to the law of the place where such an exercise must take place. It is only in virtue of these laws that such power can have any civil quality and consequent obligacy, for, while beyond the limits to which the laws of his own country are confined, those laws can produce no such effects. It follows that the law of a country is the law of every contract made within its sphere of law, for, if, in the instance of travel in which one exercises to the most limited extent the liberties of a country, that consequence would follow, it would of necessity follow in all cases. This, then, must be regarded as an important modification of personal right induced by the nature of the right of travel.

The fact that by the international law, as generally recognized, real estate must be transferred according to the law of the country where it is situated, is explainable on grounds that leave untouched the conclusions that have been expressed.

Personal rights and proprietary rights are distinguishable in many respects. Persons and property have always been considered as distinct subjects of law. The capability of certain material substances to admit of possession by man is a natural quality of those substances to which, as a habit, the principles of the law are molded. Man creates at will his personal obligations, and, within the liberty permitted by the law, makes them such as his will determines; but matter he does not make, and, at most, can only change its form. Thus the nature of the subject of property is a cause of modifying personal rights.

Immovable property admits of a very limited control, and the right of property, in its relation to that subject of property, not only takes a precise mold, but encounters the interest that the community has in that which constitutes part of the common domain, and derives modification from that source. According to the usages of primitive time, property in land was signified by its possession, and transferred by a ceremony upon the land that represented the intention of the former owner to abandon its possession in favor of a particular person, and the intention of such person to take up the vacant possession. That the act should be performed upon the land was the necessity of the nature of the transaction as a dealing with actual possession. This limitation must be regarded as impressed upon proprietary rights of that class, from natural principles, prior to the formation of civil institutions, and as perpetuated under these institutions. When, in process of time, other ceremonies were substituted for the act required to be performed upon the land, such substituted ceremonies could only take the place of the natural ceremony of the actual delivery of possession where rightfully performed; hence, forms that were not conformable to law would be inefficacious to transmit the possession. According to the primitive idea, one who was absent from the country where his land lay could not, in person, make a transfer of such possession; and if he was permitted to perform that act by an agent, the act of the agent being necessarily performed at the place of the land, it would be an act performed under the law of that place, and subjected to all its conditions. When, at length, the citizen absent could there perform ceremonies competent to express his intention of transferring possession, either permanently or for a temporary purpose, such right constituted a modification of his primitive, and, hence, fundamental right, that limited his liberty to the use of certain prescribed forms. The explanation here given is certainly in accordance with the rules of law, past and present, and tends to show that the legal idea of full proprietary right is that of the possession of material substance defended by civil obligations.

Again, the rules of the law, and the provisions of public law, giving a certain mold to the right of the proprietorship of land, are limitations of the power of control over such lands, and, as the personal powers of the individual in the use of his proprietary rights are limited by their character, only that can be done effectually which is embraced within that proprietary right.

It may, then, be asked why this is not the case with personal property, which may be transferred according to the laws of the place where the owner is present and domiciled, and with the effect allowed by those laws, when the property is within the laws of another country, provided it is not in conflict with the public law of the place of the property. In the first place, it must be understood that this effect only takes place in the absence of public law prescribing the mode of transfer, its limitations, and proper legal effect. Such laws, when binding at the place where property is situated, control the effect of transfers made, or attempted, under different laws, as completely in the case of movable property as in that of land. It is only in the absence of such laws that the effect of a transfer can be defined by the laws of any other country than that of the place of the property.

There is a satisfactory explanation of the different conclusions of the law, as it regards the effect of a transaction under the laws of a foreign country on property situated within the domestic law, as it regards movable and immovable property. The difference may be traced to the fact that, while actual delivery of possession was recognized as requisite in the case of real property, symbolical delivery was admitted in the case of personalty. The difference between actual and symbolical delivery is a technical or formal difference, as it can not be claimed that there is anything in the natural qualities of these forms of matter that suggests that the one may be delivered, in a legal sense, by mere symbol, and not the other. Accuracy of statement demands that it should be stated that the actual contract is not between action and symbol, but between action with symbol and symbol without action. The primitive forms of transferring land employed symbols, such as the delivery of a clod of the land in the name of the whole; but, the transaction being upon the land, it expressed the actual delivery of its possession. In the case of personal property, the change that is under examination involved dispensing with any act proper to actual delivery, making the symbol itself solely efficacious as a substitute for that act. There is no natural reason why the principles of the law should become molded in the form in which we find them in this particular, as there is nothing in nature to give such an impress. Then the reason of the difference must be found in social conditions, as they represent another source from which the principles of the law take impression. These social conditions are the habits of mankind, either as members of a particular community or at large. There is reason to believe that the rule of law in question as to real estate was formulated from the habit of individual communities, and as to personal property from the general habit of mankind in commercial dealing.

The language of the law constantly points to international law as the source from which that feature was derived that accredits to foreign laws an indirect power of affecting domestic rights, through the intervention of a foreign transfer of domestic property. This language warrants an inquiry whether sufficient ground exists for such a conclusion. Before examining this question, and preliminary to it, the rule as to real estate will be further considered.

The primitive custom of transferring real estate by means of a ceremony performed upon the land has already been noticed.

Such a ceremony, in view of the place where performed, contains the idea of actual delivery, and, considered as a persistent habit, it naturally gives form to the principles of the law. That impression once made, could only be erased by public law. That it never has been erased is evidenced on the one hand by the persistency of the rule as to *livery of seisin*, and on the other by the rules as to the *lex rei sitæ*, as they prevail at this day. The mode in which the necessity for livery of seisin was dispensed with in England is characteristic. The principle of the forms of assurance there substituted was that the law might transfer the title without actual delivery. In the case of a bargain and sale, the statute produced that effect; in the case of the lease and release, it was accomplished through the general principles of the law; in the case of a fine or recovery at law, it was accomplished through principles governing the administration of justice.

Turning, then, to the rule as affecting personal property, it must be observed that such property is the great subject of commerce, and, therefore, connected with the habits of commerce as they appear among mankind at large. The nature of commerce tends to separate the owner of that kind of property from his property. Especially is this true of foreign commerce, where the property of a merchant is presumably abroad on the seas or in foreign countries, in the hands of agents. So long as commerce has existed it must be assumed to have possessed that nature and tendency. Unless, then, the owner who had property abroad could make a delivery by symbol of the same, he could not use his ownership of such property for any commercial or other purpose. That the habit of transferring property by symbol was a primitive commercial habit must be concluded upon the ground of necessity already stated. The fact that such general customs tend to embody themselves in local institutions is proven by the existence of international law, and the subordinate departments of maritime and general commercial law.

As it regards the nature of the symbolical act, the present stage of the discussion only requires that the general proposition should be stated, that, when the form of the act is not ascertained by public law, the custom of general commercial dealing determines its qualities and form, the question under the general custom being, whether the mutual conduct of the parties signified an intent that immediate change of possession should take place. Symbols are a form of language, and, as such, can only serve to express the intention of those using them, while the requirements as to the character of the symbol have the effect merely to act upon the sufficiency of the evidence of intent. A deed in this respect may be regarded as a symbol, and the requirement of a deed in a particular form is in effect limiting the means of proving an intention to effect a change in the possession of land to an instrument of a certain character.

What has been said on the subject of the status of the individual who is present in a state other than that of which he is a citizen, is important as showing the effects of the law of place upon the personal rights, thereby assisting the formation of a clear conception of the estimate in which the individual is regarded under the principles of the law, and the nature of that civil endowment that attends his person. Property forms so large a part of that endowment that this conception can not be completed until a full discussion of the proprietary rights has taken place. That subject is reserved for treatment by itself, as there are general principles that have a peculiar relation to it, and that can be best understood when all the cases in which they operate are examined together. In the mean time the discussion of the principles that have a particular relation to the personal powers can only generalize the subject and prepare it for more minute examination.

Another important consequence of residence belongs rather to the subject of proprietary rights than to personal rights, but will be briefly noticed as illustrating the relative ideas involved in the distinction between permanent and temporary residence. It is the question of residence as bearing on the right of succession to the personal estate of deceased persons. Wherever one is domiciled, or, in other words, has a permanent residence, the law of such place would, on the general principles already stated, dispose, by way of succession, of all the personal estate of such person at his decease, at such place, as well as his lands there situated. The same consequences would follow a case of temporary residence, unless there is something recognizable in the consequences of a temporary residence that causes it to differ from a permanent residence in this respect.

The idea that a right of temporary residence stands on the footing of a license, rather than on the general idea that residence of any kind implies voluntary membership of the community for general purposes, appears to explain what otherwise would appear to be anomalous in the interpretation of the principles of the law. The idea of a license carries that of subjection to the laws of a country for a limited purpose, measured by the rights incident to such limited use of the liberties of such country.

The rule of the distribution of intestate estates that has just been stated is a distinct recognition that temporary residence can not displace the obligations due to permanent residence, implying that the obligations of citizenship are not dissolved by that degree of subjection to the laws of a foreign state that results from a temporary residence in such state. That this rule arises from the nature of the principles of the law is obvious from the fact that its existence is not dependent upon statutes or treaties. It affords evidence, then, that there is more than a single element in the idea of sovereignty. It shows that there are certain obligations that enter into the sovereign relation that exist independent of place, and others that arise from relationship to place; for, under the rule in question, while the satisfaction of the obligations binding the stranger by reason of his temporary residence makes the first demand upon his estate at the place of such temporary residence, yet that, after these demands are provided for, the general obligations that result from the personal relation of the subject to his proper sovereign are to be recognized by all other states.

It may be argued that there is no real distinction among the obligations to the community that attach directly to the person and those that attach by reason of place, for the reason that permanent residence gives rise to the full personal obligation; and therefore it·is, after all, a relation to place, the distinction being confined to the character of this relation, whether permanent or temporary. If there is force in the idea that all civil obligation is capable of being reduced to the idea of the law of place, or, what is equivalent, if all conceptions of sovereign power are capable of being reduced to the single form of dominion, it is important that such possibility should be appreciated as having an important influence on the whole theory of government and law.

It is true that permanent residence is the usual means of ascertaining whether the relation of sovereign and subject exists between a community and an individual found present within it. It is also true that, if he has a permanent residence in such community, the evidence of such personal obligation is indisputable. This may consist with the idea that permanent residence is the source of the personal obligations, or with the idea that it is mere evidence of the existence of conditions incident to such personal obligations. If permanent residence is the sole sanction of governmental authority, then it would follow that the obligations of a citizen, in the general sense, could only exist where the fact of a permanent residence exists. No reason appears why a person may not contract allegiance to a government without having set foot upon its territory, with all the general consequences that follow citizenship, as upon the high seas under the flag of such country, or in localities where no law exists preventing such a relation from being created. It may be that citizenship thus acquired could not receive general recognition until accompanied by permanent residence, but that might happen consistently with the existence of a personal obligation to the community.

Then, again, if permanent residence is the sole sanction of governmental authority, the moment that permanent residence ceases in any community the obligation between the community and its former citizens would be absolutely dissolved. If, then, one should leave his proper state with a fixed intention to take up a permanent residence in a foreign state, and, in passing from his former place of residence to that of his intended future residence, he should make a temporary residence in a third independent state, having personal property there, and should there die, the rule of distribution would be based upon the laws of the state of his last permanent residence, and not upon those of the state in which he intended to make a permanent residence, but failed to do so by reason of death. In other words, the consequences of a former permanent residence remain unchanged until a permanent residence is elsewhere established. If the obligation to the community depended upon the actual fact of a permanent residence in such community, then the moment such permanent residence ceased the obligation would cease also. But the rules of law do not admit of such a consequence.

As, then, one may, in accordance with the principles of the law, be bound by an obligation to the community after having left it with the intention of finding a permanent residence elsewhere, it is obvious that such obligation has a foundation other than mere relation to place. It does not by any means follow that even the establishment of a permanent residence in a foreign state dissolves the obligations due to a former permanent residence. As a general rule, the status of the individual is in such cases determined by the fact of a newly-acquired permanent residence, without regard to whether it was or was not rightfully acquired. As it regards his obligations to his former sovereign, the question is one for that sovereign to solve, should an opportunity be afforded for so doing.

In view of the foregoing comments as to the existence of a personal obligation as a sanction of governmental authority, independent of the operation of the law of place, a question may arise, whether this is reconcilable with the position previously assumed, that the right of expatriation is necessary to the idea of a government resting on the consent of the governed. That proposition, as advanced, was qualified by the statement that such a right might not exist in view of specific duties that might be conceived as binding the citizen to the state. Extreme instances will serve to show that both the rule and its limitation exist, although extreme cases have not the power of defining either rules or exceptions. If one should leave his country at a moment of peril when his personal aid was needed, or should remove himself and his property to escape contribution to public burdens, it is obvious that the principles of the law would interpret such acts as clear violations of his obligations to the community. On the other hand, should the community unjustly deny protection to one or his property, his removal with such property could not be interpreted as a violation of his obligations to the community, but, on the contrary, the community would stand in the attitude of having violated its obligation, and, therefore, as having caused that which was the natural consequence of such an act. In both of the instances cited, that may well represent great classes of cases capable of infinite variation, the essence of the wrong is the violation of a certain protective duty due by the community to the individual, and, on the other hand, by the individual to the community. It is, then, essentially a duty arising out of that mutual protective obligation that binds the community and its members together. This would lead to the conclusion that, if the community fails to afford the individual protection such as was contemplated by the common obligations, the latter may, consistently with these obligations, sever his connection with such community, and would also deprive the individual of civil power to leave the community, when such act would amount to a violation of such common obligations. This affords an illustration of the nature of the protective principle or duty.

As has been already seen, the protective principle has dominant force during the period of immaturity in the case of individuals, while at maturity it should yield to the force of the opposite principle of equal individual right. It might be inferred therefrom that the right of the individual to expatriate himself was a consequence of the principle of equal individual right. While it can not be said that the law of place, as distinguished from that of personal obligation, arises out of the principle of equal individual right, it may be affirmed that the distinction between the two is not clearly presented until the principle of equal individual right commences to have active operation. It is not until the individual can assert himself independently that the conditions appear that are the means of testing the question.

The right of expatriation, like all other rights claimed against the community, is an imperfect right, and, accordingly, it is the province of public law and common usage to adjust the relations of the individual and the community in this respect. There is an advancing tendency in the family of civilized nations to reach an equilibrium between these principles, but that adjustment is not so far advanced among nations generally as to obviate the necessity for the agency of revolution that generally represents an agency weakening the forces that counterbalance the liberalizing principles, and thus rendering possible their effective assertion. The full discussion of the law of place, in its relation to the law of personal obligations, must be deferred to a place where its essential elements can be brought into examination together.

The effect of residence on personal right is illustrated by the case of a person taking up a residence in a community that is subject to public debts, or other specific obligations or duties, the effect being that in such cases he becomes subject to bear his proportion of such public burdens in common with all other citizens who occupied that position at the time the public debts or burden was created. This result, though seemingly inequitable, is the result of the nature of the obligation fundamental to the community. As that obligation is a unit, it is impossible that one who is a party to it in a full sense should be bound by part of it and not by another part. It was this principle that led to the conclusion that one who was exercising a limited use of the privileges of citizenship, and subjected to modified consequences of the common obligations, should be regarded not as a member of the community, in a proper sense, but as having a license definable by public law or the habit of the community. When, however, a permanent residence is taken up in a community, no such limited right can exist, and the obligations that are the proper consequences of citizenship must necessarily attach. This is the law of organic assimilation, for every new unit that takes the strength of the organism takes its weaknesses also; and, as we find this principle embodied in the law, it is another evidence that the law is an organic growth following the laws of natural development.

If the several obligations that compose the general obligation thus bind all the members of a community in like manner, all the proper consequences of these obligations would be inseparable from the obligation itself, and among such consequences must be enumerated specific duties, such as public debts and burdens.

What is true of a general community in this respect is equally true of subordinate communities, such as colonies, provinces, counties, and towns. As a general rule, the contribution that each member is bound to make for the support of the community and the discharge of its obligations is ascertained under public laws or customs; but the operation of the principles of the law can be observed, in such cases, in those instances where judgments recovered against a subordinate community have been enforced against the individual property of the members of such community. Such instances show that the idea of a community —that it is an aggregate of individuals, united by a common bond and a common interest—underlies the forms of government. The fact that the enforcement of obligations, by the ordinary methods of administering justice, can not be applied to independent states, precludes the same evidence from appearing in regard to what is implied by sovereign government.

It must be added to the instances already cited, as a consequence of the same general principle, that one who enters a place where a particular law prevails, whether derived from the public authority, from common habit, or from the right of a private individual proprietorship of such place, becomes bound, in some measure, by that law, whether he enters such place for a temporary purpose, or becomes permanently united to such place. In the intercourse of society such peculiar obligations are constantly assumed as incident to every dwelling or other place that belongs to the public or a private proprietor. The violation of a license, express or implied, in such cases, is ground for the physical exclusion of the offending person, and an entry on the property of another without express license, and for a purpose not contemplated by the implied license, permitted according to the habit of the community, or of the place, is a violation of proprietary right that justifies physical exclusion.

CHAPTER XXXI.

WRONGS TO RIGHT OF CHANGE OF PLACE.

The characteristics of the right of changing place are strongly exhibited by the correlative wrongs. Every restraint of this right is in some sense an imprisonment, and, if not justifiable under proper legal authority, is a false imprisonment, and is compensated as such. As the power in question is the basis of all action, it is made the subject of punishment of the highest grade, next after the deprivation of life, for various criminal offenses. A false imprisonment implies force applied to the volition, either through the body or the mind. A person of weak mind may be thus affected by means applied to the mind, as in the case of restraint upon very young children. When any measure of physical force is employed for the purpose, the false imprisonment is complicated with what may be an assault and battery, and the two wrongs may be compensated by a general compensation. In compensating a false imprisonment, two elements of damage appear: one, the injury to the general personal right, and the other the particular injurious consequences arising from the restraint of liberty of action. If no particular grounds of damage appear, still compensation is made for the general wrong, showing that the right of moving from place to place is in itself, and apart from the uses to which it may be put, a subject of legal compensation, and, as such, estimable in terms of pecuniary value.

When a false imprisonment assumes the form of an assault and battery, the right of self-defense arises, as well as the right to use merely resistant force. The writ of *habeas corpus* is a specific remedy appropriate to the vindication of this right.

The writ is a command to the person exercising restraint upon another to appear and produce the body of his prisoner before a competent tribunal or officer, and show the cause and reasons of such imprisonment. Upon the production of the person alleged to be falsely imprisoned, he passes into the custody of the court or officer issuing the writ, and may be subjected to restraint during the continuance of the investigation. The object of the writ is accomplished by the liberation of the one under restraint. The writ of *habeas corpus* is thus to be regarded as a specific remedy, attesting the high estimate in which the law holds the right which it is intended to enforce.

The power of going from place to place may be restrained by judicial authority, as an incident of the administration of justice, as in the instances of an injunction or *ne exeat* in chancery, and by arrest, imprisonment, and bail, in both civil and criminal proceedings.

It has been already observed that the power of the individual to go at will from place to place has a relation to the means of securing obedience to public authority of the most important character. The highest punishment for public offenses is the deprivation of life, such punishment implying that, with the means, preventive and redressive, society has at hand, it is impossible to preserve the peace and order of society and at the same time preserve the life of the offenders. Such incompetency may result from either the nature of such criminal tendencies themselves, or from the condition of society itself, in the latter case the taking of life for purposes of punishment being the evidence of the existence of imperfect social conditions. Beyond doubt, both of these reasons control the extent to which capital punishment is employed at the present day, as they have exercised control in the past.

The confinement of the offender in a single place tends to deprive him, to a large extent, of the means of accomplishing his purposes; and, in addition to this, preventing intercourse with other persons is a further deprivation of individual power. This exhibits public punishment in one of its aspects, in which it is clearly in the nature of a preventive remedy. An additional feature of such punishment is the infliction of pain or inconvenience as a means of affording a motive to act upon the mind. It is not in place to consider the relative value of these punitive elements, but simply to notice the peculiar value of the power of going from place to place, as illustrated by its relation to public punishment.

CHAPTER XXXII.

LIBERTY OF SPEECH.

GENERAL liberty of action, in its relation to volition as the choice of means and ends, demands no general consideration, as its principles are illustrated in connection with the various uses to which such action may be applied. Liberty of speech is part of that voluntary power of the individual that has been denominated the right or liberty of volition. What we call a free country is one in which the liberties of the individual are formulated in perfect, or approximately perfect, harmony with the principles of the law, without restraint imposed by public laws. Such an evolution from the primitive habit of communities is the product of a long chain of causes acting upon the habits of communities, and tending to equilibrate ideas of right and public utility.

There are three radical types of government: the paternal, the militant, and the communistic, corresponding to tendencies that are found in composite governments in some condition of equilibrium. The spirit of the paternal type is to restrain the liberties of the individual when their exercise is regarded as tending to licentiousness rather than to advantageous results. The spirit of the militant type is to subordinate all individual powers to the powers of the state, exalting public interests out of proper equilibrium with individual interests. The spirit of communism is to enhance the aggregate of individual right at the expense of public right. It will, therefore, be perceived that equilibrium is only to be looked for in paternal and in composite governments. The difference in tendency between paternal governments and well-balanced composite governments is, that the former subordinate rights to ends, while the latter, constituting what we call free governments, consider that, in regulating the exercise of individual rights, the harmonious interaction of those rights should be the end of legislation rather than the benefits that may be obtained by their use. This expresses the exact difference between the law of the family and of society in the larger sense. That the paternal type was the primitive type of government is now generally conceded. The habit of governing, on the one hand, and of obedience on the other hand, would naturally prolong itself over a condition of society, partially or even wholly fitting it for a more advanced type of government, just as we observe in families that the paternal influence does not generally cease or essentially change its character at the moment a child becomes an adult and legally independent of it, but, as a persistent habit, it is only gradually extinguished as counter-habits are formed. The history of the growth of individual liberty illustrates the principles that underlie social development. It will not be disputed that the principles of liberty existed previous to the period of their special potency, and these principles of liberty are identical with the principles of the law. Liberty of speech, in a large sense, is a modern acquisition of the individual members of society, achieved through many perils, against the efforts of those wielding the powers of government, who, though in the order of nature commissioned to maintain the conditions essential to the development of society, have very generally regarded themselves as bound to suppress the natural tendencies of that development. The most general office of speech is to reproduce the thoughts and feelings of one in others. In this sense the liberty of speech is absolute, according to the principles of the law. It is impossible to conceive of an actionable wrong existing solely on the ground that one has attempted to impart his thoughts and feelings to another, unless some public law affords such remedy, or unless such speech is accompanied by some action that is an aggression on the rights of another. It is true that such an aggression does not necessarily imply the exhibition of physical force, but, when an aggression of that character appears, something in the nature of a restraint of the person will be found commingled with it and forming the basis of the wrong. Such a restraint, as has been previously said, may be exercised through the weakness of the mind of another, arising from either natural or social conditions. When freedom of speech is suppressed, its energy is usually translated into action, and its motives, becoming involved with other motives, are re-enforced, and the springs of conduct relatively hidden. The complexity of the disorder being increased, its cure is rendered the more difficult.

While, for the reasons stated, the abnormal tendencies of liberty of speech are not likely to be arrested by direct repression, so, on the other hand, the attempt to repress the normal tendencies of speech has, in its relation to the development of the powers of civil society, a tendency not altogether injurious. The influence of the principle of individual equality as a corrective of excessive paternal tendencies in government depends upon the integration of the individual elements to form a communistic body with some degree of social organization. As the militant tendency helps to strengthen the paternal principle, so the communistic principle helps to fortify that of individual right. It is obvious, from observing the course of events, that the repression of normal liberty of speech occasions a reactive influence that leads to produce the communistic integration, and thus in the end serves indirectly to bring about the proper force of the principle of individual equality.

But speech performs a special office that sometimes places it in peculiar relation to the law. It is a means of combining and constituting the common or mutual action of individuals, and, therefore, must be examined as among the means of performing such actions as depend upon co-operation. It would follow that, when an action is unlawful, speech used as a means to such end would partake of that unlawful character. This results from the fact that what is said, as well as what is done, may form part of a transaction, and thus the lawful or unlawful character imputed to such transaction must affect all the elements of that transaction. Speech in this way may be part of

FALSE SWEARING. 351

the means of connecting the action of rioters or conspirators against governments. It may even point the nature and tendency of the actions which it accompanies, and thus become a means of conferring upon them the legal character of lawfulness or unlawfulness.

So speech may, through its relation to the passions, be efficient means of securing co-operation, whether acting upon individuals or masses of individuals. It may, through the nature of the passions, be the means of uniting bodies of men incited to lawful or unlawful acts, as to acts of violence against individuals or the public authority; as of unduly influencing or compelling individuals to accommodate their actions to the wishes of another through fear or affection induced by threats or persuasion, which is a form of compulsory co-operation. In all these cases, even where the character of what is spoken determines the legal character of what is done, it is the act alone that can convert the mere use of words into violations of right. Again, speech may be used for purposes of deception, and in that case, as in the cases previously mentioned, the act of wrong is not consummated by the speech alone, but by the action induced by the speech.

In the instance of slander, words uttered may be attended by consequences rendering them injurious to the right of character. In these cases the wrong consists in what is actually or presumably done by individuals, by society at large, or by the community as a consequence of words spoken; the words in such a case being the cause of injurious consequences, are regarded as in themselves injurious.

There is an instance where, through the operation of a specific obligation, the utterance of words may become a wrong, independent of any special consequence of an injurious character arising from them, and that is in case of false swearing. Each individual is undoubtedly under a general obligation to speak the truth in all matters that concern the welfare of others, but that duty is an imperfect one in itself. When that duty is enforced by a specific obligation, as in the case of an oath taken to testify according to the truth in the administration of justice, the duty becomes a perfect duty. It is noticeable that this change of the general duty into a specific duty to speak the truth in a given case does not depend upon the voluntary acceptance of the obligation imposed by the oath, for the taking of the oath may be compulsory. There can not be any doubt that the basis of the wrong done by false swearing is the obligation that all are under to utter the truth in aid of the administration of justice, and that the oath taken is merely the formal recognition of the antecedent obligation. The nature of the administration of justice and the common duty to uphold and aid such administration of justice fully account for the existence of a perfect obligation in such cases, apart from all forms and solemnities attending the act.

The essential idea of character is that of reputation, which the law properly describes as the *speech of men*, for, although character is, accurately speaking, the result of a state of opinion, yet speech, as the organ of opinion, is the special means by which that state of opinion is produced and maintained. Any direct attempt, then, to protect character from falsehood must lay hold of speech as the means appropriate to that end. While it may be said that the liberty of speech is absolute within the limits of truth, yet the liberty of speaking falsely is subject to the limitation implied by the fact that false speech may produce a wrong either when truth is enforced by judicial forms, or where an injury to person or property is its direct consequence.

Printed and written language, and expressive symbols and pictures, are all specialized forms of speech. The relation of signs and forms to ideas, as a means of expressing them, is determined by the habit of the community, the chief element of that habit being its common language. The general duties that underlie the use of language are fundamental to all these specialized forms of that general faculty. That speech is not confined to the vocalization of the symbols of thought is implied in the common use of the term. The term written language may well stand for all transmission of thought by means of a form given to material objects external to the body, and thus contain pictures as well as both ordinary and unusual symbols.

That which distinguishes written from spoken language is

the fact that it is accompanied by a record that serves the double purpose of perpetuating it in form, and giving it diffusive power; a corresponding difference of purpose must be assumed to exist in the case of one speaking, in the ordinary sense, and writing. Hence arises the distinction between libel and defamatory words spoken. Words spoken are not necessarily, or even presumably, addressed to the community. Such words can not, as a general rule, be regarded as, by the mere speaking, put in currency. The speech of social man is a currency of ideas, and, unless falsehood is put in a condition to enter the current of public thought, injury can not be presumed from its existence; it is like forged paper that has not been uttered or placed in currency. It is true that when a forged instrument passes from its author into the hands of one ignorant of its character, in the manner usual in dealing, it is uttered, while a letter containing false and defamatory statements affecting the character of another, sent to an individual correspondent, is not the publication of such statement as a libel. The difference between the two cases arises from the fact that a commercial obligation is presumably intended for circulation, and placing it in the hands of a person ignorant of its character is in effect making him an agent for the accomplishment of such purpose, while a letter, in the ordinary sense, is a personal communication, and its publication by the receiver is not justified by any presumed assent of the writer. It would be stretching the idea of habit beyond reasonable bounds to assume that a spoken falsehood would permeate the community so as to affect the opinion in which an individual is held. It is true that a commerce in defamatory thought often exists under the name of gossip, but where an injury is capable of being presumed, as in the case of libel, from the relation that an act performed bears to the habit of the community, such habit must have a constant and organic relation to society, while such irregular and abnormal habit as that which goes by the name of gossip can give rise to no such presumptions.

Bad habits, as well as good habits, may be considered for the purpose of interpreting intention, as, for instance, the habits of burglars in entering houses for the purposes of crime. In the useful consequences of the orderly habits of the community individuals have a right, in the nature of common right, for such habits represent regular social forces analogous to the forces of nature, and where the right of an individual, as in the case of character, consists in the state of opinion, a direct product of the action of normal habit, an act tending to misdirect such habit prejudicially to such state of opinion is in itself a wrong to such right.

It is not, therefore, to be assumed that any false and defamatory spoken statement is an injury, through its action upon common opinion. Hence it is that in an action for slander, as a general rule, actual damage must be proved. On the other hand, the presumable object of writing or printing is either to perpetuate the effect of a statement, in order to transmit it to a distant place, or to cause it to be diffused through the community. It is the diffusive quality that constitutes the essential idea of a libel, and the existence of that quality is determined by the fact that there has been an act of publication. What constitutes an act of publication is a question to be solved by the habit of the community. If the tendency of an act was to give currency to a defamatory statement in writing, or its equivalent, that is a publication, and the wrong is complete, damage to some extent being presumable.

While the principle that has been illustrated places all false and defamatory statements in writing put in currency in the light of wrongs to character, its influence is not confined to violations of truth alone. As has been said, each individual owes to every other individual a certain undefined and imperfect protective duty, that has the same sanction as that of speaking the truth, which is in part made a perfect duty, through the common obligation to respect the rights of others. To make public, without just cause, the faults and vices of others is obviously an aggression upon the right of character.

When the extent of the term *just cause* is considered, it will be obvious that any attack upon the character of another, beyond that sanction, is an abuse of the right of character of such other. What is a just cause of publishing the faults of another includes not only legal occasions for complaint against others, but such as arise from the nature of social relations and duties. If the individual is bound in a general way to protect others, he is bound by a larger duty to protect society; and, if, in the performance of the more imperative duty, the character of an individual should suffer, such condition could not be imputed to an act abusive of private right, when its performance was called for by a public or social duty.

It is manifest, then, in what sense the common phrase, *the greater the truth the greater the libel*, may be taken as true. If a libel is a false defamation, it is in itself a wrong; if true, and not called for by some legal or social duty, it is also an invasion of the right of character.

What characterizes the power of speech as standing on the footing of a liberty is the fact that, independent of the force of certain specific obligations, no preventive remedy can be obtained to anticipate its exercise. Neither libel nor ordinary slander can be prevented by injunction. When certain information that appertains to the affairs of another is held by one affected by a fiduciary or a confidential relation, a preventive remedy will in some instances be afforded, as to protect a valuable secret, or individual, family, or business matters, from being communicated to improper persons, or from being made public. Such protection is sometimes afforded to prevent the improper use of letters by the receiver of them. It is manifest that in such cases the person liable to such preventive remedy has assumed some special obligation, either expressly, or as implied in some mutual dealing, that has impaired his general liberty of speech or other communication. These cases are not to be regarded as illustrating any limitation arising from the nature of the right of speech, but as the consequences of the act of the party in assuming a particular obligation implying agency.

From the nature of the right of speech, an injury to it by force must involve some form of injury or restraint applied to the person, in which the wrong is predicated upon the injury to the person, though, in compensating such wrong, regard is had to the effect upon the right of speech.

CHAPTER XXXIII.

OCCUPATION, INDUSTRY, AND ASSOCIATION.

The next general right to be considered as part of the voluntary power that each mature individual enjoys under the principles of the law, when not impaired by public law or private obligation, is, as generally conceived, a liberty rather than a right, though lacking none of the characteristics of a right, except that no specific remedy is applicable to it. It is the liberty and right to choose one's occupation or avocation in life.

From what has been said of the spirit and tendencies of paternal government, we would naturally expect to find, under such governments, some interference with the liberty of the individual in the choice of occupation or avocation. The importance to the public welfare of supporting certain industries, or suppressing others, and of exercising more or less control over all, as understood by persons assuming themselves to be clothed with parental powers over their subjects, would naturally lead to interference with individual liberty in this direction, and history verifies that deduction. Such interferences with a community fitted to commence the exercise of the liberties that belong to mature civilization can only be ascribed to repressive power, acting out of harmony with the principles of the law, and, therefore, necessarily of temporary duration. If there were any legal means by which the selection of occupation by one could, independently of some special obligation, become an injury to others, there would be some evidence of its existence, direct or indirect, in the results that have been produced upon the principles of the law by the vast body of varied circumstances that are contained in the record of the action of the law; but there are none having recognized authority. It is competent, then, to affirm that the principles of the law place no limitation on the liberty of choosing among lawful occupations, in the case of a person of mature civil rights. Infants may be trained in the practice of particular arts or industries, but they are under no general obligation to pursue them after maturity. Government may compel individuals, against their will, to serve the public as mariners or soldiers, or in other relations, but that must result from the exercise of public authority, having the sanction of public law.

To those accustomed to the measure of liberty enjoyed in a free country such liberties appear to be matters of course, but the law that holds the breathing of the air to be a common right could not be inattentive to that most important condition of social life, namely, ability to mark out the line in which the individual exertions should be directed.

The last phase of the power of voluntary exertion to be examined constitutes a right and liberty of a most important character, as affecting the relations of individuals to society. The accomplishment of individual purpose depends almost wholly on the co-operation of others. Every transaction that effects a change in relative rights and obligations demands the co-operation of two or more persons. The simplest instance of a sale or gift of an article presupposes concerted action between two or more persons. One parts with what the other gets, and the act of one in parting with the property and the act of the other in accepting it constitute the legal idea of a change of ownership. In this simple transaction the existence of association and co-operation is not forced upon the attention, and the idea can only be reached by a process of thought based upon the analogy between such a transaction and one of greater complexity, in which the facts of association and co-operation are apparent. When the idea that the law entertains of such a transaction is examined, we clearly perceive that it may be affirmed that no change in relative rights can occur without the co-operation of two or more persons. It is out of this natural necessity of association for co-operative purposes that the right of self-obligation arises, for that right, properly interpreted, is a capacity of forming associations for co-operative purposes.

The idea of association here presented covers every case where individual right is changed or modified by the concurrence of the volitions of two or more persons possessing full power of self-obligation. As the common obligations are here conceived, their effect is twofold: first, to unite all the individuals of the community in a single-associated person for the purpose of government; and, second, to separate individual right by lines of obligation tending to give to each individual the utmost amount of liberty of action consistent with the existence of civil society. Here the outlines of the civil system are marked in two opposite directions. A power is created capable of destroying all individualities, and another is brought into existence which, if unchecked by the former, would resolve society into its units. It is the function of public law and individual co-operation to harmonize these extreme and opposite tendencies, and to produce a state of equilibrium rendering social existence possible.

In the infant community the public law, inspired by the protective principles, takes relatively the first place in supplying the internal arrangements of the social organism, both legal and industrial, each function implying an associated act of individuals. As the community passes toward a mature condition, a larger reliance upon voluntary association to supply the requisite functional arrangements is possible, and is, in fact, demanded by the inspirations of the principle of individual equality.

It is by means of co-operation between individuals that that interchange of commodity and right takes place that is as distinctly the vital function of society as the circulation of the blood is a function vital to the animal system. This interchange resolves itself into the idea of change in the state of relative rights, as it regards the commodities interchanged; and, as such a change can not be induced except through the concurrent volitions of the parties to such relationships where not compelled by public law, it follows that co-operation, which is the conception of a concurrence of action, must exist wherever such a change takes place. Association expresses the condition necessary to co-operation, the object of association being to constitute some particular state of rights, as the consequence of such association.

Ordinarily, the term association is applied to such associations as involve the creation of a common interest, such as government, corporate existence, and partnership, but the term in a broad sense equally applies to those relations of individuals that produce mutual rights instead of common rights. It is apparent that permanence of either definite or indefinite duration is not essential to the idea of association; that implies union for co-operative purposes, and therefore may exist only from moment to moment, or for an unlimited period of time. It is of importance to ascertain the verity of this conception, as its tendency is to refer the great systems represented by the law of corporate organization and the law of contracts to common principles.

Unless associations could attain stability, their use could not prove efficient, and that stability is imparted by the nature of the obligations upon which they rest and the sanctions that give them their effective obligacy. Associations are either intended to establish right directly, or to create powers capable, under the conditions imposed by the law of the association, of producing rights at a future day.

The habit of mankind and the principles of the law, that assume the persistence of existing rights, acting together, have established, as a received truth, the proposition that rights thus created must continue to exist, according to the purpose of the associated effort that produced them, until a future change is impressed upon them by some new associated effort; and, further, that powers created for the purpose of bringing future rights into existence admit, according to their particular natures, of either being revoked by those whose rights they represent, or of being placed beyond the control of such persons as it regards revocation.

When individuals are found to be acting together in definite relations and for definite purposes, it must be assumed, without further evidence of the circumstances that induced and attended the formation of such association, that in forming such association they mutually exercised their power of self-obligation in the manner indicated by their conduct as associates. This is the foundation of the law of implied contracts. The conclusion that the law habitually draws from the observation of such facts points to the ground on which the argument as to the existence and nature of the common obligations depends.

If, then, the power of forming associations for co-operative purposes is a natural power, which can not be disputed, it would emerge from the act creating the civil community as a civil power, unless there is something in the nature of civil association for governmental purposes that does not admit of such a result. The delegation of sovereign power is indeed an instrumentality that may be made to work such a preventive effect, but, until it is exercised by public law so as to restrict the liberty of individual association, such a result could not ensue. The mere delegation of a power of that nature, although absolute in its nature, can not be regarded as, in itself, an abandonment of the previous right of associating in the manner most conducive to individual interest. Since that fundamental delegation was made to subserve the purposes intended by the association of men to form civil society—and such an association, so far from excluding minor associations among lesser bodies of the same aggregate of persons, must be regarded as springing from the general consciousness that by association man can alone attain the ends of life—it must be concluded that the formation of civil society left unimpaired all the qualities of the natural right of association as the proper qualities of the civil right thence arising. In a word, individuals, in associating themselves together to form civil society, must be regarded as intending protection as well for such minor associations as they might form for the better conduct of their affairs as for their individual protection. The delegation of public authority for the purposes of civil government merely implies that the occasions in which such power shall be exercised and the manner of its exercise are committed to the judgment of the whole community, to be determined according to the opinion of the major part of the members of such society.

It is true that the formation of lesser associations for the exercise of governmental powers would be inconsistent with the nature of the fundamental obligations, and, therefore, such lesser governmental associations can not be formed unless with the consent of the public authority; but associations for purposes other than those intended to be secured by the establishment of governmental power would not be affected by this consideration. It may, then, be affirmed, that, so far as appears by consulting the general object and nature of the social compact, the natural liberty of association remained unimpaired in the form of a corresponding civil right, as part of the civil liberty of the individual, according to the principles of the law.

It is important to know whether the conclusions of the law, derived from its general principles, sustain this view. There are instances where the law, in the absence of positive enactment, condemns associations for certain purposes. It condemns the association of persons for the purpose of using force to overthrow the government, or to prevent the administration of its laws. It condemns, also, combinations of individuals conspiring for the commission of crimes. It also condemns the attempt to exercise corporate powers without governmental consent, for the reason that, by the natural law of association, the act of the association is the act of each of the individuals composing it, and, consequently, the liability of all is the liability of each, while the general idea of the legal corporation is a material modification of this natural idea, the individual members being permitted to derive its benefits with some degree of immunity as it regards its obligations. Hence the right of legal corporeity can only exist under public law, either exercised in the form of a sovereign grant or a statute, and the usurpation of such a right would derogate from the right of the community.

The instances cited, and others that will readily occur to those familiar with legal procedure, exhibit the nature of the rules of law concerned as intending the suppression of certain evils that do not consist in the mere fact of association, but in the objects of certain associations. The association for an unlawful purpose, being the strength of the purpose itself, is condemned as the means to an unlawful end.

The power of association must, then, be regarded as recognized and protected by the principles of the law. As such, the association of individuals may become an unlawful instrument through the uses designed for its employment. The repressions of this power that have existed, prompted by the timidity of governing classes, when not demanded by some urgent occasion affecting the common interest, must be regarded as instances of arbitrary authority, exerted against the tendencies of the principles of the law, producing social monstrosity according to general organic laws.

As has been said, all associations are designed either to perfect certain definite rights by the act of association itself, or to create a power capable of being used for the production of future rights. The class first indicated by this distinction includes the idea of association only in a limited way, while those associations that possess a common producing power are associations in the proper institutional sense.

Associations establishing rights directly, or creating agencies of an individual character for that purpose, may be considered under the vague legal denomination of *contracts*. For the exact designation of the class creating common producing powers the law affords no single term. The term association, in common use as a means of designating classes of companies or societies, implies that they are not incorporated as such. The term societies, as used by the Roman law, has acquired with us a sense that recalls the idea of a loose association for charitable, literary, and like purposes, where the acquisition of legal rights is not an end, but a mere incident. The word company, though indefinite, has the advantage that it has acquired no exclusive sense, and, therefore, may serve the present use better than either of the terms association or society. The general subject of associations, then, resolves itself into those of contracts and companies.

CHAPTER XXXIV.

CONTRACTS.

The simplest and, as we must assume, the primitive form of a contract was a barter, by which one subject of property was exchanged for another. The exchange of labor for commodities, or for labor of another kind, implied a means of estimating labor according to quantity, for it is only a certain quantity of labor that can become the subject of an exchange, based on the idea of relative value between the subjects of the transaction, an idea inseparable from that of a barter, or of any transaction having the nature of a barter. This quantity of labor is determinable either by the length of time occupied by it, or the quantity of useful work performed. When labor was bartered for commodities, the word *hire* came to express the transaction, a hiring being a species of barter. As the idea of value is that of a certain relation to some common standard of value, it was necessary that some commodity in general use, and of such a nature that its possession was within the means of the largest number of the members of the community, should be selected as the unit of value. Thus, in pastoral countries a single sheep would naturally be the unit chosen, and other articles valued in terms of the value of sheep. If, then, in such a community, property of any kind, including a certain quantity of labor, was exchanged for so many sheep, one animal being the unit of measure, the contract itself contained all the means requisite to estimate the value put upon all the commodities or labor brought into the transaction. On the other hand, if cattle were exchanged for labor, sheep being the accepted standard there, the value of the cattle and the labor could not be estimated by means of the contract alone, but resort must be had to the habit of dealing in the community to ascertain the value of the cattle and the labor called for, in terms of the value of sheep. Then the idea of value is that of a relation to a certain standard established by common habit, and the idea of market value that of the common judgment expressed in dealings. It was a natural step of development to seek for some common standard that would adapt itself to the dealings of all classes, and unite the advantages of divisibility and small bulk. These requirements of commerce were responded to by the precious metals, an agreed quantity of a certain metal, or alloy of metals of a certain purity, being taken as the standard instead of a specific object, such as a sheep or an ox. The next step was to verify the quantity and purity of metal, in a certain mass, by putting it in a certain form, and placing indestructible marks upon it, and finally by conferring upon government the function of preparing or coining such measure of value, and surrounding it by safeguards, to prevent false coinage.

As has been stated, the inconvenience of a barter where the commodity that formed the common standard of value was not one of the articles dealt in, was that the contract did not contain within itself the means of estimating the value intended for the various articles or subjects dealt in; this naturally led to the use of contracts of sale which, while in their nature barters, had the specific quality that money is one of the subjects interchanged. In rare instances, each of two persons might possess that which the other desired to possess, and in that instance a barter might be made; but, in the ordinary course of dealings, if one has property he wishes to exchange for other property, it would be necessary to part with the property to one for the means by which the property needed may be procured from another, so that two transactions have to be made instead of one. The quality of ready convertibility peculiar to coined money fits it for such a medium of interchange as well as for the measure of value.

The purchasing power of any coined unit of value is fixed from moment to moment by the dealings of the community, precisely as in the case of any other commodity. It is possible for government to affect indirectly the judgment of the community as to the purchasing value of coin. If, for instance, the intrinsic value of the standard coin is reduced, and at the same time the reduced coin is made a compulsory tender for the payment of antecedent debts, such reduced coin may, in its power of paying former debts, have a value in excess of its intrinsic value that would, temporarily, be recognized in dealings with it. Still, the proposition remains that the judgment of the community, as expressed in actual dealings, adjusts the relative value of coin and all other commodities. When there is a departure from the tests afforded by intrinsic value and ordinary conditions of supply and demand, it is generally due to the action of the government, which becomes a disturbing influence where, as in the instance cited, it is in effect a measure for the partial discharge of debts on the principles of insolvency.

The natural tendency of barter to transform itself into sale is thus manifest. But a contract of sale does not necessarily contain all the elements necessary for a computation in terms of money of the value of the things sold, for a contract of sale may, either expressly or impliedly, call for such an amount of money as would be the market value of the property at a certain time or place. That which is, then, essential to the idea of a sale is, that the thing sold should be required to be compensated in money, in some quantity fixed or ascertainable.

It is obvious that the contract of hiring would undergo the same transformation, so that a certain quantity of labor would have a recognized relation to a certain quantity of money, variable indeed from time to time, but variable under conditions of a constant character forming a basis of computation. It would be naturally expected that—as labor is the universal means of producing all subjects of property that are the products of industry, and of applying all natural values to the needs of man, and as the operations of society are adjusted to the conditions of industrial production, rather than to those of spontaneous or natural production—if any actual relation should spring up between the value of labor and that of metal in the condition of coin, such relation would depend on the quantity of labor necessary to produce a certain coin in its material and form. It is not the province of this discussion to verify these expectations by an induction from the facts of commerce. Assuming, however, that such is the case, then a certain measure of labor, with reference to the time employed, as, for instance, a day's labor of a certain quality, would become the actual standard by which the value of money, relatively to the value of other commodities, would be ascertained. That this is the case is not only presumable, but it is so highly probable, that the fact may be assumed on higher grounds than that of hypothesis, until it can be replaced by some more perfect idea, obtained by inductive processes. If the general proposition is admitted that has been elsewhere discussed, that standards habitually spring from the nature of those elements of transactions that are of the most constant recurrence, then, as it may be said that labor is an element of value in every object that possesses value, and as this can not be said of any other single element of value, it is the element that must enter into the standard of value as a prime factor.

On this general subject all that it is here necessary to say is that the fluctuations of market value which are ascribed to other articles as compared with money are fluctuations in which the purchasing value of money participates. As the earth appears to stand still while the sun appears to be in motion, so, looking at other commodities from the stand-point of money, they appear to be the only subjects of motion, while it may be that our stand-point participates largely in that motion.

The examination of the various forms that the contract of sale assumes and its incidents appertains to the subject of proprietary rights, as these rights are modifications of personal right induced by the nature of property, property being treated as a cause of modification external to the person. Hence it is that the nature of property must be examined as a whole before its consequences as affecting personal rights can be fully accounted for.

The contract of hiring exhibits, more clearly than that of

sale, the operation of the principle of association. Take the simple case of one desiring to accomplish the performance of a certain work by means of the labor of another, and yet in the manner and with the means that he himself may select. In this case the labor of one is co-ordinated with the skill, property, and purpose of another. The essential idea of association is that of co-ordinating the labor, skill, and capital of two or more persons in the accomplishment of a certain purpose; hence, unless the circumstance that the end to be produced is for the sole benefit of one of the associates excludes the idea of an association, the case of the hiring of labor must be referred to that idea. It is true that the characteristic features of association appear when there is a common benefit to be produced, and a common interest and right to control the means of its production; but it does not follow that the principles of association are not present where that specific character does not appear. The more correct distinction appears in treating association both in its general character and its special and characteristic type, referring cases like those cited of sale and hiring to the general principle of association, but such cases as those of associations involving a common interest to a specific class. It is this distinction which is followed in treating these general subjects under the respective titles, contracts and companies.

When one employs a laborer to produce changes in the physical condition of his property, he confers upon such laborer part of his own exclusive power to deal with such property. This is a delegation of power, though in the most limited sense, that draws after it a consequence that habitually follows delegated powers of all classes—namely, an obligation, on the part of one so empowered in the affairs of another, to use active good faith, that resolves itself into one to use reasonable care, skill, and diligence in the affairs of his employer. This is essentially a protective duty, showing that the protective principle dominates in the relation of hiring, a circumstance that accounts for the peculiar personal relation that exists between master and servant, assimilating it to a domestic relation where such a power exists, if it is not actually such a relation. On the other hand, the contract of sale in its simple form puts in exercise merely the duty of passive good faith, excluding deception, showing that the principle of equal individual right dominates in that relation.

The chief object of considering contracts at this time is to trace their general relation to the wants of the individual, as the means of enabling him to exert his personal powers. The modifications that these powers undergo, through the nature of the instrument thus employed, will be considered in another place. Tracing, then, the wants of the individual step by step, we reach the first modification of the contract of hiring, where the object of the contract is to obtain the aid of special knowledge, skill, and experience. This is a contract for the hiring of labor of a certain quality—namely, skilled labor. The obligation of the employee in this case, to bring to the use of his employer skill in his affairs, is no longer a mere implication from the nature of the contract, but is the subject of an express obligation. The standard of that quality of skill demanded is that which exists in the habit of the community. This special obligation is fitted to the general obligation to active good faith, implied by a delegation of a certain power over the affairs of the employer, showing the relation that this contract bears to the ordinary contract of hiring. The contract for skilled labor implies a diminished control, on the part of the employer, over the means to be employed for the accomplishment of his ultimate purpose.

In meeting the varied wants of man, these simple contracts become combined together, as when one employs a skilled builder to furnish the materials, labor, and constructive skill, and to erect a building to accomplish a certain object, or according to a certain plan more or less detailed. If a separate price is paid for the materials, labor, and superintendence, the character of the elements of this complex contract has undergone no change; but, if, to suit the convenience of the employer, a gross sum is fixed as compensation for the whole work when complete, the separate characteristics of the elemental contract in part disappear, but in other respects their incidents remain.

The next step in the development of the idea of a contract introduces a principle of wider scope, that becomes the means of unlimited differentiation in the variation of contracts. It is an instinct and a social trait of man that he should make provision for the supply, at some future time, of wants that he anticipates will then exist, or which may come into existence upon some possible contingency. It is a necessity of society, as essential to the stability of social order, that the means of such provision should exist. Accordingly, the power of self-obligation includes that of engaging that a certain state of things shall exist absolutely at a future time, or contingently upon the event that a certain state of things shall happen. The general agreement that such a state of things shall happen at a future day becomes absolute when predicated upon a day or event that is sure to occur, and is contingent when predicated upon an event that may possibly happen, but is not certain. This agreement may assume the form of an engagement that the contracting party will himself perform an act producing certain results, either at a particular time or within a reasonable time, or upon the happening of a certain event. This is an ordinary personal contract. It may also engage that such act shall be performed by a third person, in which case it becomes a contract of guaranty or suretyship. It may also engage that a certain state of things shall exist independently of the character of the agency on which it depends. This contract contains the principles of insurance, and is a specific form of guaranty. It is obvious that a common principle underlies these three forms of contracts, and that they are in fact three aspects in which the principle of guaranty presents itself.

This feature of contracts may be applied to contracts of sale or hiring, or it may give rise to obligations that embody nothing in the nature of sale or hiring. It is easy to perceive that all contracts are capable of being resolved into one or the other, or all of these simple forms.

It is necessary to distinguish the principles that are fundamental to these several forms of simple contracts by examining their points of agreement and disagreement. A contract of sale is an obligation that assures the acquisition of the possession of something of a tangible nature, either immediately upon the completion of the engagement, or at some future time certain to occur, or contingently when a certain event possible, but not certain, shall occur. The transfer of the right of a person under an executory obligation termed an assignment is assimilated to the contract of sale. It thus contains, in a specific manner, the principle of guaranty, which is an assurance that some particular state of things shall exist upon some contemplated event. On the other hand, the contract of hiring being terminable by the death of the person when labor is the subject of the contract, for the reason that it is the consequence of an association that is dissolved by death, it is not so absolute an assurance, but still the essential idea of an assurance as to a certain state of facts is obviously present in the contract of hiring, as it is in that of sale. In both the contracts of sale and hiring the principle of guaranty is specialized, in the first instance by the nature of proprietary rights, and in the last by the nature of associative rights.

The inference would be, that the principle of guaranty is the fundamental idea of contracts, and that the contracts of sale and hiring are specialized applications of this principle. Every conceivable contract resolves itself into an obligation to perform or omit some act; in the case of the contract of sale the act to be performed is that of delivering possession of property, and, even where the payment of money is the object of the contract, the act of payment is that which is essential to its fulfillment. The term labor, in its particular sense, does not include all acts that are capable of being performed by an individual, but only such as are capable of producing some useful change in the condition or form of some subject of property, or in the relation of property to place. The hirer of labor, that is the subject of the contract of hiring, is that which, if performed without due authority, would be a trespass on the right of one in respect of whom such labor is performed. If one agrees with an artisan that the latter shall produce an article, and the artisan, according to such agreement, produces such article at his own shop, and out of his own materials, and with labor that he has the right to control, it is obvious that the act is one that does not involve any interference with the person or proprietary rights of the person for whom the article is produced; and, accordingly, no delegation of power is needed to enable the artisan to perform his agreement. The relation of master and servant that implies such a power does not therefore exist. But, if one employs an artisan to make or alter some structure upon his land, as a power to interfere with his proprietary right is necessarily involved, that element of the relation of master and servant is present. If, however, the labor employed is skilled labor, then the control of the owner of the property over the labor of such person is not complete, for, as a skilled laborer, he has a certain independence of the control of the proprietor as it regards the means employed to accomplish his work. This confines the idea of the relation of master and servant, in its primary form, to relations where a power exists to act in the affairs of another, but in the manner and by the means that the master shall prescribe. The difference between the obligation of the skilled artisan and the ordinary laborer, acting wholly under the direction of his employer, is, that the former guarantees to a certain extent the excellence or suitableness of his work, while the other is only bound by the common obligation to use reasonable care, skill, and diligence in the service of his employer, and is not answerable for results. In other words, the obligation of the artisan embraces the use of proper means, and is, in effect, a guaranty, while that of the ordinary laborer is to use such means as the master may direct.

It is apparent that a contract to make and deliver to another an article employing one's own materials and labor is, in substance and effect, a contract of sale. In these cases, where the contract calls for the labor of a particular person, as in the case of a picture by a particular artist, the character of the contract of sale is unchanged, though modified by agreed conditions.

The idea of master and servant is found embodied in the domestic relation, as defining the relation between parents and minor children, and thus existing in this primitive form gave rise to that of hiring, by the transformation of the compensations for labor, from that which was secured by the general protective duty of the head of the family, into a specific compensation to which the servant acquired an exclusive proprietary right. The consequences of the principle of equal individual right added to these means of dealing the power of interchanging commodities and labor, and obligations in the nature of a guaranty, and thus completed the elements that compose our law of contracts.

In order to understand the principles of guaranty, the different modes of its operation should be compared. These modes have already been stated in a general way. They are embodied in the particular classes of guaranty, or suretyship, of insurance, and in the general class of personal contracts in which that principle appears. These cases resolve themselves into a guaranty of one's own conduct, of the conduct of another, and of a state of things independent of particular agency. In all these instances there is a common feature—namely, that an act is to be performed, as, for instance, the payment of money upon the happening of an event either certain to occur or uncertain, but possible of occurrence.

When one engages to perform an act at a future time, he must be regarded as assuming his capacity at such time to fulfill his obligation. One who accepts such an obligation, and bases his conduct and his rights upon it, must also be regarded as assuming that the party obliged will, at the time called for by his obligation, have the capacity of fulfilling it. When the party accepting the obligation has parted with value in advance, upon the belief in the capacity of the obliged party, *credit* has been given. Credit implies belief in future capacity as its chief element. All obligations to be performed at a future day must, then, be regarded as the result of the mutual confidence of the parties that the obliged party will possess the ability to perform his obligations at the time called for. That the validity of the obligation is not dependent upon the correctness of this anticipation is established by the rules of law, for, though one may find himself wholly unable to perform his agreement, the obligation still remains. As the assumption of the capacity of a person to perform an act at a future day is the assumption that a certain state of facts will then exist, and as the obligation founded upon such an assumption is valid without regard to its correctness, it follows that it is competent for individuals to deal, upon an assumed future state of facts, with conclusive effect.

The same principle applies itself to the condition of a party who has bound himself to perform a certain act in the event that another should perform an act on his part at a future day. Although such an obligation may have been conceived for the supplying of a want which it was assumed would exist at a future time, yet, if, at the time in question, no such want actually exists, the obligation based on expectation still remains efficient. The familiar rule of the law, that a change in the situation of parties to an obligation can not destroy such obligation, unless either mutual consent exists or an act of wrong on one side liberating the other, covers the proposition that individuals may shape their obligations upon an assumed state of facts; and, if such a state of facts is possible in the nature of events, the obligation so adjusted is finally obligatory.

This principle often gives rise to great hardships, through the occurrence of unanticipated events between the time when a contract is made and the time when it is to be performed; and a very common impression exists that such a state of legal conclusion is in violation of fundamental principles of justice. It is important to show that this rule of law arises from the principles of the law that are in exact conformity with justice. The moral deficiency of an individual who seeks to profit by the misfortunes of another, or refuses to bear a due part of the burdens of misfortune resting upon another, is obvious, and needs no comment. The question is, whether the community should assume to enforce such individual moral duty.

Man in society finds himself operated upon by two principles with opposite tendencies. On the one hand, he is regarded by an irresistible power that surrounds him and is capable of controlling all his movements as a part of a great whole, and as such that his movements must be conformed to the action of that great whole; and, on the other hand, as the arbiter of his own destinies. The first stated of these principles tends to build up the whole at the expense of its parts, while the last tends to build up the integral parts at the expense of the whole. As human government exists for man, and not man for government, it is obvious that the principle that tends to solidify and give harmonious development to the individual should be regarded as the superior of the two, and that is the principle that makes man the arbiter of his own destiny, and which, as existing under legal recognition, has been termed the principle of equal individual right.

It will be admitted that individual liberty should only be restricted by two considerations: first, by what is due to the community for the preservation of its interests, and, second, by what is due to the protection of the individual on the ground of the immaturity of his powers. The modification of an obligation on the ground of hardship is not a matter that concerns the interest of the community in any other sense than as the administration of justice is a matter of interest to the community. If, then, such a measure of justice is afforded, it is to be ascribed to the protective duty to the individual. To protect an individual against the consequences of his act of voluntary self-obligation is to deny him a certain measure of liberty. In the case of immature persons this takes place.

Admitting, for the sake of argument, that entire communities may be in such a condition that governing classes may, consistently, withhold part of the liberty that belongs to mature manhood, and the whole force of the admission would amount to this, that the maturity of the individual does not necessarily imply the possession of the largest liberty due to manhood, but that the existence of such liberty is dependent upon social conditions, expressing a certain advance of the whole community toward the possession of full social power.

If one finds himself, under the law of a community, unable to control the consequences of his own power of self-obligation—that is, that the law, under the influence of certain consequences, will modify such obligation—it is for one of two reasons: either he is not an adult, or the community has not reached the experience that belongs to a mature social condition. This reason is in its nature temporary, and looks to a more perfect condition of things when that liberty can not be interfered with by the community as a higher expression of the principles of right or justice. The ultimate good lies, then, in the fact that man is allowed to be the arbiter of his own fortunes, and to state, at will, his relations to others, under existing circumstances and under anticipated future contingencies, so long as the particular interests of the community are not concerned. No difference of opinion is to be anticipated as to the ultimate truth of the proposition thus advanced. The difference arises as to the steps by which this ultimate condition is to be attained. Thinkers practically divide themselves into two classes, one of which holds that liberty is in a peculiar sense the product of knowledge, while the other class superadds another qualification to knowledge to complete the idea of experience. Those that believe in the entire efficacy of imparted knowledge as the simple condition naturally associate the idea of gaining knowledge with the discipline of external restraint, for the knowledge must be complete before the product can be realized, and in the mean time subjection to an educator must take place as a necessity. This is an amplification of the protective principle largely embodied in the idea of paternal government.

The class that attaches the highest importance to experience gives a larger definition to knowledge, making it to include the results of experience as well as of generalized or specialized study. Experience is the result of the consequences of the use of our powers realized in their exercise. According to that idea, liberty is matured through the exercise of liberty, and that implies that patient endurance of the hardships that result from the mistaken exercise of liberty. It is only when an impassable barrier is discovered as the limit of a truth that knowledge is perfected through experience; and, if society undertakes to cushion the contact with the limits of truth, it will produce something falling far short of manhood.

But, apart from the question of methods, the fact is, that man has enjoyed the degree of liberty implied by his ability to bind himself to all the consequences of his acts, in all states of society to which the term civilized is recognized as applicable, even under governments giving the largest scope to the paternal principle. If, then, it should be proposed to yield at this day the measure of individual protection such as that under discussion, the step proposed would be a backward step, implying passage from maturity to immaturity; or, if it is regarded as a step forward, it is one from maturity to senility.

That, under the operation of this principle, man has grown hardy from individual independence, so as to make a large advance toward the maturity of his powers, can not be disputed; the consequences of a larger governmental protection in this respect can only be speculatively determined. While, then, it must be concluded that the full conception of liberty must be reached by gradual steps as a growth, and that the duty of government to concede this liberty is limited to accommodating itself by gradual steps to the advance of the development of the individual, it must be recognized that the ultimate truth and highest conception of justice lie in the direction of the capacity of man to bind himself by a private law, that society can not encroach upon either to benefit or injure him. The cases of benefit and injury must here go together, for, if society can properly say that one's burdens are too large, it can also say that his profits are too large to be allowed, for that is simply taking account of the burdens of others in their relations to individual burdens.

Extreme communistic and sentimental tendencies here unite hands; the former, discovering that the individual is getting more profit than the community at large out of the obligations due him by others, propounds the fraternal measure of impairing the obligations to reduce such profit, while sentimentalism, seeing the individual overstrained and panting under the excessive weight of his obligations, propounds the same measure of relief, applied as a nursing remedy to the reciprocal obligations. Both of these tendencies, salutary when limited by the principles of social order, when unbalanced, seek to roll civilization back to the days when governing classes represented a complex father, and governed classes a complex child dependent upon paternal wisdom and providence.

The power that an individual possesses of effectually binding himself in such manner that another shall have assurance of a benefit from a certain state of things, actual, or as anticipated, applies itself as well to the present as to the future existence of such certain state of things. A guaranty of the existence of a certain quality in an article sold is an instance of the first class, while a guaranty that a certain state or condition of things shall exist at some future time, or, what is equivalent, during some period of time, which is the principle of insurance, is an instance of the latter class. The principle in question gives rise to the proposition that parties may deal together, effectually, either upon an actual existing state of facts, or upon a state of facts assumed to exist, or upon a state of facts that may actually arise at some future day, or, finally, upon a state of facts anticipated and assumed as certain to occur. To predicate a certain consequence on a state of facts assumed, either as existing, or as certain to occur, is, in substance, to assume the existence, present or future, of such state of facts, the difference being one of form alone. These principles, in their interaction, give rise to the infinite complexities of contracts resting on the two great subjects of contract, property and labor, and equally affect those of an affirmative nature, calling for the performance of particular acts, and those of a negative nature, preventing the performance of some act.

That parties may act conclusively on the assumption of an existing state of facts is abundantly verified by the action of the law. Contracts are constantly enforced where the facts actually existing at the time of the making of the contract differ from the state of facts actually represented by the contract. It is very commonly said, in such cases, that a party who has an opportunity of informing himself, and fails to do so, ought to be bound by his contract, as it regards an innocent person dealing with him. It is clear that this idea of duty is not a legal one, for if a person owes a duty to any one to inform himself of the state of affairs, with a view to conducting his business properly, he owes it to himself alone, and not to one with whom he is dealing; so that the neglect of that duty can not become an element of the right of the party with whom he is dealing. The conditions of the question are fully met by the proposition that parties may act upon a presumed state of facts as well as upon an actually existing state of facts, and, where the facts upon which they have acted differ from the actual facts, they are presumed to have acted upon an assumed state of facts. Where parties have not access to knowledge of the actual state of the facts, they frequently adopt an assumption as the basis of their agreement, such transactions being sometimes called compromises, but are to be regarded as based on conditions assumed to exist. It would follow, from this view, that, where a difference appears between a state of facts actually existing and that acted upon, an intention to base the transaction on the actual facts can not be inferred, the presumption being in the opposite direction. This would lead to the conclusion that, in order to affect the validity of a contract on the ground that the facts contemplated by the parties did not conform to the actual existing facts, it would be necessary to show, by some means external to the contract, that the parties mutually agreed to act in view of the actual state of facts, but were mutually mistaken as to the existence of such facts. This expectation is fully realized in the rule that governs the rectification of contracts, on the ground of the mutual mistake of the parties, and the rule is just the expression that the principles in question tend to give.

The general power that individuals possess of shaping their mutual obligations by the use of conditions precedent, attendant, and subsequent, has been noticed in another connection, and need not be further considered until the general question of associative rights is entered upon.

The general view of the fundamental principles of contracts is all that is needed for the purpose of outlining the scope of that liberty which the individual possesses in dealing with his rights. The particular consideration of the consequences of these principles belongs in another place. In connection with the subject of contracts, it should be observed that material means of attaining the ends of life consist in the power of delegating to others some part of that capacity that is contained within the liberty attached to rights. The creation of agencies for the accomplishment of general or particular purposes is part of every right, where the creation of such agency is for a lawful purpose. The agent, in such cases, possesses a delegated power that, in its simplest nature, may be granted or recalled at pleasure by the author of the power, although they may be created in forms not admitting of revocation at the pleasure of their author. This subject, in its details, requires to be separately considered. Wherever there is an agency created or a power delegated, there must be an act of delegation by one and acceptance by another, so that the instrument creating such a relation between parties must have the essential qualities of a contract, although, from its revocable nature, in the simplest form of delegation, it is not usually classed among contracts, but is separately denominated a power simply, or a power of attorney.

In a general sense, agency includes the ideas of a servant or laborer, as well as of one empowered to effect changes in the civil rights of another. Primarily, a servant or laborer is one who is authorized to affect in some way the condition of one's person or material property, but has no authority to modify his rights or obligations as it regards such personal or proprietary interests. That is to say, a servant or laborer can not, as such, transfer the right of his master by selling his property, nor acquire property in his behalf, nor bind him directly by obligations. Where such powers are possessed by a servant or laborer, they constitute an agency, superadded to the simple character of servant or laborer.

In the usual legal sense, an agent is one who has some power of changing the state of the rights and obligations of his principal, and thus may act directly upon his civil rights. It follows that an agency is to be regarded as a means of dealing with one's legal rights, while any employment which is not in this sense an agency is a means by which a proprietor may control the property subject to his authority. The principle fundamental to agency, however, clearly embraces both the cases of servants and laborers.

It is apparent that the means afforded by the power of delegating authority in one's affairs adds immensely to the scope of personal capacity and personal right; certain elements of such delegations, in virtue of which such agencies assume a confidential or fiduciary character, greatly enhance their value as personal aids; but the consideration of these elements must be postponed.

CHAPTER XXXV.

COMPANIES.

THE mere fact that two or more persons have a proprietary interest in the same subject of property does not constitute a community of right or interest among them, although they may have community of possession. It is evidently in reference to this community of possession, and not to any community of interest, that such independent proprietors are called, by the law of England, tenants in common. Neither of such independent proprietors of part-interests in a single subject of property of a tangible nature can modify or affect the right of another otherwise than by producing some change in the condition of the subject of property.

Community of interest implies the existence of obligations, as among the parties participating in such common interest, and when it exists, although the common property may exist in as many several equal parcels as there are persons equally participating in the common interest, that circumstance would not tend to change the character of the property as a common interest, thus showing that the existence of a common interest is independent of the divided or undivided state of the property, and, indeed, of whether it is divisible or indivisible in its nature.

The rules of law as to the relative rights of tenants in common, equally applicable to the proprietorship of personal property, are a direct consequence of the conception of rights and obligations that has been presented.

The fundamental proposition is, that rights derive their nature and form from the obligations from which they result. In the application of this proposition to proprietary rights in its relation to tangible property—that is to say, property that is made available for the uses of life by means of actual possession—it must be remembered that the right of possession looks to the fact of possession as its consummation. Again, the beneficial use of such property is a consequence of such possession. The mere fact of possession does not in itself determine the relative right of the possessors to all other persons, for there may exist in some other person a right to such possession, either immediately, or at some future day, or contingently upon the happening of some possible event. The right to maintain such possession is limited by the character of the right of the person from whom such possession was rightfully acquired. The right is ultimately determined by the character of the obligations assumed by some previous owner having full right to the possession and enjoyment of such property. The law terms the state of relative rights, embracing all persons whomsoever, under which possession may be obtained and defended, *title*. Possession is a natural act performed by one in person, or by his agent acting in his behalf, qualified as to its effect by the title of the possessor—that is, by the state of relations between the possessor and all other persons. It would follow that, as possession is that which is qualified by right, and not that which qualifies right, the fact of a common possession would not tend to produce community of right among possessors in common. Community of interest being a consequence of community of right, the conclusion would be, that a common possession might exist without tending to produce any community of right or interest modifying the right of the several independent proprietors.

But, as has been said, the beneficial use of tangible property is a consequence of possession. As such, it would be plainly inferable that a common possession must in some way affect the relative rights of the common possessors as it regards the product of the thing possessed, or, as our law terms it, the *usufruct* of the property. Being united by the fact of a common possession, the produce of the union would represent a common interest, for the reasons that will be stated.

The natural conception of community is that of independent causes operating together to produce a common product, and, therefore, as the parts of the producing cause acted together in production, the producing rights and the produced right would naturally sustain the same relation to each other. The law conforms to this idea in many ways. Where individuals unite their interests in a single obligation, the product of such obligation is their common interest, and, hence, creditors claiming under a single obligation are called joint-creditors. There can be no doubt that this was the origin of the idea of joint-tenancy, now largely modified by public law; for, as several in taking united interests under a single deed, which, as has been seen, is to be considered as an obligation of the grantor, they are in the position of voluntarily accepting the product of such obligation, and their interests are accordingly common interests. So it would follow that, in the case of a subject of property of a productive nature, belonging to several independent proprietors, but allowed to remain in the actual possession of one, the productive act must be regarded as an instance of the voluntary co-operation of their interests and rights, so as to produce a common interest, although their relation remains unchanged to the producing cause.

That this state of relations is contemplated by the rules of law is evidenced by the fact that tenants in common are bound to account with each other for the produce of the land held in common, and it is not material to this view whether the origin of that accountability is in what are termed the rules of law or equity, for both spring from the principles of the law. It must be concluded, both inductively and deductively, that a common possession can not in itself produce community of proprietary right or interest otherwise than as affecting the usufruct of the property resulting from such common possession. When a tenant in common excludes another from possession, different principles prevail as affecting the right to the realized profits of the property, that need not be at present considered.

It is necessary to examine more critically the nature of common right in consequence of its relation to the law of association. Common right, as has been stated, is produced through the operation of common obligations, and its character must be sought at its source. Common obligations are such as affect two or more persons equally, by which all are bound to each, and each to each other. The existence of such obligations, when not imposed by public law, implies some act of assent on the part of the individuals bound, in virtue of which the obligation exists. Their act may consist in an express agreement to enter together into association for some common purpose, or, impliedly, in the acceptance of a common property, or interest devoted to a common purpose. Common right must be regarded as the primitive form of right for various reasons.

In the first place, it is in the law of organic development that least developed forms first appear. Development consists in the individuation of integral parts, and their functional differentiation relatively to the whole. As applied to social development, this would imply not only that the various public functions of government must come into separate existence through a process of development, but that the function of the individual would acquire definition from the same source, for, relatively to the whole society, each individual member is a function, the word individual implying the last stage of functional divisibility.

In the next place, the acceptance of the idea of family as containing the first idea of law implies the prevalence of the conception of common right before that of individual right, for the paternal head, as such, represents the administration of common interests, though such administration naturally takes a monarchic form, as already demonstrated from facts common to all animal natures.

Finally, it is generally accepted, on historical grounds, that land, the foundation of the idea of property, was held in common before it was parceled out as a separate possession among individuals.

If it be true that common right is the source out of which individual right has been derived, then the elements of individual right must be found in the statement of the nature of common rights, and this is satisfied with the statement that common obligations are obligations of each with each. Under obligations thus constituted, the moment that a division of the common property took place the obligation of each to each would assume the form of individual right relatively to each part set apart to any individual. In other words, the origin of a usage of individual holding would produce individual proprietary rights out of the common obligation itself.

That which constitutes the subject of common right is common property, and the common purpose, expressed or implied, in the association, in its relation to the common property, constitutes the common interest. The common interest demands and implies administration, and the mode of this administration is determined by the organic law of the association. Thus, whenever there is a common interest, there must be some administration of that interest, and, for the purpose of that administration, there must be some form of organization in the concentration or distribution of the administrative function.

As it regards the administration of the common interest, every community is a unit. The moment it is stated that a particular association was produced by the associative act of individuals, and for individual purposes, it is made clear that its organic condition is determined by the principle of equal individual right, and, as such, each individual must have equal right in shaping the common purpose and effort. The effect of this principle in evolving the right of the majority to control the common interest has already been discussed. There is reason to believe that majority administration is the natural law of such associations, and, in the absence of any agreed form of rule, or any habit of the community, to interpret the intention of the act of association, the law would certainly hold the majority rule as the law of the association.

Having formed a conception of community of right and interest in its simplest form, the modifying influences tending to produce specific and varied forms can be better understood. The term part-ownership, though not very expressive in itself, is applied to describe the existence of a common interest in a particular use or employment of property held by two or more independent proprietors. The property itself may not be the subject of a common right, while its use may constitute such an interest. The familiar case is that of a ship owned by several independent proprietors, who, when they unite in employing the ship for a commercial purpose, and appoint an agent or master to carry out such purpose, are regarded as a community, as it regards such commercial purpose, although their interests in the vessel itself, apart from such use, may remain separate and independent.

A partnership is a form of community produced by the general habit of commercial dealing, though subject to modification by local usage, upon the principles of community right. Each partner has, by the general law of partnership, individual control and administrative power over the common property and affairs. This power may be modified and limited as it regards the mode of its exercise, but its nature must remain constant while the partnership exists as such.

Joint-stock companies derive their form of organization and administration either from the agreement of the parties or from public law; and in the latter case their rights and obligations are termed corporate, as they generally constitute a single legal body or person acting in a collective name. In the case of corporate companies or corporations, the general policy of the law of incorporation limits the authority of the individual stockholder to the choice of persons to administer the corporate interest for the common benefit of the stockholders.

In considering the general consequences that would flow from the principles of the law from the naked fact of the existence of a common right and interest, the fact that the legal idea of property is that of a right of possession to the subject of property would lead to the result that either of several independent proprietors of any subject of property would have authority to take or receive possession of such property from a third person. This is equally true of common proprietors, where not inconsistent with delegated administrative power, and hence it is that payment of a sum due to one of several joint-creditors is a discharge of the debt. It would also follow that property in the hands of one independent proprietor could not be compulsorily taken from him by another, for, their right of possession being equal, there is no superiority of right to warrant interference by one with the possession of another. Money is, in its legal nature, absolutely divisible, and, therefore, a refusal to divide it in a proper case by an independent or common proprietor with another such proprietor, is a wrong, in the one case, to the independent right, and, in the other, to the common obligation, considered as an obligation from each to each.

By another principle of the law, where there is a community of interest among a number of persons, a majority in interest has an implied power to direct the common interest, where there is no inconsistent delegation of administrative power. That such power resides in a majority in interest, and in a mere majority of the number of persons associated, appears from the rules of the law. As it regards the exercise of political powers, a majority in number is identical with a majority in interest, because each individual, entitled to act in a particular manner in the exercise of political powers, is assumed to have the same interest as every other person capable of acting in that manner. There is harmony, then, between these instances, both arising out of the same principle, and both are capable of being referred to the idea of majority as, primarily, one of interest.

Every administrative power is in the nature of a trust, as it is an authority over the affairs of another, granted on the ground of personal confidence. As such, it implies a protective duty, that confers on the relation a confidential character. The proper consequences of the confidential character are, first, that the information imparted for the purposes of the agency, or obtained in the course of the agency by the agent, should be guarded from unauthorized communication, and, second, that the confidential agent shall impart to his principal such information as he may possess important to the conduct of the business in his hands as such agent, and counsel and advice where the nature of the agency implies such aid.

The administrative duty becomes fiduciary when the exercise of discretionary judgment is demanded or permitted on the part of the agent, and a high degree of care, skill, and good faith of an active character are demanded. Considered as a fiduciary relation, the duty of the managers of a common interest, engaged in commerce or some form of dealing, may be called an independent fiduciary trust, to distinguish it from the trust in the hands of a formal trustee, which is dependent on the fact that the primary duty of the trustee is investment, and that he may not subject a trust fund to speculative risks, such as are incident to business adventure. Incurring such risk is, on the other hand, incident to an administration that consists in commercial or general business dealing. It follows that the discretion of the trustee is dependent upon the rules of investment, while the discretion of the managers of common interests engaged in trade, using that term in the largest sense, is not thus limited.

As the existence of an administrative power is not inconsistent with the simple relationship of part-ownership, all the incidents of such a power may be present in the relations of part-owners and their agents. Partnership, implying, as it does, the delegation of mutual powers, embodies all the rights and obligations that spring from the principle of common interest and of delegated powers. In the simplest form of partnership each partner has an equal interest, and equal power with every other, and may exercise the proprietary rights of all the partners in the manner and to the extent sanctioned by the general habit of the community, modified by the recognized habit of those dealing in the particular trade or business to which the partnership relates. Special limitations or qualifications of this power have, primarily, force only as affecting the relative rights of the partners themselves. Third persons are only affected by such limitations of ordinary powers by possessing such knowledge of them as to imply bad faith in disregarding them, while dealing in bad faith with one clothed with fiduciary powers involves the same consequences as if one so dealing was directly bound by the duty of the agent. A partner, though acting in his own interest, has a fiduciary duty as representing the interests of his associates. All persons dealing with a single partner, or an agent acting in behalf of the partnership, are presumed to know the habit of dealing of the community and particular trade, and if advantage is taken of the partnership interest, by means of unusual and unsanctioned dealing, are implicated in any wrong that such individual or agent may thereby commit against his associates or principals. Thus, if, contrary to the habit of dealing in such cases, one should obtain from a clerk having the power of a salesman, or a junior partner of limited interest and responsibility, and contrary to his duty, a bill of sale of the whole partnership effects, such person would become implicated in the wrong committed, and could gain no advantage through it. The consequences stated flow from the principles of the law taking form from the habit and particular customs of the community. It is unnecessary to point out the various sources from which this proceeds, as the rules of law in this respect are familiar, not only to professional persons, but to common understanding.

The common interest of incorporated joint-stock companies, termed capital, is in form represented as the property of the corporation as an independent legal person, distinct from the stockholders, and the stockholders are represented as creditors of the corporation, though of a class postponed to all other creditors; but, for many purposes, the law treats the stockholder as an owner of his proportion of the capital, and, notably, when a stockholder's bill is allowed to restrain the fraudulent disposition of the corporate effects by officers of the company.

The entire control of the property and administration of incorporated companies is in the hands of persons chosen by a majority in interest of the stockholders for that purpose, who are sometimes termed trustees, but very generally directors. When termed trustees, they are not such in strict legal sense, as they do not hold, individually, the right of property for the beneficial use of another, but hold an administrative power of a peculiar constitution over rights of property vested in the corporation. Their discretion is absolute within the limits imposed by the law of the corporation, though, as occupying a fiduciary relation, they are bound to active good faith. The organic law of the corporation is in form a contract, either proceeding from the public authority, and made operative by acceptance, or by the exercise of individual power, or it may in part be derived from each of these sources.

The aid afforded to personal right by these important instruments of industry is of the most important character, as operations of the greatest magnitude, that are not directly carried on by government, are necessarily accomplished by such means. The transfer of such functions from government to companies has been attended by the transfer into the hands of collective persons of an important part of that great influence that government once exercised, as the sole power capable of undertaking great industrial achievements. It is naturally to be expected that the massing of individual power should at times assume a threatening aspect. Much, indeed, might be feared from this source were not principles acting on the largest masses tending to produce equilibrium. Such a principle is that of equal individual right, combined with the co-operative principle, which, finding itself embodied in the principle of mass conservation as well as individual conservation, will in the end right itself, if the action of the public authority is kept in close relation to the principles of the law, for they possess infinite power of adjustment when free to act. To prevent, by external means, the ascendancy of great corporations, it would be necessary to destroy their power of great achievement, and that would be diminishing vital power to prevent excesses of local action, a remedy that is rendered appropriate by the presence of organic death.

CHAPTER XXXVI.

MARRIAGE.

HAVING considered association as a means of aid to personal right in its economic uses, the subject presents itself in its bearing on the domestic relations. The association that constitutes the household is an instrument of the first importance to social and individual development. Pivotal to that general relation is that of marriage, an institution that retains to the present day its most important forms and aspects, and has yielded fewer specializations under the influence of development than any other social institution. What is said of marriage will be confined to monogamy, as illustrating all the principles of marriage in their simplest form.

The primitive form of marriage was the product of the dominance of the protective principle, acted upon by conceptions of utility, based chiefly on the interest of man, the natural protector, and formulating social habits of the greatest persistency, that have as yet only yielded to a limited degree under the influence of the ultimate principle of equal individual right.

Marriage, considered from the stand-point of the principle of equal individual right, is an individual association for co-operative purposes, depending normally upon the exercise of the voluntary power of self-obligation. Civil law found the institution impressed upon the habit of society, and molded itself to that state of things. The ameliorating influences that tend to equalize the civil condition of men and women united in the marriage relation are a consequence of the operation of the principle of equal individual right on the minds of men.

The idea of injustice existing in depriving a married woman of civil power over her property held at the time of marriage, or afterward acquired, that has already mitigated the state of married women, is a recognition that the proper equilibrium of the principles of the law does not find consistent expression in the institution as existing at the present day in most countries. The ideas of right and utility are constantly in contest to find a point of equilibrium. The motives that connect themselves with ideas of utility lie on the surface of man's nature, and first assert themselves while the principles of right action lie deep, and obtain their power by slow degrees.

The early stages of the lives of individuals and societies do not admit of institutional forms of an ideal character; such lives have two distinct stages. In the first stage its chief function is to take mold from the past, in order to become the subject of future modification. The second stage, in the true course of nature, is devoted to the reception of impressions on the mold thus taken from the past, of characteristics springing in part from ultimate principles, and in part from what is, or should be, peculiar to the individuality of the person or society. Undoubtedly woman was intended to carry civilization in certain directions to a higher point than man could alone carry it. The starting-point of independent action is from that civilization that man has solidified through all the past centuries, and, as it regards time, that starting-point is practically to-day. Man is her antecedent, and his civilization must, as it has done, give her her primitive mold, upon which her individual influence must be exerted in the direction of development in order to be profitable. The institution of marriage as it has existed was a vigorous attempt to accomplish what has been stated to be essential to the first stage of woman's career of development, and she may be regarded as thoroughly impressed by man's civilization. What she can do in the future may be judged by what she has done in the past, shackled as she has been by the primitive institution, contrived to communicate qualities to her rather than to obtain them from her. She has, with all these disadvantages, shaped one side, and an important side, of society. When she passes from the condition of a subject of form to that of an author of form, it is presumable that her influence will be still more potent. As woman's natural tendency is to re-enforce the protective principle in society, it may be that her agency in that direction may be useful to counterbalance excessive tendencies in the direction of individual independence of social law, such extreme tendencies being apt to follow in the train of new dominant principles, calling for what would seem superficially a retrogressive adjustment.

It is evident that the form of the marriage relation has not yet become a true expression of the tendencies of the principles of the law. On the other hand, it is equally evident that considerations of utility are relatively losing weight in the discussion and action that are taking place in regard to the form of the marriage relation, and that the principle of equality is obtaining increased relative weight. From these facts we must infer that the forms of that institution are changing in the direction of a higher conformity to the principles of the law. It might be possible to state what these relations would be if the principles of the law were allowed to determine results independent of antecedent forms; but, what the form in any particular age should be, it is impossible to state from the principles of the law alone. It is not the province of science to determine such a fact. Science can, however, say what is possible and impossible in any given case when determined by the law of development, and can go further and ascertain that there is a certain sequence in the order in which variable influences are applied and forms produced, and on this ground can advance from the apprehension of possibilities to that of probabilities. The arts of life can alone dictate what forms shall arise, and what shall not, within the liberty allowed by the law of nature and society. Hence it is that the question of what precise institutional form is proper to replace an existing form is a question of policy, taking that term in its proper sense, as embodying both considerations of utility and right, and therefore is beyond the sphere of science, that only presumes from existing facts to state rules and principles, but can not predicate the actual existence of any formal fact from such principles with any greater degree of certainty than that which is expressed by probability.

It is clear, however, that, in the absence of any institutional form controlling the question, the law would conclude that the persons uniting their civil powers for a particular end intended the creation of a common interest and administrative power, and would apply to such relations all the principles of co-operative association. But institutional forms place in the husband alone an irresponsible administrative power over all that can be regarded as appertaining to the common interest. The principles of the law contain no direct power to reverse the sentence of society.

When a woman marries, she presumably exercises her power of self-obligation. She may use any amount of liberty in the exercise of that right that is consistent with the habit of the community of which she is a member. The marriage contract, interpreted by that habit, is an assent to the consequences of the marriage relation as existing in such community. Having determined her power of self-obligation in this respect, the principles of the law, interpreting her civil right, take their mold from the marriage as a fact of intention. It may be, morally speaking, that woman is not a free agent in contracting marriage, but that is a circumstance of no legal importance, for, as she has the legal right to remain single, the change in her condition by marriage must be ascribed to voluntary choice.

The existence of absolute administrative power in the husband, over that which in other associated relations would be regarded as a common interest, does not necessarily exclude the idea that a common interest exists. We have already seen that the existence of absolute sovereignty in the community does not interfere with the idea of a community of interest, although the exercise of such power may involve the destruction of all liberties and communities of interest. The power delegated to the husband by the marriage contract must be regarded as of a governmental type, having a common nature with sovereignty. The principles of the law that respect the idea of common right, arising from the fundamental social obligation, notwithstanding the existence of absolute sovereignty, may well conceive a common interest and right as involved in the married relation, notwithstanding the sole and irresponsible administrative power of the husband. That the law does so consider it, is manifest by its action in certain cases. The mode in which courts of equity interfere to protect the proprietary rights of married women may be referred to these principles. Equity springs from the principles of the law, as well as from those formal rules that are distinguished as the rules of law. Indeed, the common law, using that term in the sense of formal law, is that side of law that is most influenced by institutional habit and form, while the free play of the principles of the law is observed in the action of equity.

The courts of equity can not deprive a husband of his administrative power, because that would be denying the proper force of the power of self-obligation, unless a forfeiture of that power has arisen from its abuse. What they can do, and habitually do, in certain cases, is to prevent the property of the wife from passing into that common fund, and thus becoming subject to the administrative control of the husband. There is no other instance in which a common interest is created for a legitimate purpose where the law assists one of the associates to retain from the common fund anything that should properly go into it. In diverting the wife's property from the common fund, and placing it in the state of a separate fund, in the hands of a trustee, it is obvious that the law does not consider itself as withholding from the husband that which is his individual right by marriage, for the principles of the law would not admit of such action. Evidently the idea is that the fund represents a common interest, and that, as it regards the wife's share in this common fund, the husband's power is administrative merely.

The usual ground on which equity makes a separate provision for the wife is to provide for its security. As it is not confined to cases where there has been a maladministration on the part of the husband, it is clearly the enforcement of a rule of prudence in the administration of the wife's estate. The husband's administration admits of subjecting the wife's interest to speculative risks with the view to profit. The interference of equity amounts to an indirect control of the administration by placing a proper part of the wife's estate in a condition subject only to the risks incident to investment. Although this is accomplished by preventing the separate estate from passing under the husband's control, instead of directly controlling the functions of the administrator, it is in ultimate effect the same, and is a recognition that his relation to his wife's estate has a fiduciary basis.

If the foregoing is assumed, it is possible to account for the general ground on which funds of the wife are diverted from the administrative control of the husband. If property passes into the hands of the wife, impressed with a different character as it regards its administrative control, secured through the proprietary right of a former owner, as where that control is placed in a trustee, it is consistent with the principles of the law that these conditions should be maintained. So, if resort must be had to a court of equity, as an extraordinary tribunal, to recover what is due the wife, the court of equity regards itself as standing in the place of a former proprietor, as it regards an impression on the future administration of property so recovered, and in that way a course is opened for administration by a trustee. It was just said that this is the only instance where a court of equity diverts property from a common fund, established for a legitimate purpose, in the interest of an associate. The reason of this is, that it is the only relation in which the property of an individual, in its entirety, passes by operation of law into a common fund. The formal principle of equitable interference in such cases has a technical aspect; but the vital ground of action is the fiduciary character of the husband's administration, that naturally subjects it to such prudential rules as that which places part of the estate in a position in which it would sustain the minimum of risk.

It may be said that the right of the husband, as existing at common law, to the personal estate of the wife is inconsistent with the idea that his position is that of an administrator of a common fund. Whatever the husband disposes of under his administrative power, either by an assertion of individual right or by transfer to another, is obviously removed from the condition of a common fund, for his administrative capacity is absolute; and his theoretical right to possess himself, individually, of his wife's personal estate, results compensatively from his liability for her debts before marriage. If, however, he should fail to exercise such administrative power, then, if the character of a common fund can be ascribed to the property of the wife in the husband's hands until affected by actual administration, that fact would appear when a failure to exercise such power has taken place. Such is, indeed, the case, for, if the husband dies without reducing his wife's chattels to possession—that is, without an effectual assertion of individual right over it—it returns to her estate.

It may well be considered whether the tendency of legislation at the present day, to place the property of the wife on the footing of a separate interest, is not a confession that the means of administration of a common fund in such cases are inadequate. Certainly the action of the courts of equity, already noticed, bears such an implication. It does not follow, by any means, that such changes indicate a conclusion that a common interest, independently of the question of the mode of administration, would not be congenial and useful to the marriage relation. On the other hand, it admits of question whether the abolition of the community of proprietary interest between husband and wife, not merely by limiting its scope but destroying its existence, would not destroy one of the natural incidents of the marriage relation, and thus place it out of relation to the natural wants of mankind.

Beyond question, some modification of the idea of master and servant entered into the primitive idea of the marriage relation. Whether that idea was distinctly present, or merged in the superior idea of a certain governmental power lodged in the husband, need not be considered, for its origin was institutional, and, in the change of institutions, became nearly obliterated, and can no longer be regarded as a distinctive feature of the marriage relation. A marked distinction between the relation that subsists between the sovereign and subject on the one hand, and the master and servant on the other, in the nature of the powers exercised in the respective cases, is, that in the one case they serve a community of interest, and in the other individual interest. Unquestionably the husband and wife have a community of interest in the government of the family, although that government is of the monarchic type. It is difficult to reach a point of conciliation between these opposite ideas. That difficulty suggests that the existing institutional form of marriage looks only to two states of society as entirely agreeable to its incidents—namely, that in which the husband exercises absolute authority, and that in which this authority is equal and balanced. Society has passed beyond the first of these states, and has not reached the second, and at this day represents a changing equilibrium necessarily characterized by disorders.

The law recognizes that the husband has a valuable interest in the companionship and services of the wife, and protects such rights, and compensates injury to them. This suggests a vestige of the relation of master and servant; but, on the other hand, the husband has not a vendible interest in the service of his wife, which supports a contrary inference. It may be safe to say that the relation of master and servant does not exist between husband and wife, but that a common nature embraces the two relations.

CHAPTER XXXVII.

THE FAMILY.

INTIMATELY connected with that form of association denominated marriage is that of the family. The family in its simplest form is to be regarded as consisting of parents, united by the marriage relation, and their children. The addition of domestic servants, additional permanent members and guests, produces various modifications of this simple form. The law of the family is obviously derived from that of marriage. What has been said of the law of marriage is true of the law of the family, the latter being developed from the relations between the parents. The parental power is governmental in its nature, and is generally regarded as the primitive form that human government assumed. As the law of the family is evolved from that of the compact of marriage, that compact must be regarded as the primitive governmental institution, and thus the source of origin of all those institutional forms that enter into the structure of society. The particular consideration of the family relation belongs to another place in the general discussion, but the mode in which it enlarges the sphere of personal right may be noticed in a general manner.

The parental idea contains three distinct elements: that of ruler of the household (Rex), of a master controlling the labor and service of the immature children (Magister), and of the owner of the family domain and property (Dominus). In the primitive family the powers corresponding to these sources of authority were full. The feature of the primitive family, that gave the father the right of a master over the services of the minor child, still remains, while in other respects but a shadow of the former power is left. A subordinate government still remains, and the product of the labor of the minor children is still his property; but property acquired by them by other means does not pass under his dominion, or even administrative control as parent. His power of control over the person of his wife, children, and other members of the family, where not taken away by absorption into that of the community, is limited to that which is conformable to the habit of the particular community. Within these limits he possesses both coercive and punitive power over his children, and, as the result of his proprietary right, some measure of coercive power over all other members of his family, and some authority to control the conduct of strangers to the family within the family domain. His general duty to his family is that of protection, to his wife and children maintenance, and to his children discipline, including instruction. The right of the family is a personal right, and may be asserted at any place, though that element that springs out of proprietary right is dependent on a relation to place. The family association is coercive upon children while remaining immature, but may be dissolved at will after maturity. Wife, children, and domestic servants usually exercise some degree of agency for the head of the family, either under the operation of the habit of the community by giving rise to a presumption of such agency, or the habit of the family, in the express delegation of such power; but, independently of these sources, neither a wife, child, nor other member of the family has power to impose directly any obligation on the head of the family.

As these powers, which we find expanded into an elaborate system in the organism of civil government, were antecedently in the family as original powers, it is of interest to observe their germs in the family relation, and compare them with their matured condition in the fabric of civil society; and also to notice the course of that evolution by which such changes are produced.

The origin of the parental power must be ascribed to three natural sources of authority, two of which give rise to what has been termed the law of person, and the third to the law of place. The basis of the idea is that there is an obligation imposed on the parent to protect, maintain, and discipline his children during their minority, which, in its primitive form, was a natural obligation, subsequently transformed into a civil obligation, to the community. As incident to these duties, there are certain necessary complementary rights. The duty of protection and discipline implies power to regulate the conduct in a governmental sense, of which general rules applicable to all in like conditions contain the typical idea. The duty of maintenance implies the possession of the means of maintenance, and, as the labor of the individual is the primary means of individual maintenance, the parent is endowed with the right to the labor of his minor children as part of the means of their maintenance. This implies the power of imposing particular laws upon the individual, embracing the idea of determining the ends and means of his individual exertion. This particular law at maturity is evolved as the function of the voluntary power of self-obligation, and thus assumes the form to which the name of private law has been applied. In addition to this, the parent becomes a master in another sense through the obligation to discipline; as he is charged with the duty of developing the individual powers of the child under that obligation, he has, as the proper means to that end, the right to control the thought and exertion of the child, as material to the educative process, and may delegate such power to an educator. Finally, the duty of protection connects itself with the means afforded for that purpose by the nature of the proprietary interest, and thus the law of place becomes interwoven into the general parental power.

With regard to the stages of transition from the primitive parental form to the civil condition, all that need be said at the present time is that at maturity the power of the parent potentially passes into the mature individual, and there rests as an original power, and thence passes in the form of delegated power into the community in the manner that has already been pointed out.

CHAPTER XXXVIII.

ASSOCIATION—COMMUNAL AND GENERAL.

ANOTHER form of association is involved in the relation of the individual to some community of a local character endowed with powers of government of a subordinate character, such as provincial, departmental, or municipal government. As general liability as a member of such community depends on the fact of residence, and as residence, upon the principles of the law, is voluntary, the connection of the individual with any particular subordinate community must be regarded as voluntary, notwithstanding it may be necessary that each individual in the general community should be a member of some subordinate community.

The foregoing statement indicates that the law of subordinate political communities is based upon the law of place, and hence is termed local law, to distinguish it from those obligations that bind the individual to the general community personally and independently of place.

The relation of the individual to the subordinate community is usually defined by public law, but rests on principles that are illustrated more fully in their relation to the state or general community.

The nature of political government depends on that of political power, which is the same whether exercised directly through a sovereign or by local communities of limited authority. The liability of an individual assuming residence in a local community for all the obligations binding the community at the time of commencing such residence has already been commented upon. The correlative truth that that liability ceases, unless affected by public law, the moment he ceases to reside in such community, through residence acquired elsewhere, flows from the principle already stated.

For the facilities and the protection afforded by local government, a general indefinite duty exists to contribute to the maintenance of such local government, which is made definite by public law, either that of the community at large, or of the local community, if possessed of that power. The local community has the obligations and the rights of an individual, within the limits of public law, modified by the possession of political powers; so that, while bound by the obligation to respect the rights of others, and to exercise prudent care in the use of its own individual rights, and of the public powers committed to it, it is not responsible as an individual for the exercise of political discretion. Such communities are usually endowed with the custody and care of certain common rights, such as the right of public way, and with power to enforce contributions of money or services for improving, extending, and repairing public ways. Municipal communities, including cities, towns, and villages, are primarily clothed with police powers in some degree, and with power to regulate the exercise of trades and callings.

The many modes in which an individual becomes associated with others in the course of the affairs of life—that need not be classified, as they sustain only a general relation to personal right—embrace industrial, religious, educational, charitable, and political associations. The liberty of association, as we find it in a free government, is large, as has already been commented upon. It is involved with the liberty of speech; indeed, the liberty of speech becomes a matter of public importance principally through its agency in consummating the purposes of associated bodies of men. If the condition of a government is such that public measures should originate with those controlling public affairs, and the origin of such measures in popular discussion is regarded as an interference with the proper functions of the public authority, it is manifest that restraint of the power of association, and of the liberty of speech incident thereto, must ensue. If a government of such principles does not put restraint upon such means of forming the popular judgment, it can only be ascribed to the fear of consequences that might result from such attempt. Such restraints are essential to the perpetuity of such forms of government; and, when we see the people of such a state freely discussing public measures in associations, we may be assured that the government has entered a period of change, and that public opinion, as a means of enforcing a policy of government, is organizing into a form that will compel a change in the principles of the government. The presence of the vital means of normal political development carries an assurance that the normal course of such development will follow.

A free government is, then, one in which public measures may originate in the popular mind under such conditions as to become a part of the policy of the state. But, even in free governments, associations may have an unlawful character, under the principles of the law, when seeking to change the form or action of government by means inconsistent with the principles of the law. In such cases, as has been said, the use of the power of association, and of speech only, becomes inconsistent with the principles of the law, and, therefore, inherently unlawful, through the ends to which they are applied.

It can not be doubted that there is such an indefinite right as that of revolution. The existence of such a right is a necessary deduction, from the view that has been expressed in regard to the nature of civil society. According to this view, the right to establish a form of government rests with the majority of the members of the community. If, then, we should conceive that the members of such a community should make an actual compact corresponding to the fundamental obligations of society, and one of their number should immediately seize the reins of government without the consent of the majority, and supported by a clear minority, it is obvious that the majority would have a clear right to enforce the purpose of their compact by physical force. If this be true in a case of that particular character, it must be equally true after any lapse of time. When a right is lost, such loss occurs either through the operation of public law or of some general custom to which it may be referred. But the conduct of a usurper can neither give rise to such a law nor to a custom having such an effect. The fact of the submission of a people, for an indefinite period, to a usurper of public authority, is not in any sense a custom carrying such a consequence. Its origin is in duress, while all customs are in their nature voluntarily imposed obligations. Conceding that the sovereignty as delegated is absolute in its nature, still it only possesses that quality in the hands of one to whom it has been delegated for exercise, and not in a mere usurper.

It must be conceded that a usurper, coming in without a proper delegation, may acquire one through the acquiescence of the people governed, but not necessarily through their submission. But the principle may be carried a step farther; if at any time the majority of the people of a state desire to change the form of government, it is a necessary consequence of the nature of civil society that they may rightfully do so. That the power of the majority to organize government is a continuing power, so as to warrant its exercise in changing the government as once established, is clear. As a political power, it is presumably a continuing power. The sanctions that originate government must constantly minister to its support.

General political powers are in their nature vital powers that must always be in exercise. Particular exertions of political power may, like motions of the limbs, be intermitted indefinitely; but general political powers are like the pulses of the circulation, that must be maintained as the condition of life. It is manifest that the right of the majority of a community to change the form of government is a vital function of society, and, as such, a continuing power.

The question then arises, Why are not public associations for the purpose of revolutionizing the government by force conformable to the principles of the law? The answer appears to lie in the nature of the means by which such an attempt must be consummated. An act of revolution is in its nature an act of war, and the fact that war is internal does not change its nature, though it affects materially its incidents. The justification of a war of revolution can only appear in its result, and then only as an inference. If the people of a community are strong enough to overcome the governmental power and change the government, it is presumable that they embrace at least a majority of that community. It is not to be doubted that a much larger proportion than one half must be presumed to have contributed in some manner toward the result in order to render a revolution successful. It follows that no possible means exist for making it appear that a majority of the people desire a particular change of government, nor could that evidence be afforded unless through the aid of the government, which can not be anticipated when the laws of the country make no provision for a change of governmental forms. It must happen, then, that associations to revolutionize the government by force are unlawful as well in their relation to the principles of the law as to the public law, and there is nothing that can change that presumption until the work of revolution is consummated; hence it is that, while it is consistent with the principles of the law that the majority should control the form of government, yet the law can draw no distinction between associations agitating a change by force, whether the desire for that change is limited or general. This anomaly in the operation of the principles of the law points to the fact that a system of government that makes no provision for a change of the form of government is an anomalous system. As change in this respect is the constant order of events, the fact that no provision is made for such change implies that the development of governmental form is committed to the law of force, the whole anomaly arising from the relation of aggressive force to the right of self-preservation, as applied to the conservation of social forms. A corresponding anomalous condition of the animal economy would arise where an animal, whose function it is to change its skin, should have no muscular adaptation for such purpose.

When it is considered, on the one hand, that the unrestrained liberty of association and the associated liberty of speech are inconsistent with the preservation of certain forms of government, and, on the other hand, that they are the means by which the change from the government of the few to the government of the many must be effected, the reason is apparent why political changes in that direction are generally accomplished by disruptive forces. To conceive of a government that would permit causes in their nature capable of being governed, and tending to destroy the foundation on which it rests, is to speculate in reference to conditions that have nowhere appeared historically, and which are inconsistent with the natural instinct of self-preservation with which communities, as well as individuals, are endowed. It is asking of a state more than can be expected of an individual to require that it shall consider its present form a mere incident, that should admit of ready change, and that its instincts of self-preservation shall center around an ideal conception of itself, admitting of formulation in an indefinite series of forms. That this is not the quality of all changes of form is obvious, being confined to those that affect vital functions.

The relation that exists between the various phases of national life, when an absolute monarchy is changed to a limited monarchy, or parliamentary government, and such governments are replaced by popular institutions, is like those transformations in animal life in which an earlier form of life is destroyed, and replaced by a new derivative form.

Institutional law adheres to existing forms and habits, as they are its life. That which has been called the spirit of the laws, but is more accurately described as its principle, acts as well against forms as through them. A sense of injustice communicated by these principles generally accompanies movements for a change in the form of government where that change is upon the line of normal development. But, though a sense of justice may excite revolutionary conditions, it does not control the formal results of revolutions. The fact that motives of interest are combined with the tendencies that arise from a sense of justice in the complex conditions that constitute revolution, prevents the higher of these motives from dictating results. Utility, when co-operating with the sense of justice, always carries off the lion's share. Hence it is that revolutions ordinarily disappoint the expectations of those who study them as acts of justice. As the highest organic condition of society is attended, as well as produced, by the relative dominance of ideas of justice, so the lowest forms are products of unbalanced utilitarianism. The principles of the law are, therefore, responsible for inspiring the spirit of change which they can not control, and, in this respect, are a force acting against the tendencies of institutional law. The conception is here forced upon the mind that the principles of the law must exist in two distinct forms in order to sustain this dual relation to human affairs. As formulated with the habit of communities, they appear as the source of orderly progress, while in a more general form they are the inspirations of liberty; that produces organic changes in society, acting through the individual in his relations to society, just as the principles of animal life in their productive form tend to prolong and perfect the career of the individual, while, in their broader relation to unitary life, they are the means by which individual life passes from form to form through disruptive changes. As, in the case of animal life, general classes are produced by the operation of universal characteristics upon the individual, so, in the development of governmental forms, universal principles operating upon individual man, the unit of the system formulates such generalized conditions as are termed forms of government. If the structure of the government admits of the statement of a definite relation between the individual and the process of producing organic change, then such processes may be worked out by normal and orderly methods; but, if such adaptations to the conditions of development do not exist, the cause of development must assume the form of individual force, and the method of its realization must be the disruptive agency of revolution.

In studying the principles of the law, we have to deal especially with them as formulated by the forms and habits of mankind; but it is material to understand the more general interpretation of which they admit to comprehend their full nature and function.

The various forms that have been assumed by industrial

associations, and notably by the guilds, are interesting to the study of political development; only a passing notice can be taken of that fruitful field of inquiry. It may be remarked that individual liberty of industry appears to have been preceded by that of associated bodies or guilds. The liberty of industry was conceived in early times as a franchise appertaining primarily to the government, and passed in that form to trade associations, or guilds. The idea of the guild was based more or less upon the conception that the special knowledge that is attained in the practice of an industrial art was a subject of property. The guilds, as the recipients of the requisite franchise, were associations to which this kind of property of the trade at large was committed for custody and exercise. The incidental powers as to the admissions of apprentices, and regulating the conduct of particular industries, show that the liberty of industry was acquired by associations of men before becoming the right of the individual. The creation of guilds was an act of public authority, but the dissemination of the liberty of industry, in the form of an individual liberty, was the result of a change in the habit of the community, induced by the operation of more general principles.

The change was no doubt greatly facilitated by the policy of granting letters-patent for new inventions. Such letters-patent represented the acquisition of individual industrial rights, and were thus contrary to the ideas of the guilds. The guilds sought to perpetuate, in a certain body, as a secret and mystery, all that appertained to the practice of a particular art, while the principle of the patent system was to divulge methods employed in the practice of the arts, and to create individual rights to pursue certain industries, as against the monopolies that claimed to act under the sanction of a function of the government.

Without doubt the tendency to representative forms of government was intimately connected with the existence of the guild, acting through the influence that the guild exercised in local governments. The relation of the liberty of association to the progress of general liberty is here illustrated in a manner that places the power of association in the position of that from which the liberty attached to individual right has been achieved. The same truth will be found represented in the history of modern republics. The city and borough have been important instruments in affecting changes from absolute to limited monarchy, and from the latter to republican government. These complex bodies have been found capable of retaining the impress of liberal ideas, as against governmental forces that individuals could not withstand.

Associations of laborers to enhance the price of labor may be regarded in two aspects: First, as intended to overcome some force that prevents the law of supply and demand from arbitrating the price of labor; and, second, as intended to produce an enhancement of the value of labor beyond what the law of supply and demand would produce. In the first of these aspects they resemble in nature those associations that have been the instruments of transferring authority from government to individuals, while in the second aspect they are instrumentalities running counter to social influences that are essential to the legal idea of society. The relation of the habit of the community to the law implies the proposition that the varied operations of society tend to find a certain equilibrium or balance, which, when sufficiently stable, engenders fixed habits, that become part of the structure and function of society itself. That money values are fixed in the course of trade as the result of all the influences that can possibly affect such values in public estimation is a commonly observed fact. There must be in every community influences of both normal and abnormal tendencies operating on modes of estimating value. Among normal tendencies there are those who, by ordinary means, are striving to get the best price for their commodities; but these efforts are balanced by the efforts of those who are striving to purchase at the lowest rates. The abnormal influences are chiefly in combinations to enhance or depress prices, that tend to deny to the principles of trade their proper influence. While these combinations are casual, and of a limited character, they tend to balance themselves by combinations of an opposite character, and hence it is that the policy of government, which was formerly energetic in the restraint of such combinations, has become molded to the idea that an actual tendency to balance will leave the law of trade in the end effective. When, however, such combinations should assume the form of co-operation between all producers of a particular commodity, or of all dealers in or consumers of a commodity, to fix its price by arbitrary means, it is obvious that the legal idea of a market value, as the result of natural equilibrium, disappears, and the methods of the law are in that respect defeated.

The question of the policy of government, in view of these propositions, can not be here discussed; but it is evident that if such abnormal tendencies as have been noticed tend to call up counter-tendencies of an equilibrating tendency, then the proper function of public law, in its general character, is simple, as it consists merely in guarding the transition from the class of dangers to which all transition states are exposed.

The invariable tendency of religion is to associate men together for co-operative purposes; therefore, to deny the power of association for any religious purpose, is to affirm the unlawfulness of the purpose itself. That an association intended merely to conserve and propagate a state of opinion or belief on any subject should be unlawful, inherently, and by virtue of the principles of the law, is impossible. Especially is this true of a belief in reference to the relations existing between Deity and man, and between man and man in consequence of relationship to Deity. All restrictions of the power of association for religious purposes must be ascribed wholly to utilitarian tendencies in the policy of government. As the proper function of religion is to recognize obligation and not to create it, and to inspire conduct and not to control it, it is obvious that, unless associations for religious purposes exceed the sphere of religious action, it is impossible that they should antagonize the principles of the law. They are objects moving on parallel lines that can not meet, and, where the contrary is supposed, it arises from mistaking perspective for fact, through obliquity of foresight. The habitudes connected with religious conviction may or may not conform to those civil conditions contemplated by the principles of the law, and, therefore, may be lawful or unlawful in a civil sense; but form of worship, or religious conduct, is an accessory to the central religious purpose, that consists in the conservation and propagation of a particular religious belief; and the possibility of repressing conduct springing from a religious motive does not imply the possibility of the restraint of the primary motive itself, as by restraining associations for such purpose.

If, then, the actual restriction of the liberty of association for religious purposes is found to exist in any community, it arises, necessarily, from the public law of that community, as no possible action of the principles of the law can account for it. In the application of the principles stated, it is of particular interest to know what are the tests by which the existence of a religious character, in the case of an association of persons, can be ascertained. If the professed object of an association is religious, and its particular purposes are consistent with such character, no difficulty can arise. If, however, the particular or active purpose of the association points to a general political or civil purpose, as to revolutionize the government by force, or to accomplish purposes unlawful in themselves, such particular force, not being capable of being referred to a general religious purpose, may confer upon the association the character of an unlawful conspiracy upon the principles of the law alone.

So far as the law confers civil functions upon bodies associated for religious purposes, its action may be properly based upon considerations of utility. But the denial of the right of association for religious purposes, except with the sanction of the public authority, must rest on the idea that some form of religion is more congenial to the policy of the state than some other, unless a wider departure from the proper conception of the tendencies of the law is fundamental to such policy—namely, that such liberty of association does not exist apart from the positive permission of the public authority.

The question of the liberty of religious association may become involved with the idea that the tendency of a particular association is inimical to the prevailing form of government. Such a tendency is involved in all associations that touch public questions, and associations, as has been shown, are the proper means by which public judgment is formulated with a view to changes in the government. Where the direct tendency of such associations is to induce a change in the government, and the form of government does not admit of change, the question as one of public law is simple.

In such governments the necessity exists of arresting development, for development implies change of form, and that the formal constitution of the government does not admit of. That such instances have a present as well as an historical existence, is a fact that appears to be accounted for by the dominance of a sentiment of reverence for a dead ancestry that overpowers the sense of protective duty to the living and the generations to come, if not sufficiently accounted for by the lust for power.

As religious development directly stimulates social development, the arrest of the latter implies the arrest of the former. The first step of religious development is the differentiation of form and function, and, until such differentiation takes place, integration has nothing to act progressively upon. It follows that it is necessary to the perpetuation of any particular form of government that the condition of both social and religious development should be suppressed, and a dynasty intent on conserving forms, and yet permitting any considerable degree of liberty of religious or social association, is in the condition of having desires without the means of gratifying them, and of being affected by the incipient stages of revolution.

Where, however, the power of majorities to change the form of government is recognized, such associations can not be regarded as illegal upon general principles, unless they exercise means for carrying out such a purpose, that imply war against the existing government. It is, therefore, impossible to conceive that, upon the principles of the law, a religious association could ever be regarded as beyond the proper liberty of association, whatever might be its indirect tendency.

The right of individuals may be violated by associated bodies as well as by individuals. If an association is a legal person or corporation, its general, as well as its special obligations, remain under the same sanctions as those of individuals, the association, and not the individuals composing it, being the legal person on whom the obligation is binding. This liability is sometimes transmitted in some form to the persons composing the corporation, but that is produced by public law, and not under the operation of general institutional forms. If the associated body has no corporate capacity in a legal sense, the law regards the action in question as the action of the individuals composing the association, as the source from which the power to perform the act has sprung.

There are two propositions that can be gathered from the distinction pointed out between the liabilities of individual associates in the two cases of corporations, made such by public law and voluntary association. The first of these propositions is that, according to the principles of the law, an association is an aggregation of individuals, in which the personality of the individual members is not merged in that of the aggregate body, but the associative rights are qualifications of the several individual rights composing the aggregate; hence, when such a body demands the enforcement of obligations due to it, or when it is proceeded against to compel it to perform its obligations, the individual members maintain the controversy. The second proposition is, that the qualities of a corporation, as created by public grant or law, so far as the individual members are detached from the collective obligation, depend upon public law, and such individual immunity is, properly speaking, what it has been called, a franchise—that is, a freedom from an ordinary legal consequence attached to the rights of an individual associated with others.

As the quality of the individual act is not changed by the fact that two or more have co-operated to bring the act about, the reason of the general rule just stated is obvious. This proposition is not only illustrated in the class of cases that involve the efficacy of obligations created by, or otherwise affecting aggregates of, individuals, but in the foundation of criminal proceedings against conspirators to commit crime, and of the doctrine as to accomplices in crime.

CHAPTER XXXIX.

LIBERTY OF JUDGMENT.

THE next aspect of the right of person, as connected with the liberty of self-exertion, is that which is here termed the liberty of judgment. Although this subject presents a very general aspect of personal right, and is usually, in its relation to particular rights, treated as an element of the question of the voluntary character of certain action, yet it is worthy of separate consideration, as showing in what light the law regards the relation of mental conditions to individual right. A determination of the will may be attended by a conscious exercise of the faculty of judgment, or it may be of so spontaneous a nature as to be attended by no such distinct consciousness. The consequences that flow from the actions of individuals are not dependent, in a legal sense, upon the quantity or the quality of the exercise of judgment from which they spring. There must, however, be some exercise of judgment, and the absence of any conduct on the part of one seeking benefit through such an act, tending to prevent the exercise of judgment, either through force or deception. It is evident, then, that the law does distinctly recognize an obligation as binding all persons to respect the right of the individual to govern his conduct in the exercise of his rights, as it regards the means afforded for that purpose by the nature of his mental constitution; and the violation of such obligation gives rise to definite legal consequences.

The relation of this subject to questions of mental competency to manage one's affairs, and to the effect of duress and deceit, is apparent. Actions, in their relation to judgment, are either deliberate or impulsive. Actions may, through physical duress, be regarded as involuntary, but, for the present purpose, they will be considered as free from physical necessity, but affected by want or defective action of judgment. A want of judgment exists in cases of idiocy, and may exist, either permanently or as a temporary condition, in cases of insanity. A want of judgment also exists in the early stages of infancy, and is followed by an imperfect condition that remains until maturity. For legal purposes, the period of maturity is arbitrarily fixed at a certain age. Imbecility and weakness of judgment are instances of a defective exercise of judgment, not necessarily implying a total want of judgment.

All acts that proceed from a want of the power of judgment must be put in the class of purely impulsive acts. In the same general class must be placed all acts in which there is a defect in the exercise of judgment, for impulse is the prime mover of all action and judgment, the quality that confers on such impulsive tendency a rational character; hence, if the function of judgment is defectively exercised, the resulting conduct must be in some degree dominated by the impulsive tendency, instead of by the deliberate judgment, as it should be; the fact of such dominance of the impulsive tendency in the consequences produced tends to characterizing such action, wholly or in part, according to the dominant tendency, as an impulsive act.

Deliberate acts, on the other hand, may be affected by deceit, through control exerted over the means of forming a deliberate judgment. The case of impulsive acts will be first considered with reference to their relation to the idea that the law recognizes a certain right of judgment as inherent in personal right.

On what principle, then, does the law refuse to enforce an obligation made by, and prejudicial to, one wanting in the power of judgment? It is clearly not because an act wanting in judgment is necessarily defective as a voluntary act, for the function of volition is ordinarily present in persons of the class under consideration, and often attains great force and persistency, as in the case of the insane. Nor is it the fact that an action has not actually proceeded from a deliberative judgment that its legal inutility arises; for, if one possessed of the power of judgment, and with the means of exercising that judgment, neglects to exercise it, that circumstance affords no relief from the consequences of such action. It is, then, incapability of exercising judgment on the one hand, or the presence of a certain duress of mind or deception, that separates such an act from its ordinary legal consequences.

The nature of rights is the same in the hands of persons incapable of using them as in the hands of persons possessing full powers. If an idiot, or a lunatic in a state of delirium, should chance to make a valuable contract that involved parting with some right that he possessed, the law would not deprive him of the benefit of such contract, but would recognize his capacity of self-obligation, and enforce, accordingly, the obligation of the other party based upon it. It can not, therefore, be affirmed that incapacity of judgment is equivalent to a want of the power of self-obligation. When the law invalidates a contract, it must either be on the ground that it is a nullity in itself, or that it is affected by a wrong done by one asserting a benefit claimed under it. As the contract of an incapable person is not void, irrespective of its consequences, it is obvious that, when invalidated in the interest of an incapable person, a violation of some obligation must be attributable to the person against whom it is invalidated. Such an obligation must be general in its character, and can only be interpreted as binding the party to something that is included under the general idea of an obligation to respect the right of judgment of the person with whom he deals. If a person meeting another walking in his sleep, and knowing him to be in that condition, and irresponsible for his conduct, should have valuable property offered to him in the pantomime of sleep, and should accept it and carry it away, and appropriate it to his own use, it certainly would be a fraud, if not a theft. The essence of such fraud consists in the wrong done to the right of one to exercise his judgment in his affairs, and, when one sees that judgment is asleep, to deal with a waking faculty is a violation of good faith. It may be urged that there is no voluntary power in such case, but that fact would be difficult to establish. There may be no memory of a transaction that was voluntary at the moment it was performed, but that does not imply that the act does not proceed from the will. It is true that there is no complete act of volition, for such an act can only exist where judgment is exercised or its suggestions consciously declined.

It is necessary, then, to inquire what is implied in the general duty to respect the right of judgment of an incapable person— that is, of one who does not possess the power of exercising deliberate choice in the control of his rights. That obligation, as has already been seen, in its relation to persons of mature and full power of self-obligation, demands merely the exercise of passive good faith, or, in other words, that nothing should be said or done tending to mislead one in the use of his rights. In its application to persons who are incapable, the rule of law has been found to go beyond this point, and to exact a certain duty of active good faith. Whenever such an active duty exists, as has been shown, there must exist some protective duty out of which it springs, as illustrated in cases involving the various grades of confidential relationship. It would follow that the rule of law covers the idea of a certain protective duty on the part of all persons toward such as are in a legal sense incapable. The same principles obviously underlie both the cases of immaturity and general incapability. The legitimacy, in accordance with the principles of the law, of a certain control over the incapable, that would not consist with the principle of equal individual right where fully operative, has already been attributed to a certain protective duty that society at large owes to such persons on natural principles. Such a duty as a collective duty would naturally be reflected on the individual on principles of association, already demonstrated, and thus the recognition of such an individual duty by the rules of law is accounted for.

As has been previously demonstrated, the efficacy of an obligation may be impaired by showing, in the interest of a party, that the equality of position of the parties had been destroyed by an act of the opposite party, operating against such interest. The equality of position has been shown to consist in the fact that there has been a performance of all obligations defining the relations of parties dealing together. If, then, one dealing with an incapable person takes advantage of the imperfect condition of the power of such person, this is a clear violation of an obligation fundamental to the validity of such dealing, and the efficacy of the dealing is disturbed.

But assume the case of one dealing with an incapable person without knowledge of such incapability; that would not prevent the dealing from being affected prejudicially, and a very clear principle, derived from protective relationships, accounts for such result. If, by any accident, a person should gain an advantage over another where a fiduciary relationship exists, as to the subject of such dealing, an attempt to insist upon such advantage, after being informed that it arose from an accidental non-performance of duty, would be a clear wrong. This principle clearly accounts for the rules under consideration.

Where power of exercising judgment is not wanting, but the mind is in a weak condition, whether that condition is permanent or temporary, if means are employed to induce or compel the performance of an act prejudicial to the right of a party thus situated, and the character of the means is such as to take advantage of such mental weakness, a clear wrong is done to the right of exercising the faculty of judgment.

Two degrees of weakness are characteristic of minds—one of a general, and the other of a specific character. Liability to depart from the suggestions of judgment through the impulsive force of fear is common to mankind. The difference among men in this respect, as a general rule, is as to the degree to which fear must be exerted in order to overcome the judgment. Wherever means appear to have been employed adequate to produce that effect in any given case, and an act prejudicial to the subject of such fear has been performed under its influence, a wrong is consummated, although initiated as such, the moment the application of such means commenced. The application to the mind of another of means for causing an act to be performed through the impulse of fear is a form of duress. Under the normal operation of the judgment, the condition of the mind in dealing with one's rights is that of choosing between apparent advantages. This action is reversed when the choice is between evils, as it is in all cases where action arises from the impulse of fear. One may be compelled by circumstances to choose between evils, and yet bound by his choice. But, if one claiming an advantage under such an act is chargeable with wrongfully producing such state of mind, the act, as to him, is invalid. This exhibits the fact that an assault upon the mind, tending to deprive it of the benefit of a deliberate judgment, is the basis of relief in such cases; and this resolves itself into a violation of the general obligation to respect the right of judgment in others.

The other case of weakness of mind, which has been termed specific, exhibits a different class of external phenomena. In that case the existence of favor or affection for the person of another, inducing a prejudicial act, may be the noticeable fact. In very young children, and wherever a certain degree of mental weakness exists, mere force and persistence of will and sympathy may control conduct, as well as the means of exciting conscious fear. The controlling action of one will over another, especially when there is less than ordinary strength of mind, must be referred to fear, conscious or unconscious. It may be worthy of inquiry whether it is not a sense of the want of protection that produces the condition of sympathy in such cases. At all events, that state of favor and affection that is regarded by the law as the product of wrongful means must be considered as ultimately founded either upon fear or deception, for in the absence of these motives it must be regarded as the natural reward of good character and conduct, and, as such, a conservative force that could not be denied by the law. The subject of deception will be considered in another place, upon different principles.

The arbitrary rule of the law as to the duration of the period of immaturity shuts out of view many complicated questions which would be presented if the actual condition of a person passing through the successive stages of immaturity toward maturity were necessary to be considered in connection with the question of legal capacity. The questions that most commonly arise grow out of either bodily or mental infirmity, or the approach of death. These two causes of mental weakness are to be carefully distinguished. Infirmity of body may impair the power of attention to the circumstances that are essential to a full act of judgment without impairing the power of rightfully disposing of those matters that can be held before the mind for a sufficient duration of time. It tends to produce indifference to ordinary consequences whenever the motive that arises from the fear of death is present. A consciousness of the uncertainty of life carries with it, in most minds, a sense of fear, and always produces some degree of indifference to ordinary consequences. It is quite certain that, whenever disease or the apprehension of death gives occasion to the origin of a feeling of affection, it is from a sense of dependence caused by fear. The approach of death is assumed to cause fear producing both indifference to ordinary consequences and deprivation, more or less, of the means of conducting one's affairs. The actual state of the mind in such cases is ascertained by its actions and declarations, upon the general presumptions as to the tendency of such causes in general.

It is with testamentary disposition that these internal states are required to be most carefully investigated. Such questions are complicated by the fact that the undue means employed to influence testamentary disposition are not an injury, in a pecuniary sense, to the person wronged. That the wrong in such cases must be regarded as such in its relation to the right of judgment involved in testamentary disposition, and not to any supposed right in those entitled by way of succession in the case of intestacy, is manifest. The right of succession does not arise until the death of the person in whose right it is claimed, and, accordingly, is not in a condition to become the subject of a wrong at any time while such person is capable of making a testamentary disposition.

The principles governing dealings with persons not altogether wanting the power of judgment, but exposed, by reason of infirmity of body or mind, to undue influences, may readily be apprehended from what has been previously said. To the degree that incapability exists, though not amounting to total want of the power of judgment, the protective principle applies, charging those dealing with such persons with active good faith; and when such protective relationship does not exist, and merely passive good faith is demanded, the condition of the person affected by such infirmity is to be considered in judging of the sufficiency of the means of exercising undue control, for the tendency of such means is exaggerated by the diminution of the power of resisting them.

Deception must be regarded, in its essential nature, as a wrong to the right to the exercise of judgment, for knowledge is the means by which judgment is formed, notwithstanding an act of judgment may include facts merely assumed to exist. To deprive one of the means of exercising his judgment, with the intention to prevent its proper action, is manifestly a violation of the obligation that binds each individual to respect the rights of every other. Misrepresentation involves the performance of some act tending to deprive another of knowledge, which may be necessary to the proper exercise of his rights; the object of representing a false state of facts includes that of hiding the truth. The concealment of the truth by an act intended for that purpose is the substance of the wrong. This end may be attained by creating a false appearance of truth. There is, therefore, no difference in nature between what may be called an active concealment of truth and misrepresentation. A passive concealment contains other principles. The general obligation to good faith, as has already been seen, demands only passive good faith, or, what is equivalent, excludes only active bad faith; consequently, the obligation to respect the rights of others being of that nature, only concealment that is produced by some affirmative act is a violation of such common obligation. Where an obligation to active good faith exists, or where a protective duty is present, passive concealment becomes a violation of the obligation. While thus the mere withholding of truth by one bound to give counsel is a violation of what is implied by that relation, it is not a violation of any duty that springs unmodified from the common obligation to respect the rights of others.

It appears from the foregoing that all the consequences that result from dealing with one destitute of the power of judgment, or dealing unfairly with one of weak judgment, and from the use of deceptive means, are attributable to the common obligation that binds every individual to respect the rights of others by using good faith in his dealings with them, either simply, or as affected by the nature of protective duty.

The duties of giving information and counsel depend upon the same general principles, and these general principles underlie the whole doctrine of agency. It is obvious, on the principles already presented, that one who gives false information to another, tending to cause, and that actually causes, an injury to the right of the latter, violates the common obligation accessory to such right, and, therefore, is the cause of the injury thereby sustained to such right.

Where there is a specific obligation to give certain information, as where it is promised to be given for an equivalent, the extent of that duty is materially affected by the consideration whether such duty involves an agency to obtain information, or merely to communicate such information as the party may possess. Wherever there is an agency, there is a specific obligation to use prudent care and good faith in its exercise; and, hence, if one is employed to obtain information, inasmuch as he undertakes to perform an active service, he is an agent, and, as such, bound to use the degree of care and the means that, according to the habit of the community, or of any industry to which such agency may relate, are the ordinary mode of performing such duties. If one volunteers as an agent without compensation, he is bound to the extent that he acts as such by the same general obligation, as compensation is not essential to the idea of protective relationship, although he can not be compelled to act in such cases. Independently of such an agency, the obligation to communicate information calls for nothing beyond what the party obliged possesses, and is not a guaranty of its fullness or accuracy.

An obligation to afford counsel to another is shown, by its consequences, to be in the nature of a delegation of the power of judgment. In other words, one thus obliged must act as if the power of applying a deliberate judgment to the affairs of the one he counsels were in his own hands for exercise to the extent of the duty of counsel imposed. It is, then, apparent that the principles of agency affect such relations, although an agency in its formal character may not exist. It is the presence of an agency of a delegation of the power of exercising deliberative judgment that constitutes the fiduciary character. It is obvious, therefore, that, in every instance where one applies to another for counsel, such an obligation in the nature of an agency does not exist, and that, where one expresses an opinion to another concerning his affairs, he is not necessarily in the position of one who has voluntarily assumed an agency in the affairs of another. According to general habit, the duty of counsel is assigned to professional advisers, and the presumption from this habit is against interpreting the seeking of counsel from non-professional persons, and its offer by such persons, or implying any obligation other than that of exercising general good faith.

Professional advisers are regarded as representing themselves to possess special knowledge and skill in the arts they profess, and the assumed possession of these qualities is considered the reason why their services are sought for such purpose in preference to those of other classes of persons. It is obvious that the specific obligations they assume toward those who seek counsel must contain these elements. They bind themselves, it is true, only to ordinary care and skill, but the habit of their profession is the standard to which the term ordinary is here applied.

The question in hand affords an opportunity for examining more carefully the proposition that the common habit is the means of ascertaining what measure should be applied to the mode in which duty is performed. If one employs a physician or a lawyer notoriously unskillful in his profession, and for a compensation that implies professional inferiority, it is manifest that if he suffers by such want of skill his right to redress must, to some extent, be affected by these circumstances. The brief way of putting the case is to say that his injury is the product of his own folly, but the proper solution lies deeper. If one employs another having actual or presumable knowledge of the limit of his skill or general capability, it is not to be assumed that he expected or engaged for more than the known capacity of the person employed could insure. In his case, the question as to what constituted due performance would involve special features precluding recourse to the habit of the community, as the means of its measure. On the other hand, if a stranger, having no opportunities for judging of relative professional skill, employs a person holding himself out as proficient in his profession, and is injured by malpractice, it is perfectly clear that it would afford no justification or ground for diminishing damages that the practice in the case was conformable to the general practice of that particular practitioner. Such a defense would be equivalent to that of a merchant justifying the delivery of an unmerchantable article on the ground that he was in the habit of selling articles of that condition, without going a step farther, and showing that the purchaser had reasonable knowledge that such was the character of the commodities dealt in. In practice, these niceties of distinction, as it regards the proper qualities of counsel, do not appear, as men bear the consequences and injustice of bad advice more patiently than any other class of evils, and seldom bring breaches of professional duty to the attention of the courts, unless flagrant violations of that duty exist, or are believed to exist.

The constitution of juries affords peculiar means of applying to cases those limitations of right and duty that are imposed by the habit of the community. The fact that they are taken from the vicinage assures, in a general way, their familiarity with those habits and customs of a general nature by which the rights and duties of parties are affected, and with their local modifications. Their acquaintance with the general and local community is the source from which they are presumed to draw their knowledge of the general standards that obtain in the popular judgment. While the estimation in which the community holds the value of a commodity dealt in is the subject of proof, as it is a variable expression of the constant element or general standard, yet the fixed standards themselves do not demand extrinsic proof. Of such a nature is the common judgment as to what constitutes due and ordinary care and skill, as to which matters the jury represents the community at large.

From this view of the constitution of the jury, it is evident that it sustains an important administrative function of the law that adheres closely to its principles, by bringing the limits of rights and duties to the crucial test of the habit of the community. Professional judges of fact would be apt to replace these practical standards by ideal ones, and disassociate the law from its proper relation to the actual facts of life. The idealization of the law would destroy its applicability to existing society, and convert it into a rigid mold, to which society could only be adjusted by the constant application of external force.

CHAPTER XL.

LIBERTY OF SELF-GRATIFICATION.

THE liberty or right of self-gratification is the conservator of those susceptibilities of man to external impressions of a pleasurable or painful character which are here treated as the power or faculty of sensibility; and, as the distribution of states of pain and pleasure is the prime mover of society, it is obviously necessary that the protective sphere of the law should environ and guard these sources of human energy. The fact that this right is protected through the office of accessory rights hides it from ordinary view in the practical administration of the law. It enters, however, frequently, as an element, into the constitution of damages where a wrong has been sustained to some other right of a more positive or objective character, which evinces the fact, not only that it is esteemed a right in itself, but that other rights may stand as accessory to it, through which it may be compensated.

The idea of self-gratification is not to be limited to equivalence with that of self-indulgence, but has a much more comprehensive significance. One may find his gratification in industry, another in acts of benevolence or intellectual studies, while others may seek only the gratifications of their tastes and appetites. The right of self-gratification is, then, the right to propound the general and specific ends toward which the exertions of life shall be addressed. Whatever indirect motives the policy of government may afford to induce habits of industry, still its principles are based on the idea that, whether man chooses his purposes in life well or ill, he is entitled to protection in the use of such rights. Whether he seeks to possess himself of property or rights in order to squander such possessions, or is disposed to be a prudent and useful citizen, the same measure of protection and redress is intended to be afforded him. Nothing can display more clearly the large conceptions of liberty to which the principles of the law have given rise. Under the most despotic governments, whether of a paternal or militant type, this character has been possessed by these principles, and in every age they have produced fruit that evinced their continued life.

The general law of development seems to demand that duality of function should be replaced by a system of related single functions. Primitive government represented the naturalistic stage of blended function. Government affecting the parental instincts, assumes to be not only a ruler, but a providence. But humanity is passing the limits of immaturity, and entering a *régime* characterized by the largest legal liberty. The highest conception of civil government is that which imposes no greater necessity on conduct than such as is required to compact a solid social substratum, on which man may found his individual powers. Having attained that point, man confronts singly that system that connects his conduct with his destiny.

The conception that those tendencies that shape the ultimate destiny of man are parts of a system is compelled by the fixed laws of organic life. For the higher phases of life the only conceptions are organic life, or nothing, of which the nature of our consciousness compels the selection of the former. One of the characteristics of developed conditions is that as function is separated it is intensified. If, then, man is entering a *régime* in which the exercise of providential care over him is passing out of the hands of human government, he must anticipate higher functional activity in that system that replaces this governmental function.

It is natural that the protective sentiment should take alarm at the responsibilities that attend the full conception of legal liberty; and that a paternal impulse should exert itself to postpone the danger by delaying the acquisition of liberty; but that the period for such a change is at hand is evinced by the fact that repressive efforts appear to be engendering the worst tendencies and instincts, embodying immense disruptive social forces. In such an exigency, the nearer the policy of government is conformed to the principles of the law, the less will be the shock attending that stage of civil development that is impending.

THE END.

www.ingramcontent.com/pod-product-compliance
Lightning Source LLC
Chambersburg PA
CBHW022105290426
44112CB00008B/555